Information Systems in Organizations

Information Systems in Organizations

Improving business processes

Richard Maddison and Geoffrey Darnton

CHAPMAN & HALL

London · Glasgow · Weinheim · New York · Tokyo · Melbourne · Madras

Published by Chapman & Hall, 2–6 Boundary Row, London SE1 8HN

Chapman & Hall, 2–6 Boundary Row, London SE1 8HN

Blackie Academic & Professional, Wester Cleddens Road, Bishopbriggs, Glasgow G64 2NZ, UK

Chapman & Hall GmbH, Pappelallee 3, 69469 Weinheim, Germany

Chapman & Hall USA, 115 Fifth Avenue, New York, NY 10003, USA

Chapman & Hall Japan, ITP-Japan, Kyowa Building, 3F, 2–2–1 Hirakawacho, Chiyoda-ku, Tokyo 102, Japan

Chapman & Hall Australia, 102 Dodds Street, South Melbourne, Victoria 3205, Australia

Chapman & Hall India, R. Seshadri, 32 Second Main Road, CIT East, Madras 600 035, India

First edition 1996

Typeset in Times by WestKey Ltd, Falmouth, Cornwall
Printed in England by Clays Ltd, St Ives plc

ISBN 0 412 62530 X

A catalogue record for this book is available from the British Library

Library of Congress Catalog Card Number: 95–74661

Printed on permanent acid-free text paper, manufactured in accordance with ANSI/NISO Z39.48–1992 and ANSI/NISO Z39.48–1984 (Permanence of Paper).

Contents

Preface

As people design new business processes of greater novelty and complexity, and as enterprises are connected more extensively by information systems to support new processes, so education and training needs grow. Some time after their initial education about business and computers – perhaps at university or college or during their employment – thousands of people need knowledge of the principles, approaches, methods and techniques of analysing and improving business processes and information systems, including information system development and management. This book includes material for a successful first course on these topics.

The fundamental problem – to produce good working models of business processes and information systems that support people in their work – is much wider than information technology and computerized information systems. Human and technical issues abound and interact. Previous books have generally not considered these underlying issues. After reading this book, people should be able to discuss the underlying key concepts and their application.

Rationale

This book is for students and practitioners. It aims to explain the principles of analysing and modelling business process and information systems requirements. It may suit second or third year university and college students, postgraduates and people in their early years of employment. We hope it will be suitable for self study and for those attending a course. It may need 100 hours of study, including the exercises, to pass an examination based on it, and perhaps another 100 hours to put its material into commercial practice. Some topics are intellectually challenging. However, most of the book should present little difficulty to any student or professional willing to invest time and discipline.

The positioning of the book may be problematic. We realize that many people will be tempted to see the text as mainly suitable to support postgraduate courses. But that is precisely because many undergraduate courses do not equip their students for employment in the information systems world. We believe this book will be suitable for undergraduate and professional courses aimed at correcting that current bias.

We discuss and explain the following issues.

1. This book supplements the ideas presented in many previous books on business process design and re-engineering, and information system development methods. We take many analytical and other techniques to the depth that the professional analyst requires.
2. Much popular literature on modelling things such as business processes and information systems over-simplifies the characteristics of the processes involved. In our experience the actual modelling of a typical real business involves understanding many hundreds or thousands of components all linked together in many ways. Practitioners need ways of handling this modelling 'richness'. We suggest ways of doing so.
3. There is a need for the development of an analysis profession. Analysts are frequently faced with a large number of business-determined restrictions and approaches that may inhibit taking a professional approach. We identify a set of key elements for professional analysis work.
4. Much existing business process re-engineering (BPR) literature has a bias towards seeing business processes in process flow terms; we explain alternative ways of modelling processes. Our emphasis is on analysis and modelling, rather than on design.
5. Many previous business methods either assumed and had built into them the traditional structure of stages such as requirements, analysis, design, code, test and operate – along with associated documentation standards – or else emphasized a prototyping approach. The fundamental problem with these two alternatives is that each only fits certain sizes of organization, and neither can be scaled in the direction of the other. But the business analyst, the developer and the provider need to understand such scalability problems, so we cover this issue.
6. Much of the past work on business and IT development placed its emphasis on the software aspects of the system. Our more contemporary view sees development and provision in the wider context of business functions and processes. Indeed thinking of business processes is sometimes preferable to thinking of business functions. Many existing analysis techniques can be adapted to give a clearer understanding of processes that embed software.

Earlier versions of some of the material used for this book were presented in a very brief, summary-like, way, which has proved particularly helpful to students and practitioners who wish to look something up without having to read pages of text. We have retained this style for appropriate parts of this book.

The behavioural objectives may be split into those achievable short-term, at work on the Monday after attending a course; and longer-term education and skills understanding that may come through months or years of practice and experience. We aim to include both, and distinguish them. For example after attending a course some people may be under pressure the following week to achieve something new almost immediately, so people may need to know what can be done at that point – the short-term abilities. The longer-term abilities cannot be tested in an end-of-course examination. Our book also includes both short and longer exercises that require thought to apply the concepts to real or realistic situations, and we provide solutions.

Book objectives

The overall book objectives are the following.

- To explain how business processes and the corresponding information systems should encompass solutions to the overall needs of an enterprise – fitting its strategy, plans, success factors, culture, environment and people – so that the enterprise's managers are helped in achieving the enterprise's objectives and continually improving its performance.
- To explain why the information systems needed to support business processes are not just computerized systems.
- To provide support for the development and provision of business systems and information systems – explaining approaches, methods, techniques, tools, management considerations and planning, and giving sound reasons.
- To assist those who wish to select and implement within their organization a methods framework.
- To provide clear recommendations to relevant managers, user representatives, and specialists.

Reader's objectives

After studying the book or attending a face-to-face course based on it, a person should be able to achieve the following objectives. The reader should understand and be able to discuss and use in practice, in addition to specific skills, several abstract but key concepts.

- The issues and ideas for business processes and their related information systems and how to make appropriate representations of both the real world and hypothetical variations such as the consequence of proposals and plans. This includes ideas about actions, selections, relevance, procedures, criteria, purposes and dynamics – not just objects and relationships or data and processes.
- Ideas about wisdom, knowledge, information, and the fundamental problem which is how these are wider than information technology (IT) and information systems, and why some problems are not suitable for IT; and related ideas.
- How a practitioner helps a client to solve a problem – including points about mental images, descriptions, communication and the sequencing and overlap of actions –

applying these to the management of specialists helping the development of new business processes and information systems, and extending these ideas to the ways that business processes support work in its usual contexts.

- Issues about change, evolution, pressures, planning and decision making, including subservient terms and actions such as business and information systems planning, information architectures, management control cycle, feasibility, review, control, feedback, costs, benefits, perceived maintenance, hidden IT development, quality and standards.
- Some commonly encountered approaches, methods and techniques for the identification, planning, development and deployment of business processes, including the problems and issues that these approaches, methods and techniques face and the key features of some of the most widely used business process and information system development methods.
- Many terms about business processes, information systems and methods, including connotations and assumptions – some of which are often hidden or not stated.
- Issues concerning the selection of techniques and methods to use, so that a solution for a set of requirements may involve a combination of manual and technology-assisted components.

The book may be used to support an appropriate UK National/Scottish Vocational Qualifications (NVQ/SVQ) Level 5 course.

Substructure

The book's substructure interleaves topics, allowing gradual understanding of the relationships between them. But for easier use later, the book's outer structure mostly puts all material pertaining to a major topic together. Some terms in Chapters 1 and 2 are marked †, to indicate that they are defined a few pages after they are first used, in order to avoid interrupting the early flow by such definitions. Please use the index to find explanations and definitions if you need to.

The text has interleaved exercises to help you learn. We suggest that you should cover the solutions at a ruled line whenever you turn to a new page. Attempting them may help you to learn and understand the ideas. We do not expect you always to get the right solutions to such exercises, and we may make new points in our solutions to them.

At the end of each chapter we give objectives and further questions as a self check. These have solutions in Appendix, and usually do not make new points. But they give practice which you may need before studying the next chapter.

Richard Maddison, Bedford, England
Geoffrey Darnton, Titchfield, England
October 1995

Acknowledgements

Both The Open University and Digital Equipment Corporation have provided useful and stimulating environments over many years for the development, testing and use of the ideas presented here. However the particular combination we give is our own responsibility. We thank Lynn Darnton for drafting part of Chapter 5, Moksha Darnton and Fiona Jackson for help with the manuscript and diagram preparation, Frank Poole for helpful comments and suggestions, and Ingmar Folkmans for encouragement and guidance about publishing.

Overview

Chapters 1–4

Organizations need to improve continually. They need regular measurements of external-value and internal performance. To monitor and improve the uses of resources in an environment needs periodic control.

At each moment many issues and problems compete for action. They ought to be allocated optimally to the available staff, but to do so is impossible. To create information systems that ensure that the right knowledge and information is selected and sent to the right people for action is also impossible.

Staff can achieve small improvements within existing resources and business processes. Greater improvements need changes to resources, processes and information systems. Such changes need thought and planning. The planning, development and provision of the new facilities and processes may itself become a huge set of actions. People have different views on how to plan, analyse requirements and develop the facilities. Human issues abound. Large organizations need continual ongoing planning, with feedback, overlapping actions and iteratively improving products such as business processes and information system facilities.

An action involves interleaving the various aspects of planning, performing the actual action, monitoring the results and instituting corrective measures to conform to plan. The amount of this activity relative to the amount involved in carrying out the perceived work should roughly match patterns that result in optimization of the whole. If slightly more would produce greater savings from reduced waste than the cost of the extra work, then planning and control should be increased. Information and appropriate processes are needed to determine that.

Information exploitation is preferable to MIS-centric systems. Ongoing reductionist planning involves over 20 steps covering objectives, strengths, weaknesses, opportunities, threats, critical factors, metrics, gaps, strategies, responsibilities, control mechanisms, tactics, projects and other actions.

Planning actions involves identifying options, assessing feasibility, having criteria by which to evaluate each alternative, selecting from alternatives, and making optimum decisions about the relative amounts of planning, control and client involvement, against the amount of the work itself. For small actions these are trivial, but for future business actions using major information systems, the planning and development activity is itself the main work.

Management involves directing, organizing, initiating and controlling appropriate work. Management styles can affect the provision of systems and how people behave. There are limitations on what can be done. Middle managers may amplify or attenuate information. Information systems may flatten management reporting structures. Managers need long-term, medium-term and short-term control cycles and points of control.

Human issues are often more important than processes and technical facilities. Appropriate management styles, participation by all stakeholders, top management commitment, adequate resources and timescales and never pressuring others to promise the unachievable are all contributors to success and need to be combined with the technical issues.

Chapters 5 & 6

A process can be described richly. Its models include many kinds of generalizations, information flow diagrams, entity–attribute–relationship diagrams, identifiers, events that trigger, conditions, sources of information, synonyms, rules, context, processors, decision making, responsibilities, which data is used how for what, what information is generated, timing, starting and finishing. Processes are associated with other processes through timing, interruptions, and structures such as data activity interaction. Diagram conventions aid clarity and understanding, and provide shortcuts. Associated text is needed. Forms may be created and used to record such rich descriptions and to aid systematic work. Many people can use such forms and richness after a week long course. Processes may be decomposed into subprocesses within appropriate guidelines, balancing and levelling. Subprocesses may be equally richly modelled.

Some of an organization's processes are essential to it. They are stable and will continue. The higher organizational structures are less stable and liable to unpredictable restructuring. The computing facilities and lowest level operations are similarly unstable. Improved IT products lead to continual pressure for change. Information systems should be based on the relatively stable essential processes and their corresponding essential and stable data types and behaviour, so that the information systems have the features and flexibility to survive long-term without a huge amount of rework every time the relatively unstable aspects of the organization or the IT products change.

Chapters 6 & 11

Modelling may be further generalized into metamodels. These are models of models and represent rules about rules. They may be expressed as object–property–relationship structures, completeness and consistency standards, and associated processes. They give form to how the rich analysis of a process was achieved.

Functional dependencies between attributes aid their grouping. This leads to aggregates and/or normalized entity types. Practitioners need to be able to handle entity–relationship representations, aggregates, normalized structures, object oriented features, and various metamodels, and to transform between representations.

Typical organizational situations involve relationships between more than two entity types, so such complex relationships and their associated rules have to be modelled.

These various models, metamodels, rules and behaviour have to be converted into the features of the information systems for use by other staff of the enterprise. The underlying models, design and implementation should have the right features for providing staff with easy to use unified facilities, so an occurrence of something can be handled the same way in all circumstances.

Chapter 7

Selecting a few key priorities should indicate an approach – how and where to start and why, or even whether to. Many information system development methods have underlying and sometimes unstated assumptions. Some assume that the client organization has a problem and its solution needs a computer system, and analysis and design for developing that system is the most important part. Many methods make the tripartite assumption that everything can be modelled as processes, data and behaviour, perhaps with behaviour controlled by the computer user. These assumptions miss many aspects.

We recommend a contingency approach with interleaving and gradual development of products. In appropriate situations this may be combined with suitable aspects of other approaches: waterfall, structured, systems, planning, information architecture, data analysis, prototyping, product set, participative, automated tools and computer-aided software engineering. Some of the approaches and tools cannot be scaled from the small to the large, or vice versa.

Chapter 8

Many physical and mental concepts form the foundations. People can act, be concerned with impact, distinguish, select, and form new concepts and representations. Abstractions include existence, indication, symbols, attributes, values, classification, association, aggregates and generalizations. Describing and modelling the relevant part of the universe, or a hypothetical universe of discourse such as a plan, includes representing facts and assertions, deducing consequences, making predictions and handling associated times.

Privacy is a moral right, ensured by appropriate security mechanisms. Integrity, correctness, accuracy, precision, consistency and completeness are desirable features which are ensured by information capture, reliability, various checks, internal processes and recovery mechanisms.

In many contexts, problem solving involves a client getting help from a specialist. In simple cases the specialist solves the problem. In more complicated cases the specialist may develop more general processes and tools for the client to use in solving many similar problems, then build the tools and give training to the client. Contexts include: staff getting help from specialists; users getting help from computer-based systems; customers getting help, information, products and services from suppliers; staff getting help in the form of points of control, strategy, tactics and performance information to optimize the running of their resources in the changing environment; and organizations getting help from specialists, including their own staff and/or consultants, to improve their business processes and information systems. Information systems should have the right facilities for aiding such problem solving.

Chapters 2, 4, 9

Information systems development is a huge problem and to ease comprehension it may be separated into overlapping subproblems – each with their own specialists, models, phases, activities, methods, techniques and tools. The subproblems involve developing corresponding models of the real world and organizational requirements, mental models, conceptual models, logical models, physical models, designs, implemented systems, and changes to these thereafter. Project management may envisage overlapping phases such as strategy, analysis, user design, technical design, implementation, use, maintenance and removal. The actions are structured into information systems developments, phases, activities, tasks and operations. Each of these may use methods, techniques and tools. Each phase or action has or may have purposes, prerequisites and deliverables for various audiences. Teams are needed, with appropriate education, skills, motivation and management. Through its products, analysis has to supply to later phases, such as design and programming, the right knowledge for their actions. Similarly, design provides knowledge for implementation, training and use. Each phase has many activities, some have completeness and consistency checks and other techniques applicable to partial products. Some actions are deliberately never completed.

Points of control and control cycles need to be analysed and modelled like real-time systems, using appropriate techniques and representations. Process behaviour can be modelled using structure charts. State-transition diagrams and pseudocode help communication from analyst and designer to programmer where these are different people, as occurs when the programming is subcontracted. Decision tables help in specifying every action for every combination of conditions, but alternative structures are often preferable. Entity life histories cover specifying the behavioural life of an entity, and indicate which associated entities are involved in the functions and processes occurring during its life. These help to indicate database logical schemas and subschemas as structures of records that application programs use to access records. They may similarly indicate spreadsheet structures.

Chapter 10

One of the main motives for improving business processes and information systems is cost. Cost is one component of the work involved in creating, providing and improving information systems and business processes. The communication gulf between finance staff/ accountants and analysts/developers may be partly bridged by including some understanding of issues about costs in the latter's education. Key cost concepts include cost classification, cost centre, cost objectives, product and infrastructure costs, allocating overheads, opportunity costs and activity-based costing.

Chapter 12

The whole of the above forms aspects of a framework for managers and practitioners. We emphasize contingency and flexibility. An organizational decision to standardize on a particular method will usually eventually lead to deeper problems because the method does not include the right rationale, assumptions, modelling techniques and other facilities to solve the organization's future problems. The other way round is also impossible – organizations cannot solve their future problems before deciding what method to standardize on to solve those as yet unknown problems.

Appropriate styles of development may need to be combined to fit differing circumstances, even within one organization. Metamodels can be developed and usefully compared. Rationalizing a business process involves factor efficiency, substitutability, behaviour and organizational learning. Information systems need to provide ways of measuring performance before and after changes, and facilities for points of control.

Chapter 13

Our conclusions combine topics in various ways and give advice to managers and practitioners. We hope that readers gain intellectual pleasure from achieving increased understanding.

Some actors

In parts of the book we adopt a discursive style involving the needs and actions of various characters who perform and distinguish various roles. We give their names here for you.

Aggie is one of Anna's colleagues.

Anna is an analyst, widened to a specialist in analysing business processes and ideas for change, in analysing needs, and in developing and providing information systems.

Claire is George's client or customer. She wants him to do something. She wants to receive some product or service from him. She may be within the enterprise or an outside client or customer. Later, in Chapter 8, Claire may be a client, a customer, or someone in a part of the organization with a problem, or even represent the whole organization with the problem of needing improvements to itself.

David is a developer of better software, hardware, processes, procedures and facilities. David can develop better processes and tools, including better ISs, for George to use.

Eric is one of Anna's colleagues.

George is any general member of the staff of an organization, e.g. the person who has to do the relevant work in the current context.

Graham is the manager responsible for a general part of the business, the part where George works.

Gwen is Graham's manager or Mark's manager or some more senior manager.

Idris has ideas, and is asked to work on ideas, e.g. for improved business processes and/or improved information systems.

Isobel is a person within an information system, doing part of the work within it, and helping others such as George who are its users.

Mark is the manager responsible for the current information system that George uses, and for information systems development.

Nora is one of Anna's colleagues.

Obadiah is one of Anna's colleagues.

Peter provides things, e.g. is responsible for providing better information systems.

Sophie is a specialist who helps a client such as Claire to solve a problem. In Chapter 8, as an actor Sophie may represent a whole organization, or a business system or IS within it, or a person such as Anna, David, Peter or Isobel, or a consultant, or a subcontractor.

Susan makes suggestions for improvements.

Each of these named people may represent a group or team of such, without us explicitly and tediously saying so.

1 Basics and the fundamental problem

Initial overview

Why mix business process concepts and information system concepts?

People sometimes think of a part of the world, such as a business organization, as a system†. The business organization has both business process† aspects and information system† aspects. In Figure 1.1, we suggest that many methods† to provide and to improve businesses apply to both aspects.

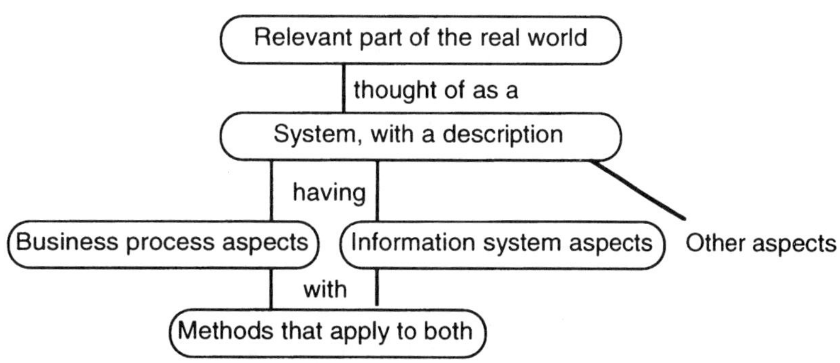

FIGURE 1.1
The structure of the initial ideas.

Terms marked † are explained and defined later in order to allow you to read on without breaking the flow of ideas with a lot of definitions, knowing that the terms will be explained a few pages later. Not all defined terms are marked. You can find our definitions from the index. We develop explanations of terms and ideas gradually and relate them together, rather than try to give full definitions where the terms first appear.

Much contemporary professional and popular literature about business processes portrays processes, information systems and information technology as inextricably bound together. We aim to help you to understand how they are interrelated.

A description of a business process is a model† – like the models used by analysts† who contribute to the development and provision of information systems. An information system is a tool that holds a working model of the relevant business processes and handles information. Use of the information system is usually central to operating the business processes successfully. Information technology enables people to design and implement improvements, including new processes and facilities of increasing complexity and novelty.

Computers are part of a much longer line of technology. Such technology has impact on processes, for example making new processes technically feasible and cheaper, and hence worthwhile. Changing technology has impacted business processes for centuries. New technology is an enabler of further such evolution of business processes and facilities.

George's story

We tell a story showing some general principles. As you read it you may begin to form some ideas in your mind that have wider applicability.

George enjoys life. He talks in a friendly way, aware of what others want. He deals with things that need attention. He belongs to the committee of a local sailing club. They plan, agree a programme, and send it out to members. People in the club often discuss what has happened and make suggestions to George who responds with appropriate actions, including sometimes changing the plans. George uses both new information and previous knowledge in whatever he does, discussing issues, making judgements, deciding priorities and allocating time and resources. The committee predicts, plans, takes action and evaluates, and these actions generate new information both to George and to other members. They also learn from experience, generating new knowledge. The committee members cooperate with each other as a group, trying to identify and solve their problems.

The committee sees different business issues from the members. The committee has to ensure the long-term stability of the club together with satisfactory finances and membership. It arranges permission for people to sail on the lake, insurance, boat and building maintenance, the purchasing of equipment and spares, security, safety and rescue and emergency facilities. Whereas the members sail boats, the committee performs other processes which the members hardly see. The members mostly take these for granted – they just come and sail when they want.

Memory

George remembers most things but because his memory fades he also makes notes. He and the committee communicate the final programme details to the members in writing. People cannot take in a lot of detail and remember it so the written programme avoids arguments. It informs members and gives a permanent version which they keep until the relevant dates.

Communications

George communicates by speech, by body language and in writing. When speaking, George uses gestures and listeners may nod in response. George phones people and obtains information by others telling him things, by receiving minutes and circulars and, occasionally, by overhearing a snippet of conversation. He may need to act on the information immediately or keep it until later. Sometimes George receives a message that is not clear and if he does not understand it fully he has to ask the sender to clarify it.

Usually George intends particular information for particular recipients but sometimes he makes it available more widely. If someone is not available when George wishes to say something he leaves a note or he phones later. He cannot communicate the information on a printed document by phone directly, and he has to read it to them since most of his friends do not have fax machines.

Improvements

Suppose George and his friends want better club activities and better ways of informing each other and the club members. The patterns may be the same as in the past or they could change, e.g. if the club changes in some unexpected way such as having different kinds of boats or a different programme of events – perhaps needing a change to the committee structure and processes. The committee members may be unable to think of all the possible needs and may disagree over what is required, having different priorities, intentions and views. They could be unaware of what equipment has recently reached the shops. They may disagree over how to provide the facilities; is it better to change gradually or perhaps there is no halfway point, as indeed there is no halfway point between sailing on an inland lake and in larger boats on the sea.

George and his sailing friends have several distinct kinds of possible improvements.

- Perhaps they could improve their sailing ability slightly – with training and practice they may knock a few percent from their times in races.
- The committee may improve the products and services it offers to members – better boat storage and better programme content achieved by the officers and committee managing[†] the club better; and a better looking programme or magazine by using word-processing facilities and printing instead of the existing old typewriter and duplicator.
- Introducing sea-going voyages in cruisers with cabins and berths in addition to dinghy sailing on the local lake would provide major new attractions and opportunities to members. It may need a lot of planning and work.

The above simple story has parallels in most organizations. Large organizations employ hundreds of staff who carry out business processes and handle knowledge and information. We aim to explain some generalizations that apply to many organizations.

Exercise 1.1

Form some generalizations from the above. Look for ideas about people, information, and actions. If you have difficulty with this, or any later exercise in the book, please just read the solution below. It runs on into the following text.

Hereafter when you turn to a new page please start by covering whatever is below an exercise box like this with a piece of paper.

People communicate information to others. They predict the possible outcomes of alternative courses of action and plan, take action and evaluate the results. These actions are often triggered by new information received. During such actions people use knowledge gained from experience as well as new information. The actions may generate further information.

Most people enjoy belonging to and working in groups. Different groups deal with different kinds of issues. The committee has to manage many business affairs that underlie the members' sailing.

People's memory fades and so they need more permanent records, such as paper, in case they need to recall knowledge later. Such representations are also used to pass information and detailed knowledge to others. A person may receive information because its originator so intended and communicated it to them. Alternatively they get it because they want it and arrange to obtain it, or because they receive it unexpectedly.

Representations and timing

George can store or delay the transmission of information. He can store knowledge from its creation until he or others need it. His facilities are not integrated but with improvements they might be combined in some integrated whole. They should include ways of representing knowledge in suitably permanent forms, ways of converting between such representations and the communication methods that people use, e.g. speech, vision and hearing, and ways of arranging appropriate timing.

For confirmation of understanding, communication channels need to be bi-directional

A recipient might not understand a message and consequently has to determine its meaning either when received or when used. The originator may be asked for further explanation. Both of them want to ensure that the information passes satisfactorily, so they need to communicate confirmation or other responses. Their communication channel, therefore, usually has to be **bi-directional**, even if the main information is thought of as flowing only or mainly in the one direction from originator to recipient. The languages and representations used in the two directions, however, need not be the same.

As in a club, so in a business, gradual improvements and occasional new facilities are needed to satisfy people – members/staff, customers, suppliers and people in other organizations. The management must think about business issues and they must ensure acceptable processes, facilities and arrangements. These underlie good-quality products and services.

Businesses can have improvements such as the following.

- Perhaps the staff can improve their performance of the existing procedures – with training they might improve a few percent.
- The managers could improve the products and services to customers – better management and better information.
- Introducing new business processes and information handling facilities could provide major new opportunities. It would need a lot of planning and work.

Business processes

This leads us to an initial explanation of what a business process is. Here is a first definition.

> A **business process** is a collection of interdependent actions that together produce outcomes which contribute to the business success of an organization.

For example, the following are business processes: developing a new product, achieving adequate sales, providing an integrated information system, and employing staff. A subprocess can also be a business process. Some people think of an enterprise as having a few tens of such processes, others visualize thousands. Usually a business process crosses the boundaries of traditional departmental structures. It needs active cooperative work from staff in several areas.

The term business process is used in a wider sense than 'business procedure'. A **business procedure** corresponds to detailed work conforming to lower-level actions, typically in circumstances where staff have limited discretion to take decisions. By extension it also corresponds to the design and specification of such lower-level procedures.

The hidden essence and connotation of the term business process is *not* whether or not it is a *process*. The features are as shown in Figure 1.2.

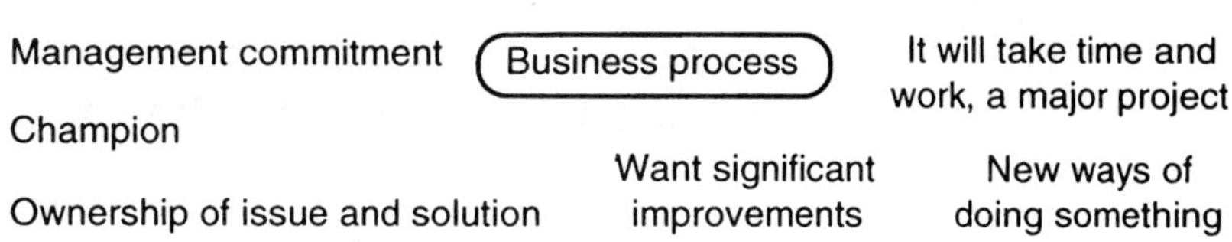

FIGURE 1.2 Some features of a business process.

The essence is *managerial* – having a high-level and senior-management commitment, having a champion and a team, and feeling ownership of a big issue and its solution. It means focusing on looking for significant improvements when appropriate, perhaps having high-level objectives with measures of performance, and hence thinking of longer-term major improvements in performance. This implies having a major project with suitable terms of reference, resources and objectives. The project objectives will include significant improvements, usually from devising and making suitable changes to the organization or one or more business processes. The changes may be changes to existing business processes, but need not be, and usually concentrate on changing *how* things are done.

Examples of business processes are:

- planning the strategy of the business, managing the business and ensuring achievement of business objectives, deciding tactics, managing the operations, products and services; (management includes directing, controlling, initiating work, monitoring and assessing performance);
- capturing marketing information, attracting and retaining customers, selecting appropriate markets;
- providing support services to staff, human resource management, ensuring appropriate internal culture and management styles;
- research, design and development for new products and enhancements to existing products;
- developing new services to customers and clients, ensuring customer needs are fulfilled, capturing and acting on feedback from customers and those who were potential customers but did not purchase;
- managing supplier relations and logistics;
- financial planning and services, asset management, capital, buildings, leases, cashflow, liabilities, control of gearing and debt;
- dealing with external organizations, legislation, governments and their agencies, external relations, publicity, public relations, public image and the consequences of all of these.

People in different organizations may view their business as having different numbers of business processes, and may or may not view them as capable of being subdivided. As stated above, business processes often cross business functions and traditional departmental structures, and should not be confused with business functions or departmental responsibilities.

Performance measurement

This leads on to needing to know how well current processes and procedures are being done, or whether a real improvement has been made. Managers need a *way of measuring or comparing*. Ideally the answer has to be a number, a value, a percentage, or some quantity. Fuzzy words such as satisfactory and good, which do not give a quantified measure of performance, may be useful for comparisons.

A **performance measurement** is a variable that is quantified and measurable or comparable. Usually obtained for each time period its value shows to what extent a performance objective has been achieved during that period, or gives a useful comparison.

For example: how many errors occurred per 1000 products during a week's production? What percentage of products were delivered fault-free to customers on the correct date as agreed when the order was placed? What percentage were delivered within half an hour of the delivery time as agreed before the delivery? What percentage did not result in any query or complaint within a month of delivery? What percentage of the staff went to a particular meeting? Has customer satisfaction improved?

Exercise 1.2

Managers should define the performance measurements appropriately otherwise performance could seem to be better or worse than it really is. Which of the following three is the appropriate choice for ensuring customer satisfaction? Should a manager choose to count the percentage of products delivered on the promised day as a fraction of: (a) all orders received in a given week; (b) all orders delivered in a given week; or (c) all orders that should have been delivered in a given week?

Either the first or third alternative is appropriate. The second does not include orders that are not delivered and therefore its value will be misleadingly high. The second may be useful to managers for other purposes but does not indicate customer dissatisfaction from non-delivery.

Some people distinguish measures of things that are **internal**, within the enterprise, such as how many staff attended a meeting, from things that are **external**, e.g. affecting or affected by suppliers, customers or other outside organizations and pressures. Managers need a measure of how outsiders view some aspect of the enterprise.

An **external-value metric** is a measure of some external factor relevant to the organization, such as the value of a product or service as perceived by a customer, client, supplier or other external organization.

The definition should lead to a quantified figure as the answer. To obtain this often involves a survey of customers or the appropriate external group and could be done by means of a questionnaire, or by phoning them to get their views on the product or service or about what would be advantageous to them. The survey could be based on feedback from each customer or on a sample.

Suppliers might want better advance information about the expected patterns of future orders to help their logistics. Customers might want improvements in size, shape, colour, finish or accuracy. They might prefer shorter leadtimes from order to delivery, or to be allowed to order in smaller quantities, or some change of packaging such as how many inner items to each outer carton, or better reliability or durability. The survey results might show that one of these would be far more useful than a price reduction.

Not everything is possible. Where significant random variations can occur in the durations of some activities, buffering between them is needed to maintain high throughput and efficiency. The buffering shows as queues, stock waiting for the next operation or on shelves, unanswered letters and memos waiting in people's in-trays, and software[†] improvements held up waiting to be programmed. These can be revealed in appropriately defined performance measurements.

The complete collection of performance measurements and external-value metrics in a large organization may include incompatibility. Perfect just-in-time supply, manufacture and delivery, without anything waiting or wasted at any stage, is impossible. It would require and imply no errors, no stock held, no administrative delays, no reserves and no random variations in the time taken to do any action. For example, it would be impracticable for a hospital to ensure that *every* person who arrived at the accident and emergency desk was seen by a doctor within one minute. Coping with a busload who suddenly arrived after a road accident would need a corresponding number of doctors at that minute, most of whom would be idle much of the remaining time.

Compromise involving some waiting, queues, delays, spares, reserves and non-perfection is the best that can be achieved.

Exercise 1.3

If managers want a significant improvement in the business, should they concentrate on achieving near 100% against the main performance measurements, or against the main external-value metrics, or something else?

Often the lower-level operations and middle managers will be achieving fairly high scores on the current performance measurements, and it may be difficult to produce significant improvements in the short term without changes of processes, facilities and resources. Significant improvements may require thinking hard about the issues that underlie the performance measurements.

Some people use the term **breakpoint** for a significant achievement in performance against an external-value metric, e.g. quartering the leadtime or quartering the minimum order quantity. Customers will recognize the huge advantage and that it corresponds to what they wanted. So increased sales and increased market share should result, at least until competitors achieve the same. Similarly supplier logistics may be substantially improved.

Business functions

The above leads us to give examples of business functions.

Examples of **business functions** are sales, accounting, personnel, manufacturing, marketing, transport and maintenance.

Alternatively a business function may be regarded as a unit of business work as perceived by the user of a system†. Usually business functions can be analysed into lower-level units. The subdivision may be continued as far as is useful. The first one or two levels of analysis may give named processes such as sales order processing, invoicing, stock control, purchasing, recruitment, subcontracting and training.

The need for information

Information must mean something to whoever or whatever receives it. **Useful** implies relevant to some purpose

About half the employees in major developed countries perform information work. Essentially **information** implies a *useful communication* received by a *person*. This means an **information flow** from someone or something to *someone*. Nowadays, however, one can also say information flows *to something* – such as to a computer system if that system† is capable of interpreting the information and acting appropriately on it by processing it and creating further information.

Information is not the same as data. Essentially **data** is a structured collection of symbols that represents something about the real world, but might not be relevant or meaningful to a person or to equipment holding, sending or receiving it. A radio operator transmitting and receiving messages sees them as data and need not understand the messages. The messages could be in codes only understood by the originator and recipient. We define data later in Chapter 2 (p. 52). Our definitions of information above, and others later, are intended to aid your initial understanding.

Exercise 1.4

Think of at least six general purposes of information, giving explanations or examples of each.

Information is produced and used for many purposes.

- **Communicating** the current or past situation, or the intention, hope, desire or expectation about the future and communicating thoughts, reasons, ideas and the other things listed below.
- **Planning** – discussing various alternatives of what might happen in the future and choosing between these, making decisions and communicating their consequences. This may include rules, procedures, laws, constraints and justifications about plans.
- Carrying out the **transactions of a business** – about products, services, marketing, purchases, sales, personnel and accounts and about dealing with staff, customers, suppliers, shareholders and local and national authorities.
- **Integrating** – ensuring good morale and unifying people. Within an organization this includes keeping people informed of what is going on and what is expected of them – in order to promote motivation and commitment. Organizations that deal with other people, e.g. as suppliers, customers, clients or the public, need appropriate relationships and coordination. Many staff are suppliers of information to other staff within their own organization as well as to people outside and, vice versa, are customers or clients receiving information from others within their organization as well as from outside.
- **Innovating** – supporting and encouraging creativity, solving problems, doing research and development, making decisions and adapting to changes such as those in the external environment or the rest of the organization.
- **Managing** – including directing, controlling, initiating work, monitoring and assessing performance.
- Creating and **keeping records** of what is happening and has happened, in case knowledge about the past may be needed in the future. This includes analysing data about sales, customers and transactions in order to determine trends and hence make predictions.
- **Social contact** – smalltalk, greetings, friendship and human relations.
- **Services** for providing all these kinds of information and the management of the information services.

> Information is important to people. Ideas, values, attitudes and constraints on behaviour are profound human uses of information.

Information services needed

Organizational survival depends on good products, services and relationships with other organizations. For these, good information services for sound decision making and management are essential.

Managers:

- ensure that information systems† exist to handle relevant information;
- understand the provision and use of information systems and services, including IT-based† information systems where these are appropriate;
- use such systems themselves to generate and receive information, including information about the effectiveness and management of the information systems;
- understand issues such as the impact of information systems on people and organizations.

In most organizations a person may be the manager who provides the information systems that are used, as well as being a user. But for clarity to you, we distinguish between the roles by introducing **Mark**, who is the manager responsible for the information systems that George uses. We also introduce **Graham**, who is the manager responsible for a part of the business, the part where George works. The four items above apply to both Mark and Graham, and to George where appropriate.

Information system

We lead you next into ideas about information systems (ISs), information technology and systems. You will see that the definitions are such that an information system is a system. Suppose **Isobel** works in an office, perhaps with other people as a team. She has paper in files in filing cabinets, communicates by post, fax and telephone, and uses appropriate office equipment. She receives data and information from outside, stores and processes it, and produces information for other people outside the office. She can change her procedures to adapt to external pressures and events. She helps those who need information from her system. An external observer who was not allowed to see inside the office might not be able to decide whether the office contained a computer or not. To someone outside, she and everything around her together form an **information system** (IS).

> Information systems do not necessarily use computers.

An information system should suit the needs and activities of the people who use it. So business information systems should support the organization's objectives, strategy and needs. Such systems should also help cooperation and relationships between people and between organizations such as customers and suppliers. We gradually build up to a definition of an information system near the end of Chapter 2 but as an initial definition we offer the following.

An **information system** is a collection of people or equipment that performs purposeful operations on information.

An information system has the features of a system and we explain that next. It could include some IT-based parts as explained in Chapter 2, p. 56.

Information technology (IT) means the study and use of the artefacts of the technologies associated with handling information. This includes computers, computer peripherals, data communications and networks that link computers, printing, telephones, radio, television, satellite communications and similar technologies used to create and handle information and knowledge. It also includes how IT artefacts are used to achieve objectives and purposes such as products and services.

System

In order to lead you gradually into the features of a system, either a business system or an IS, we start by explaining the systems approach. An **approach**, as explained later, means an overall way of thinking about or doing something, often regarding one or two aspects as the most important.

The **systems approach** to understanding how the relevant part of the real world works is based on the following two ideas.

- The relevant part of the real world may be thought of as having **purposeful** human-activity **systems that are of interest**. These systems **interact** with each other and with the natural, economic, political, social and other environments in which they are embedded. Each viable system can **adapt** to external changes.
- A system may be viewed as having several **parts**. Each part contributes to the purpose of the whole. So the whole would be affected if a part were to leave the system. Each part has **interfaces** where objects, energy, people or information pass across its boundary to and from other parts and to and from systems external to the whole. In some cases a part is able to **adapt** to changes external to itself (changes in other parts or in the external environment of the whole system).

So a system will have features which match those two points about the systems approach.

A **system** has parts that contribute to the purpose, interact, and can adapt.

Many of the parts are **subsystems** – conforming to the definition of a system.

Hereafter for brevity we may put **real world** or **world** or **reality** for the relevant part of the real world. For example, people interested in a business called ABC, its events and its processes would be interested to know that ABC is an organization which manufactures engines; that on a particular date a sales clerk, Mr Smith, received an order from a particular customer for 18 of a particular model of engine; that these will be manufactured and that they will be delivered on a certain date. They would not, necessarily, be interested in how Mr Smith opened the envelope containing the order, or in minor interruptions occurring while the order was dealt with or during manufacture (although a process analyst might need to understand interruptions).

The systems are whatever people think are of interest. People may differ over the purposes and what is included in a system.

Through an understanding gained by thinking of the world working in this way, it may be possible to think of ways of intervening in these systems to improve their operation and performance. People looking at the same set of operations will often see quite different systems and certainly **different purposes**. For example, a factory may be viewed as a means of providing the following: employment and economic support for the local community; profit for the owners; products to the customers; taxation income to the government; and contribution to the gross national product for the country. From different viewpoints other aspects can seem relatively more important.

Thus a **system** may be considered as follows.

- A system is an assembly of components connected together in an organized way.
- Each component is affected by being in the system. If a component were to be removed from the system or another component added, then the behaviour of the system might be changed.
- This organized assembly of components does something; it may appear to have a purpose or perform some function.
- This assembly has been selected as being of particular interest, and hence has been defined.
- What is perceived as a component at one level may be perceived as a system at another level – some people call this phenomenon an **unfolding of complexity** (discussed p. 15).

Here **issue** includes problem, need for a decision, plan, something needing action or requirements of any kind. It means business issues relating to the business functions of the organization, their consequences and all subservient issues such as all incoming communications and objects, such as mail, telephone calls and items delivered; anything that should produce something that flows out; and issues arising externally which may need action just to make someone in the organization aware that an external situation has arisen. These issues also include similar internal flows of objects and information.

> The **fundamental problem** addressed in this book is how to produce good working business processes and information systems that support people in their work.

This is much wider than information technology and computerized information systems. Human and technical issues abound and combine. Specifying and producing these processes and IS facilities needs planning and models.

To deal with something, George needs information and knowledge

For George to deal with some issue he needs to receive or have access to all relevant information and knowledge that he does not have already. When a new issue arises that George should deal with, new information needs to be sent to him to inform him that action is needed and to advise him of the current situation.

Relevant knowledge held elsewhere or only known to certain others should also be selected and sent to him. We include the case of sending information to George which implies that he should *not* act where otherwise he would have acted, and we will not be explicitly mentioning it at each occasion.

Information triggers action

For each issue needing action, information is needed by someone. For each occasion where someone should take some action, information is needed by that person to highlight the need to act. Figure 1.3 illustrates the fundamental organizational problem. Actions can generate further issues and information and so the cycles continue – some starting with a message from outside, others starting from an internal need or action.

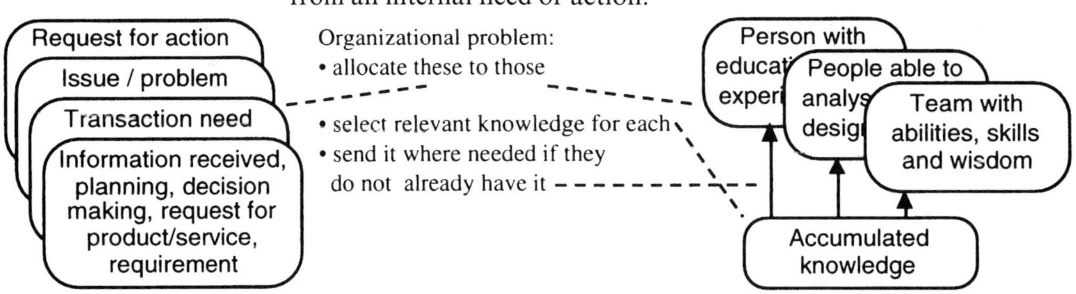

FIGURE 1.3
The need to pass information and knowledge to appropriate people.

This collective organizational problem has several aspects:

- how to know what all the issues are – an information capture problem;
- how best to allocate these issues to the available people – a resource allocation problem;

- how to get the appropriate knowledge and information about each issue to the right people – an information handling problem;
- providing the right processes, facilities and equipment, and providing in advance information such as training so that the staff can undertake the right actions – a business process problem;
- how to know the effectiveness of all that has been done – a management feedback and control problem.

This collective organizational problem is about how to create organizational structures that provide optimum structures for the work that needs to be done, and about locating the points of control in the 'right' places. The information handling problem is supplying the information systems for the appropriate amplification and attenuation of information and knowledge in every situation. Amplification means more out than in, and attenuation means less out than in, as explained in Chapter 4 near Figures 4.5 and 4.6 (pp. 121–2). Most IS developments have concentrated on attenuation rather than amplification.

From hour to hour the set of issues and the situations change so that continual action is needed.

The above states the problems of business processes. Some group, such as the board or top managers, should know the issues about business processes. In principle they should allocate the right people to deal with these issues and arrange that they receive relevant information, including ideas about what changes are likely to be feasible.

Resource and information handling problems

Many such activities and tasks have to be handled by the staff. This gives a resource allocation problem.

> The people **resource problem** is to allocate the tasks optimally among the staff, given the abilities of each person and given the kinds of education, skills and wisdom needed for each task.

The criterion here is to optimize the whole. This does not necessarily optimize the handling of each required task nor the use made at any instant of each person's wisdom, education, knowledge and skills.

The staff need to organize themselves so as to get the right information about each business issue to the right person. Their problems include how to organize themselves and how to handle information, as well as the actions to deal with the issues. This compounds the people resource allocation problem with the information handling problem.

people in different areas is essential. It is not effective or efficient for all such coordination information to flow upwards to someone senior and then down a different branch of the tree to whoever needs it. Therefore information tends to flow across the hierarchical management reporting structures to other staff at about the same level; this is called **horizontal information flow**. Some organizations recognize the value of horizontal flow and use alternative structures such as teams.

Many flows are to and from **external** people, systems and organizations. Many of these flows are essential, particularly for customers, suppliers, legal and government purposes.

People also exchange information as part of deliberate social **networking**, to make friends and to belong to groups both at work and elsewhere. People are often not happy unless they belong to some group or groups and the exchanges of informal information help to create relationships that are desirable for satisfactory discussions, planning and actions.

> **Vertical information flow** is up and down the management reporting structure. **Horizontal information flow** runs across, e.g. to coordinate work in different sections and departments, without going through any higher managers. Business needs both of these types of flow and also **external** flows.

Working parties and teams

Many people have a variety of abilities that are not restricted to and do not necessarily match their place in the hierarchy. So in tackling significant problems, and to ensure cross-hierarchy cooperation, other structures – working parties, committees, matrix structures and teams – are set up. These aim to bring together people with the required wisdom and skills to deal with a collection of suitably similar issues. The members of a particular team may have differing skills, but each skill the issue requires is available amongst either the team members or others on whom the team may call for appropriate expertise. For coordination of their actions, appropriate information then has to flow among the various members of these structures. They meet, discuss, plan and exchange knowledge and information. Most of such information flows will not be vertically up and down the hierarchical management reporting structures. Groups can achieve far more than the sum of the individual contributions but this demands collaborative working. However, coordination of the activities of the team members creates extra work and extra information needs.

From years of education, training and work, people acquire knowledge, skills and experience. Even so, each individual's abilities are small compared to the total capability required for a successful typical large organization and many, varied contributions are required for success.

People may be selected for membership of groups and teams for major new requirements through the use of informal knowledge that their colleagues have of them and through requests for volunteers and representatives from the various sections of the organization that might be involved. Personnel sections often keep formal records of each person's qualifications, training and CV, and these may be consulted to find appropriate people for a new requirement. For large requirements, new posts are created and people apply. Such procedures, although the best that can be done easily, do not always achieve the hoped-for ideal.

The organizational information systems problem

The **organizational information systems problem** is how best to provide and use information systems and services to support the people and activities within the organization. This means providing the facilities for getting the right information and knowledge in the right form to the right people at the right time. It assumes that the organizational problem of allocating tasks and responsibilities has been acceptably solved, or else that its partial solution is included. The problem has many aspects.

At work, at his sailing club and at home George faces issues such as human relations, motivations, reasons, hidden agendas and leadership. For success he has to tackle complex problems and know how to start, how to continue and when to stop. He has to think ahead, plan before he acts and be aware of the outcomes, results and effects of his actions.

In making plans George thinks of several alternatives and perhaps unconsciously forms some criteria for choosing between them. He is aware of moral and philosophical principles, external pressures and what kinds of actions are acceptable in his situation and society.

He handles and manages information and knowledge continually, and doesn't just use information systems and information technology. He receives some information because others talk to him or send him mail. He should select correctly what he wants from the mass of other information that is offered or is available to him. He should interpret each message correctly, become aware of its deeper meaning and consequences, and decide its priority against other messages that he receives. He may see its purpose, priority and implications differently from its originator. All these aspects help George to decide what to do initially and why.

George and his colleagues each play many roles, such as planners, thinkers, actors undertaking actions and communicators. In discussions and other communications they need representations of almost anything in the universe – representations of artefacts, services, requirements, proposals, alternatives, timing – and of the structures of these representations.

Their purposes and intentions will differ. Each may or may not want his or her intentions, priorities, beliefs, desires, hopes, secrets and knowledge or ignorance to become known to certain other people. In their activities they use information and knowledge, and create yet more. In the same situation, such as receiving the same

whole organization would be impossible or costly. If Mark's boss insists on standardization, people may grumble at the extra overheads and delays.

Business process and analysis issues

Making improvements to processes and facilities can be complicated. Extensive planning and work are needed. A key issue is to analyse the business requirements as later work could be useless if the facilities thus provided do not fit the requirements. The whole involves many choices and constraints, hidden aims and how to decide priorities. Many methods have been tried some of which have evolved into proprietary methods recommended by their authors. We gradually explain these.

Methods of developing and providing improved processes and facilities

Since the late 1950s people have proposed many methods† of analysing processes and developing computer-based information systems. Most of these methods have *not* gained widespread acceptance and have not lasted. Some have been merged and a few have continually evolved and become virtual standards.

Computer and related technology has continually improved. So some user facilities and corresponding IS development methods that were not feasible during one decade became cheap and easy to provide during the next. The emphasis has shifted from the complexities of programming with large teams of programmers, through the stage of having teams of analysts† and developers finding out needs and creating bespoke systems for routine operational work in individual organizations, towards users each individually using large software† packages on their own computers.

Ways of providing business processes and IT-based facilities for groups of staff such as George and others have evolved continually and somewhat pragmatically throughout the last 40 or so years. The current ways can, however, still be improved and the optimum way of providing processes and facilities is not yet known.

Different Georges and Grahams need appropriate variations in the facilities to match their differing skills and their personalities as well as their business needs, their patterns of work and responsibilities. Their equipment should have appropriate compatibility.

Many methods†, techniques† and tools† for information system development have been proposed. Most of them aimed to help with only a part of the whole problem, although as the years have rolled on some have been widened to cover more of the work.

A few practitioners tried to develop methods that might be applicable generally in many situations and that covered many of the complexities of managing, developing and maintaining information systems for business processes†. Some of their methods have been called **methodologies**† as we explain later (p. 31).

A typical information system development method of the 1970s and 1980s recommended several identified and named **phases**/stages, with several activities in each phase. The phases were recommended to be done in sequence so that the products of one phase, such as analysis, could be used in a later phase, such as design, and so that the products of each phase could be signed off as approved by managers who accepted that the end-of-the-phase milestone had been reached and subcontractors should be paid. We do not recommend having distinct phases. Instead we advise overlapping so that, before completion of an activity, any potentially difficult parts of later activities should be addressed in order to provide feedback.

Analysis

Here is our first definition of analysis, in the context of the analysis of business and information systems and requirements.

> **Analysis** means the study of a concept, or a system or requirements for a system, by breaking it/them down into parts and determining the relationships between the parts so as to research and describe the whole, according to an identified set of analysis rules.

Later (pp. 71–3), we explain alternative ways of undertaking analysis, including alternative kinds of parts and alternative relationships between parts.

The essence of analysis is really to specify a requirement or problem with sufficient correctness, completeness and consistency. This means breaking it down into smaller parts each of which can be specified so that the way that the parts fit together can also be specified. It is usually done either by an *ad hoc* one-off method invented as the analyst goes along or by applying a previously understood collection of methods and techniques to the problem, and thus producing a model of the problem and perhaps also producing a model of its solution.

The fundamental underlying reason for such analysis and planning effort before starting work on design and implementation such as programming, is that it makes success more likely. It reduces what might otherwise be higher development and maintenance costs. Rectifying mistakes spotted during analysis costs perhaps one tenth of rectifying them during programming, and can avoid the huge losses and waste during use which occur if the mistakes go undiscovered and the systems provided to George do not meet his needs.

The **scope of the analysis** should include, insofar as each of these is worthwhile:

- **completeness**, going into details;
- **consistency**, ensured by appropriate crosschecks;
- **correctness**, agreement with reality.

We use the term **analyst** for a person who contributes to business

alternative sequences, products and ways of undertaking an action. This means many decisions each of which should be based on appropriate evaluation of the advantages and disadvantages and the application of suitable criteria – unless the cost of the evaluation is not worthwhile. Anna and others have many choices here in how they work.

Anna may have many pressures on her. The objectives may be any combination of wanting:

- to help improve an existing business process or processes by improving George's actions or by improving the ISs that he uses, or both;
- to contribute to the development of an improvement that makes better use of some new opportunity, e.g. new technology, new methods of management, a new method of manufacture, automation, CAD/CAM or robotics. The most common of these are computers and IT;
- to contribute to the investigation of some major new product or service, for example, the building and use of the Channel Tunnel between England and France, a new pipeline, an oil rig, a new satellite, a new manufacturing site, building a new town or main road or developing a new product line. The planning and analysis work to investigate a major change can be extensive.

We explain the various kinds of analysis later (p. 71–3).

Constraints on changing the business processes

The above also gives constraints on changes to business processes. For a new or changed business process to be achievable several roles are needed as well as George's role in carrying out the process. These roles can be combined, although for clarity we distinguish them. Someone, e.g. **Susan**, must suggest something that starts the whole activity. Someone, e.g. **Idris**, must have ideas and help to think out the requirements, details and arrangements. Someone must have the ability to analyse, particularly in complicated situations, e.g. **Anna**. Someone, e.g. **David**, must develop any new tools and training needed and devise a way of changing from the existing to the new. The availability of such people, ideas, expertise, tools, and migration possibilities constrains what can be achieved.

Constraints may arise because the existing processes and culture prevent someone thinking of the new or thinking out its details, because, for example, of management pressures and current workload. Driving vehicles on the right or left in different countries is an example where no way exists of moving gradually from the existing system to the new. No worthwhile and acceptable way of arranging the transition to a new situation with all countries the same has been devised, so the existing pattern continues.

In most organizations the existing IT systems and associated staff skills prevent certain kinds of change. In fact, the existing IT and associated processes and data arrangements can be the biggest constraint on certain desirable kinds of change. Managers concerned with changes to business processes need to understand the constraints that arise from the existing systems – both from their technical design and facilities and from what the staff know about how to use them. These constraints have far more effect than if past investment in the systems were written off early.

Computers and IT have been one of the main sources of significant business process improvements for the last thirty years. New IT products continually reach the shops and their prices in real terms fall. But one year's wonder purchase may be the seed of a later year's constraint.

Hidden aims of analysis

The work of systems analysts was not just analysis as defined above. Usually the work had a hidden agenda – to invent significantly improved business processes by using computer-based information systems. This hidden objective was usually not stated openly in order to avoid opposition from existing staff whose jobs might disappear or change unacceptably.

In practice the improvements were usually gradual, not innovative. It was too difficult to envisage any major innovative changes. The systems analysts did not have the training and seniority to propose major changes and, fearing for their job security, would not propose anything that might upset their bosses and other top managers. Senior managers usually did not have the time to understand how the various systems and the business objectives were interrelated, so they could not help the systems analysts by discussing the relevant interrelationships with them. Systems analysts did not have a body of knowledge, methods and skills to do the work.

Some proprietary information system development methods ('methodologies†') recommended analysing the existing systems as a start. The hidden reasoning was both to get the systems analysts, user representatives and managers talking together, about something uncontroversial, and to give hidden training opportunities to the analysts, who were usually dealing with something new to them. After a limited amount of such discussion, managers usually opted out saying they had to return to their normal work and could not afford more time. So they did not continue the discussions long enough to produce the details of useful improvements and innovations.

The distinction between improvement and innovation is usually not very useful to the practitioner. Any useful major innovation usually takes several years and is actually composed of many component parts. Each has taken significant work to develop and test – by gradual improvements to each part. People cannot think of, and implement, major innovations overnight. The many details need planning, design and implementation and the impacts of any proposed change have to be thought through and agreed by those affected.

The above raises many questions. How should Anna and others allocate their priorities? What should she do next at each point and why? How should she carry out the various activities? Who else

known that the whole must finish in a finite time. So in a finite time either the correct result is found or it is established that there is no solution. An algorithm can be programmed and it is known in advance that the computer run will terminate, whatever the data. ISD methods are not algorithmic, although some operations within them are.

Methodology correctly means 'the science of method; a treatise or dissertation on method'; 'a body of methods used in a particular branch or activity'; or 'the science of method in scientific procedure'. Given the widely accepted correct meaning of methodology and the inconsistent use of the term in the fields of business process and information systems development methods, we use the terms **ISD method** and **proprietary ISD method** in preference to methodology.

An ISD method will recommend a certain collection of techniques, and sometimes its authors or their collaborators have provided computer-based tools to help their customer's equivalent of Anna to use the method. So we need to define technique and tool, but first we explain the term style of development, which allows methods to be combined, perhaps after making some assumptions.

Style of development

Several ISD methods may be combined to give a **style of development**.

We use this term to mean a recommendable collection of methods (or parts from several methods) that could be used in an ISD project or business process improvement project. Other concurrent ISD and business projects in the same organization might use different styles of development. A style has more detail than an approach[†], may be management oriented, and may include how to interleave and improve products incrementally by combining methods. The same idea of style of development can be applied to a business process improvement. Various styles of development and life cycles will be presented in Chapters 7, 9 and 12.

Techniques, tools and computers

A **technique** is a describable and specifiable way of performing a fairly low-level operation – a mechanical-like skill. It may be sophisticated and dependent on non-trivial mathematics or other knowledge. A particular technique may be appropriate in certain circumstances so that if these change different techniques could become more suitable.

A **tool** is an artefact to enable an operation or operations to be performed. In IT the term is used specifically to mean a software package running on suitable hardware to enable someone to do something. The term tool is sometimes misused to mean 'technique'.

A **computer** is an electronic machine with circuits that can store and process data under the control of a program. The program is essentially held in the same way as the data, so a computer can create data and use it later as a new program, giving great flexibility to create increasingly complicated and powerful programs.

Hardware refers to the physical components – the circuits, input and output peripheral devices such as keyboard, screen and printer, storage devices such as memory and disks, a processing unit for arithmetic and other logic, and communications equipment. Essentially a computer has a store or memory that holds the program and data, and a control unit that fetches each program instruction in turn from the memory, and sends out signals that cause the rest of the hardware to execute (= carry out) the instruction. Computers can execute millions of instructions per second. Execution speed and memory logical size continually improve, although the physical size of the circuits tends to become smaller.

Software means the totality of all the programs, associated documentation and facilities. This includes: the application programs that do the users' perceived main work; programming language facilities and packages such as compilers and editors that programmers use to create the application programs; operating systems that are programs that manage the transfers to peripherals and control the running of application programs; and software packages of programs for applications such as payroll, accounting, graphics, wordprocessing, spreadsheets, scientific calculations, linear programming optimization and electronic mail.

Computer technology limits what can be provided to George in the way of facilities and tools. Application programs essentially can only do algorithmic processes, otherwise the user could not know whether the process will finish satisfactorily. Even networks of computers and parallel processors have limitations.

Management and human aspects

All the above are to be done in an organizational environment where external and internal pressures, cultures, management styles and other factors will affect people's behaviour and the outcomes. Human aspects – participation, cooperation, acceptance – can be more important than technical features. As the environment and technology change so the purposes, objectives, compromises, development methods and feasibility aspects should evolve. So flexibility to change in a dynamic and proactive environment should be built in since the patterns of changes of facilities and developments will be unpredictable. Anna has problems.

Management aspects such as planning, organizing, directing and controlling apply to all actions – those concerned with the organization's business and those concerned with the provisions and use of its information systems. The right managers should receive appropriate information promptly about the performance of the business and the information systems. They need feedback. Mark and Anna both need such information on Anna's progress.

The business managers also need to plan ahead, in ways such as making appropriate production or marketing plans. This may involve holding a representation of the relevant features of the business in an information system which provides the range of functions to hold and handle such representations. Indeed holding and evaluating several alternative versions is usually needed – alternative proposals, contingency plans for various situations that might happen and

might have occurred in the past, be being done currently or be done in the future. George has several possible plans as alternative futures. He sees order and structure in things. Knowledge and information involve many kinds of representations. People think – involving ideas of intellect, reasoning, cause and effect, ethics, space and time, and change.

Exercise 1.7

Create a list of about 30 terms that cover classes of ideas about describing the real world and life. Think particularly of terms that could apply to business organizations, their processes and information.

You might have highlighted terms in the text above, and extended the list as in Figure 1.4 (p. 38, to avoid you seeing it accidentally). A dictionary or a thesaurus would give a far longer list.

We have chosen to mention terms associated with business processes and information systems both in the paragraph above about Anna's observations and in Figure 1.4. Defining all these terms is not the point. They serve to illustrate the huge variety of concepts that information systems may need to handle to represent effectively a part of the real world.

Providing information systems that can just handle terms representing these concepts, however, does not meet the full need. Just providing word processors that can store and print such words achieves little more than typewriters did beyond easier correction, editing and handling of styles, fonts and formats.

To be useful the information systems should have facilities for handling the concepts themselves – their structures and associations – for checking the completeness and consistency of derived products, and particularly for improving the effectiveness of the appropriate business processes.

Self check

Please spend some time reviewing what you have read. We suggest that you look again at the summary boxes, definitions and margin notes. Do not worry about terms that have not yet been defined – we define them in Chapter 2. If you need to read text more than once you may like to try reading Chapter 2 before rereading this first chapter.

Objectives

After reading this chapter you should be able to:

- state some generalizations about people, information and actions;

- explain why permanent records of information and knowledge are needed;
- explain why most information flows need two-way communication facilities;
- explain various general purposes of information;
- discuss some of what managers have to do regarding information service facilities;
- discuss some of the main kinds of uncertainties in providing information services;
- explain the collective organizational problem of allocating issues to staff;
- explain the kinds of information that flow vertically up and down a management reporting structure, and the reasons for horizontal and other flows;
- use the following terms, insofar as they have been explained: information, information system, system, subsystem, approach, systems approach, ISD method, optimize, vertical information flow, horizontal information flow, methodology, algorithm, style of development, technique, tool, computer, hardware, software.

The exercises in the text above and the questions below test these points.

Questions

Please do *all* the questions *in writing* before checking with the solutions in Appendix B at the back of the book. Educationally, most people are more likely to find their misunderstandings and to remember new knowledge if they have made it their own by writing something, rather than just reading a question and thinking 'Oh yes, that's right' when glancing at the solution.

Most of these questions test your understanding of the material so far. The questions at the ends of some later chapters include longer exercises that illustrate how concepts apply in real situations, or make minor new points.

1.1 Decide whether each of the following assertions is true. If it is only partly correct, or is vague, muddled or misses the point, then write a correction.

(a) Business processes are the basis for structuring staff into departments.

(b) A business process starts to happen when all the appropriate information reaches the appropriate person.

(c) Analysing information about past sales may create data that is not useful for planning future marketing.

(d) An information system is an assembly of computer and communication system parts that has interfaces for information to flow across its boundary and that provides facilities to its users.

(e) A person's manager is responsible for the provision of satisfactory information handling facilities for that person's work.

2

Modelling business and information needs

We explain how actions benefit from planning, review and control as a management control cycle. In some situations the planning and control work may be far larger than doing the action. This leads on to how actions and facilities such as information systems have well-structured limitations. George is limited by what is provided to him and his current knowledge, education and experience. These are a subset of what could be provided within available resources which themselves are a subset of what is available or could be developed. Those in turn are a subset of what could be achieved within current technology and the totality of current knowledge worldwide which are a subset of what is theoretically possible. Any of these may or may not be worthwhile or culturally acceptable.

So managers face problems in how to decide what processes George should do and what IS facilities should be provided. Further problems arise because those involved may not be able to analyse and plan what is really needed. Pressures arise not only from the objectives and strategy of the business, but also from human issues and patterns of work. Some problems are well defined, others are not so well defined and some have a combination of well and ill defined components.

Many modelling issues arise. Data is a representation of reality and is handled by appropriate processes that mirror corresponding real situations and changes. The situations are dynamic, not only because they change with time but also because the rules change. Ideally, the facilities and procedures will have the features for coping with these aspects.

An information system consists of people who undertake manual parts, and it usually also has automated parts that include IT-based parts and non-IT parts. It is a system working within an environment and so needs the right features for success in that environment – fitting the organization's objectives and strategy, fitting the people and fitting the management style.

Developers face problems in trying to decide about standards: what should be automated, what should be IT-based, whether to develop a bespoke one-off process and IS or purchase whatever is the best available from suppliers. They also face many soft issues that managers may disagree about, including how to make decisions about these and other issues.

Modelling the real world, and modelling many possible futures such as the alternative plans that George and Graham might invent and want to simulate or evaluate before deciding between them, involves many complexities. George's IS becomes a working model of reality. Information flows to and from the IS, not only to and from him but also to and from many other people. It also has processes and built-in rules that help it to keep an accurate and consistent model of the continually changing relevant part of the real world.

Anna, Idris, Mark and others envisage the whole of that modelling in different ways. Additionally, as they discuss future business processes and future information systems, they impose their modelling of the information systems and processes, and the dynamic changes to them. Because of the many unknowns, and because organizational survival may depend on what they provide to George, their plans must be well founded. Because of external uncertainties and the likely need for future evolution, flexibility is needed. One way towards achieving these objectives is by having many independent parts in the created systems.

Anna and Idris need ways of representing their models and proposals during discussions and as documentation. They may use diagrams and text. They may be helped by computer-based tools. In their minds, they separate their mental models, their conceptual models created as representations of requirements that are free of rules that would otherwise constrain them in undesirable ways, their logical models of how they or George would view things and the physical models of how things are or will be behind the scenes.

They make choices about how they structure their work. For example they may regard a development as having activities and tasks within it. These may or may not overlap. They may do many kinds of analysis: of requirements, of processes, of data, of business functions, of behaviour, of responsibilities, of volatility. These various kinds of analysis lead to creating many models of differing aspects. As analysis continues these models are extended. The models need to be merged and unified. Consistency and completeness checks may be done, or it may not be worthwhile to continue too far. That is another issue which needs continual decisions.

The eventual systems will have the Georges and Grahams as performers of the business actions and users of the ISs, and other people as developers, providers and administrators. Integrated systems where data is shared between many users, perhaps having differing views of the structures and kinds of data that they handle, may need database management system software, particularly in large organizations or organizations with many transactions involving numerous clients or customers.

Richard's story

To introduce some ideas we start with a short story.

In 1958–9 Richard Maddison did some research on commercial applications of computers. In those days there were few computers,

First, planning then becomes a larger part of the whole, perhaps even dwarfing doing the work itself, reviewing it and effecting control. Mistakes in planning could mean that everything done later is wasted. That may be avoided by increased planning which should reduce the risk of errors and failures later.

Second, where George needs tools that are not readily available, extra planning is needed to acquire the tools. Perhaps the tools have to be specially built as part of the planning. Even if the tool can be purchased, the selecting and purchasing actions to acquire the best tool may take more time than George takes doing the job itself. If George needs training to use the tools then that entails extra planning action preceding the work. Similarly, if George has to use some new or changed procedure, then extra planning and training will be needed. Again this can take longer than George takes doing the work itself.

> The more complex the action, the more disproportionate the amount of planning.

This increased-planning feature was explained in the contexts of creating changed business processes, changed information system facilities or other tools for George. Planning becomes the main action and work. But the planning can itself become so large and complex that the action applies to doing the planning. The first and second aspects just described then again apply to those actions that are the planning for George's action. Extra work is needed to plan Anna, Idris and David's actions and to provide resources and tools for them.

In his story Richard spent months developing a computer-based tool and associated human processes that were quite different from the current processes performed at the store, although equivalent in the sense that the final results in terms of paying suppliers and producing accounts were essentially indistinguishable. The store's Georges were trained to work Richard's processes, and they could deal with one month's invoices in far less time than Richard had spent on planning, analysis, development of programs and other procedures, human relations, and so forth.

Just as the store had many invoices every month, similarly George might have many fairly similar actions. So the planning is done only once for all the set of George's actions, except perhaps for a trivial amount of planning for each individual action within the set. Similarly review and control is mostly done only once for the set. The whole set is regarded as being undertaken for the same client, Claire, even though the actions may be parts of work for many separate customers of the organization. The planning also includes all of the work involved in setting up the above, including providing facilities for the review and control actions undertaken by George and Claire.

Complicated planning and provision of tools such as ISs is done once, and it is worthwhile in situations where George will have many somewhat similar future actions and can apply the same processes and tools to each of them.

Optimization of each pattern of work

How should a good pattern of work be arranged? Suppose George has a proposed pattern for a set of actions. This includes a certain amount of work doing each item within the set. He also does a certain amount of the following: planning done once for the complete set, planning for each individual item within the set, control by him for the set as a whole, control by him for each item, where reviewing is done once for the set perhaps by testing and checking a sample, and a certain amount of redoing what is unsatisfactory. The proposed pattern will include certain amounts of all the corresponding planning and reviews and control actions by Claire. The relative amounts and the actual amounts of each of these kinds of action will be varied.

George and Claire have many kinds of work – such as planning, reviewing, control, checking and redoing – where the amounts of each element and their relative amounts may be varied. One problem is how the optimum should be determined.

First George and Claire need to know what to optimize. Suppose their time costs so much per hour, and that for simplicity we ignore other factors. The objective is therefore to choose the correct amount of each kind of work to minimize their total time taken.

Think of climbing a hill. At the top, if you go in any direction you will be going down from the top. Think of two variables in the list above, say the amount of planning done once and the amount of control by George while doing each item, as represented by north and east. The optimum pattern will be such that if the planning were increased, like going north, the overall total would be made worse, like spending too much on planning. If the planning were reduced, going south, the result would also be worse because the increased costs of the increased scrap and reworking would be more than the reduction in the planning costs. Similarly going east or west by increasing or reducing the amount of control would make overall total costs worse. So the amounts of each variable should be such that if any were either increased or decreased the result would be worse.

The above corresponds to altering one variable at a time, keeping the others unchanged. On a hill the local terrain can be like a **saddle point**, as shown in Figure 2.2. On a north–south road, comparable to varying only one variable at a time, it is a maximum. Similarly for east–west. But a suitable combination of changes to both variables could give a significant improvement. Such a saddle point is *not* an optimum. It corresponds to where the two factors interact. Appropriate specialists know the relevant mathematics to handle and optimize such situations, provided someone can specify how height varies as a function of the variables, of which there can be far more than two.

FIGURE 2.2
A saddle point that is not an optimum place of maximum height.

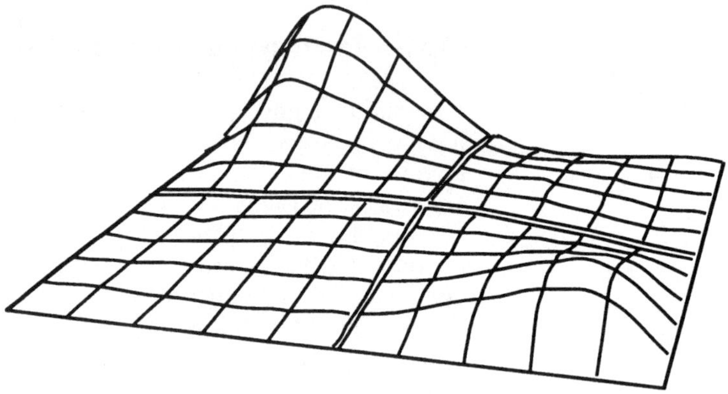

Usually in practice George and Claire do not have the information enabling them to know the effects of increasing or decreasing the variables above. Over a long period they may try small variations. They may make a minor change to a variable concerning how things are done for a week, and they have some measure of performance or cost that can easily be evaluated each week. This is a trial-and-error way of gradually improving a variable in a process and may be the only way to try to optimize it. Rarely, if ever, can George and Claire work out or acquire the knowledge of how the variables above interact, such as what would happen if they increased planning and also reduced control.

Optimizing the wider whole system or organization

The above was described in terms of just Claire and George. In principle the idea may be extended to the whole organization or to a part such as a business system. In practice Claire and George as individuals, and the managers of a large organization, cannot obtain the information to perform such global optimization. Cross-charging between departments may help, such as Claire being charged for George's work, but it could distort the underlying real situation.

Optimization needs the *variation* in the value of George's scrap and rework to be taken into account, and the *variation* in Claire's planning contributions, and so on. To set up information systems to do all that is hardly feasible. The costs of those systems themselves, and the time taken by George and Claire in accounting for how they spent their time in sufficient detail for *variations* to be observable with confidence, is unlikely to be worthwhile. The whole is also affected by the continually changing external environment, which could dwarf the effects.

At a human level Claire and George might also object, regarding the system as providing them with an unacceptable working environment and management burden. Leaving each small group such as George and Claire to discuss its local actions and coordination, usually gives the best achievable result.

> The pattern of optimum ratios between planning, doing actions, and review and control is unlikely to be achieved. The information needed to determine the optimum is probably not available and cannot be made available. Some approximation to it can be achieved by commonsense.

The above applies not just to Claire and George as described, but also to all those involved in management, those trying to improve business processes and those trying to improve information systems. Their work is essentially composed of actions that represent planning for some other actions later. They may miss the availability of some new knowledge such as a research result published in another country, which could have been applied in a way that would have been beneficial in their work. They are unlikely ever to know.

Factors affecting improvement in processes and actions

Suppose someone, Susan, thinks of an improvement. More usually she may think of some vague idea, without all its details. The idea indicates something that is probably worth investigating and Susan suggests the change to her manager or feeds it into the organization's suggestions scheme. If it is a very small change, affecting only Susan and perhaps her colleagues, her manager may consult those affected, agree it and authorize any small expenditure needed.

A team is formed to work on the suggestion

A slightly larger suggested change may need a small team to discuss it and decide about it. If it affects a wider group of people or is a more major change then it should be passed to some appropriate group in the organization whose members will discuss it and make some decision as to whether and how to pursue it further. If it seems likely to be worth some work, we assume that it is passed to Idris and Anna and an appropriate team is asked to work on it. For a really large project a fresh team may need to be assembled, perhaps by seconding staff from their current jobs or by creating new jobs. The team considers the suggestion, perhaps develops a related but better alternative, and does all the work leading to the implemented change.

People move so knowledge is lost

In theory the team, including Idris and Anna, should presumably have appropriate knowledge of all aspects of the current systems from the documentation and from experience in creating them. In practice this is not so. After doing a major piece of work people often move on to something else or have a rest. Others are recruited and promoted and move to gain experience. So the availability of those with the experience and knowledge of the details of previous projects and existing systems, and how to do such work, becomes lost.

In order to avoid repetition, we assume the work entails the following: appropriate evaluations of alternatives, planning of actions, making recommendations and decisions; resources for, and the management of, the whole process; correctness and quality of the various products; liaison and cooperation between those involved; and ensuring that the whole is done satisfactorily to an agreed overall plan. Work may stop at any stage where it does not seem worthwhile to pursue a particular line further.

Exercise 2.1

Under what circumstances are Idris and Anna likely not to have such knowledge of a current business process or an information system's details? In what situation are they likely to have to start from scratch?

Idris and Anna will not have such knowledge if they have been recently recruited, if previous work was not documented or if the current system was supplied externally by being purchased as a package or supplied by a consultant. If they and Mark think a really large project is needed, then maybe they should start from scratch to avoid wasted work. We summarize this start-from-scratch situation next, but ask you to remember that Idris and Anna may rely on existing knowledge and do only the appropriate minimum work, and that the whole could be an ongoing activity.

For a complete ISD (information systems development) project, Idris and Anna find out the organization's objectives, strategy and tactics, or the relevant part of them as explained in Chapter 3. They find out the consequential information needs of everyone in the relevant part of the organization. Different people, George and his friends, will be expected to have different needs and these will probably change gradually. Here **information needs** means not just the information they receive and generate, and where such information flows from and to. Rather it also includes finding out enough about the underlying work, actions, reasons and patterns. The team bear in mind the likely future and perhaps several alternative futures; they do not think only of the current patterns. This is one approach to **analysis**.

The team think of alternatives that are likely to be improvements. They select from among these in increasing detail. They design George's future methods of working and the changed information systems (ISs) and facilities – if and where changes are needed. They build the new information handling facilities. They install the equipment and train George to use it.

Impacts of changes

IT may reduce human contact

The team think of the likely effects of changes. The information handling facilities can affect not just how George does his ordinary work, but also how George communicates with others. For example, horizontal information flows from George to staff in other departments may in future flow through the new information handling facilities instead of George having a face-to-face meeting, phoning or sending a memo through the internal mail. After a few years, perhaps the Georges hardly know their opposite numbers in other departments. At most they phone each other or send memos when the information systems seem to indicate some exception that needs clarifying or rectifying. Such phone calls and memos are essential for the smooth working of the whole, and such information flow facilities must be provided. IT systems alone are not sufficient.

Exercise 2.2

How can vertical information flows be affected?

Vertical filtering and power reduced by IT

George's manager, Graham, may receive some information about George's work and performance in new ways from the changed information systems and not, as previously, from George himself. More generally the content of the vertical information flows may change significantly. Graham's manager, Gwen, may get information directly from a computer system instead of in the form of a progress report from Graham. So Graham can no longer delay or filter information about George's results on its way to Gwen. Graham and George lose power.

Conflicting factors

George wants pleasing processes and interesting information facilities for job satisfaction. The fancier they are, the more they cost and the longer they take to provide.

Mark feels that ISs are to be planned and provided using the same kind of decision-making procedures as other investment. The IS developments may need complex work to analyse what is needed and to decide upon the design, implementation and installation details. So Mark cannot be given an exact specification of the equipment and its cost before Anna has done the analysis and design work. Thus he has a timing problem of how and when a reasoned proposal can be formed, with costs fully known, before significant expenditure is incurred on work by the team.

Managers might be unable to say what is really needed

George and his manager, Graham, and Graham's manager, Gwen, and their colleagues have other pressures on their time. Perhaps they cannot spend as long as Anna would like in order to discuss and explain their needs to her. They may be frightened of changes – maybe even of losing their jobs. They could have other hidden reasons for not wanting to cooperate – such as fear of being shown as ignorant or unable to discuss and explain. Perhaps they have an expertise that they regard as essential to the organization and fear that if they disclose it to Anna then computerization could make them redundant.

They might not have the education and training to explain and document their procedures and priorities, so they may find it difficult to specify what they really need. They might not be able to visualize a substantially changed situation that Anna might suggest – involving new information, new procedures and new methods of working. Problems of workload, fears and hidden agendas can hinder effective communication.

The organization is longterm unstable

The organization's strategy, tactics and information needs could change in the future in ways that cannot currently be known to anyone. Restructuring disrupts. Mark and George will not know about such possible future changes and so certainly will not be in a position to suggest them to Anna. Anna can hardly be expected to think of all the possible future changes of organizational strategy, never mind build-in all the facilities and flexibility that would be needed to cope with their consequences!

Flexibility, if it can be afforded

The patterns of George's work and his detailed information needs may alter as the patterns of business operations vary with changing customers and suppliers, changing external pressures and changes to the products and services that the organization produces. George's use of the IS facilities will change as he gains familiarity and confidence. So Mark should encourage, and Anna should incorporate if possible, flexibility in the ways that George may use the IS facilities to be provided.

Table 2.1 Soft and har[illegible]aches

Soft means:	*Hard means:*
• not sure what the problem is	• know what the problem is
• not sure what needs to be known	• know all that needs to be known
• unstructured, messy, ambiguous	• structured, clear-cut, definite
• no obvious way of working it out	• clear methods for working it out
• solution might be any one of many things	• solution can only be one thing
• uncertainty whether or not a claimed solution is correct	• a solution, when found, is usually widely agreed as being correct
• people disagree, even over priorities	• generally everyone involved agrees — as people do about science findings
• does not have agreed assumptions about what can be done, and applies to ill-defined ways to aid understanding and clarify work, e.g. ways to decide business and requirements and designs	• has agreed assumptions about ways to proceed, well-defined, well-structured steps, with a traditionally simplistic cookbook approach to ISD
• stresses the importance of people and systems, allowing controversy over boundaries, responsibilities, specifications	• emphasizes data and computer processes, with well-structured specifications and models
• perceives software development as primarily an organizational issue	• perceives software development as primarily a technical issue
• does not assume the final goals, so the nature of what is needed is unspecified; but instead tries to help with clarifying and defining the *what*, as well as perhaps to a lesser extent *how*	• assumes the ultimate goal, the nature of what is needed, is an IT-based IS and so concentrates on *how* to develop the IT-based parts; or assumes the goal is a new business system so concentrates on how to create it
• concentrates on a project's early stages, e.g. the human relations in getting started	• gives greater emphasis to the project's later stages

TABLE 2.1
Soft and hard, as applied to problems, methods and approaches

Thus for many reasons the team can have difficulty in deciding what is really needed and what to provide. Even if Anna could get a specification of what was required it would be partially unknown and excessively flexible, missing many details and containing too many alternatives. Anna would have the problem of turning that specification

Difficult to decide what is really needed and what to provide

into software and hardware and into programs and data where everything is predefined and coded as clear-cut processes and data structured suitably for George to use. This is a problem of transforming the soft, uncertain and incomplete into the hard, definite and complete.

Table 2.1 explains the terms **soft** and **hard**. These terms were originally applied to classifying problems, sometimes alternatively called **issues**. They were later applied to the kinds of ways that people tackle problems, including approaches and methods. Think of these terms as extremes of a continuum, rather like a spectrum with many combinations in between.

To some people the term problem has the connotations of problems in mathematics and sciences, where usually they are hard as defined above. We do *not* imply this when we use the terms **problem** or **issue**.

All the above factors are soft issues.

Exercise 2.3

Pause and think to what extent you prefer soft or hard problems, thinking of examples of each class from your work or studies. Then think of some of your colleagues: which are they best at?

Many IT specialists are not happy working with soft issues such as those explained above. Some scientists and engineers are similar. These specialists prefer the definite, such as finding out the names of the types of data that George uses and the details of his corresponding processes, and programming these as database structures and programs. They dislike writing project proposals involving uncertainty, and dealing with conflicts of opinions.

On the other hand many managers are downcast when required to apply the hard methods of science, engineering and technology, preferring to debate softer issues and human problems. For example, some people cannot express themselves correctly in English or manipulate what mathematicians see as equations involving differentials, such as how the rate of change of some variable depends on certain other variables, or how and why something oscillates around a stable equilibrium.

Few people are equally good with both soft and hard problems.

Issues about modelling

Next we explore how a relevant part of the real world, or a proposal or plan, can be modelled. In most sciences various things in the real world are represented by symbols on paper and these symbols are manipulated according to rules, like solving equations. One objective is to have sufficiently correct rules so that the deductions from the manipulated symbols correspond to the way that the relevant part of the real world behaves. Think of the computer as having within itself the symbols, perhaps held as data, and the rules of manipulation, perhaps held as programs. The people who use and operate the computer, by giving it commands, manually control how and when the computer performs the manipulation processes. The people, computer and software and the associated knowledge, documentation and human procedures together form a system.

Data

Data is:

- a **representation** of some part of reality, usually recorded in a form (= representation) in which it can be processed by equipment operating automatically, e.g. computers under control of a program;
- typically groups of characters, representing part or the whole of raw **facts**, e.g.: 'BN3333';
- a **structured** collection of **symbols** that is made up from allowable symbols.

Data can involve symbols, characters, codes, syntax and structure representing information and knowledge. In some sense the **allowable symbols** are an agreed set. Examples include: all the printable, control and other symbols that are available on a keyboard; or all those allowed in a computer representation of a wordprocessing document; or all those allowed in a programming language. In a programming language the allowed symbols can be listed. For example, 'begin' is a single allowable symbol.

We distinguish data in example situations, such as BN3333 above, by using a different font to help you. We also use another particular font for reserved symbols such as begin to help you to distinguish them.

More difficult to envisage initially is the set of words allowed in a language such as English but restricted by an agreed set of editorial conventions that include preferred spellings. Here the words are symbols that cannot be *meaningfully* decomposed into letters, such as begin above. The term **element**, as in chemistry, and derived terms such as **elementary data item** and **elementary process**, are such that they cannot be meaningfully subdivided within the current viewpoint.

Coded characters are ways of embedding meaning by suitable structure and choice of characters in data. For example nearly all UK vehicle registration numbers have a letter indicating the year of first registration, and two letters indicating where it was registered. UK postcodes and zip codes in some other countries have similar features.

Names, types and occurrences

A particular object and its representations, such as 'the sun', has (or can have) three associations:

- the actual **object** that can be seen in the sky;
- a **logical name** associated with it, such as 'The sun was shining when …';

- a **data** string representing the object, e.g. the sound patterns when reading the word 'sun', or electronic patterns representing the same sounds, or binary patterns representing the letters of the word, or some other representation such as a picture, abbreviation or representation in shorthand.

Additionally, as you read this, you form or recall mental images of the object, the name and other words, and the image of the physical print on the paper and you associate these ideas correctly together.

That idea applies to single unique physical objects, but can also apply to abstract objects like the day, Monday 28 March 1994. George has to distinguish the following: that period of 24 hours; the words in and for the logical name associated with it, such as 'Monday' 'March' '28' '1994'; and corresponding data such as `1994.03.28`, `28/3/94`, and `3/28/94`.

In general a particular object may have more than one acceptable logical name, and may have different representations as data in different human systems, computer systems or in different parts of a human or computer system. Additionally, an object may have several names, minor variants of the names and synonyms within any one language; and the world has many natural languages and many computer languages.

Synonyms are two or more words, terms or names for the same thing, such as Product-no, Part-no, Material-item-no. Minor variants of Product-no include Product#, Prod#, ProductNo, ProdNo, P#. **Homonyms** are two or more meanings or objects for a particular name or word. Homonyms of Product include meanings as something produced by manufacturing, something supplied, a result, a work, offspring and a number obtained by multiplication.

Sometimes a unique object does not have a corresponding unique name, so a phrase or clause is needed to describe it. For example you are (presumably) reading a particular copy of this book, but that copy might not have a unique logical name. If you have two copies and have numbered them you might refer to 'My Copy 2 of that book'. If you have not numbered or marked the copies in any way, they can probably be distinguished only by their physical positions at particular times, e.g. the copy that was on the kitchen table yesterday afternoon.

Terms like 'car' and 'brick' can be used in ways that do not refer to unique objects. They are typically a logical name for a **class** (= **type**) of similar objects. In using such a term, George has created a classification, classifying all the relevant actual objects into the named class. George may define the class either by listing all its members, as a school lists all the pupils in a particular class on a particular date, or George could give a rule that defines the class, such as all the employees of The Open University employed in the UK on a particular date. There may be none or millions of instances, that is occurrences of actual corresponding objects in the relevant real world.

Idris and Anna then think of a further generalization – collections of members at different times and dates. For example, you could think of the set of all vehicles licensed in the UK on the first day of the next month after the day that you are reading this sentence. No one yet knows which vehicles will be included. On the day you are reading this no one can even know how many such vehicles there will be. But the set can be defined and discussed.

The set that Anna thinks *could* occur may be even larger. For example the set of all possible vehicle registration numbers for that month is far greater than those that will actually occur.

When discussing information systems and processes for George to handle future occurrences, Idris and Anna may be able to estimate the population. The processes and facilities should allow for all reasonable possibilities so that George has no problem when the actual ones arise.

Exercise 2.4

Under what circumstances can there be infinitely many members of a set of possible occurrences of a named class that George uses?

How could all bricks or trees be distinguished?

Some people might think incorrectly that most such classes could have an infinite number of member occurrences. However, the number of cars in the world is finite, even if large. Similarly the allowable registration numbers are finite, though larger than the number of vehicles. The number of combinations of a finite number of letters forming a string of not more than a certain length is finite. From, say, 36 symbols in eight positions, only 36 to the power 8 vehicle registration numbers can be formed, perhaps less if the positions of spaces are not distinguished.

Similarly the number of atoms in the universe is finite, believed to be about 10 to the power 80. The earth has about 10 to the power 50 atoms. So the finite number of bricks is less than that divided by the number of atoms in a brick.

Objects such as bricks and trees, which have no **identifying** name, can be distinguished by referring to their **physical position at a particular time**. For example, one can indicate a particular object by combining map grid reference, height above sea level or some other datum, date and time – each specified to sufficient accuracy.

Most of the descriptions of the relevant part of reality that Anna handles involve **classes** or **types** of objects and ideas, and associations between them. Here the term **object** becomes widened to include almost anything – actions, behaviour and all the concepts in Figure 1.4 (p. 38).

Simple models

To a young child a toy is a model of part of reality, as well as being a real object. For effectiveness people usually choose the part of the real world that fits their current interest or their needs and omit other parts. For example, a road map represents only certain selected roads in a selected part of the world. Bends, junctions, bridges and other features are either omitted or clarified by exaggeration and conventional signs. To the user what matters are the features such as accuracy, completeness, consistency, usefulness and ease of use.

The designer of the map, or the designer of the toy, took particular viewpoints about how the product would be used and hence decided what to create a model of, what features to include, and how the user would use the product. Different maps are produced for long-distance motoring and for streets and buildings in towns. If the choices made by the designer of the map are not suitable for the current user's need, poor decisions may follow. Different users, or a single user on different occasions, may want different details for different uses. Similarly, if the child's toy does not appear to model the imagined reality satisfactorily then the child will be less happy with it.

Each model is produced for a particular purpose which may or may not be what is wanted.

Similarly, the providers of information systems make assumptions about the intended purposes and uses of the systems. Such assumptions may be explicitly stated but often are not thought out and remain unstated. Providers also make assumptions about the skills of the imagined future users and therefore the ISs will be able to handle only the data and processes that the designer imagines will be wanted. Designers and providers are limited by the available technology but rarely tell the user what assumptions they built in, and how these limited the facilities.

This idea of models such as maps and simple toys has some oversimplifications. A map is a *static* representation of reality and corresponds to a fixed state at only one instant of time. In contrast, information systems have two *dynamic* aspects.

Dynamic models

Firstly, think of a model railway. The trains move along the track and stop at stations and signals. The model can be controlled and operated to match real railway situations. People operating it can observe what happens and discuss it, propose and plan future model train movements, and then try them and watch them happen.

Secondly, they can alter and reconstruct the track layout, move the stations, alter the rolling stock, reposition the signals and try different safety rules. Perhaps the model itself is changed significantly to match a different real railway or some imaginary situation. After trying something on the model railway satisfactorily, perhaps the operators can get permission to try the same arrangement on a real railway.

Dynamic models allow the items in the model to change to match corresponding real-world changes, or changes in some imagined situation as time goes on. They also allow for alterations to the rules and structure to be made occasionally.

Models where the data is held in an information system, whether on paper or as data in a computer, have both these features. As transactions happen more paper or data is added and also the rules about what is allowed may also change. Idris and Anna bear these principles in mind when discussing proposals for systems that George will use, and George runs a system that is dynamic in both senses.

Introduction to the IS modelling problem

Anna's typical objective may be to produce or improve an information system which is a working model or part of the world, as in Figure 2.3. Every such system is a combination of **manual parts** and **automated parts**, which may be **IT-based** or **non-IT based**. The system operates within an environment.

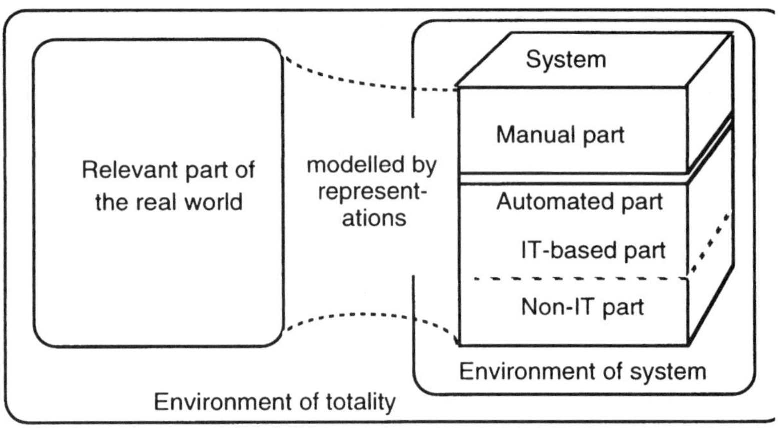

FIGURE 2.3
Modelling part of the world by a system.

The **environment** is everything normally regarded as outside the system but having impact on it, or interfacing with it or on which it has impact. It includes human issues and the management and control of the system.

Figure 2.3 distinguishes and shows no overlap (= intersection) between the relevant part of the real world represented and the environment of the system. In practice these do overlap and this can confuse some people initially. For example, a computer system may be within a company and hold within itself accounts that include the cost of everything in the company, including the cost of the computer. It is like a piece of paper which has written on it symbols that describe the piece of paper and its cost.

The term **IT-based information system** means an IS that includes IT-based parts where these are an important feature in the current point of view. It is a common unfortunate tendency for authors of ISD methods and those involved in developing information systems to focus on the IT-based part rather than on both that and the non-IT based parts.

Exercise 2.5

List about six features that are important for success of any IT-based IS project. Which of your list are hard and which soft?

In practice the important **features for success** include: fitting the organization's **objectives**, business strategy, tactics, budget, timing; the **human relations**; fitting the culture and **management style** of the organization; **acceptance** by the users and managers; **ease of use;** and **perceived usefulness**. All the above are **soft** issues in that people may disagree over the extent to which they have been achieved and how best to solve each one.

The information system **manipulates representations** of real-world **objects** – including **actions involving those objects**. For a particular organization, finding out about these and modelling them may be complex. Specifying and building a tailor-made information system can be very complex. Methods, techniques and tools help with this.

The alternative for a particular organization is to buy a software package that has most of the required features, and then adapt it to fit as closely as possible by setting the options in the package and by having appropriate manual procedures to cover anything else needed.

The **relevant part of the real world** may mean the following.

- Appropriately selected **actual** things and actions – such as certain goods, services, transactions and operations in a business. This can extend to the actual past, the current time and the actual future.
- The equivalents in some **hypothetical** world – considering situations such as what would happen under a particular proposal or assumption, or as intended with an agreed future plan or in an imaginary situation that could have existed but did not.
- A **combination** of reality and several alternative possibilities.

We use the terms **relevant part of the real world**, **real world** and **reality** to include such alternatives without saying so on each occasion.

The term **universe of discourse** (UOD) means everything that was, is or might be under some overall hypothesis, either a hypothetical world or the real world under some plan or assumption, or the real world as it is without any assumption. The objects in the UOD may have many associations between them. A UOD is a mathematical **set** and may have infinitely many elements.

Whereas George handles a finite representation of reality or a particular UOD, Anna and others may think of analysing, designing for and programming all the possibilities of a UOD or even allowing for many UODs.

Exercise 2.6

What combination of the above is being used when an organization's production planners create several alternative outline plans as spreadsheets and choose between them, and then make a computer form a detailed plan that takes into account the current outstanding orders to schedule the desirable optimum production as a plan for the next month?

In this exercise scenario the IT-based IS holds several alternative outline plans. These are evaluated partly by computer (to do the spreadsheet calculations), and partly by management discussion (to take account of external factors and to fit the current strategy). This gives the tactical plan, selected from many hypothetical possibilities. Within the rules of this tactical plan the computer is then used again at a more detailed level to produce an optimum schedule for the coming month. This becomes the actual plan for operations. The IS manipulates data representing the new situation – including the rules of the tactical plan, orders, plant, manufacturing operations, time, resources and everything else which is relevant.

It is desirable that the IS has facilities so that if the strategy is slightly different next year, e.g. to deal with a cashflow problem, the spreadsheets can be modified to show the effects of each alternative on the cashflow. It is also desirable that the facilities provided for the second part, the longer monthly scheduling calculations, have facilities so that slightly different tactical rules can be input quickly and easily. Also, perhaps the layout and details of the outputs need to be changed by appropriate options in the software so as to show the effects of delays if actual production does not keep up exactly with the computed monthly plan. In addition, managers might want to change from monthly to fortnightly or weekly recomputing of the schedule.

Anna's problems in programming the ISs, or in selecting a software package, include the uncertainties of not being able to predict such changes of strategy and tactics. Also she does not want to waste a lot of time programming possibilities that will never be needed. George could want some unexpected change made quickly to enable the organization successfully to ride the cashflow or whatever other situation arises. The survival of the organization may depend on such flexibility.

Furthermore, the organization needs to be able to enhance or replace any component of the IS fairly easily, without affecting George and his work too much.

Exercise 2.7

Give three reasons for needing enhancements or replacements.

Replacements may be needed because of any of the following: obsolescence, caused by factors such as new standards or new interfaces between components; because the business changes so that new facilities are needed; and because developments in IT or production engineering or some other branch of knowledge mean that the products, services or methods need to change to maintain the organization's position, image, effectiveness, market share, profitability and viability.

Some simple modelling

Some readers may need examples of simple modelling as a basis for what follows here and in later chapters, so the following are some examples and exercises involving processes and knowledge. We explain the underlying rules and justification in Chapters 5 and 6 (pp. 146–158; 174–195). These exercises may help you to feel that you have begun to learn a new skill.

We start with a little carefully worded text and create a corresponding diagram.

Scenario

Suppose ABC Manufacturing sends an enquiry about a particular product to a supplier, asking the price and leadtime from order to delivery. The supplier responds by sending that information about the product. The customer then sends a purchase order to the supplier. The supplier next sends the goods to the customer and sends an invoice requesting payment. The customer sends the payment information.

Exercise 2.8

Draw a diagram corresponding to the above scenario showing only the information flows. Draw a box with rounded corners for each person or organization sending or receiving information. Draw a line with an arrowhead for each flow. Against each line write a few words to describe the information represented. Do not invent and add more detail than was given in the scenario. For each flow show the main direction by an arrow, do not include bi-directional communication.

Figure 2.4 is printed overleaf so that you do not see it accidentally before trying to draw the diagram. In this figure, which is an **information flow diagram** (IFD), we show information flows but do not show the physical flow of the goods. In practice the goods may have an advice note, which is information, and this would be shown, but we asked you not to invent further detail. We have used curly brackets in the figure to illustrate an alternative that would be equally correct.

Strictly speaking, no knowledge is carried by the physical layout of the diagram, such as the sequence of the information flow lines down the page. However in Figure 2.4 the sequence corresponds to that described in the scenario. Our convention is that **soft boxes** correspond to how people think about the real-world situation. Soft boxes have rounded corners, or could be hexagons but not rectangles or squares. Later we shall use **rectangular** boxes to depict how things are actually done, or how people view them, in logical models. Also we use named and unshaded boxes for **types** of things. In reality there will be many actual suppliers, invoices and so on, called **occurrences**.

An **Information flow diagram** (IFD) shows information flows between people, areas of responsibility, business systems, information systems and external objects – each represented as a named soft-shaped box. Each flow is a named arrowed line corresponding to the main direction. The purpose is to explain that aspect of the requirements or processes.

We continue with the scenario. Our text here has been carefully worded.

A supplier is sent a purchase order. A supplier can supply a part. The purchase order contains a purchase line item. The part is ordered in the purchase line item.

Exercise 2.9

The above is knowledge about the types of entities (= objects) involved, and how they are related to each other. The nouns are the names of the entity types and the verbs are the names of the relationship types between these entities. Each sentence explains one relationship.

Draw a diagram corresponding to the structure of the entity types and how they are related. Each entity is to be represented by a named box with rounded corners. Each relationship is to be represented by a named line between the appropriate boxes.

Figure 2.5 gives a solution. This diagram is called an **entity–relationship diagram** or an **entity–relationship model**. We have chosen to have all the boxes the same size but that is not necessary. We have also chosen to have names that start with a capital (= upper case) letter; that is also not necessary, although usually done in practice. We have used singular names, as explained in Chapter 1 (p. 26). Usually no knowledge is carried by the physical layout on the page.

We explain more about these diagrams in Chapters 5, 6 and 11. Our purpose here is to give readers who are not familiar with simple diagrams a brief introduction, which may help them in the next few sections.

An **entity–relationship** (ER) **diagram** has named soft boxes representing entity types, and named lines between them representing relationships or associations. Note that this is our form of representation and some other writers use alternative representations.

Modelling the real world

We turn next to some general principles of modelling. Figure 2.6 represents *part* of the real world, a model of it, a change and a changed model.

This can be viewed in two ways.

- Starting from a real-world situation (top left) and its model (lower left), an **actual** change gives a changed real-world situation (top right); the lower right model **should correctly model** that. This corresponds to going *clockwise* round the diagram from top left to lower right.
- Starting from a real-world situation (top left) and a model of it (lower left), a change to the model gives a changed model (lower right); this should correctly **predict** the corresponding future real-world situation (top right). This corresponds to going *anticlockwise* round the diagram from top left to top right.

FIGURE 2.4
Information-flow diagram for customer and supplier.

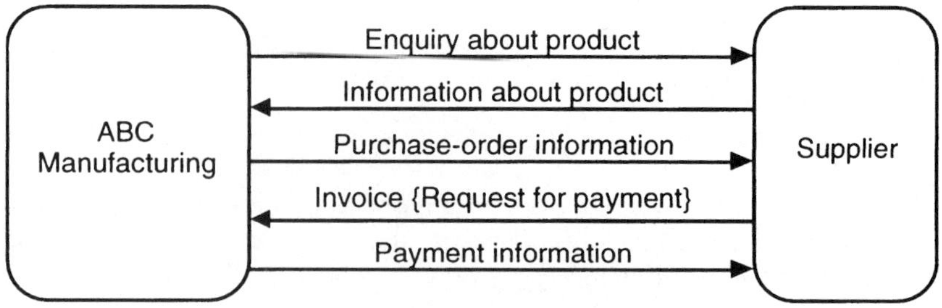

FIGURE 2.5
Example entity types and relationship types.

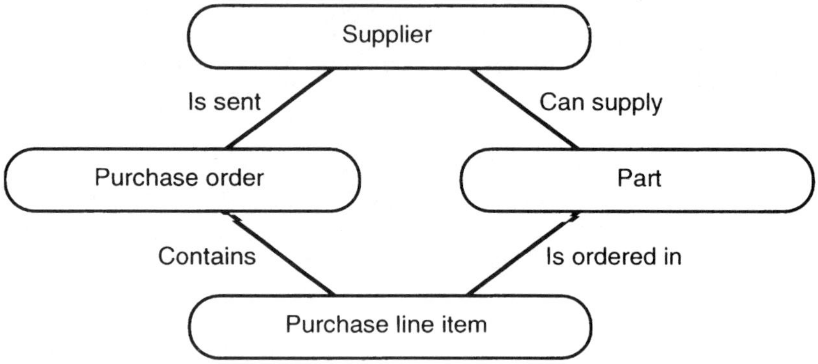

FIGURE 2.6
As the world changes so should the model.

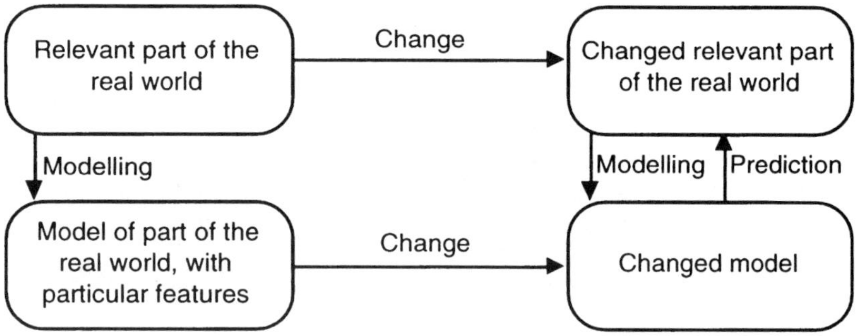

The modelling of changes

The way that the model changes must correspond to the way the real world changes. There must be satisfactory ways of modelling all possible real-world changes, as in Figure 2.7 and, vice versa, all possible changes to the model should have real-world equivalents.

FIGURE 2.7
Changes must be modelled correctly.

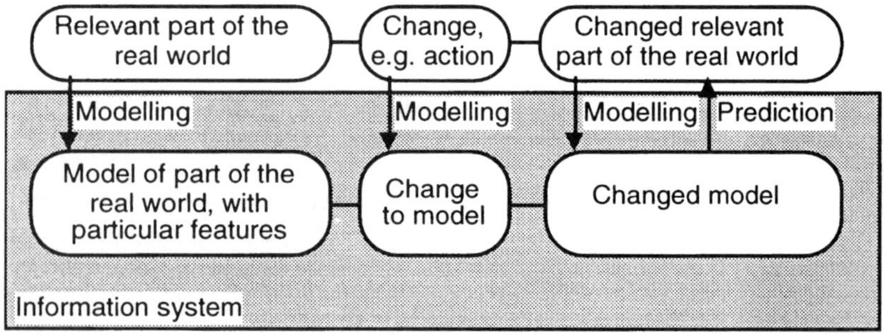

Exercise 2.10

Think of examples of each of these two ways of using such a model – the clockwise and the anticlockwise. Think of situations in which they are combined.

The clockwise first way has a real-world situation and a change to it, and the model should change to match. This applies to recording past events that involve change such as: accounting; recording the history of something (ownership or uses of building, land or equipment); recording customers' transactions as in banks and insurance; and keeping medical and school records. Each real-world object – customer's account, building, policy, person, and so forth – has its own equivalent diagram in which the upper half represents the object and the lower half represents the corresponding records on paper or wherever.

In the anticlockwise second way, the model is changed, processed or calculated to yield a new model which is then interpreted for prediction. This applies in such areas as: weather forecasting; calculating the interest that would be received if some money were to receive interest; calculating the future movements of the earth and moon; estimating a future quantity from the known past pattern and assuming the pattern will continue; and combinations of such. Where the mathematics of the model involves equations, methods of solution must be known so as to be able to calculate forward.

In practice these situations are widely combined, for example estimating or predicting a future situation from continuing the pattern of historical records, and then deciding on a particular real-world action that makes an acceptable change. Some people manage bank account transactions in this way. Organizations use such models to decide how many of what to reorder when.

Modelling as an information system

An IS is a **working model** of part of the real world. The current state of the real world is represented by data and as the real-world situation changes the corresponding data changes. Information flows to and from users such as George. The totality forms a larger system as seen in Figure 2.8.

For a single occurrence of an information system, that is one version, the information and data within that IS is part of the model. Therefore as *small* changes occur, for instance a transaction, the information system has the information change 'fed' into it. In effect it is constantly trying to keep pace with changes in the real world.

George will make **enquiries** and expect the system to provide appropriate information.

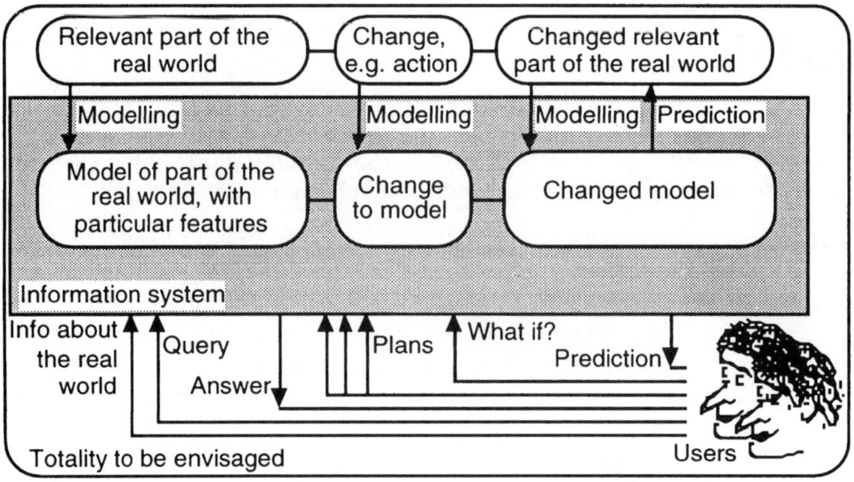

FIGURE 2.8
The total system envisaged includes: the real-world part, its changes, the IS, users and information flows.

Modelling collections of alternative plans

George may input several **plans**, and try 'What if …' scenarios in order to make **predictions**. This involves the IS modelling many different alternative future scenarios. Modelling many such possibilities is far more complex than just modelling the current state of the relevant real-world part.

ISs need to be usable in order to **model actual changes**, and to keep records of the past and the present states of affairs, and also to **model predicted changes**, holding plans and calculating predictions based on them, and also answering hypothetical 'What if …' questions based on variations from the future plans. The IS has to handle many possible changes to the model of the real world, and all the consequences of many changed models, as Figure 2.9 shows.

As well as the stored data changing continually to represent the continually changing current real-world state, the IS's facilities and features could need to be changed gradually to match the changes in requirements and the ways the data is used.

As IT costs fall and new technical developments appear on the market, an IT system may need to be changed to utilize the new possibilities, reduce costs and give (or avoid loss of) competitive advantage. ISs have to last and Mark and Anna should consider:

- how robust are the models for coping with expected business changes? and how long will the system last without needing changes to the functions it can do?
- can the system and its models continue effectively and economically without costly continual evolution to keep up with IT developments?
- what if the supplier ceases trading or ceases supporting the products that are used to hold the models?

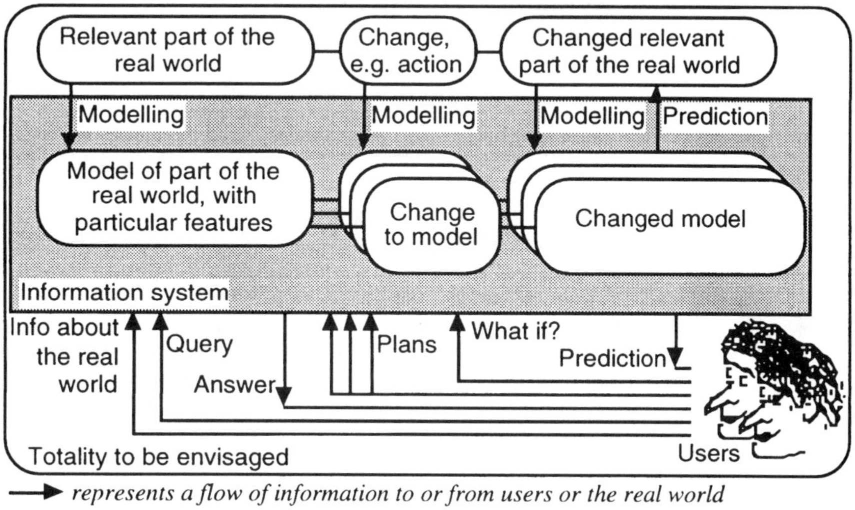

FIGURE 2.9
Many possible plans can be modelled and the best then selected.

Modelling current to future IS

The model of the real world as an IS above needs extending in two ways:

- to form a model of the whole, that is to describe the requirements and modelling of the real world part, the IS, the users, and information flows;
- to describe (like a model) a new IS corresponding to some change, for example before building the new IS.

These two extensions correspond to the lower left box and the right side of Figure 2.10.

This shows the models that Anna works with. Mark and George envisage the same models when discussing future changes to the IS with her. How to do all this modelling, and the design and implementation of the new changed IS in a complex situation, is the issue. The beginning should have been a description of requirements and systems, forming a **conceptual model** – an agreed description for effective communication.

A major change, to strategy for example, usually means that the existing information system either can no longer model part of the real world satisfactorily or does not model some other part of the real world now required. Consequently a new version of the system will have to be envisaged, developed and built. Developing new systems doesn't *sound* too bad – but think of a complex case, such as a large company where migration plans can span years.

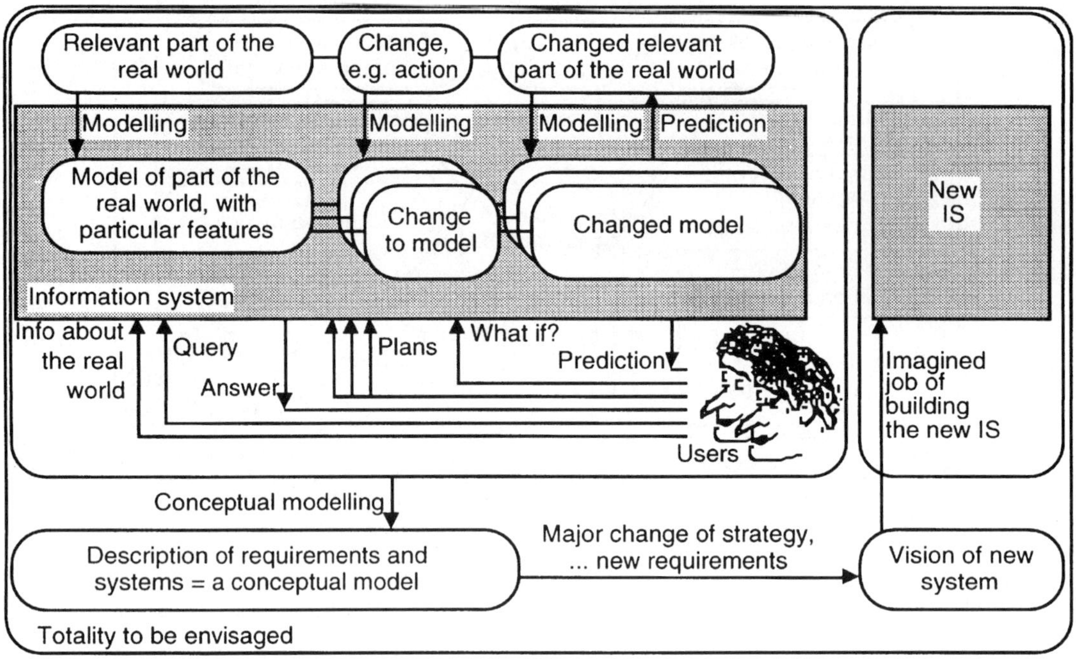

FIGURE 2.10
Current to future IS.

Modelling issues – many representations

In the late 1970s data analysis methods and techniques changed significantly. These were used by Anna during requirements analysis and data analysis as part of the development of computerized information systems. Corresponding software packages for database systems were developed in the same five to ten years. Through the 1980s, database techniques were applied in commerce, industry and public services.

We explain several kinds of analysis later in this chapter (p. 71–3), and more about how to do it all in later chapters.

Many models

Many models, descriptions, specifications, codings and representations are involved in the numerous stages of envisaging the business processes, envisaging an IS, assessing feasibility, specifying and analysing requirements, and in designing, programming, constructing, building, installing, using and retiring an IS.

Features of diagrams and models

Building, using and changing information systems and business processes requires models. Diagrams are used extensively in discussions and modelling. They help communication and expression of ideas during discussion and in documentation. A model is a simplified description of relevant aspects of a system or of part of it, aiding explanation, communication of ideas, calculations and predictions.

We distinguish a particular **model**, one actual product; **models**, features of many such; and **modelling**, ways of doing it. Similarly one can distinguish a design, designs, designing; plan, plans, planning; and so on.

Exercise 2.11

To be useful, what features should a model have? And what features should good diagrams have?

To be useful a model should be smaller, cheaper, easier to use, simpler and faster than its corresponding full system and also correct, relevant, understandable and workable. Or at least have some of these advantages – enough to be worthwhile, i.e. the benefits should outweigh the costs.

A model can simulate and represent part of the real world. The model might do both or either. For example, computer calculations can work out a mathematical model (i.e. solve the equations) of the motion of the air, calculating the pressure at various points. From this the weather can be forecast. The controls of an aircraft flight simulator can be connected to a computer system whose output controls what the pilot under training sees, hears and feels. A computer-based information system can hold data that represents real-world information and can perform processes (e.g. calculations) on it that simulate real-world processes.

Diagrams are used to represent models of processes, information systems requirements and actual information systems. Good diagrams to represent IS models should have the right features. They supplement text and can clarify thinking and help to achieve effective communication. It usually helps to have simple diagram conventions and consistency.

Modelling stages – mental, conceptual, logical and physical

Ignoring various complexities, the main models in transforming the relevant part of the real world into its IS equivalent are *usually* roughly as shown in Figure 2.11. In practice the distinction between the conceptual, logical and physical models is not clear cut and we have tried below to distinguish them in a way that should help an *initial* understanding by those not familiar with these three models and their corresponding development stages. The stages could overlap, depending on organizational management procedures and tactics for a particular project and the details of what is included at which stage may vary from what we give here.

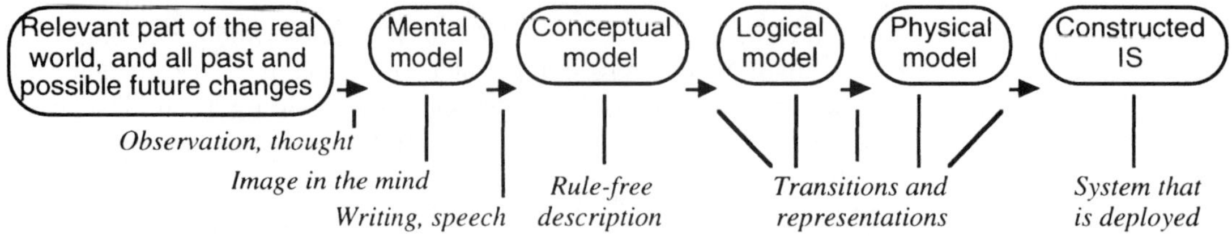

FIGURE 2.11
Some possible models from requirements to deployment.

Each model in such a sequence should carry particular knowledge and details correctly. Figure 2.11 omits several intermediate models, e.g. program code and compiled and linked equivalents. Table 2.2 gives the main properties of each model and a similar sequence may be created for a process. An idea in someone's mind is expressed as a conceptual model with text and diagrams and this is transformed into the logic of how the process will be done using available tools. That in turn is converted into a physical design which is then implemented to give a constructed system for George to use in carrying out the process.

Model	*Main property*
Mental model	Ideas in a person's mind, inaccessible by others
Conceptual model	Rule-free, independent of hardware and software constraints, indicates requirements, helps understanding; can use agreed representations such as EAR and IFDs where the audience understand these
Logical model	A detailed representation based on the conceptual model and created by applying formal modelling techniques.
Physical model	Buildable, as it actually is or will be, within the constraints of the implementation and operational tools, including design details that need not be known to users
Constructed IS	Actually built, provided for use

Some people use terms differently, e.g. logical model to mean as people view the system, or how a proposed system would seem to work or appear to be, with processes arranged to fit particular hardware and software tools; or cognitive model means as users will view the system.

TABLE 2.2
Main property of each type of model

Many versions of the conceptual, logical and physical models may be created as the models are gradually developed. But in practice the **models are never completed** – or even anywhere near completed. They serve different purposes, have different objectives and involve different people because they expect different particular skills of those involved. These three types of model may use different kinds of abbreviations and conventions. At each stage except perhaps the last, the people involved assume that many details can be deferred and dealt with later. Commonsense and defaults are assumed without being stated.

Some people use the terms introduced here – mental model, conceptual model, physical model and logical model – with different meanings from ours.

Conceptual modelling

Rule-free has two meanings: (a) free of rules of software and IT; (b) free of imposing rules of diagrams

The crucial characteristic of a **conceptual model** is that it is as 'rule-free' as possible. **Rule-free** means that no particular rules are imposed, such as rules of software packages or unnecessary diagramming techniques. Conceptual models should be, as far as possible, independent of hardware and software constraints. **Hardware and software independent** means that the description and model at this stage should be independent of the technical features and facilities of any particular implementation. It may not even be known whether a target IS will need computers or not. It may, however, be based on known overall general constraints.

Conceptual modelling typically **produces an articulation of requirements**. These include business requirements, descriptions of who needs what and why, description of the environment, business rules, descriptions of the kinds of information and knowledge handled, and also information system requirements. Conceptual models *should in principle* satisfy completeness criteria, but in practice to do the work required for completeness may take more effort than many analysts are willing to apply. In practice it is not worthwhile if the completeness and consistency criteria are too rigorous for initial conceptual modelling.

User representatives and analysts should use whatever means of communication and representations seem best able to communicate effectively full details of the requirements and underlying reasons. Information for the conceptual model should be gathered and represented in whatever way works. Non-specialists may fail to communicate relevant information if specialists impose particular diagram techniques. If, however, the people involved are familiar with and prefer more formal techniques then these could be used to supplement the ways information is represented.

Many kinds of diagrams may be used for effective communication and representations. These include activity-on-arrow network, activity-on-node network, activity–sequence diagram, bar chart, control loop diagram, critical path network, data flow diagram, effect-correspondence diagram, entity–attribute–relationship diagram, entity life cycle diagram, entity life history diagram, flow-block diagram, flow-process diagram, functional dependency diagram, Gantt chart, influence diagram, information flow diagram, input–output diagram, mind map, multiple cause diagram, project management diagrams and system map.

Logical modelling

Logical modelling typically **produces a functional specification**. This explains how all the functions and processes will appear to work. A **logical model** is the result of formal analysis and considerations of user aspects of design and takes into account features of information technology in so far as it offers automation and efficiency possibilities. Logical models will also specify human procedures and the logical flow of information between people and systems. However, logical models should not normally indicate the physical forms, such as whether information comes on paper or on a particular type of disk, or whether by post, electronic mail, fax or phone. Logical modelling should be sufficiently complete to enable decisions to be taken about how the target IS could be implemented.

Physical modelling

Physical modelling involves making any necessary changes to the logical models to take account of the selection of technology and products to be used for building the information system. It includes technical design and other details that depend on products. The essential characteristic of a **physical model** is that it is **buildable**, i.e. it is constrained by what can be constructed and implemented. These constraints will also be documented.

Physical modelling should take account of the following points: performance requirements; general business and user requirements and rules; technology products selected for implementation; skills and learning; integration with other systems; maintenance, support, enhancement and legal requirements (current and anticipated); management or marketing preferences, strategic decisions, and standards. Human–computer interfaces, computer–computer interfaces and interfaces with communications equipment are specified. Physical modelling typically **produces a design specification**. It includes the layout of data on disks or in documents, the physical flow of data in networks and the physical layout or storing of objects during and between processes.

Transitions between the various models

The transitions between models in a sequence such as that in Figure 2.11 may mark phases, stages or project milestones, as Figure 2.12 shows. In practice, as explained in Chapters 4, 7 and 8 these could be overlapped.

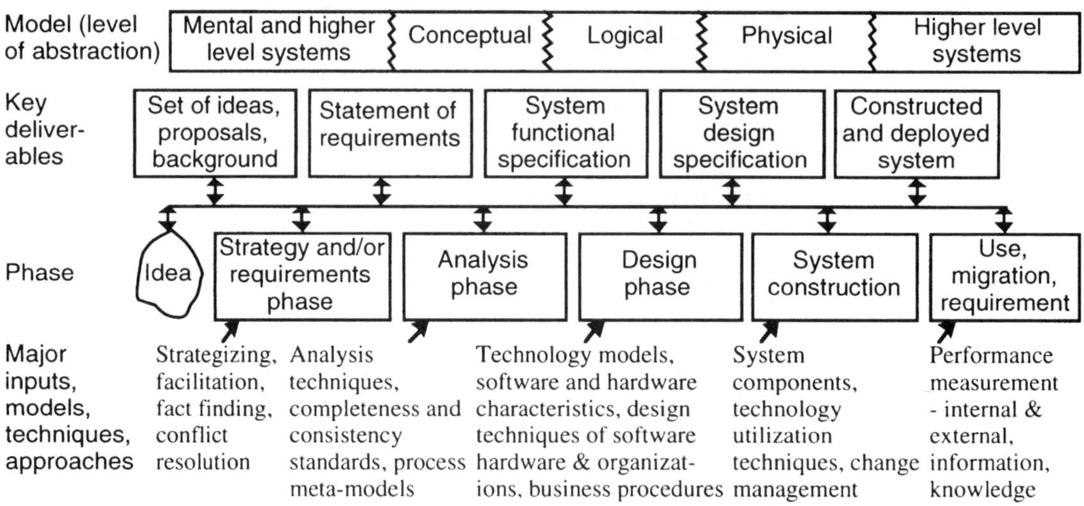

FIGURE 2.12
Some possible modelling phases.

Transition from one stage to the next means transformation between different models. In principle, the various models each represent the requirements but at varying stages between the initial idea and the final implementation of a system to serve the purpose. So each model should be somewhat nearer the implemented system than the previous model. Each transition will involve many subsidiary mental models, processes, actions and documentation which are not shown here. Table 2.3 shows the possible principal phases in which the various models are created or derived.

Model produced	*Phase that produces that model*
Conceptual model	Strategy phase and/or Requirements phase and/or Analysis phase
Logical model	Analysis phase and/or User-design phase
Physical model	Design phase or Technical-design phase
Constructed IS	Construction phase

TABLE 2.3
Which phase produces which model

These phases correspond to a simplified view of part of a software life cycle†. A phase applies to a major collection of activities and tasks. A **life cycle** is a set of phases to be performed in a specified sequence. Usually it starts with, for example, strategy or planning for an ISD and finishes with removal of the IS. It specifies the phases, the deliverables at the end of each phase, the tasks, activities and roles (e.g. analyst, designer, ...), and perhaps the management methods (e.g. review and report at each stage).

A **life cycle model** is a model that is a candidate that might be recommended for many ISD projects or ISs. Typically, it specifies a structure of phases and the activities within each of them. We explain later (Chapters 7 and 12) that there are many life cycle models, some of which are very different from Figure 2.12.

Analysis methods and skills

Next we explain various kinds of analysis. Analysts need methods of analysing the business processes and the kinds of information that can flow to and from staff and be held as data. If the fundamental nature of the structure of the business processes and the information is not understood correctly, then the IT-based information systems are likely to be implemented in ways that make later evolution difficult.

How does one ensure the analysis is correct? There is no universal answer but there is a body of techniques that have been found useful in practical situations. Many alternative methods of analysis and of structuring information have been proposed and the more successful ones are explained later in Chapters 7, 9 and 11.

Analysis can be divided crudely into the kinds listed below. These kinds of analysis overlap and generally may be done in any sequence, in parallel or in any combination. Each kind may be pursued as far as is judged worthwhile or relevant. Good analysts can change between these kinds of analysis from hour to hour.

Each kind of analysis is both a human relations task, getting managers involved, and a technically complex task requiring many skills to create clear, unambiguous specifications and getting agreement to them. Each involves finding out and documenting the details in ways such that everyone involved can agree them and use them. Although summarized here, some of these kinds of analysis are explained more fully later in Chapters 5–9 and 11.

- **Requirements analysis** (RA) means finding out what the system requirements are. Many people say their needs are just to perform an operation faster or more effectively.

- **Systems analysis** (SA) consists of collecting, organizing and evaluating facts about a system, actual or envisaged, and the environment with which it interacts.
- **Functional analysis** (FA) concentrates on business *functions*, such as manufacturing, marketing and accounting, and subdividing each of them. A functional area may be a department, division, group, section, company, subsidiary, location, site, building or generally any sensible part of the whole organization. Functional analysis implies analysing each functional area to create a model of that area.
- **Process analysis** (PA) concentrates on the processes (i.e. procedures) that staff or machines perform, and the processing done or to be done by IT or other technology. Think of a manual of office procedures and of the processing carried out by a computer program when run. Process analysis concentrates on activities, events, operations and flows of resources and information between situations where processes are undertaken – somewhat irrespective of the functional areas of the organization.
- **Data analysis** (DA) concentrates on the structure of information, assuming that the underlying information structures will remain for many years without much change, and that the business products and the processes will change more often. Data analysis is out of its 1970s research phase and has become accepted as a practical discipline.
- **Behaviour analysis** concentrates on how the activities, events, functions, data and other parts behave as systems. This includes timing, dynamic behaviour, conditions for starting and finishing an action or process, what triggers or causes what to happen when and, in each case, why. **System dynamics** has the same meaning.
- **Transaction analysis** means analysing each transaction, such as dealing with an incoming order or making a payment.
- **Transform analysis** means analysing subprocesses that change incoming resources into some other form, usually algorithmically.
- **Analysis of responsibilities** considers how decisions are made, reporting structures, authority and responsibility. A starting point may be how strategies, business processes, business functions, critical success factors and objectives are mapped to each other and to various people's responsibilities.

  For significant improvements or innovation in business processes the patterns of responsibilities may eventually have to evolve. Priorities may have to change. Cross-functional and cross-responsibility processes and corresponding information systems are usually controversial, leading to interpersonal issues and interdepartmental politics. Staff in different departments may want different views of collectively shared information, and could see different priorities among the various processes. Extensive work and a long-term confidence in others – analysts and managers – are needed to specify, develop and provide such processes and information systems.

- **Business process analysis** (BPA) concentrates on analysing the business processes that are performed by the organization, e.g. a new product or service. Such analysis cuts across traditional departmental structures and could include any or all of the other kinds of analysis above. **Business process re-engineering** (BPR) usually means rethinking business processes as opposed to gradual improvement. BPR can start from a manager's hunch, ideas and table thumping, or from the results of good BPA.
- **Volume analysis** considers how many of each kind of data, process, event, activity, resource, message, user, ... will occur on average, e.g. how many of each kind of data and process occur, where and when.
- **Volatility analysis** considers how often something unusual happens, seasonal changes of the volume patterns and the uncertainties of each such pattern. This widens into how often the business strategy, the business processes, the external environment, the management structures, the requirements, the responsibilities, the kinds of information needed and the operational processes are likely to change. Each could experience gradual or sudden changes.

Exercise 2.12

List at least six aspects of a business process that should be understood and documented as a product of analysis.

A model of a business process, or of a collection of business processes, should include the following, where worthwhile.

- The objectives of the process, or of each process and of the whole.
- The resources needed, including staff, types of data, equipment, tools, training, skills, buildings, facilities and money flow.
- Processes and algorithms, both computer-programmed and human. How are rare exceptions to be spotted and handled? How much relies on George's commonsense? What checks are to be done where and when in the processes and algorithms?
- Process dynamics and behaviour. What events will George observe and how he should act in each situation?
- Privacy, security and integrity aspects and requirements that may arise during development or use or both. For example, what privacy and access authorization is needed? How is consistency of the data and incoming and outgoing messages ensured? How is unauthorized access to data and the running of computer-based processes prevented and detected? How is attempted fraud detected and dealt with?

- George's requirements as a typical performer of or user of a process.
- Volume information both during the provision of the system and during eventual use. For example, how many orders, customers, parts or insurance policies are there? How is all the relevant data about them all going to be captured? How long will it take to build up that volume? How many transactions an hour or day will George have to deal with? How often do rarer processes occur, e.g. the frequency of planning cycles?
- Test criteria, e.g. how will the providers know, prove and show that the systems work correctly; what test results should be shown to managers such as Mark and users such as George, and will George need some test situations for his training and experimentation.
- Interfaces to other existing processes that may share some of the data or be affected by the new business processes. Often other systems are not well defined and so Anna has to start work in this area knowing uncertainties will be found.
- Process topology. How are the various processes that George and his colleagues use distributed? Are they sequences to be done to time and in the right order? Are they different people's responsibilities, so that the people have to act in sequence, or do the people have to collaborate or all be present simultaneously? Where are different processes performed by which organizational units?

Exercise 2.13

Think of at least six reasons for volatility in business processes and information needs.

Things change with time because of:

- changing demands and abilities of customers, clients, suppliers and banks, and external changes that affect the products and services;
- changes of legislation, national and local government policies, environmental issues and public image issues;
- mergers, takeovers, business expansion or contraction and reorganizations;
- changing management styles, methods and responsibilities brought about by changes to the board and senior managers whose different ideas can affect management delegation;
- changing inflation and interest rates which affect criteria for cost-effectiveness and the desirability of borrowing and investment;
- cashflow issues, availability of credit and new priorities;
- seasonal and economic cycle variations and changes of strategy and tactics;

- poor formulation of the business processes and information needs leading to better changed formulation.

Each of these kinds of analysis can be applied to a part or an aspect of an organization and the result contributes to a conceptual model of that part or aspect.

Extending and merging models

Models are gradually extended and merged

As analysis continues, a conceptual model is extended into neighbouring parts or has increasing detail added. Analysts can, for example, develop a conceptual model of a functional area or a business process and merge and extend such models. In order to ensure that the requirements are clear, analysts have ways of representing various situations and, rather like architects' plans and accountants' sheets, the analysts' diagrams and tables have conventions. For communicating details of requirements, specialists also have terminology and conventions for describing and representing the structures and properties of knowledge, information and data; the structures and properties of processes; and the structures and properties of information flows and communications. They also have ways of handling the structure and properties of all sorts of objects, e.g. events, conditions, information flows, relationships, associations, entities, attributes and many abstractions. These more formal representations and techniques have rules applied to evolve a conceptual model into a logical model.

Managers and user representatives should be able to discuss the correctness of analysis products. They should be able to confirm correctness or to indicate errors and be able to discuss the merits of alternatives. However, they might not need the higher skills and understanding to do all the analysis tasks.

The problem is to create, sufficiently quickly and cheaply, a specification of the strategy and needs so that designers and constructors can build a system that meets the needs. Just as building costs far exceed architects' costs, so programming, construction, deployment, installation and training far exceed the cost of analysis and design. A system that does not meet the requirements is a waste of resources to build. Such waste should be avoided.

User, developer and administrator

Analysts also have to think out the roles that various people will play during the use of a system and analyse the need for integrity and security and how these can be achieved.

A **user** means any person who is part of a system. This does not include the analysts or constructors who provide it. For simplicity we use singular terms and refer to everyone in a group as a user. The term **end user** was coined to mean the same thing, the non-specialist user of a system. **Developer** includes analyst, designer, programmer, installer and maintainer, e.g. David. The user's system is called the **target system** and the system used to develop that is called a **development system**. A person responsible for organizing and controlling information exchange and storage, including integrity, security and recovery, is an **administrator**.

Integrity, databases and security

Users of business systems and information systems need **integrity**, i.e. all the resource flows between each user and the system must be consistent. If a user inputs a fact then any subsequent output to any user should be consistent with that fact. This integrity is difficult to achieve if the system has two or more copies of a particular fact, e.g. if there are files with similar data items that are repeated. If one file is used for one user and another file for answering a different user's query then inconsistency can occur.

With particular reference to databases, one solution is to have a shared pool of data that represents all the facts but without **redundancy**, i.e. each fact is represented essentially only once in the stored data. We do not here count safety copies kept solely for recovery after an accident. A pool of such data gives the idea of a database. A **database** is a collection of stored data organized so that *all* users' data requirements can be satisfied. In general there is only one representation of each fact although there may be some controlled repetition for efficiency. Controlling the repetition will be the responsibility of the **database administrator**. Database administration includes organizing the initial specification of the structure of the database and the way it is to be controlled, monitoring the use of the database to ensure that the design is operating satisfactorily and that the users are adhering to the controls, and initiating evolutionary changes as required.

A database administrator ensures integrity and **security** (mechanisms to ensure protection of data against unauthorized access, modification or loss). Sometimes other people use the terms database, integrity and security with meanings slightly different from ours.

Some conceptual modelling issues and terms

In principle managers should know as much about business processes, ISs and computers as about production, marketing, engineering, accounting, technology and so on. A manager cannot afford the time to do all the work of developing processes for the organization and so must delegate. In practice, people must specialize and all organizations need specialists.

Flexibility through many independent parts

In general, in order to minimize the cost of subsequent improvements, each process should have features that allow for many kinds of evolution – wherever such features can be built in cheaply. Thus the system should initially be built of many fairly independent parts such that any one part could be upgraded later without affecting others – and it should not even be necessary to check whether or not such other parts need attention. The system should be designed and built such that any likely improvements can be made easily – for example data in a database being structured so that later new applications can be developed with minimal restructuring or reprogramming.

When new technology is announced, incorporating it should be easier because of standard interfaces between parts and compatibility. Naturally, wherever possible suppliers who are likely to continue in business should be chosen, so that spares, service and improvements will be available.

Build in hooks for future improvements

Nowadays most large organizations already have extensive computer-based business processes. But as organizations grow, evolve, merge or are involved in takeovers, their needs will change substantially and as business strategy develops continual system changes may be needed. Good process managers and developers build into their systems particular features that may mean little or no technology change is needed when a future change in requirements occurs. This flexibility and independence avoids problems in the long term, but the wisdom of creating the hooks for future flexibility is sometimes not appreciated in the short term. **Independence** here means that something can be changed without affecting something else.

Issues, problems and concepts can sometimes be classified as bounded or unbounded, as in Table 2.4. This is *not* the same as hard versus soft. Small changes are usually bounded since the resources and timescale to solve them can be estimated, and if their method of solution is known they are also hard. But by contrast, proposed big developments and changes in business processes and ISs are initially not only soft messy problems without an agreed method of solution, but also unbounded because the alternatives and the resources and timescales for each alternative are unknown. It is impossible to list what is known and what is wanted and also impossible to estimate the resources and timescale optimally to find out and solve it all. Who is affected is unclear. Who should be involved in what ways and at what stages is unclear. What the many alternatives are is unclear. What is needed is unclear. How to solve it is unclear. The whole seems complex. The whole will involve planning, analysis and work to even decide what has to be done. To some extent, one objective is to discuss the unbounded initial problem, or any part of it, and form a bounded and agreed statement. Hence a need for flexibility.

Unbounded means:	*Bounded means:*
• unknown large number of alternatives	• limited number of alternatives
• not sure what the issue is	• know what the problem is
• priorities uncertain or questioned	• priorities clear
• resources uncertain	• resources known to be available
• long uncertain timescale	• limited timescale
• can't be disentangled from its context	• can be treated as a separate issue
• many people involved – not sure who	• limited number of people involved
• no recognizable solutions	• know what could be a solution
• don't know what needs to be known or found out	• know what needs to be known or found out
• can't list what we know, and what we want	• can list what we know, and what we want
• involves uncertainty, vague, fuzzy	• accurate and precise information available
• human feelings important	• no human feelings
• social aspects	• technical or mathematical aspects

TABLE 2.4
Features of unbounded and bounded problems

Exercise 2.14

Try to create a better definition of the term information, bringing in several points from Chapters 1 and 2.

Information is any form of **communication** that provides understandable and useful knowledge to the person receiving it, including data with **meaning**, usually received as the result of a process, e.g. as a reply to a query: 'That person's Badge Number is BN3333'. Equivalently, information should be: **useful**, relevant to some action or purpose; **understandable**, in both a form and language that can be understood; and **received** at an appropriate time, to fit its implied purpose. The purpose may be already known or recognized, or may be implied in the information.

Telecommunications technology has a technical definition of information. A **message** is one of many that can be made up from an alphabet of allowable symbols. The **measure of information** is related to the probability of the event the information represents. An unexpected message carries more information than a string of 'A's.

Some messages and communications, or parts of them, carry meaning just by their existence. The data or words used are almost irrelevant. For example, greetings, reflective responses, fillers, acknowledgements and farewells. Each of these can take many forms and wordings but the alternatives carry the same socially acceptable interaction information. Most IT systems lack such facilities.

The difference between **data** and **information** is that:

information = data + meaning + process + flow

For example, receiving an understandable and useful message is information. Here 'receiving' is a process and implies flow, 'understandable and useful' implies meaning, and a 'message' otherwise would be data. Alternatively, data is information represented in a form in which it can be processed by equipment such as computers operating automatically.

The translations between data and information or knowledge are human processes – usually involving interpreting given data as meaning facts about the world or creating suitable data to represent selected facts.

Information and meaning are not the same. The term **meaning** refers to the significance in a person's mind, the sense intended. This implies a mental process.

Exercise 2.15

Next try creating a better definition of information system, and a definition of user.

An **information system** is:

- a means of catering for the flow and storage of knowledge and information to satisfy the needs of all users;
- any system, usually but not necessarily computerized, which provides information to any type of organization – including real-time systems, embedded systems, management information systems, and so on;
- a system that accepts data representing knowledge and information, stores it, processes it and outputs information for people (= users) to use.

Information systems may be computerized or non-computerized, but many people (wrongly) mean only computerized ISs when they use the term.

An IS could include any of the following: people, books, papers, photographs, storage – such as filing cabinets; transport; communications – such as speech, radio, television, telephones; and electronic equipment, mechanical equipment, IT equipment.

A **user** of an IS is any person (or by extension it may cover a group of people) who has requirements which involve providing input or receiving output. Information systems should fit the information needs of the organization, which is usually regarded as derived from its objectives and strategy. We have not yet explained how Anna and Idris should do that, but we shall do so in Chapter 3.

Objectives

People participating in organizations and systems have objectives and so we need to define and explain that term and some other terms needed for later chapters.

Exercise 2.16

From your previous education, can you define objective, behavioural objective, project objective, mission statement, aim and goal so as to distinguish them appropriately? If you cannot, then please read on.

An **objective** is a statement of a result or product that it is intended should be achieved by the time an action ends. There should be a way of determining whether the objective has been achieved by the time stated. Usually it is quantified, that is it can be measured or expressed, or it has a corresponding performance measurement.

Objectives should be worded to be SMART: specific, measurable, achievable, realistic, time-limited

A **behavioural objective** typically has the form 'After doing ..., the person will be able to ...'. It describes a behaviour that is to be achieved. A **project objective** may be of the form 'By the end of this project the following will have been produced or achieved ...' A strategic or business objective could be more long term, quantified but perhaps less precise (e.g. implying an improvement but not by precisely how much), or perhaps political. For example, 'to continue in business and continue to employ current staff' is an objective – achieved if the business is still trading and no redundancies have occurred at the specified future date.

A **mission statement** is a business oriented assertion statement of long-term intentions, which may include measurable objectives on product quality, manufacturing performance, and personnel. An **aim** is a less detailed intention, which may not be achieved – and is perhaps not even expressed in measurable terms. Both aim and **goal** mean a vaguely stated objective of work, effort or ambition, usually without being specific, measurable or time-limited.

Aspects of information system development

Information system development (ISD) involves many aspects, as in Figure 2.13. Each can take many alternative forms in a particular organizational situation. They may be combined in many ways.

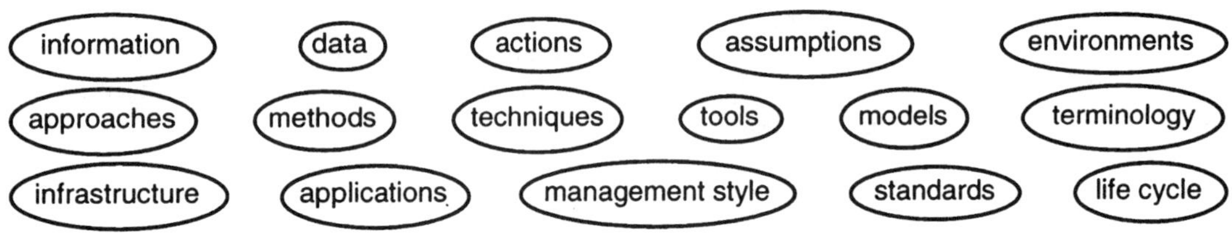

FIGURE 2.13
Some key aspects of business processes and ISD.

In a book or course such aspects might be presented in many different sequences. They have to be in some sequence and a choice also has to be made as to how much detail to include. Later chapters have some interleaving which allows you gradually increasing understanding of these various aspects and of the ways they interrelate.

Self check

Please spend some time reviewing what you have read. We suggest that you look again at the summary boxes, definitions and margin notes.

Objectives

After reading this chapter you should be able to:

- explain reasons for continual enhancements to systems and processes;
- explain why and how Anna's analysis should be wider than just finding out about current needs;
- discuss the systems approach and what should be optimized;
- justify the gradual iterative development of facilities and evolutionary change;
- explain how the relevant part of the real world is modelled in a system; and that the system is not just IT but has other non-IT parts;
- explain and use the various models, modelling stages and products needed in analysis discussions;
- begin to appreciate what we mean by a framework;
- use the following terms: analysis, design, build, install, soft, hard, data, name, type, occurrence, environment, manual part, automated part, IT-based part, non-IT-based part, relevant part of the real world, universe of discourse, IFD, ER model, mental model, conceptual model, logical model, physical model, constructed IS, development, phase/stage, activity, task, operation, objective;
- create simple IFD and ER diagrams from well-worded text or explanations.

The exercises in the text above and the questions below test these points. Some are also tested in later chapters.

Questions

Please do all of the questions before checking with the solutions in Appendix B. Whereas the questions at the end of Chapter 1 did not introduce anything extra, some of the questions here extend beyond the chapter text and give further knowledge and skills.

2.1 Decide whether each of the following assertions is true. If it is only partly correct, or is vague, muddled or misses the point, then write a correction.

(a) An information system holds data representing part of the real world.

(b) An action that is planned correctly should not go wrong.

(c) Longer actions require more planning.

(d) If a variation is made in the way something is being done and the result is worse, then the way it was originally being done must be the best.

(e) If information systems were such that all vertical information flows were through them, then meetings would not be needed.

(f) A framework will tell a developer which method to use in a particular situation.

(g) Hard problems can be programmed to produce a solution, but soft ones cannot.
(h) Data is characters which may be in a code.
(i) Conceptual models are rule-free, having no rules, but logical models are logical and have rules.

2.2 Richard's story at the start of this chapter describes a research project. What differences would there be if nowadays Anna were asked to develop a similar software package for a large department store? Assume for simplicity that the store is not part of a larger chain of stores, and that it would not be satisfactory to purchase a software package.

2.3 Draw a diagram showing all the models implied by the following, all of which are to be modelled in the IS.

The current real-world situation will change as a result of the current strategy being applied over the next year. George wants the IS to answer now queries about the predicted effects of an alternative strategy if that strategy were to occur through the coming year.

2.4 Explain the terms real world, hypothetical and UOD as applied to a child playing with some physical toy. Consider two children in the same room speaking into toy telephones pretending to communicate through them; is their UOD different from what it would be if they had real telephones?

2.5 Write a paragraph on the management view of information systems – no technical definition please.

2.6 Write a paragraph on possible differing views of a particular IS.

2.7 Interpret the following data, i.e. what does each item represent? `020920, 15:53:47, London.` State the underlying principle.

2.8 Explain three different meanings of 'The Eiffel Tower'.

2.9 Think of some other examples of coded characters in data, including some international ones.

2.10 Give an example of an infinite UOD, starting from a finite set of 10 objects that are members of that UOD.

If George is allowed to have data about objects in such an infinite set, how can Anna envisage a computer system with a finite size of store and backing memory that is likely to cater for George's needs?

2.11 In a manufacturing business employing 500 people, with mostly satisfactory business processes and information systems, and where competitive businesses are beginning to grow, which kinds of analysis are likely to have been done satisfactorily in the past and which kinds of analysis are likely to be needed to maintain sales income?

2.12 Classify each of the following as hard or soft. We accept that at this stage in the book you have not yet read all about these methods, techniques and approaches, so just think of the main feature of each and make a decision. No marks for saying 'mixture', since many things have some hard and some soft features and we have not included things that are mainly a mixture.

(a) a structured analysis and structured design method;
(b) the waterfall approach, having well-defined non-overlapping stages separated by milestones;
(c) using semi-automated computer-aided tools;
(d) prototyping, creating a simple version and extending it based on the result obtained from operating the simple version;
(e) conceptual modelling;
(f) a method of starting that aims to get people to understand a problem with the intention of initiating later some action towards improvement but making no attempt to decide the solution yet.

2.13 Is Question 2.12 above hard, soft or a mixture?

2.14 (a) Write a paragraph on what makes an information system acceptable to a user; (b) write a paragraph on what makes a process acceptable to a person who has to perform it.

2.15 This question extends the ER diagram in Figure 2.5. Add an m, for many, near the end of a relationship line where many of that entity could occur for each occurrence of the entity at the other end of the relationship line. For example, a Supplier is sent many purchase orders. So add an m near the Purchase-order end of the Is-sent relationship line. The Supplier end of that line does not have an m, since each Purchase order is not sent to more than one Supplier. Suppose the organizational rules are as follows.

A supplier is sent many purchase orders. Each purchase order is not sent to more than one supplier. A supplier can supply many parts. Some parts can be supplied by more than one, i.e. many, suppliers. A purchase order contains many purchase line items. Each purchase line item is contained in only one purchase order. A part is ordered in many purchase line items. Each purchase line item is an order for one part.

3 Business planning and strategy

Most people would agree that some planning is essential for improvements to business processes and for information systems provision, but many have difficulties over:

- what the planning activities are;
- when they should be done;
- how they should be done;
- who should do them.

Be warned. This chapter contains a lot of detail. Some of it applies to some organizations, other parts of it to others. Small or static organizations that continue with the same policy and work do not need most of this and those in such a situation may find it best to skim or omit much of this chapter, or use it for reference when needed.

Organizations have various aims, goals, mission statements and objectives, applying strategies and tactics to achieve them. The strategies and tactics usually include the use of processes and ISs. If this is not explicit, then the use of appropriate processes and ISs is usually a hidden assumption that has not been articulated. The organization should have performance indicators to measure the extent to which it achieves its objectives. Managers may argue about IS strategic and tactical issues, and the desirability or otherwise of changing a process or an IS in various ways. We explain various aspects of strategy and plans, and a set of steps that can be used to create them.

Here is a shortened simple example **mission statement**, based on that of a real medium-sized manufacturing business.

> ***'Our policy is to ensure customers are satisfied by our products and services at competitive prices. Customers should be able to communicate with us. We should listen and respond. We should be reliable, do what we promise and deliver the right products on the right day, with no defects in our products, services, information and advice. Our staff should produce quality products with no defects – right first time. Each employee has internal or external customers – those for whom we do our work. Our aim is to maintain and if possible increase customer satisfaction.***

We have performance indicators to measure our quality, defects, timing and delivery errors, if any. We collaborate with our suppliers over logistics. We plan ahead long term over three to five years, medium term over a year or so and short term over three months. Our strategy is to complete projects within their timescales, develop new products within two years, use appropriate technology, use proven processes, achieve particular performance metrics each within a stated small percentage at stated dates, achieve delivery leadtimes of so-many days for 90% of all sales, and develop and reward staff – encouraging them to support us.'

Planning of business processes and information systems

Terms

The planning of business processes is usually merged with the planning of information systems since many business process improvements depend on ISs. Many analytical techniques are applicable to both.

In Chapters 1 and 2 we explained the terms business process, information, system, information system, action, planning and some analysis issues. Essentially these terms can be combined appropriately. **Information systems planning** is all the planning for the ISs of an organization – for providing, using, changing and removing ISs. Similarly we have **business process planning**, **business system**, **business systems planning** and **business systems analysis**.

MIS-centric or information exploitation

We distinguish viewing an information system as a **management information system** (MIS), where the emphasis is on providing information for management, from viewing an information system as having information to be **exploited**. This distinction, seen in Figure 3.1, is central to both business process engineering and information systems planning – and planning is itself a particular way of using information. **Business process engineering** means applying engineering principles to providing and changing business processes – although a great deal of 'poetic' licence is involved by the use of the term engineering.

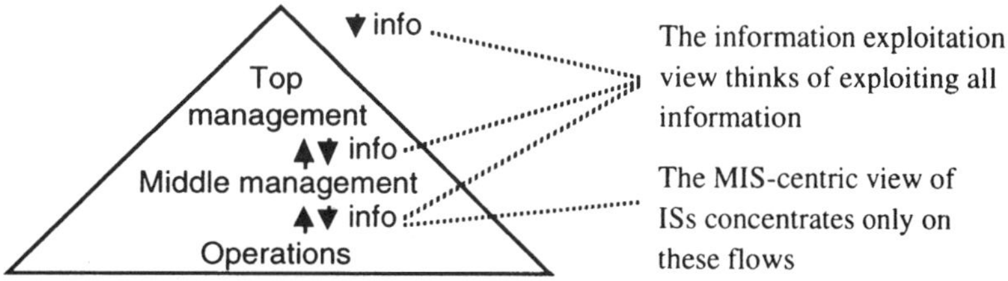

FIGURE 3.1
MIS and information exploitation views of information flows.

MIS-centric view of IS planning

The **MIS-centric** view of information systems planning (ISP) sees the problem mainly as one of identifying those information systems (ISs) that are needed to support the business, particularly the main business operations and processes. Business needs is the point of importance, and ISs are designed around those needs in a supporting role. They are to be provided and used both for the information needs of the actual operational processes and for MIS purposes to provide management with the information to manage those business operational processes – to initiate, direct, review and control them. So an MIS should provide managers with appropriate information to plan, initiate and direct operations, and appropriate information to control the quality of the outcomes, the products and services. Therefore most of the information flowing downwards concerns plans, direction, the availability of resources, the implementation of higher level decisions and, particularly, the processes to be done. The information that flows upwards is regarded as mainly for control and assessment purposes.

Information exploitation

Information exploitation sees the relationship between business planning and information systems planning very differently. When *information* is taken as the point of importance, it is seen as a set of assets, and business processes are constructed to make a business around exploiting the use of those assets. Information here includes knowledge and new uses of data for new ideas and processes. George has information relevant to his work but where performance is not satisfactory and management approval is wanted for more or better resources, his bid for this will flow upwards. In this sense the management and exploitation of information is an integral part of many business processes. Information assets can be used as a key supporting resource to optimize not just the execution of business processes but also their improvement. Everyone is likely to be aware of new information, from the news, current affairs, meetings, education, training courses and the grapevine. That totality brought together appropriately may lead to thoughts for improvements. The ideas and associated knowledge become part of the available information to be exploited. The ISs provide for this and mean that good IS facilities for handling a huge variety of incoming information are needed.

The business processes should be easy to change when exploitation opportunities arise. The decision-making arrangements need to encourage the flexibility. Various managers should use part of their time to gather information about what is going on around them and also more widely, and to think of and discuss possible consequences and business developments. The reductionist ways of planning may still be used.

Information systems are inseparable from business processes in the following very important ways.

- **Measurement requirements**. A frequent need associated with a business process is to know how 'successful' it is. This involves a need to define ways of measuring and monitoring processes and their products.

- **Control requirements**. In some sense, this builds on a more detailed aspect of measurement requirements in that control implies knowledge of performance and measurement against some benchmark. But equally as important as the need for information to exercise control is the need to deploy information to exercise control. This dual nature of information is explained further in Chapter 4 as **attenuation** and **amplification**.
- **Communication requirements**. Many business processes would be impossible without the communication of information.
- **Decision requirements**. Decision requirements can be considered as a more general form of control requirements.

Choices during planning

Before any significant action people choose and plan what they are going to do, the aim being to think ahead and avoid wasted actions. The planning involves making choices between alternatives which result from predicting likely outcomes. Usually one alternative is to take no action or make no change from current practice and expectations. For small actions the choice can be made mentally on the job but larger actions, such as changing business processes and ISs, need more work.

Actions have purposes and making a choice will be based on evaluating each alternative to assess how it contributes to the purpose in mind. People may not have complete information for this and it may not be worthwhile trying to obtain it, for example where the effort of doing so is greater than the likely difference in benefits or costs.

After the action has been completed, retrospective assessment could be made but for large actions, such as creating a business system or an IS, such retrospective action to discover whether the right choices were made is more difficult.

Criteria for making choices

Most choices in principle have some **criteria**, which may or may not be stated and justified rationally, such as a combination of purposes, desirables, advantages and gains, assuming each alternative is feasible. Assessing feasibility is explained in Chapter 4.

Exercise 3.1

List at least six kinds of desirables, advantages or benefits that might arise in a typical situation.

Benefits include such things as:

- increased flexibility, profit, revenue, happiness, success, satisfaction, speed of action and response;

- better qualified, trained and more knowledgeable staff;
- improved services, products, quality, environment, image, effectiveness, support and survival;
- being more competitive, perhaps evidenced by keeping or increasing sales and market share;
- reduced costs, loss, dissatisfaction or resources needed. Resources include equipment, tools, people's time, materials, space and cost;
- less deterioration, disruption, catastrophe, failure and claims;
- ensuring continuing employment, financial stability and success;
- playing safe – avoiding high risks and being sure of continuing reliable service;
- good return on investment and improved cash flow;
- avoiding losses, undesirables and the opposites of all the above.

Perfection is impossible

Each alternative may offer several of the above to some extent. A criterion implies some way of combining the relative merits and importance of each gain for each alternative, and comparing the results. The criterion should seem rational and justifiable, although people may differ over the relative importance of the various aspects and purpose. Different people's ideals are sometimes incompatible and, even if they agree an objective, they may disagree over how to achieve it, and hence over shorter-term choices. Selection often has to be made on incomplete information.

Exercise 3.2

List at least six issues over which initially there could be uncertainty or compromise when a decision between alternatives has to be made.

Making a choice, with its implied criterion, could involve uncertainties and compromise, such as uncertainty over:

- the **cost of the evaluation** of each alternative;
- **how to combine** different kinds of advantages into a single criterion, where they are not all quantifiable into money;
- the **relative value** of making some decision now versus making a better decision later with an extra loss from the delay;
- **conflicts** where people have different views;
- lack of **resources**, **time** and **expertise**, perhaps because people cannot devote the time needed to do the work properly, or do not have the necessary expertise;

- whether it will be worthwhile to obtain and use **software** for evaluation, planning, scheduling and project management;
- whether to try to find out if a similar **problem has occurred before**, and if so what was done then and why;
- whether to comply with various **standards**;
- **risk**, to what extent to play safe or try some more uncertain innovation;
- **management style** issues and whether major re-organization could affect the decision.

These points are often seen to apply to large projects but some also apply to smaller issues and all could apply to decisions taken during the development and use of business processes and ISs.

Taking a long-term view of an organization, its management may consider whether to select a particular proprietary ISD method and standardize on it, a choice that can be treated as above. After making such a decision, however, subsequent choice will be restricted as it will be far more difficult to change again to a different method since the staff will have been trained and become accustomed to the one selected. The same points could apply to major changes of large computer installations – particularly if the change involved moving to a different manufacturer.

Exercise 3.3

What do Mark and Anna, in an organization using a supplied proprietary ISD method want from the supplier? What should be the supplier's aims?

Mark and Anna should want the supplier to remain in business for many years and continue to develop and release improved versions of the products – software or method and its associated techniques and tools. Possibly they would also like the method gradually to evolve to include features found in some competitors' methods. These are far more important than a slight reduction in the price of the tools and the licence. No marks for Mark if he just wants a price war among suppliers!

Suppliers want sales income, profit, to continue in business and protection of their investment in research and development. Suppliers therefore tend to develop general-purpose systems that can be tailored by installers and users to fit individual requirements. In order to protect know-how they tend to build in special features making illegal use difficult. For efficiency they use computer systems to help automate parts of certain development processes and to help monitor, control and improve their existing products.

Facets of business systems and information systems planning

Specifying the purposes of the systems and how to go about acquiring, developing and using them requires process and **IS planning**. For large organizations, this includes:

- business strategic planning – for the whole business, explained later;
- information systems strategic planning – for all lower level systems;
- information system tactical planning – for each system;
- information system project planning – for each project.

Similarly, specifying and implementing business systems requires planning, which may be substructured similarly to IS planning. Thus we have **business systems strategic planning**, **business system tactical planning** for each business system needing it, and **business system project planning** for each project needing it.

For small organizations or a small change to an existing IS or business system, only part of each of the above kinds of planning will be needed. It could be done mentally or by means of a short meeting. However, we shall describe the general case below and assume Anna and Mark will select appropriately in a particular situation. The general case assumes that the whole is so large that such planning will be worthwhile. We explain the **reductionist** logic next and then some facets of each piece of planning.

Planning is a vital activity. The relevant managers coordinate and decide the overall aims, goals, objectives and mission of the organization at the corporate level. From these and the overall situation and environment they determine the strategy of the organization, producing the business strategic plan (BSP). This helps to establish relationships between the organization as a whole, expressed in its overall plans and needs, and the overall views governing the definition of its business and information systems (not usually involving technical issues).

From strategy, ISSP specifies what ISs are needed

From these, managers may decide the overall strategy and architecture of its ISs and business systems, i.e. produce an information systems strategy and a business systems strategy. These activities are **information systems strategic planning** (ISSP) and **business systems strategic planning** (BSSP). These extend the strategy and cover the overall planning and coordination of ISs and business systems including their identification and the specification of their structure and terms of reference. Like strategy, systems planning is only concerned with specifying plans in outline since the detailed state of the organization and its environment is continually changing. Business systems planning, ISSP and BSSP should be the **ongoing** joint responsibility of senior managers in both user departments and information services or management services departments. The policies, directions, constraints and resources of the systems are determined. ISSP and BSSP concern identifying, in general terms, the systems needed to fulfil the strategic plans and needs of the organization.

In our framework ISSP applies to information systems, but ISTP and ISPP apply to *one* IS or to *part* of one IS

From these, for each part of the business, the managers create the shorter-term tactics, i.e. the **tactical plan** for each IS and for each business system. These relate to the analysis, design and development of any *one* business system, one IS or one related group of them. These are **information system tactical planning** (ISTP) and **business system tactical planning** (BSTP). Each ISTP or BSTP concerns *one* system and the coordination of its parts. An individual system can be large or small and may comprise many related applications, e.g. sharing processes, resources, technology or information. Over the years each system's plan may change, due to changes in technology, in the higher strategies or for other reasons. One possibility is for no change in the medium term because the existing is satisfactory.

From these, for each system, where a project is needed the managers should create a **project plan**. A project may be a phase of a development, such as its analysis, design or construction, and includes **short-term** developments and improvements to each system – including conducting evaluations, reviews and providing better short-term control. Also from the tactical plan, the business operational **short-term plans** and IS operational plans are created.

Exercise 3.4

To help you to analyse the flow of information and logic in the above description of business systems planning, draw a diagram showing what is derived from what. Ignore issues such as iteration, gradual improvements and evolution with time. Give some reasons why managers may not behave in that way in a real organizational situation.

See Figure 3.2.

In practice the managers that undertake the above may decide to use their time and resources on other issues which they regard as having higher priority or giving greater pleasure. Some may not have the education and ability to do it, others may not consider it as having high enough priority at any time. Some may deliberately not do it – their hidden agenda being to avoid some undesirable outcome.

Facets of planning

Each plan will state **how** the whole is to be done, by breaking the project into pieces such as phases, activities and tasks, all linked by suitable events to assist review and control. It will schedule **when** each action should occur, **estimating** for each action the **resources** involved and **allocating** appropriate resources to each action. Techniques and tools are secondary to all the above.

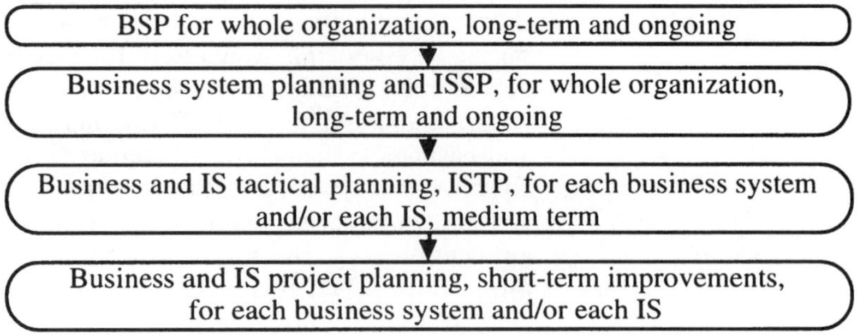

FIGURE 3.2
Possible reductionist logic of decision making for planning.

Business strategic planning

Forming business strategy

BSP yields several kinds of strategic plan, as illustrated in Figure 3.3, all of which interact and affect ISSP and BSSP which must therefore take into account the decisions about human resources, buildings, plant and equipment, service and delivery, and so forth. In our framework we aim to connect ISD and BSP through business processes.

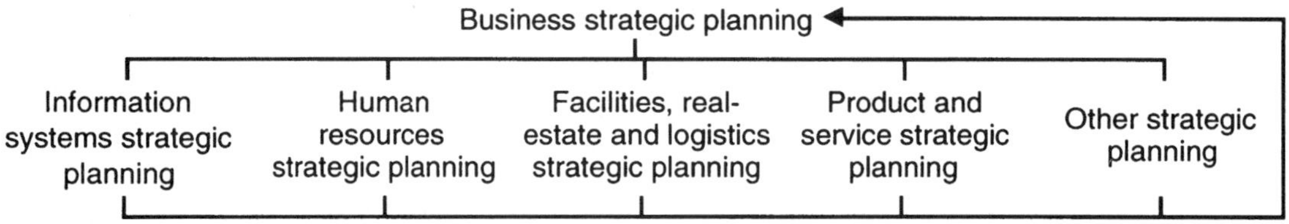

FIGURE 3.3
Business strategic planning context.

BSP interacts with information systems strategic planning (ISSP) precisely because ISSP is concerned to identify those information systems needed to support the whole enterprise.

Reductionist and ongoing views

Business Strategic Planning is conducted in at least two different ways. The common way is that it is the first in a set of stages starting with strategy formulation and ending, as far as information systems are concerned, with a set of implemented information systems and with other kinds of systems such as manufacturing, personnel, logistics, and so forth. This is **reductionist**.

A less common, but perhaps more realistic, view considers BSP as an **ongoing central strategic service** that performs the tasks and generates products such as those described in this chapter.

According to the reductionist view, BSP is a prerequisite for other activities, and a certain minimum amount of BSP activity should be done before other activities can be performed. This is an idealistic position but, in reality, very many enterprises do not have an overall business strategic plan, or are not able to overcome organizational barriers to create such a plan.

According to the ongoing central service view, an enterprise should be as responsive as possible to, and focus on, core competencies and the needs of customers and other partners. Strategic planning becomes a central service provided to improve the flexibility of the whole enterprise.

Such different views will have a major impact on the results of BSP, ISSP and BSSP, and also on the ISs.

Very large organizations, such as multinational companies, cannot conduct BSP from the top, as the organization is too large. The top management is concerned with overall issues such as major policy, profit, cashflow, dividends, size, group structure, major investments, restructuring and takeovers. Business planning, business functions and ISSP arise only at divisional level in *large* organizations. Small organizations hardly need any strategic planning at all, unless they intend to grow. However they usually need a business plan and tactics to avoid cashflow or other problems.

IT developments in the last ten years may make BSP easier but the improved IT does not justify doing more strategic planning than is worthwhile. Many organizations do not achieve this ideal BSP – they do not have an overall strategic plan and cannot overcome the barriers to creating it. Possibly they do not have the infrastructure needed for BSP, they cannot assemble the right people and achieving the participation of all stakeholders is too difficult.

The argument that business strategy should precede information strategy, without feedback, is flawed. Business strategy and the corresponding information needs should be realistic and achievable, although derived independently of IT implementation constraints. Business strategy is not the same thing as information needs, information strategy or IT needs.

Objectives of BSP

BSP takes place in order to satisfy a set of objectives. The BSP objectives should be realistic within its time period, and may include:

- establish or continue the strategic capability to perform BSP as an ongoing process, and ensure the future evolution of the plans and products;
- provide first drafts of the initial deliverables from BSP;
- enable managers to articulate the mission statement, the corporate objectives, the plans and strategies to achieve them, and how each achievement is to be measured;
- deliver the products from the activities as described later;
- provide the prerequisites for other strategic plans of all business units, where such unit strategic plans will show the equivalents of the above for each unit.

The BSP should cover an agreed time horizon, stating quantified observable objectives against which the overall performance of the organization can be measured. A long-term plan should state a target organizational pattern, say five to ten years hence. This may be developed into more detailed medium-term targets that lie on an appropriate development path from the present situation towards the long-term pattern. The plans should allow flexibility for change and evolution when unexpected factors arise.

Alternative view of BSP framework diagram

Figure 3.4 shows one possible set of main components of BSP and summarizes the related information relevance. BSP involves iteratively doing the activities on the left, with appropriate feedback and feedforward. Each of these activities could involve any or all of the **information relevant aspects** on the right.

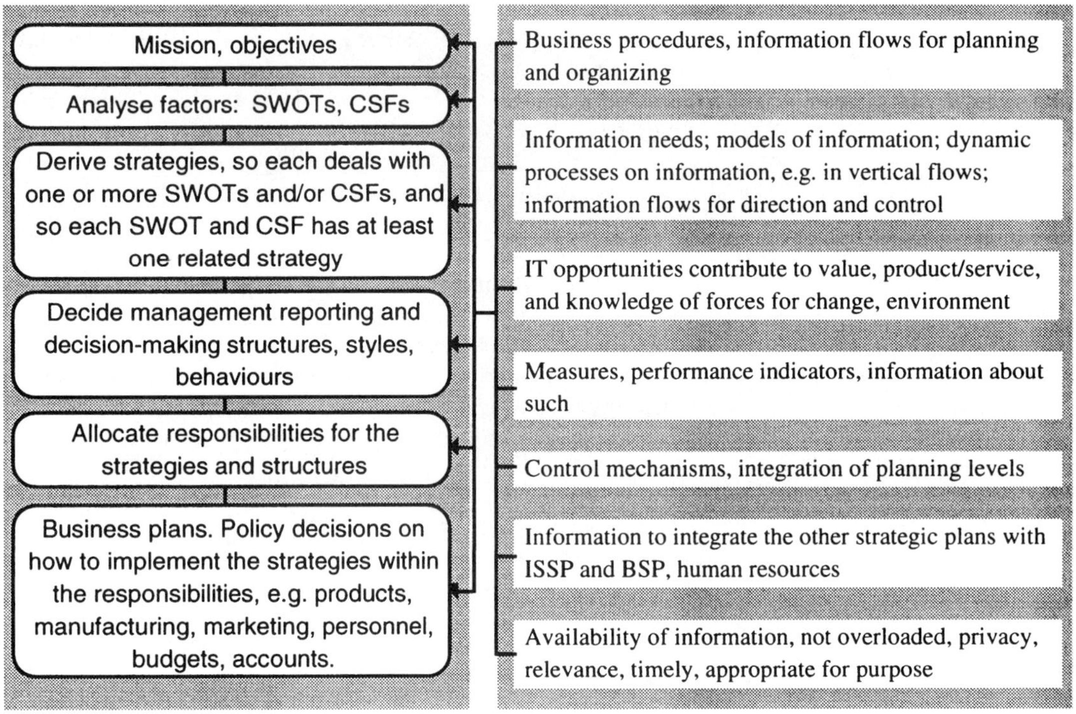

FIGURE 3.4
BSP framework. The right-side aspects may apply to each left-side BSP action.

Figure 3.5 shows the key supporting activities for BSP. This is a list of things that should be done by people who undertake or sponsor BSP. Each of these could be larger than an activity in a project network. We explain all the activities later.

FIGURE 3.5
Alternative view of key BSP supporting activities.

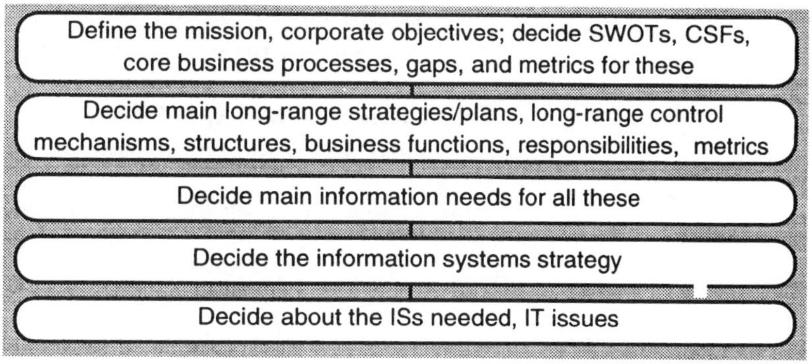

Exercise 3.5

Give a definition of BSP in about two sentences.

Business strategic planning develops and documents a clear understanding of the nature of the organization – why it exists, its core objectives and top management's long-term strategic plans. This process should be going on continually among top management. It provides a continual top-level framework for ISs, organizational units and other systems.

Here is an alternative definition.

A **business strategic plan** establishes a clear understanding of the nature of the enterprise and its main objectives and activities. It provides a top-level framework within which information systems, organizational units and other kinds of systems can be placed in context, with interrelationships clearly understood.

Metrics

Business processes should have performance measurements associated with them and related information systems are required to monitor and control the processes. This is a particularly intimate connection between business processes and information systems. Each critical factor and each strategy can have values of three quantified metrics:

- **actual current performance**, also called **actuality** – what the enterprise is achieving now.

- **present potential capability** – what an enterprise could be doing now within existing constraints but with some process rationalization.
- **future potential expandability**, also called **potentiality** – what an enterprise could achieve with radical process redesign.

This applies to the business as a whole, to each part of it, to the business systems and ISs as a whole and to each system. Thus the tactics, projects, plans and actual processes and services should fit the organization's strategy. Usually for each area of performance there should be measured actuality values and perhaps the other two will have values. Figure 3.6 shows two ratios that can be derived for monitoring performance.

Actual current performance, and trend of recent performance, e.g. 90

Performance gap = productivity gap = actuality to present capability, e.g. 90/100

Present capability, what could be achieved with current constraints and resources if the business were excellently managed, derived from long-range projection of situation and trends, e.g. 100

Strategic gap between present capability and potentiality, e.g. 150/100

Desired long-range future performance = potentiality – ought to, future intentions, derived from objectives but freed from current constraints, e.g. 150

FIGURE 3.6 Measurements of performance. Actuality, capability, and potentiality compared.

A major action for information systems planning is to understand the metrics that are needed, and to identify the information systems that will provide the necessary information for establishing the values of those metrics. For business process measurement and improvement, three steps can make use of these performance measurements.

1. For an existing process, identify the many ways in which the process is done currently – these all give measures of the actuality of the process.
2. Identify the best-in-class way of performing the process in order to give a measure of capability. By promoting this best-in-class method, the enterprise should be able to achieve improvements in cost or resource utilization.
3. To identify measures of potentiality, the process should be examined for fundamental changes that could be achieved by dealing with existing constraints or resources.

Scope of BSP

Ideally, BSP is for the whole enterprise. In practice the relevant minimum BSP often covers only one or two strategic business units, or the relevant minimum for ISs. BSP crosses the boundaries between business functions and can cause changes to these. It should transcend the priorities and views of individuals.

Essentially BSP is concerned with the identification of future hopes and expectations by senior management, contrasting these with the projections of the organization's past performance and deciding appropriate courses of action in general terms. BSP deals with reviewing the organization as a whole, adapting it to its changing environment and deciding on its products and services and to what markets they should be offered. The actions involve discovering information from many sources and forming realistic long-term strategic plans. Incomplete information and uncertainty abound. Human-relations issues arise.

Many enterprises undertake traditional **strategizing**, that is defining mission, objectives, and strategies. Some evaluate IT opportunities but very few attempt to apply information theory to understanding information needs and exploitation at the overall enterprise level.

We recommend that as a minimum BSP should establish the information relevant aspects of the enterprise and its various strategies. When considering information systems, two important decisions for the scope of BSP and the identification of the required information systems arise. How far is consideration given to information that is not handled by computer-supported technology? and is IT considered as only computers and networks and their related software or does it also include other forms of information technology such as telephones, faxes, printing, photocopying and measuring instruments?

Surprisingly, many enterprises' efforts at overall information modelling are very much biased towards computers and IT-networks because considerations of information are restricted to the information handled by computers. An enterprise embarking on the definition of an enterprise-wide set of interrelated and interconnected information systems must decide the scope of the work. We strongly advise that as far as BSP is concerned, information and knowledge are considered completely independently of technology, organizational structure and information processing IT applications.

BSP activities

BSP activity descriptions

We give detailed descriptions for the actions. These activities could all overlap and give feedback one to another. At most, the sequence here may suggest a logical order of starting, but in practice one starts in any way that seems feasible, given the current situation and context.

Mission

Action 1 Get agreement on the **mission** for the organization and each **strategic business unit** (SBU). Produce an agreed mission statement giving long-range aims and goals. Depending on the scope of the BSP, a mission statement could concisely state the principal objective of the enterprise or SBU.

Organizational objectives

Following on from a Mission statement, senior members of the enterprise, either alone or in conjunction with other enterprise stakeholders, will outline the key objectives of the enterprise or SBU. A **stakeholder** is anyone who has an interest in the enterprise including suppliers, stockholders, customers, employees and any other kind of partner. Outlining key objectives involves creating a vision of what the enterprise should look like at a certain future time. The objectives are then derived from such a vision.

Objectives and strategies are not the same. However, some people have no clear agreed understanding about the use of these terms, and it would be inappropriate to characterize any particular use as right or wrong; hence it is advisable to define how terms such as objective and strategy will be used in each particular case.

Action 2 Get agreement on the objectives of the whole organization and of each functional unit. These specify what should be achieved by when, and are measurable. The objectives may evolve with changing environment, and social, cultural, behavioural and economic issues. Stakeholders should agree that they are realistic.

SWOT analysis

Action 3 Agree the **state of the organization and its environment**. Ideally this can be obtained readily from top managers, otherwise the team must carry out fact-finding interviews and study whatever documents are available to discover the **current** and **desired (= future potential expandability) position** for each area of the organization. This could be done by a SWOT analysis – looking at strengths, weaknesses, opportunities and threats. This may differ from internally accepted thinking and assumed norms. A SWOT analysis requires an understanding of the current internal and external environments of the enterprise.

Internal strengths and weaknesses

Note the distinction in a SWOT analysis between internal forces for change, factors and decisions over which staff and managers have influence; and external forces, factors and decisions over which they have little or no influence

Strengths and weaknesses are mainly **internal** properties. They evaluate strengths and weaknesses in relation to what the enterprise is able to do or how it makes use of its resources. This covers:

- state of plant technology, capacity and capability; finance; and how plant and distribution centres are located with respect to markets;
- what products and services are offered, research and development, product innovation;
- managerial effectiveness, techniques, technology, age distribution, adaptability and morale; and management styles;
- work force size, skills, adaptability, morale and expectations;
- basic philosophy of the organization at the key management levels: Board, Chief Executive, executives and middle management;
- reporting and decision-making structures: what types of

control are tightly held centrally, what types are delegated to regional and line management, what boards and committees exist with what terms of reference, how long various kinds of decisions take and long-range control loops;
- specific objectives, goals and targets; detailed enough for information systems strategy;
- plans: success rate of past and current plans.

These factors must be assessed realistically.

External opportunities and threats

Opportunities and threats are mainly **external** properties and refer to opportunities presented by the current (or future) states of the markets and industries and threats arising from the activities of other players in the same field. This covers:

- reactions of customers, clients, suppliers, partners and other organizations;
- market details: share, location, characteristics, distribution, technology and trends;
- impact of interest groups such as government, trade unions, consumers and shareholders and of environmental issues;
- legal issues arising from legislative requirements and changes to them, professional codes of practice and industry standards.

Critical factors

Critical factors, which are those expected to be particularly significant in terms of success or failure, need to be associated with objectives and SWOTs.

Action 4 Agree with all stakeholders, including top management, those **critical factors** (CFs) likely to affect the achievement of the stated corporate objectives, goals and targets. Each CF and each objective should be stated in terms that can be observed, measured or calculated at specified dates in order to serve as a performance indicator. CFs can also be stated as **critical success factors** (CSFs), **critical failure factors** (CFFs) and **critical existence factors** (CEFs).

Strategies for achieving objectives

Some writers deal with strategies in a way that is somewhat similar to objectives and certainly some statements of strategy are indistinguishable from statements of objective. We suggest a more formal approach to strategy formulation. A strategy statement should be related directly to an objective and critical factors by indicating how the various critical factors will be dealt with in order to achieve the objective. For example, if the objective is quadruple turnover within three years and SWOT analysis shows that a particular competitor's strength is one of the critical factors preventing this, the strategy adopted might be to acquire that company.

Action 5 Agree strategies, plans, functions and methods to handle each CF and objective. Each objective and CF should have at least one related strategy and, *vice versa*, each strategy should be for at least one objective or CF. This really does mean identifying specific plans and projects to be implemented, not just creating papers to be filed and revised sometime in the future! This is where BSP is viewed as an **ongoing strategic service** to the organization – continually producing new strategies and plans as situations evolve. From the strategic plans flow policy decisions regarding products, services, R & D, manufacturing, marketing, human resources, personnel and administrative matters, and finances including investment, budgeting and accounting.

Metrics – how to measure achievement

Statements of strategy and objective are frequently qualitative but less often quantitative. It is, however, advisable to identify and define metrics that will show the following: if each objective is being achieved; if each objective is still appropriate; the strength of each critical factor; the degree to which a strategy is attenuating a critical factor; the extent to which a strategy is being pursued (i.e. does the enterprise know if the strategy is actually being pursued or not?); and whether each strategy is right.

Action 6 Decide upon the **metrics** for each objective and CF and each strategy, plan or function. These should be quantitative and should also show whether the objective or CF is being achieved, whether it is still appropriate, its relative importance, the extent to which it is being pursued and whether the organization has any gap in the long term.

Identify information needs

An overall business strategy is far more extensive than an information strategy. The many components of the BSP must be examined, along with interactions between the components, to identify the information needed. Information is needed for all objectives, strategies, SWOTs, critical factors and business processes. All this information is needed in order to know if the enterprise is on-target or out of control. Having such knowledge only as data is not adequate because it must be processed and placed in context to support decision-making activities. Then after decisions have been taken, information amplification mechanisms will be needed to support the implementation of those decisions and the subsequent monitoring of their effects.

It is also necessary to identify the underlying information needed for the many defined metrics. Such information will often require extensive statistical and arithmetic aggregation. Here the term **information needs** includes **knowledge**.

A frequent error in information analysis is to place undue emphasis on the information for which there is a high expectation of computer assistance. For the purposes of BSP, information needs should be identified independently of technology.

Action 7 Agree the main **information needs** of the organization for the management of all the above actions 1–6. Each component of the BSP, along with the many ways the various systems interface and interact, should be examined to determine the knowledge and main information needed. The **components** include mission, objectives, SWOTs, CFs, core business processes, strategies, plans, procedures, reporting and decision-making structures and business functions. Each of these components has information needs for its metrics, gaps, responsibilities and control mechanisms – with appropriate aggregation, attenuation, amplification, procedures, information flows and so on. Leave some details out to avoid being overwhelmed. Also avoid the mistake of considering only IT-based information needs and knowledge here, the information needs should be identified independently of IT. Some tasks that belong to ISSP and other phases may have to be partly done here to ensure accuracy and feasibility.

Estimate effects of loss of control

Indicating where the enterprise or SBUs could be considered to be out of control is needed in order to determine the information needs of the enterprise.

Action 8 Identify major ways in which the organization or business units may be out of control – any strategic **gaps**. These could indicate missing kinds of information or control systems.

Define control mechanisms

Homeostatic means self-regulating

Specify the control (and homeostatic) mechanisms needed for the enterprise. Such mechanisms will usually require the eventual support of information systems to ensure that decisions related to the exercise of control are amplified, and the operation of homeostatic mechanisms will also generally involve information (although some of them may be mechanical or electro-mechanical).

Action 9 Specify what high-level, long-range **control mechanisms** are needed. These may need amplification of information about decisions and control, and may need attenuation of other information. As well as long-range feedback, information from many external sources could be needed.

Consider alternative organizational structures

There are many possible kinds of organizational structure. Some business critical factors have associated with them specific kinds of organizational structure without which problems can be expected. There are also many kinds of organizational structure (such as networks and virtual teams) that will require the support of information systems to function efficiently. BSP should consider the interactions between strategy, business policy and forms of organizational structure.

Action 10 Consider alternative **organizational structures** – decision-making, reporting, matrix, work-breakdown, administrative and staffing. Are the financial structures for budgeting, approval, commitment and accounting satisfactory? BSP should consider the interaction between strategy, policy and various forms of organizational structure. Different structures could imply different kinds of ISs, information needs and features. Organizations need to **adapt** – adjust their behaviour, procedures and structures to accommodate plans to fit their changing environment. Creating a new structure is not enough for success; it also needs the support of appropriate people and cultural acceptance. The existing culture, structures and systems are forces opposing change, so changes tend to be delayed.

Define organizational metrics for the structures

Financial metrics are widely used to analyse and compare enterprises, or to provide some measures of the efficiency of resource usage. Clearly such metrics need information systems for support. Operational metrics are also needed to measure the non-financial aspects of operations and resource utilization (as well as the implementation of objectives). Metrics should be designed for organizational components in order to be able to understand the whole performance of different organizational units (and not just their financial performance).

Action 11 Agree metrics for the organizational structures. Financial metrics are widely used to analyse and compare organizations, and to measure the effectiveness of using resources. Operational metrics such as performance indicators are needed for non-financial components. The metrics should show the performance of different components – such as by objectives, CFs, gaps, structures, systems, functions and responsibilities.

Identify technology opportunities

BSP is not performed in a technological vacuum (hence the idea of BSP followed by IT or other technology planning is fundamentally flawed). Indeed the literature contains an extensive discussion of matters such as the use of IT to gain competitive advantage. In a similar way, activities such as BSP were not in vogue until recently, and there is good reason to suppose that one reason for this is that technology itself is an enabling mechanism for taking and implementing strategic decisions across the whole enterprise, whereas previously it was not feasible technologically to define and implement extensive strategies.

Action 12 Part of BSP could therefore be to match the opportunity that IT and other technology provide for new information exploitation and new processes to achieve enterprise objectives.

Define enterprise processes

To the reductionist, a business strategy must precede an information or IT strategy. Whilst in some senses this is desirable it is not always a prerequisite. For example, there are many business processes that should be performed independently of the organizational structure of the enterprise and of the technology employed – such as selling, purchasing, employing and telephone-call handling. All the key processes in the enterprise should be identified, and in most cases the interconnection between the various processes will need the support of information flows and operations on information.

Action 13 Agree the **business functions** needed, the core business processes, main procedures and **systems**. For some of these, IT may be essential – they might not be achievable without IT-based ISs. This involves boundaries and interfaces, and vertical and horizontal information flows.

Investigate similarities between enterprise processes and IT

In some cases there will be mutual critical factors between enterprise processes and IT; in others there will be a greater degree of independence. When considering enterprise processes and possible support from IT, therefore, one should bear in mind that IT is much more extensive than just computers, networks and related artefacts.

Action 14 Check whether the enterprise-oriented and the IS-oriented CFs, processes and artefacts fit together.

Create and maintain strategic plans

BSP is an activity that occasionally results in strategies being produced which are never implemented and which become shelfware. To try to avoid this, BSP should be carried out so as to indicate specific plans and programs for implementation. ISSP activity is one way to take BSP activity forward, and other kinds of strategy processes (BSSPs) complement ISSP. A far more satisfactory approach is to treat BSP more as an ongoing strategic service available to the enterprise, rather than to treat BSP as a project or program that *may* be revised at some time in the future.

Action 15 Arrange that BSP will be an ongoing central activity, at least in changing and large organizations.

Assign responsibilities

Particular people should be made responsible for the appropriate business processes and information systems to achieve their objectives, just as for human resources, logistics, manufacturing, buildings, plant and equipment. Responsibilities should be assigned for objectives, processes, critical factors, environmental monitoring, organizational units and the ongoing BSP activity. BSP includes the strategic planning of various business units – covering people, logistics, products, services, manufacturing, property and assets, as well as ISs. This assignment of responsibilities should be done within the context of decisions about the organizational structure.

Actions 16–18 Assign **responsibilities** and get people's agreement for their part in achieving the objectives (16); strategies, plans, functions, structures and processes (17); and organizational units (18).

Define information attenuation and amplification mechanisms

Many enterprises suffer from information pollution. It may also prove difficult to obtain *appropriate* information presented in the right way in order to maximize support for key decision-making processes, and to ensure control of the enterprise. This need to supply appropriate information requires the definition of enterprise information attenuation mechanisms. After objectives have been defined and decisions taken, it is necessary to apply defined enterprise information amplification mechanisms.

Actions 19–20 Decide upon the organizational guidelines on information – including attenuation mechanisms (19) and amplification mechanisms (20). For each main kind of information determine its availability, privacy and security – including how to ensure each kind is presented in an appropriate way to maximize support for the main management procedures such as planning, organizing, directing and control, and how to ensure avoiding information overload.

IS objectives and strategy

Action 21 Indicate and describe the **IS objectives** and hence the **IS strategy**, including the goals and objectives of the existing and evolving future information systems as seen by top management and representative user managers. This overlaps ISSP and Actions 22–28 below.

What ISs are needed

Action 22 Describe the main underlying ISs needed for all the above. Describe the profile of existing ISs, both computerized and manual, in terms of their main successes, problems, assets, technology, staff, history and plans. Here 'existing' includes anything for which decisions have been made and resources committed, even if not yet implemented. The top management view is required.

IS performance gaps

Action 23 Describe any gap between recent past performance and future hopes, intentions and expectations from the existing ISs, manual and computerized, as perceived by top and user management. Ideally, the ISs should cover all information needs for the management of the whole organization, consequent on the implementation of the BSP. This includes features to measure gaps in the ISs.

Relevant issues, alternatives

Action 24 Identify the main relevant issues and **alternatives**, and whether and how they could affect the ISs, as seen by top management. These issues may be areas of the organization that have problems or seem to be in some way in an unsatisfactory muddle or out of control. For example, the organization's top plans may include moving into new products, new engineering or production methods, new financial or legal situations and new methods of sales and marketing. The continual improvements in computer, control and automation technology may affect the organization, its internal methods of operation and management, the external customer demand for its products and services, or its external suppliers.

For each issue the **alternatives** could include or lead to the following: more or fewer employees; higher or lower use of IT; higher or lower expenditure, income, investment and assets; restructuring, takeover, forming new companies or subsidiaries, joint ventures, mergers, consolidation or divestment. Top management should be able to list those main issues and alternatives, or at least the relevant minimum needed for information systems planning.

Organizational and IS recommendations

Action 25 Define and agree the priorities and **recommendations**, including criteria and desirable time-scales, for each organizational requirement. This means corporate organizational objectives, not just information system ones. Personal and political issues may be as important as the logical and reductionist approach implied elsewhere in this chapter. The key tasks of highest priority for implementation of the BSP should be identified and agreed.

Prepare report

Action 26 Write the report on strategic planning, outlining overall feasibility and limitations of requirements, stating next steps – proceed or review – and stating the necessary organization commitments for the next phases.

Form steering group?

Action 27 Consider whether to recommend that top management should set up a **steering group** or committee for strategic planning reviews. If so, think out the justification and plan for it.

Presentations, publicity, get acceptance

Action 28 Prepare and give appropriate presentations to key organization executives, and user and computer management, on the recommendations and next steps. Give out copies of the reports. The objective of a formal presentation is to gain acceptance of the main recommendations at the end of a phase of work.

Lobbying

The preparations include discussing and deciding upon the programme and the roles of the various individuals, e.g. for each point who is the best person to explain it. The discussion should identify which executives hold key opinions and which are key decision-makers. Perhaps some of the main points should be explained to certain executives individually in private before the formal presentation, so that they have understood the main points and thus may help guide the discussion at the presentation rather than asking awkward or sidetracking questions.

Major products from BSP

We give a candidate list of products that may be generated during BSP:

- mission statement for the enterprise or strategic business unit;
- objectives of the enterprise or SBU;
- statement and analysis of the enterprise's strengths, weaknesses, opportunities and threats;

- critical factors that can affect the success or failure of the enterprise;
- strategies for relevant SWOTs and critical factors;
- metrics for the strategies to know if they are on target or not;
- analysis of the information needed for defined metrics;
- control and homeostatic mechanisms needed for the enterprise;
- statement of the organizational structure of the enterprise;
- handbook of metrics for each organizational component;
- analysis of IT opportunities;
- definitions of key enterprise processes;
- strategic plans;
- statements of responsibilities for objectives;
- statements of responsibilities for enterprise processes;
- statements of responsibilities for enterprise organizational units;
- definitions of enterprise information attenuation mechanisms;
- definitions of enterprise information amplification mechanisms.

Resources for BSP

Broadly speaking, the resource requirements for BSP are an investigating team which has appropriate experience of management and ISD, together with some other senior managers' time and some expenses. BSP is an intellectual task. The investigating team should:

- have broad experience in quick investigations into defining the business performance of organizations;
- be effective at communicating from shop-floor to boardroom;
- be proficient in the technical skills of analysis and synthesis, such as accounting, finance, forecasting and the interpretation of company ratios; and in project management and planning and control techniques such as PERT;
- be a good judge of managerial abilities;
- have sufficient understanding of computer technology and techniques to work effectively with analysts;
- be skilful in handling personal relations at all levels;
- be experienced in translating business process and systems requirements into an outline of IT and computer systems quickly and correctly;
- be able to call up support from practitioners experienced in analysis and applied information theory;
- have an in-depth grasp of IT, computer systems and languages, and be fully aware of the cost and time-scale problems of systems from the strategic planning stage to implementation;
- be able to envisage alternative technology configurations to fit the functions, circumstances and personalities of user managers;
- be understanding and sympathetic to the business problems and information requirements of non-technical users;
- be capable of devising an IS/IT strategy from the information needs.

The team will need to inspire confidence in all managers, minimizing the interference with their daily work by conducting fact-finding interviews in a planned, structured way, and by keeping records. Cost and time estimates may include obtaining information for business analysis purposes, specialist research reports and intercompany comparisons. The true costs of computers and word processors may be hidden. The largest cost, management time, could be difficult to estimate and may be regarded as an overhead on the whole organization.

This chapter has explained many aspects of the planning of business systems and information systems, which those involved in such organizational situations should take into account. Information opportunities can be exploited and not just used in a MIS-centric way. For effective improvement planning is usually essential, particularly in larger and more complicated situations. Creating the objectives, strategy, tactics and performance indicators, and planning suitable projects should be an ongoing exercise.

Self check

Please spend some time reviewing what you have read and doing the questions below.

Objectives

After reading this chapter you should be able to do the following.

- Explain the following terms: business strategic planning, business system, information systems planning, business process planning, business systems analysis, MIS-centric, reductionist, information exploitation, metrics, control requirements, alternatives, criterion, contingency, iteratively overlapped, information systems strategic planning, information system tactical planning, actuality, capability, potentiality, stakeholder, SWOT, critical success factors, organizational structures.
- Contribute to business and IS planning in appropriate situations and understand the dependence on business objectives, key factors for success, strategy and business functions, and also why completeness should not be attempted.
- Discuss the scope, objectives, minimum actions of, steps, products and resources for BSP.
- Recommend steps for a particular organizational situation; and contribute to applying those steps and producing the various kinds of planning.

Questions

Please do the following questions in writing. In these questions marks are indicated. The mark scheme gives two marks for a well-worded point and a reason or example, typically two sentences or a sentence containing both the point and justification or example. Give yourself half marks for implying the answer but not actually stating it, or for a point without its justification or example.

3.1 Explain two ways to distinguish internal from external. (4 marks)
3.2 List six ways that ISs have impacts on the organization in which they function. (6)
3.3 IT features improve significantly every few years. What are the main forces driving such improvements? (4)
3.4 Think about the forces for change in your organization, if any. Try to think not only about its IT-based ISs but about its strategy and decision making, whether its management style is changing and other issues mentioned in this chapter. Is it proactive? Do middle managers amplify or attenuate information flows? Do the ISs, and the ways that they change, match? What is the management style? If you are in a large organization is the style the same at a local and at top level?
3.5 (a) Is a reductionist approach hard or soft? Why? (b) Is information exploitation hard or soft, bounded or unbounded? Why? (4)
3.6 What is the main issue that business strategic planning (BSP) focuses managers' attention on? What needs are thus indicated and hence eventually specified? (10)
3.7 List the prerequisites for starting BSP in an enterprise where it is not ongoing and has not been done for two years, but is probably needed. (4)
3.8 Start to think about your own organization, as follows:
    - Does your organization have staff with the vision and skills to do the BSP work and develop the IS strategy?
    - Are you aware of the aims, goals, mission statement, objectives, strategy, tactics and plans for your organization or your part of it?
    - What are the critical factors for the success of your organization or your area?
    - Is the planning, design and provision of ISs in your organization integrated with its strategies?
    - Does your organization have metrics, e.g. performance indicators, for measuring the achievement of objectives, plans and strategy? Does it have long-range control systems as well as medium- and short-term controls? Has it a performance/productivity gap or a strategic gap?

4 Management

Managing means directing, controlling, initiating work, assessing performance, and monitoring.

In this chapter we explain how management style may affect business systems and ISs and the ways these are provided. How to manage starting to change a system can be controversial, so we explain various approaches and making a choice between the kinds of models needed. What can be provided is limited by feasibility, time, resources and costs. We explain the purpose and steps of assessing feasibility in both implicit and explicit feasibility study situations.

What is theoretically computable is wider than what can be achieved on currently available computers, which itself is wider than what is worthwhile on the computers within a particular enterprise. ISD methods, ISs and the facilities for George to use in his processes have similar nested structures.

As George gains familiarity and confidence, there is a gradual change in the facilities he would like to have. This affects what should be provided and the analysis of requirements. Managers also face decisions about standards, what to automate, appropriate use of IT, the impacts of such IT use, whether to develop or purchase and other soft issues.

Business system developments and IS developments are sometimes so big that teams are needed, demanding team management actions and consequential extra information. The management control cycle for an action explained earlier is extended to cater for nested and interleaved actions, for repeating parts of actions in various ways and for ways of reviewing and controlling during long actions.

The patterns of vertical information flow differ between the proactive and the reactive; and middle managers may amplify or attenuate. Managers have a role in using ISs to control correctly the resources that are their responsibility, making decisions continually based on both feedback about the resources and environment, and the objectives derived from higher-level decisions. We explain various views of such control cycles and how short-, medium- and long-term control cycles work together.

The people to whom information requirements and needs are presented face management issues in continually determining what their problems and priorities are, and how best to use their time.

Management styles

Over a long period of time the culture of an organization can have changed insidiously without top management necessarily taking decisions to do so. Management styles evolve continually and imperceptibly and the impact of IT has contributed to these changes. Fewer lower managers and fewer levels are now needed, a characteristic called **flattening**. Those remaining managers are able to produce more effective management and should have more decision-making delegated to them. Some 20–30 years ago the top management style was usually characterized by centralized control, with a hierarchical reporting structure having many levels of middle and lower management. Nowadays the style has moved more towards decentralized control and responsibility, with fewer management reporting levels.

Management issues of starting and of modelling

An approach to starting to improve a process or facility concentrates on a few chosen issues

How to start changing business processes and IS facilities is a controversial issue. For example, for a particular change to the IT-based ISs in a particular organization managers may argue about what is the most important aspect. This leads to the idea of an **approach**. Possible approaches include concentrating on one or two of the alternatives below, which are not all compatible. Management styles and people's personalities and previous experiences may be the dominating factors over what is decided.

Alternative approaches include: **planning** the business processes and ISs properly with information exploitation or being reductionist to determine what is needed; selecting and managing the right **team** to do the job; selecting and using a recommended or proprietary **method**; pushing for **participation** and involvement of all the appropriate people, by approaches such as prototyping, discussions and demonstrations; having project management with well-defined non-overlapping **stages** that can be subcontracted and signed off when completed – often done in large enterprises; aiming for quality and productivity by using software-engineering **tools**; allowing **interleaving**, iteration, gradual developments and change; and having a **systems approach**.

Small enterprises hardly need to consider these alternatives since few people will be involved. Managers in larger organizations, however, should consciously consider them.

Exercise 4.1

Which of the above alternatives did Richard use in his story near the start of Chapter 2?

Richard's story in Chapter 2 combined prototyping, participation, and iteration and gradual development. In his story Richard used weekly iteration in developing his whole system – part of which was computer-based. The store did not correspondingly change its actual procedures. Indeed when Richard started, he and the store's managers and staff knew that his research project was unlikely to produce any computer-based way from which the store would benefit by improving its procedures, management or decision-making, or reducing its costs.

Adopting an approach as described above is often not sufficient guidance. No single person can acquire all of the skills and expertise needed by people combining those of Mark, Anna, Isobel and George. Within a particular organization even forming a team with all the required expertise may be impossible. Staff may not be available.

People in a particular organization might not even agree on how to decide about such issues.

Impact on people and people's impact

As well as tackling these issues the people involved have to remember that a new or changed process or IS is itself in the real world, so it will affect the people and the part of the world around it. The world, the processes and the ISs interact, and each **impacts** on the others.

How to ensure that a new or changed process or IS is satisfactory and successful may become an issue. If an IS has many users, they may have different abilities, skills and understanding of its features, and hence different attitudes to it. Different people may perform a process in different ways.

People will disagree over the criteria for success and satisfaction. In some large IS and business process projects the activities of deciding what should be created and the activities of creating the whole may each be complex and controversial. People do not always agree on: what the problems are, how to tackle them, what the priorities are, what should be done, and in what order. They may argue over which activities, products, techniques and methods should be used when. Complex processes and complex IS developments need to be developed as a sequence of models and developments that in some way specify and implement the whole.

Choosing the kinds of models needed

Problems that arise at the initial proposal stage for a new business process, a new information system or a change to an existing process or IS include the following. For large projects these may be controversial.

- What to include: what are the relevant objects, actions, interfaces, events, situations and environment that will be involved in the new process, its tools, its facilities and its products and services?
- How to model: what are the relevant features of each of the above objects and so on? How should each be represented at each stage? How should managers and staff contribute to and handle these models?
- Whether to develop the whole or each part such as models and specifications of each process and information requirement. Is the proposed process or proposed IS facility cheaper, faster, better, more effective, relevant, worthwhile, cost-effective, technically feasible, legal, politically and culturally acceptable, and does it provide an improved service or product? Is it worth the development?
- Building the new: how should the team implement, build, install, test, ensure correctness, train staff, and ensure completeness and operation to specification?
- Running the new: how to enable people to carry out the new process or use the IS facilities satisfactorily. This includes future training, operation, help and maintenance. Privacy, security, integrity and long-term reliability should be ensured.
- Management: how to organize the whole project, how to direct and control those who analyse, design, build and run it; how to decide about and control future changes; how to ensure that what is done is done within the available budget, timescale and resources; and how to ensure that the new satisfactorily and successfully meets the needs.

Feasibility

Next we explain how to assess feasibility during the planning of actions, and various limitations on what facilities can be provided and what processes can be done.

Some things are feasible, some are not. The idea of feasibility may be applied to any action. For small actions it is done mentally and for large ones it becomes an action itself that is part of planning the main action. To be **feasible** an action must be achievable within a reasonable time, with the available resources, such as people, equipment and tools and expense budget, and subject to restrictions such as cash flow constraints.

Feasibility implies judging in advance whether a proposal is possible, and includes making wise choices between alternatives. Whenever an action is large enough, it is possible to carry out the extra action of investigating its feasibility. Feasibility may be regarded either as part of planning or as a stand-alone activity. In either case it can involve doing a little of various lower-level actions, e.g. estimating the benefits, performance or cost of a proposed system or a proposed design detail. Chapter 3 (pp. 87–9) amplifies what follows here.

An action may be so large that investigating its feasibility is treated as a project or phase and is itself an action. For small actions, judging feasibility and choosing between alternatives is done mentally or perhaps with a brief discussion.

Exercise 4.2

Is the following correct? An information system development or a business system development should start with a **feasibility study** phase that checks whether the whole is feasible, and thereafter no further checking of feasibility will be needed.

We do *not* agree with the above, although some proprietary ISD methods recommend an initial stage called the Feasibility study. For a major project it is advisable at some early stage to try to ensure that it is likely that all future problems will be solvable. In each case, the more certain one is that it will be solvable the less necessary will be investigation in advance. Such bridges should only be crossed when they are reached. Feasibility should be checked only where appropriate.

The feasibility of an action is studied before doing it in order to reduce uncertainty and **risk**, and to make success first time more likely. Risk management involves difficult decisions where a project involves high-risk items. Generally the advice is to avoid risk or reduce it to a minimum. Most actions are such as to make a **small improvement** to a current situation as people usually cannot think out large feasible actions and purposes that give huge improvements in a single step. **Gradual improvements** may work better and have less risk.

Any action may have an associated feasibility study. The feasibility study includes evaluating each alternative against the criteria, involves thinking ahead, considering 'what if ...', and needs wise assessment and estimating. It should lead to making a decision to accept or reject a proposal as achievable, and to choosing between alternatives. For success, participation and commitment of the people who will be responsible for the action are essential.

Able to act within reasonable time, cost and resources

A feasibility study may arise in either of two situations: **implicitly**, as part of the detailed planning of some already-agreed larger action; or **explicitly**, as an action in its own right. An explicit feasibility study may have its own management control cycle of planning, doing and reviewing and controlling; its own terms of reference and meetings and working papers. Either kind may arise during any business process or during the development of facilities such as ISs for future actions.

The **purpose** of assessing feasibility is generally to determine which of various possibilities seem practicable and justifiable. Then from the alternatives a best choice may be made. Generally there will be: **an area of study**; various **assumptions** – about policy, costs, resources and priorities; various **alternatives**, each of which may or may not be feasible; a need for a **criterion** for assessing each alternative; and various **people** involved – the client who knows the area of study, the specialist on the alternatives, people who can advise on the assumptions, the person who will carry out the chosen action and a specialist in feasibility.

Assessing feasibility may involve the actions in Figure 4.1. The order in which the activities may start is shown from left to right.

Specify the area of study and check the assumptions	Agree the alternatives	Agree the criteria for selection between the alternatives	Evaluate each alternative against the criteria	Recommend and hence make a decision between the alternatives.

FIGURE 4.1
Actions of a feasibility study.

The **criteria** may have several aspects: technical efficiency, increased revenue, reduced costs, better products, safety, legal, other benefits. In many situations the eventual ideal and the criteria may be unclear and choosing them may be trivial or controversial.

In comparing **costs** it is important to relate them to a common point in time since £100 spent this year is not equivalent to £100 spent in four years time. This can be done by applying discounted cash flow tables to reduce each cost to its Net Present Value (NPV) by means of which the effects of interest and inflation can be taken into account.

Technical limitations

In considering technical and economic criteria for computers, we distinguish three levels or sets of what is computable.

1. What is **theoretically computable**, with no limitations on computer speed or other complexity, limited only by the mathematical properties of what is computable.
2. What is computable on **current computers** that are available in the marketplace, limited by software and technical facilities.
3. What is **economically** feasible, limited by what will provide cost-effective benefit to the organization, taking account of the existing computers within the organization.

Level 3 is a subset of 2, and 2 is a subset of 1.

Nesting of limitations

This three-level nesting generalizes to any action that has a tool, and hence to where improved tools such as ISs are developed. Business processes and methods of working have similarly structured limitations. So we explain that structure next.

IS facilities and business process facilities that could be provided within a particular organization may be classified as follows:

- what is **theoretically possible**;
- what is **achievable with current technology** and scientific and social knowledge, including the results of research;

- what is **available**, such as the products on the market;
- what is **acceptable** within the organization and externally, e.g. culturally and within current attitudes to jobs and employment;
- what is **worthwhile** – e.g. judged cost-effective, beneficial and hence economically feasible;
- what **can be provided** within the enterprise's **resources** and a reasonable timescale, e.g. keeping up as needs change;
- what actually **is provided**.

Exercise 4.3

Draw a **Venn diagram** showing how the above sets are related (subsets are to be drawn nested). As a hint, think of some examples and decide which sets are within which others. A further hint: five of the seven sets are nested; the other two depend on opinions about the state of the organization.

In Figure 4.2 the five solid sets are nested. Those named in plain font do not depend on the organization's current state.

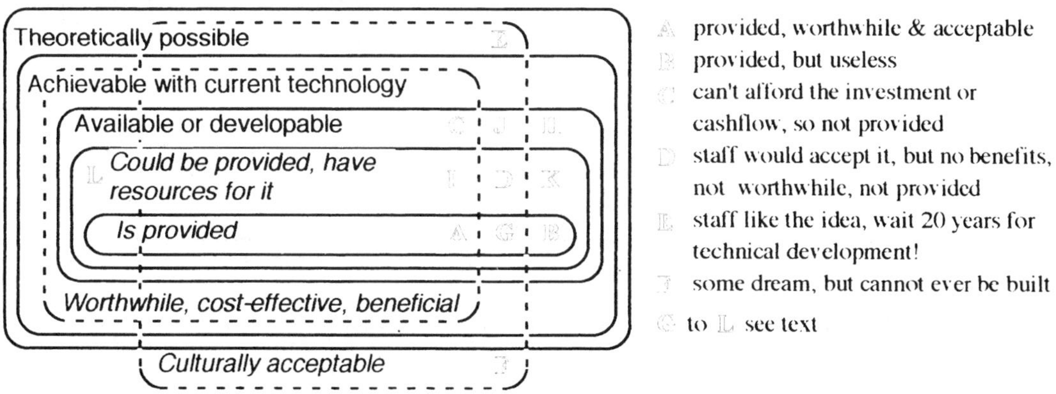

FIGURE 4.2
Venn diagram of how various sets of possible products are related.

Exercise 4.4

In the Venn diagram what do G, H and I represent? What is the difference between C and I?

G represents something provided and accepted by the staff, but not cost-effective, e.g. expensive to provide or not giving much benefit. H represents a product that could be provided but that would not be worthwhile and not acceptable to staff. I represents what should be provided but currently is not – the organization would benefit by more than it would cost, and the organization has the money to buy it and staff to use it. C is also worthwhile but correctly is not provided because the organization does not have some of the resources that would be needed such as cash available, floorspace or the right staff.

The Venn diagram relates together seven sets of possible ISs for an organization. A similar diagram can be created for Anna's **methods** of developing and providing such ISs, and for George's **processes** and actions.

The corresponding diagram for methods and actions is essentially the same. Just change 'product' to 'method' or 'action', change 'provided' to 'used', and widen 'technology' to 'knowledge', as Figure 4.3 shows. We can make the generalization that with appropriate rewording this structure applies to any product, to any service and to any action.

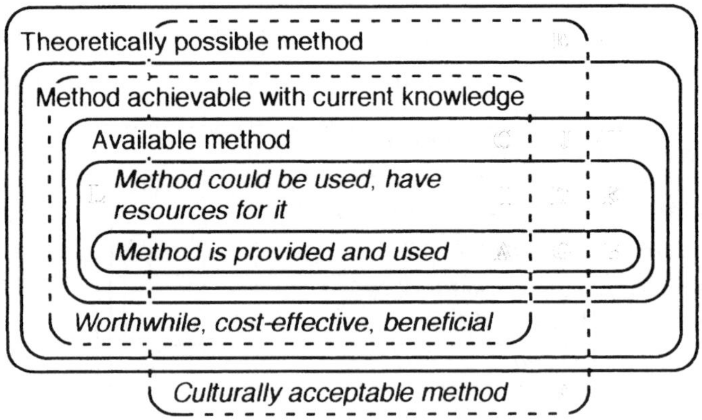

FIGURE 4.3
Venn diagram for methods.

Exercise 4.5

Draw a Venn diagram representing the use of products. Facilities here plays the same role as products. The solution is overleaf to avoid you seeing it here.

Developing this Venn diagram requires two diagrams, for products and for use, then merging them knowing something can only be used if available. The result is seen in Figure 4.4 (p. 118). The innermost oval represents what is usefully provided. Adjacent areas represent things for possible consideration and which constraints have to be overcome.

What facilities to provide

Choosing and deciding what IS facilities to provide for staff to use is a management issue. It involves considering facilities and methods of use; and the means of developing and providing them. Useful improvements are those lying within area I in the Venn diagram, Figure 4.3. The issue appears to be to think of ideas that may be in that area, to assess each such idea to decide whether it is, and if so then provide it.

As the manager responsible for the IS facilities that George uses, in principle Mark should decide what IS facilities to provide for each person, such as George, to use. In some situations George himself may take this role, deciding this or recommending that, but for clarity we distinguish Mark's role of decision-making about the facilities from George's use of them. The work leading to such decisions may be extensive, may be delegated, may involve teams of people, and may continue for years. We assume Anna is a typical specialist in such a team.

Ideally Anna should provide George and his colleagues with individual variants that evolve with familiarity and use

What is ideal for one person may not be for another. Because of people's differences it is more difficult to create a system that is ideal for everyone. The more users, the more this applies. Also, as a George's skill and knowledge change, he may want different facilities. With familiarity he may want shortcuts and abbreviations, new combinations of commands, changed layouts and new information structures. As each person's skills and information needs evolve, so the facilities ought to evolve to match. People like Anna and Mark do not always see or hear of these desires, however.

In principle, Anna might try to decide what IS facilities George needs for his work by finding out what actions George actually does, how he does them, what information he receives, what information he generates and to whom this information flows.

Exercise 4.6

What aspects of George's work does the above sentence miss? And what wider principle does it miss?

Anna should also take into account how the whole may be improved and changed by providing further facilities and better information. This is analogous to providing different tools and methods for someone's work.

More widely Anna should look at all of the work done by groups of staff, not just that of an individual such as George. For example IT opportunities may continually change the nature of the work staff do in ways similar to the way that engineering technology has continually changed industrial production methods.

More widely also, the IS facilities have to fit the broader needs of the whole organization. The objective is to optimize the whole,

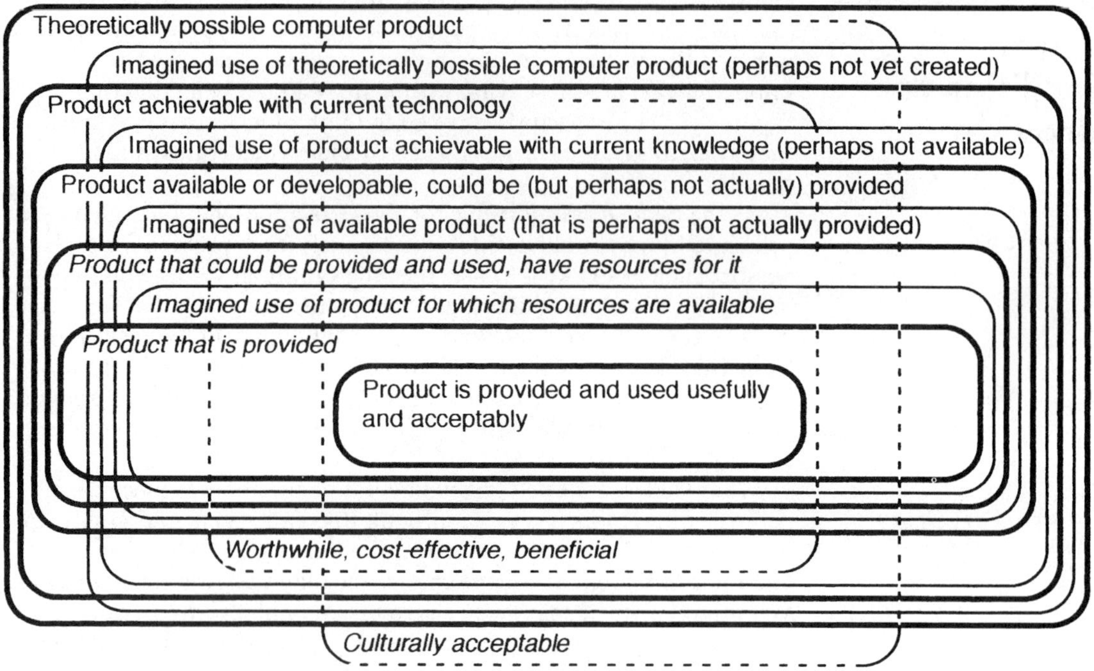

FIGURE 4.4
Venn diagram for availability and use of products.

The needs form a chain or network back to higher objectives and strategy

perhaps by change and evolution, rather than to optimize just George's current work.

The issues about what information George needs to do his job, and why, are subservient to issues about George's actions and job in the organization. George's information needs are subservient to his work which is part of the work of the group to which he belongs. Ultimately the paths lead to the nature, strategy and objectives of the whole organization. In the same way as each group's work should fit with the objectives of the whole, the IS facilities should fit with the objectives of the whole.

Exercise 4.7

Should the work of each group be optimized? If not, explain why. How should this affect the IS facilities?

The overall aim is to optimize the whole organization. It may be impossible to optimize a particular part, such as a group of staff, as this may be incompatible with optimizing the whole. Indeed it usually is. Examples abound, such as applications of linear programming to transport and to blending, which optimize the whole and thus determine how each part should operate but do not optimize any part in isolation. Similarly the IS facilities should be arranged to contribute their part to the optimization of the whole, and not be individually optimized.

Change involves a migration from existing to new

Most situations do not start from the hypothetical green-field site where some planned ideal may be built from scratch. One starts with existing arrangements: staff with their existing skills and training; buildings, equipment, tools, finance and other resources; suppliers, customers, clients, government and other agencies; methods of working, procedures, standards, expertise, quality, image, management style and expectations; and the existing IS facilities and correspondingly trained staff. Most of these cannot change quickly and easily, though they may evolve gradually.

Exercise 4.8

How does deciding about and managing the IS facilities differ from other management decisions? Or are they similar?

The above suggests that decisions about the IS facilities should be made in the same way as other management decisions. Each decision is usually about making a change to existing arrangements. Each alternative competes for favour, investment and even the manager's time to discuss and decide about it. IT decisions should be made in the same way as, and in competition with, other decisions, aiming to contribute to optimizing the whole.

Principles of modelling and provision

Next we look at some underlying principles that affect how Anna and George will describe and build models and provide information systems that represent objects, rules and other features of the relevant part of the real world.

Standards

Some people (wrongly) say that **standards** are only for the software part of the system. In fact they may apply to all parts of ISs. Anna's and Mark's successors will find their problems easier if Anna and Mark have conformed to appropriate standards, or even created such where standards did not exist.

George also wants his current names for types of data to be used in discussions with Idris, Mark and Anna. So they have a problem where different names are already in use in different departments of the organization and a proposed IS is to handle and integrate data used in both areas.

What to automate

The issue of the balance between **manual versus automated** solutions poses many questions which apply to each situation where there is a choice to be made for each part of the IS. These choices have an impact on jobs and morale since IT can be used to automate work and replace staff.

George should make appropriate use of technology. Organizational structures can affect what technology to use and the ways people expect it will be used. Anna and others should also use appropriate technology, tools and methods when developing facilities for George.

Impacts

The use of the IT will have an **impact** on the organization, affecting its culture, structure, capabilities and success. Conversely, the organization's culture and structure have impact on IT developments. The long-term trend indicates increasing numbers and types of successful applications of IT so that managers are gradually getting better information and better information handling facilities.

Change of management structure

IT-based ISs tend slowly to flatten the organizational hierarchy

Generally, with improved ISs a middle manager should be able to supervise a larger number of subordinates since the ISs provide improved facilities. A manager can be enabled to work more effectively and give greater added value to the organization's overall productivity by being provided sooner with better formal information to support activities and responsibilities. Fewer managers are needed for a given turnover and so large organizations gradually tend towards fewer levels of management – a process known as **flattening**.

IT has produced continual change and people and organizations have had to cope with both internal and external changes.

People cannot predict major disasters, changes of local and national government policy, changes of exchange rates between currencies and other economic effects. Staff cannot predict future organizational changes such as restructuring, changes of responsibilities, changes of managerial style, cultural changes, and reversals of policy and strategy. Occasionally organizations have to save money, leading to decisions such as to reduce all IT costs suddenly and substantially, or to close down a particular line of business, or to cross-charge between departments in some new way. Even if Mark or Anna could forecast such internal and external situation changes, it would not be practicable to build into the ISs the facilities and flexibility to handle them. To do so might be politically controversial and the jobs of the proposers could be threatened.

Attenuation and amplification

Defective previous ISD biases towards lower-level operations and MIS-centric

Many past ISD methods were biased towards helping lower-level business operations because they were initially the most cost-effective applications of IT. They were also MIS-centric to give management information for scheduling and control of the operations. Methods and IS products were also biased towards attenuation†, where summaries flowed upwards. We explain the terms first, then explain teams and actions, and then the control mechanisms.

Upper-level decision-making cannot be improved significantly by current (1994) IT. This is a cybernetic issue and most previous publications have omitted it. **Cybernetics**, plural in form but treated as though singular, means the study of communication and control mechanisms in machines, living creatures, organizations, and so forth.

For example, in discussing a financial issue the top managers and board may be concerned about the rate of return on investment (ROI), and they need ways to handle information about such. But at lower operational levels the nature of the ISs and the ways that information is handled are quite different, and involve quite different ways of thinking. In general, the ROI of each part of each business function cannot be calculated easily to give useful information about each contribution to the ROI, and thus give appropriate information to flow upwards within the existing ISs. Similarly, directives about ROI and how these should affect lower-level decisions and operations cannot flow downwards in existing ISs.

Transformations needed in vertical flows

Part of the issue here is information amplification† by managers. Flowing downwards, the upper-level objectives and metrics that measure overall performance need translating not only into lower-level decisions, but also into quite different kinds of lower-level performance measurements from the forms in which the upper-level objectives, strategy and metrics were expressed. Flowing upwards, the information wanted at the top level needs to be calculated from many other different kinds of lower-level performance measurements – that may not even be available. Complex transformations are needed in both attenuating and amplifying information flows.

Attenuation

When exceptions and summaries are produced for management, the information flows at the subsequent levels summarize information from the original flow. This is called **attenuation**, as Figure 4.5 shows. It can happen anywhere.

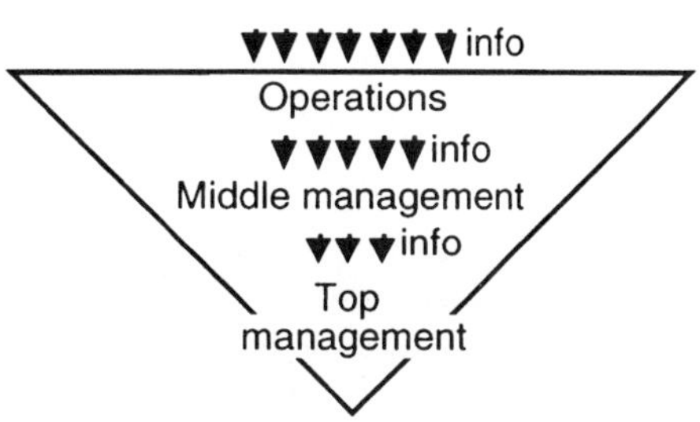

FIGURE 4.5 Attenuating information flows – less out than in.

Amplification

When management (or others) expand policy, strategy, tactics and detail they pass on more information than they receive. This is called **amplification**, as Figure 4.6 shows. It can be done anywhere and information flowing upwards can also be amplified. Amplification implies more than just broadcasting. For example, high-level sales targets are amplified by expressing them as sales targets for each salesperson, not just by broadcasting the overall sales goals. The individual sales targets must also be based on some test of reasonableness such as past performance or good prospects.

FIGURE 4.6
Amplifying information flows – more out than in.

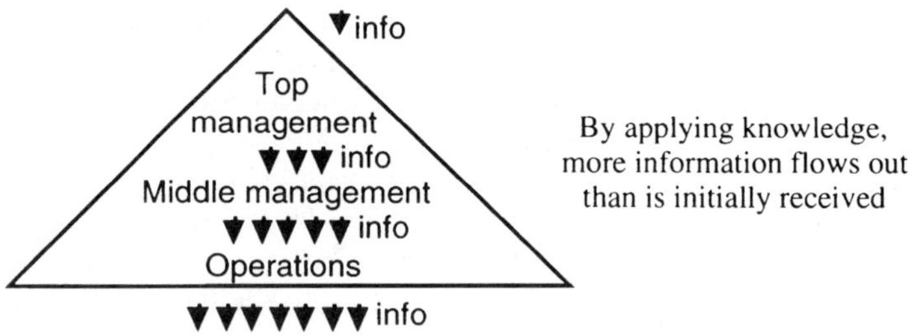

> **Exercise 4.9**
>
> List alternative ways that a middle manager, Graham, may handle a memo coming downwards requesting action by staff under him. Think about passing the information on and perhaps adding value by contributing wisdom, knowledge and experience.

Graham, who receives a memo coming downwards requesting action by staff under him, may act in various ways, some of which add information value.

- He may duplicate the incoming information to all who are to act. The minimum contribution is selecting the recipients. This adds no value, it is merely broadcasting.
- He may apply some knowledge and experience, for example draw up a plan of how the whole should be divided among those available, create a schedule and pass these on as commands to the staff. This appears to add some value.
- He may consult the staff and form a plan that they feel is feasible and that they support. Thus his reply gives estimated completion information and indicates the difficulties.

Where the incoming request corresponds roughly to the expected and maximum performance of the staff available, and if that is already being achieved, then the middle manager cannot add much of value anyway.

Teams

In practice many business and IS projects are so big that they need a team of people. The development and implementation activities need management, the planning activities that precede them are so big that they need management, and the team needs managing and coordination to help its members work together.

> Teams, as opposed to work done by a single individual, need extra activities. Extra planning arises to decide who in the team will do what. Extra control arises to coordinate the members during the work. Extra cross-checking arises to ensure the parts done by the different members fit together.

The quality of the work and the achievement of objectives depend not only on doing the appropriate activities when scheduled, but also on the personalities of the people involved. Having good people is fundamental. They must appreciate human issues and human behaviour as well as technical details. Good management implies the ability to lead others, work in a team and make excellent decisions; it implies integrity, conscientiousness, reliability and achieving objectives. Team management is not a new problem. Many people and business organizations have succeeded at it.

Teams ought to be drawn from across departments and functions to aid comprehension where requirements cross such boundaries. Only then can they make proposals leading to changes that integrate and optimize the whole. Indeed, having people from external organizations such as suppliers or customers in a team may be desirable where the objectives include optimizing systems that interact with them. Teams also need to have people from different jobs, different levels in the organization, different education and backgrounds. However the creation of cross-departmental, cross-organizational, and multi-level teams is often prevented by existing power structures, dominant personalities and management reporting structures. Teams need a culture and encouragement to manage themselves and to think out how to improve the business processes and ISs.

Actions and managing them

An action has conditions which indicate when to start. It usually needs products of earlier actions as **prerequisites**. Decisions are needed as to when to finish. Issues arise of how to estimate the duration and what to count. A collection of activities in a project needs project management which may involve PERT for scheduling.

Actions need feedback to those doing them during the process and afterwards. Actions may need to be repeated in various ways. Actions may be interrupted.

> We use the term **action** for any one of a development, a phase, an activity, a task or an operation in order to describe the various possible sequencing structures later.

Often methods, **techniques** and **tools** are used for each activity or task. These activities and tasks have various features such as the ways their inner management control cycles are nested and interleaved.

An action may produce **products** (i.e. deliverable goods), services, knowledge, or information. Formal actions have prestated **terms of reference**, objectives, scope; and perhaps agreed **resources**. Actions may have a **timescale** within an agreed work programme. During an action **resources** are consumed, but **tools** are not.

Actions need **points of control**. The structure of this control typically has long-, medium- and short-term cycles that are nested. Improved resources are decided in the outer medium- and long-term cycles. The short-term control cycles take the resources as given.

An action, such as George making something, has internal (by George) and external (by George's manager, Graham) control, each with appropriate feedback and decisions. Viewed a different way, Graham controls resources in an environment. He receives strategy and tactics guidance from higher decisions, receives data about the resources and the environment, and carries out appropriate processes to make decisions or small adjustments to control future performance. The provision of information systems and business processes should take account of these management aspects.

Sequencing of actions

An action may be **repeated** in various ways. **Backtracking** can undo mistakes and errors, and allow one to redo with improvements. The action may be **refined iteratively** – developing **prototype** products and improving them gradually.

How actions may overlap

Two or more actions may be done in **sequence**, one after another; or in **parallel**, concurrently; or partially overlapping and with deliberate **interleaving**, which allows each to benefit from the other.

> Where a **product** of one action is required as **prerequisite** for another, usually the **second action can be started**, but not finished, when the first action has produced a primitive version of the relevant product. In general each **action can start** as soon as previous actions have started and progressed far enough. Usually an action cannot finish until appropriate previous actions have finished.

Interruptions

People may **interrupt** a particular action, do some other action, which need not be of the same type, and then return to the interrupted action. The action's elapsed time increases by more than the duration of the interruption because of the need for extra time (and resources) for changeovers.

Start from requirements and planning

Usually an **action starts** from requirements as part of the controlling information received, and has a **management control cycle** as in Figure 4.7, which is an expanded form of Figure 2.1 (p. 43).

Requirements already known and agreed in outline or to appropriate detail
→ Plan an action, e.g. a change, development, phase, activity, task, operation
Produce and agree terms of reference, work programme, schedule, budget ←
→ Do the work itself
Produce deliverables: products, documents, working systems, trained staff
Evaluate, review and control the above during and after it
Produce progress report, time report, accounts, list of further requirements ←

Management control cycle deliverables

Feedback and evaluation may lead to gradual improvement by repeating the cycle or part of it

FIGURE 4.7
A management cycle for an action.

The flow means the order in which **actions may start**, but it does not imply priority or finishing one before starting another.

An action may start as soon as enough information has been received, such as requirements and drafts of products from the **prerequisites**.

For large actions, such as a major part of a business system or IS change and development, the **plan** can take the following form.

- Define the objectives and **terms of reference**.
- State the phases, activities, and perhaps tasks to be performed and provide time and cost estimates for them: the **work programme**, and hence the **budget**. Some items are only a **cost,** e.g. insurance, expenses and certain overheads; some need only **time**, e.g.waiting for suppliers to deliver; and some are proper **work packages** that achieve something that has an associated **performance measurement** or **metric**. Each work package will indicate the scope of the work needed in that package; state the activities, inputs required, and outputs to be produced; and specify resources such as labour, materials, assemblies, equipment, facilities and costs.
- Establish start and end dates for each of the phases and activities, and perhaps tasks: the **schedule**.

Completion of any action occurs at the production of the required end-products. A deliverable is not necessarily tangible. For internal review and control, time reports and accounts should give the resources used. The **end of any management control cycle** is usually when agreement is reached that the actions have been successful and the objectives achieved effectively. This may follow an evaluation and progress report. A major event is called a **milestone**, which means a management checkpoint or a technical or development highlight.

PERT

Programme (or project) **evaluation and review technique** (PERT) is a project control method of scheduling activities. Actions can be sequenced, such as one finishing before another starts, or laddered, where the first part of a second activity is done at the same time as the second part of the first, or overlapped in various other ways.

The constraints between two activities may be any of the four following kinds. From start of first activity to start of second (SS) allows the second to start soon after the first has started, e.g. when a first draft of a product from the first is available to start the second. The SS assumption is that work on the second may start as soon as a first draft is available of a product created by the first and needed for the second. From finish of first to start of second (FS) is the usual sequencing, meaning the first must finish before the second can start. From start of first to finish of second (SF) means the second may not finish until the first has started; this constraint is rare. From finish of first to finish of second (FF) means the final versions of some products of the first must be used or checked in the steps of the second so the first cannot finish until that has happened.

The logic of the activities can be shown as a network in which the activities are the nodes and the events are the lines or arcs joining them or, alternatively, a network in which the events are the nodes and the activities are the arcs or lines. For complicated projects activity on node is more usual.

PERT is attractive as a project management method because it can be used to yield a **critical path**, indicating the sequence of activities which determines the duration of the whole project. Managers should concentrate on these if they wish to speed up the project completion, and to avoid slippage. Identifying a critical path from a PERT network is applying the Critical Path Method (CPM).

The first stage is to calculate the earliest date that each activity can start and finish, taking account of all logically earlier activities and the constraints. To do this one works forwards through the PERT network from the project start date. These dates may be regarded as planned start and finish dates for each activity. This stage also gives an earliest project finishing date.

The second stage is to calculate the latest date by which each activity must start and finish in order to complete the whole project by the finishing date. To do this one works backwards through the network from the finishing date.

For projects of not more than a few tens of activities these calculations can be done by hand on a suitably drawn network. For more complicated projects the management may need a suitable software package.

Getting three estimates is better than just one, but rarely done

When planning a project, a manager should ensure that on average each activity can be achieved within its allocated time and resources. All persons who will be involved should be consulted to plan their contributions. Where estimating the durations is controversial or subject to uncertainty, three estimates should be obtained. This is not often done, on the grounds that it is believed not worthwhile. How to do it is straightforward. The project manager should ask the person responsible for an activity to give three estimates of its duration: (a) the minimum or best if everything goes well; (b) the likely expected; and (c) the maximum or worst if many things go wrong. The calculated mean expected is $(a + 4 \times b + c)/6$. Its calculated spread is $(c - a)/6$. The calculated mean expected is usually more than the original single estimate (b), and is usually more realistic. PERT and CPM software packages have the facilities to handle and combine three such durations for each activity; by hand it is too tedious. For cost estimates people usually want a single figure.

When asking for estimates the project manager should distinguish time spent doing the actions from elapsed time in days and weeks. Interruptions and other work have to be allowed for and consideration given to bank holidays, annual leave, sickness probabilities and so on. Are these to be included in each estimate or applied afterwards?

Planners often do not allow for statistical variations in times taken on tasks. Suppose a specialist has to do many activities servicing a queue. The queue may become unexpectedly long, for example where each task takes on average 4 days and tasks arrive randomly averaging one every 5 days, statistically the queue will become on average $1/(1 - 4/5) = 5$ tasks long. So jobs expected to take a week will on average wait a month.

Continual review of actions

Feedback is needed during actions

Most actions need some way in which the person involved can see continually how the work is progressing – by self-evaluation and by **feedback** to themselves from observations of the current state of whatever they are doing. Without it they may make small errors that gradually build up to noticeably larger ones. The feedback may be continual, but not necessarily continuous. Thus they can judge success and when to stop. The need for continual feedback and control applies to both small and large actions, and to actions by individuals, teams and systems.

The activity of obtaining feedback and conducting an assessment may be viewed in two ways. Firstly, when all goes to plan it provides a check that an action has been finished satisfactorily thus triggering the start of a future action. Secondly, if progress is not going according to plan it enables that fact to be known at an early stage and suitable corrective measures to be applied.

The management cycle is a continual loop, the plan being continually revised in the light of progress and changing requirements

Review and control should be an ongoing process ensuring effective progress, use of resources and completion on the agreed schedule. For project control, key variables such as time spent, value of work done, and quality of work performed need to be monitored. Review and control may involve people who were not those doing the work, and the feedback may generate further requirements.

Having phases

Managers responsible for the investment in a major project may be unwilling to commit all of their resources to a project and then await delivery of the final product. This mode has risks and instead most managers like to take things a step at a time. If the project is not going according to plan there is then the opportunity to stop it and thus minimize any losses. Alternatively, at any step they may decide to change the product specification to ensure that it can still be developed within an acceptable budget.

For any organization the construction of a new business or information system can be a major investment, so the entire development may be broken into **phases**. At the end of each phase the managers responsible for the investment decisions will be presented with a report of the work completed, a list of available options and estimates of the costs and benefits associated with each option. Investment decisions, such as those described above, can then be taken between each phase.

Major deliverables may be suitable **breakpoints** between phases

With any project the difficulty lies in identifying suitable breakpoints between phases. The differences between many proprietary ISD methods show that professionals do not agree on how many phases there should be and what they should be called. To identify the phases within our framework we tried to list the major deliverables of interest to managers responsible for making decisions. The following observable deliverables are possible outcomes of each phase:

- a report on the likely benefits and costs of the entire project (feasibility phase);
- a project plan (project definition phase);
- a statement of requirements in detail (requirements analysis phase);
- a conceptual model of the system including a description of the proposed system's main facilities and features from the users' viewpoint (systems analysis phase);
- a complete specification of the system, a logical model (system design phase);
- a working system (handover phase).

The above phases reflect periods of increasing expenditure commitment, suggesting breakpoints between them for review before authorising the next phase.

Exercise 4.10

List some possible management decisions from a review.

The managers may:

- request **more information**, more detailed assessment of progress and performance, further planning, risk analysis, or better cost analysis;
- request **further work** to be done: maybe redoing something from a past phase that is now judged not entirely satisfactory;
- give approval to go ahead with the next phase as previously planned; perhaps subject to qualifications, policy changes and new directives;
- delay, curtail, reduce or stop the project: divert resources to a different project;
- make no decision.

Structure of actions as having parts

Sometimes an action may be viewed as consisting of several parts. In some authors' views the structure of an action is a sequence of subactions, but this is misleading as even for a time-oriented view it is too narrow.

People may differ in their views of the ways an action is structured. Structures may depend on any combination of breakdown by: time, resources, tools, location, size, importance, risk or other criteria. Where an action is viewed as having a time-oriented substructure, the subactions need not be done in sequence – e.g. they can be overlapping, or a subsubaction may form part of each of two subactions – as in a network structure.

Phases, activities, tasks, operations

Our framework structure to describe the development of business processes or information systems uses the terms in Table 4.1. We shall explain it gradually.

A **project** may be any size and, typically, have many activities.

An IS **development** is bigger than a phase. It involves many **phases / stages**. Each is a major part, made up of many **activities** meaning a schedulable action, which includes many **tasks** meaning a piece of work set or undertaken, which includes many **operations**. Each is a (small or single) action or process carried out – as a unit. Elementary operation means not meaningfully subdivided.	Actions to which the management cycle applies

TABLE 4.1
ISD action terms to which a management cycle applies

Each of the actions in Table 4.1 may use any of the terms about how to do actions from Table 4.2.

TABLE 4.2
Terms that apply to an action

Methods, which may use many **Techniques**, which may use many **Tools**	Terms about ways of doing actions

Terms for sizes of actions include: development, phase, stage, activity, task, operation. Terms concerning ways of doing an action include method, technique, using a tool; and, more vaguely, approach, style.

Nested management control cycles

A major change to an existing IS or the development of a new one may involve a nested set of phases, activities, tasks and operations each with their own management control cycle at increasing levels of detail, as Figure 4.8 shows.

In general our framework allows one or more of the actions to be partly planned before the first action is started. Planning and actions may be interleaved.

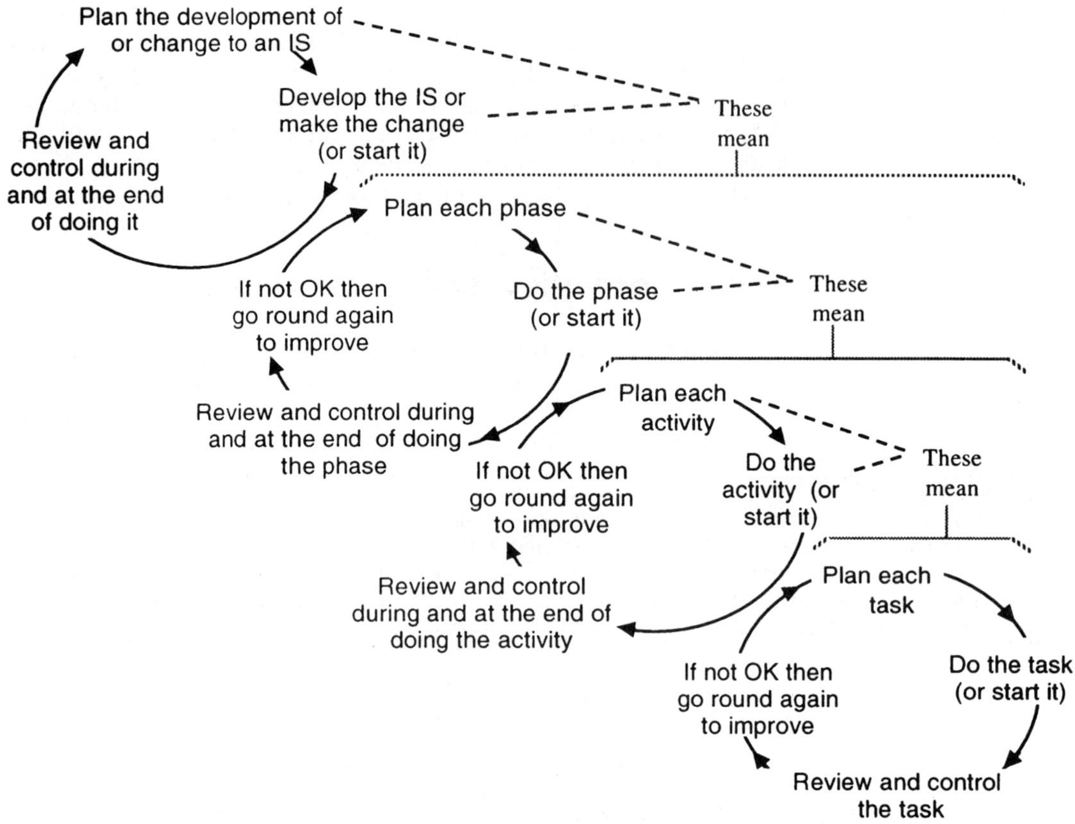

FIGURE 4.8
Nesting of development, phase, activity, task; with plan, do and review of each action.

Control aspects of managing

Wherever George, Graham or anyone else makes decisions that control something is a **point of control**. Management of a business unit is a point of control. This involves defining who can take what decisions, where the points of control are placed in the organizational structure, what are the decision-making criteria for each point – perhaps coming from some higher objective, what information is needed to support decisions at the point of control, and the need for recursiveness in control networks. A point of control should account for the use of business assets and resources under it, and account for all transactions for which it is responsible.

Short-, medium- and long-term control cycles

The integration of planning and control cycles, seen in Figure 4.9, is essential to success.

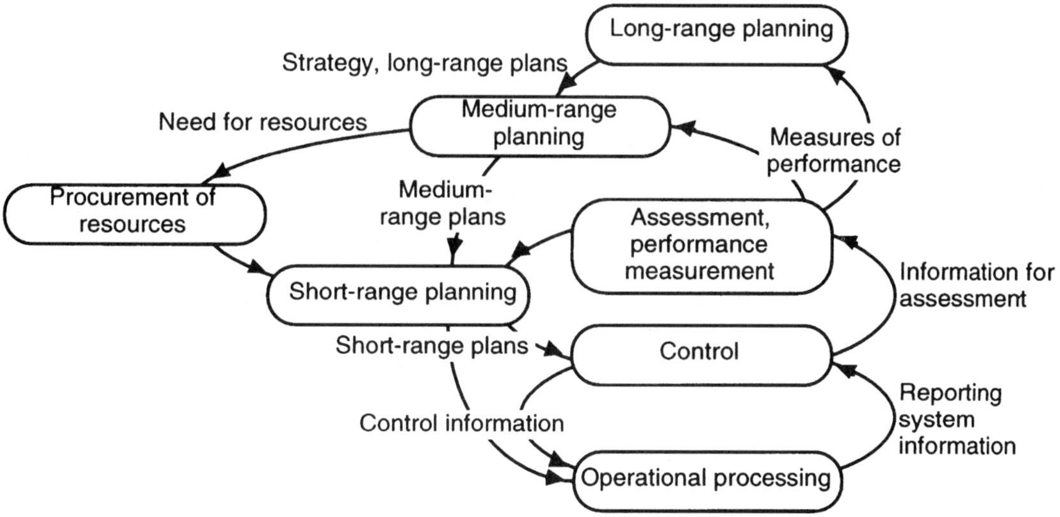

FIGURE 4.9
Continual planning and control with an integration of different timescales.

Long-range plans, strategy

Long-range planning is different from medium- and short-term planning. Long-range planning is an economic task, affected by the external environment. It is concerned not with resource management but with the broad direction and strategy in which the management intend the organization to go. Long-range plans should be feasible in order that subservient levels of planning can develop achievable, more detailed objectives and plans.

The service and support being given to an organization by IT should be evaluated periodically, perhaps every two years. Changes in the information systems strategic and tactical plans may be needed. Assessing what might be obtained in the future needs faith and imagination. Alternatively this can be an ongoing central service.

Medium-term plans and tactics

From such long-range planning the medium-term tactical planning will be developed and this does concern the availability of resources. If the current performance is not as good as is desired long term, then the medium-term plans will include making arrangements for changed or enhanced resources.

Short-term plans

Finally, short-term planning produces a schedule of the allocation and intended use of the resources available to provide the products and services. Short-term planning, because the timescale is short, does not include the capability of changing the available resources. It does allow for emergency changes of plans and ways to cope with breakdowns or late deliveries, where the resources and materials are not quite as expected.

The operational processes consume materials and energy and produce goods, products and services. They use resources.

Exercise 4.11

What information flows are omitted for simplicity in Figure 4.9?

Figure 4.9 omits feedback between the various planning processes, e.g. flows from short-range planning to medium-range planning saying whether or not or to what extent problems might arise within the current planning period. Similarly the figure omits feedback from medium-range tactical planning to the long-range strategic planning processes.

The figure also omits flows of information to all levels from outside, including information about the expected availability of resources and technology. Flows of information about incoming and outgoing materials, products and services at the operational level are likewise omitted.

Allowing for these, control of an action, such as George making something during a business process, involves internal and external controls, with several information flows, as in Figure 4.10. The same applies with appropriate change of wording to Anna producing something during an ISD activity, where the top-left objectives are those of the organization as a whole.

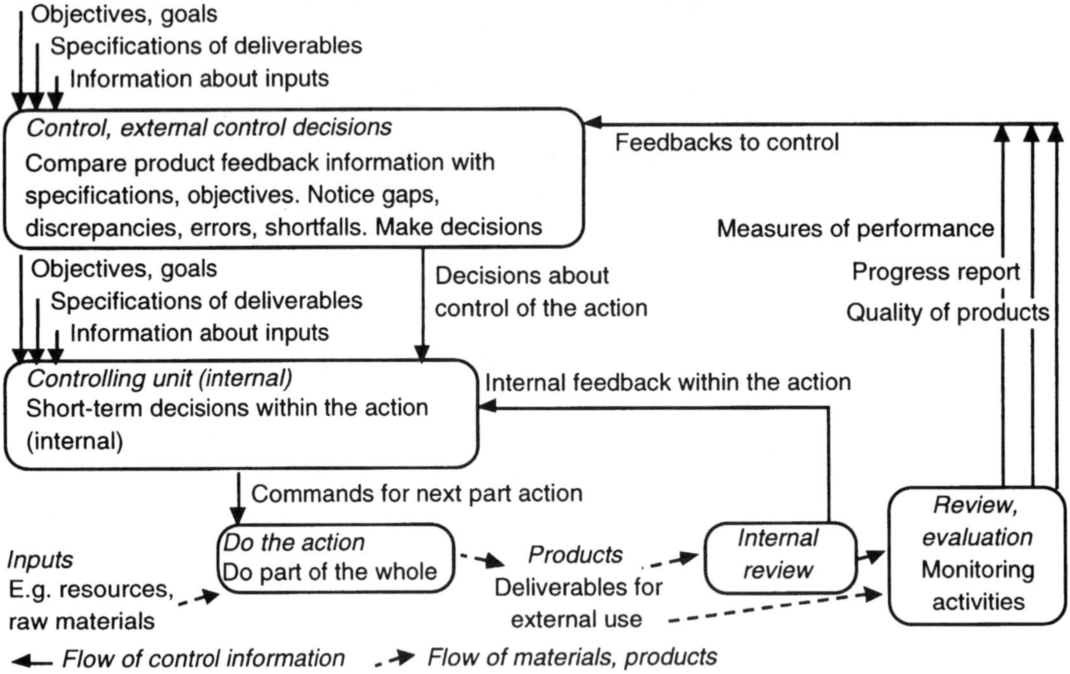

FIGURE 4.10
Control cycles for an action with internal control and external control decisions – each being closed loops.

Role of managers using information systems for control

Next we view the same control aspects from a different standpoint, that of the manager trying to control some resource in an environment, and wanting the right information and knowledge. The IS needs to provide the right information and facilities.

Many people wrongly see managers and decision makers as being external to the ISs. They see ISs as providing information to decision makers who then take decisions and issue directives and instructions for control purposes. Figure 4.11 shows in a **cybernetic** way that in fact a decision-making manager processes information and creates further information that controls resources.

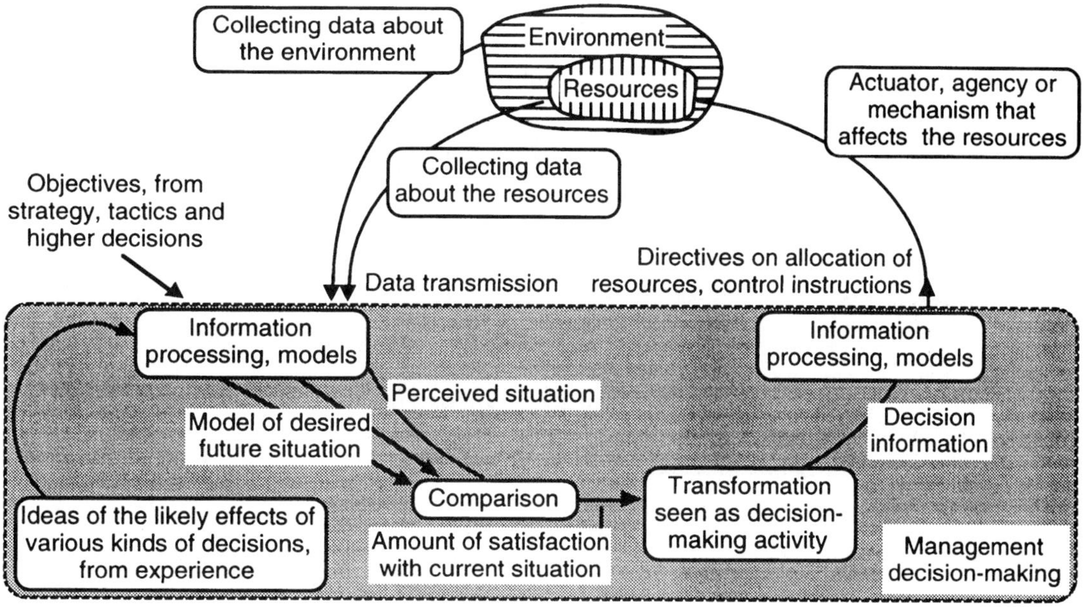

FIGURE 4.11
A system to make decisions and control resources in an environment. The lower shaded area represents the manager.

Decision-making involves:

- transforming information about the state of resources, the organization and its environment into new information;
- comparing perceived states with desired states;
- making decisions that should improve the situation, e.g. by changing the use of resources or altering priorities.

Managers are themselves part of the information processing system. When people talk about models of reality, the organization and its environment, they should remember that these models are not all explicit, and not all held in computer or IT-based systems. The people like George, and managers like Graham, are themselves part of the ISs. To a large extent the models are implicit and held in people's heads.

Availability of information for control

Figure 4.11 applies at several levels. At an operational level George controls certain resources such as machines, materials and energy. These operate like the top part of the figure and George performs the functions corresponding to the lower rectangle.

Graham, George's manager, also behaves like the lower rectangle, regarding George and everything George is responsible for as within the upper resource. Graham may perhaps be more concerned with tactics or medium-term planning or considering whether improved resources should be considered. Similarly Gwen has a higher management view, regarding Graham and George as part of her resources, and perhaps being far more concerned with strategy and major improvements in performance.

The ISs should provide these three quite different views of the activities in appropriate forms to George, Graham and Gwen.

Exercise 4.12

Under what circumstances should George's view be available to Graham? Under what circumstances should Graham's view be available to George?

Many people may say, traditionally, that Graham should have access to George's view in order to manage George; and others that Graham should only need or want George's view in exceptional situations as otherwise Graham is just duplicating George's work. Graham needs a different view, that shows whether what has happened, is happening or is about to happen, is satisfactory. George acts. Graham plans, organizes, directs and controls.

Some people may say that George does not need Graham's view and should not have access to it, thus preserving power for Graham. However, the aim is to optimize the whole and where George can check for deviations from plan in the same way as Graham, and can do this before Graham's regular time of doing so, George can rectify the matter. Thus effectiveness is improved.

In providing and managing ISs a **chicken and egg** situation exists. Which comes first, the IS to hold the objectives, strategy, plans and information; or the strategy, plans and approvals to create the ISs? Also which comes first, the business process or the IS to hold information about it and control it, particularly where the IS is itself part of the process? Managers have to accept compromises over this. The ISs cannot be perfect. In practice existing ISs are used to hold information about the next generation of strategy, plans and processes.

Management involves directing, controlling, initiating work and reviewing. Management styles affect processes, plans and products. People have differing opinions on how to tackle large improvements. What can be provided, IT-based facilities and the availability of tools and methods are limited in ways that nest the theoretical, the available and what is worthwhile at any time. What should be provided is affected by people's familiarity and understanding. So management decisions on what to automate, which business systems are appropriate, and other soft issues interact. Large projects need teams and project management and consequently have extra complications. Management control cycles of the planning, doing and reviewing of actions have to be applied to nested and structured collections of actions such as developments, phases, activities, tasks and operations. Review and control occurs during and after actions, and may be done by the person doing the action or by the manager. Controlling resources in an environment involves points of control and decision processes. Long-, medium- and short-term control cycles are nested, on the assumption that it takes time to obtain resources.

Self check

Please spend some time reviewing what you have read and doing the questions below.

Objectives

After reading this chapter you should be able to:

- explain what management means;
- discuss some of the management issues of information, information systems, ISD and IS use; the various impacts and management difficulties;
- explain various issues about starting to improve a business system or the facilities of an IS;
- explain feasibility, listing appropriate steps;
- explain criteria for choosing between alternatives; and the desirable benefits and avoidable costs of a typical situation; and uncertainty and compromise in such situations;
- explain the intersecting sets of what could be provided in theory, what could be provided with current technology, and what is actually provided, acceptable and worthwhile; and equivalents for possible methods and products;
- discuss organizational issues about what to automate, IT budgets, and custom design and development versus purchasing a standard system;
- explain the necessity for, and the features of, working in teams and the extra actions, processes and kinds of information thus needed; and how these should be arranged and managed;
- explain the management control cycle applied to actions; the structure of actions; terms such as development, phase or

stage, activity, task and operation; the general properties of actions; and their possible nesting and sequencing;

- explain review and control of actions, and possible outcomes;
- explain amplification, attenuation and control and evaluation information flows;
- explain how these ideas apply to managers in their roles of using information for control of processes and resources;
- explain the nesting of long-, medium- and short-term control cycles, and what kinds of information and decisions are needed in each; and the need for ISs to provide the appropriate information flows and products.

Questions

Some of these questions extend the points in the earlier text.

4.1 Which of the lettered areas in the Venn diagram of Figure 4.2 (p. 115) could something which is currently in E and something which is currently in F move into in 20 years time? (4 marks)

4.2 A food manufacturer's top management allowed each of its divisions, which made different kinds of foods, to create its own IT-based ISs to support its sales and marketing to suit that division's information needs – some divisions had only a few outlets. This company's dynamic top management decided centrally to expand into neighbouring countries in Europe. What do you think happened and why? (3 marks)

4.3 The top management of the holding company of a dynamic large international oil conglomerate, with five companies in the group, decided that each company should be free to make its own decisions about IT expenditure and standards, subject to one condition which arose from the need to produce corporate accounts. What do you think the condition was? (3)

4.4 In the Venn diagrams (Figures 4.2 and 4.3) showing how various possibilities are related, we showed certain sets with solid edges and others dashed, and some with names in italic. Why? (3)

4.5 A highly centralized organization, HC, and a decentralized one, D, behaved differently and had different strategies. Each was fairly large with several operating divisions making and selling various products. How did their physical distribution and sales analysis ISs differ? (4)

4.6 Fill in Table 4.3. In each cell put a number from 0 (no effect) to 5 (major effect) corresponding to how much effect you think the item at the left has on the item at the top of a column. In the headings 'its' means the organization's. You may be reductionist or assume ongoing BSP – both should give the same. (7)

4.7 What kind of organization would allow many different managers each to set up their own spreadsheets to plan their tactics or as a basis for discussing short-term operational plans with colleagues? Is this likely to be organizationally advantageous? (4)

	... its organ- izational objectives	... its management style	... its product / service	... the market for its products	... its selection of IT applications	... successful use of its ISs
The organizational objectives affect ...	-					
Its management style affects ...		-				
Its external environment affects ...						
The market for its products affects ...				-		
Its selection of IT application areas affects ...					-	
Successful use of its IT-based ISs affects ...						-

TABLE 4.3
See Question 4.6

4.8 What are likely to be the effects of successful IT-based ISs on the management styles of lower to middle managers, and on near-top managers, and why? (10)

4.9 How have the attenuation and amplification activities of middle managers been affected by IT in the last ten years, and what has been the consequence? (4)

5 What is a process?

Structured systems analysis and design techniques were popular for well over 20 years. More recently, '**Business Process Re-engineering**' (BPR), '**Business Process Improvement**' and so on have become the vogue panaceas that herald orders-of-magnitude efficiency improvement. One would imagine, therefore, that the anatomy of a process is now understood clearly and that people don't need yet another dissertation on this subject. Contemporary and demonstrably expert authors, whose literature is rich with dazzling success stories, bear evidence to the relative effectiveness of current business process re-engineering thinking.

However, nowhere in the most popular expert business re-engineering literature available could we find (a) any consensus about the definition of 'business process' or (b) a formal definition of 'process' that is sufficient for use by process engineers and system builders. How incredible that such improvements have been managed without a satisfactory generic metamodel and corresponding notation for expressing the anatomy and dynamics of a process! This would be similar to medical practitioners having no formal representations of anatomy, physiology, psychology and biochemistry; or financial controllers without formal accounting analysis techniques.

Be able to create a **level I process description**

After studying this chapter and the next you should be able to create appropriate blank forms corresponding to the various kinds of knowledge needed about a business process, and fill these in for an actual business process in your organization. We gradually build up to that objective. Our aim is to show you how to do useful process analysis. Some books on business processes may enthuse top managers into initiating work on changes but often do not explain how the analysts, managers and other staff who are required to do the detailed analysis work should do it. Our objective is to explain to you how it might be done, so that you could do likewise in your own organization.

The principles in this chapter apply to business processes and not just to computer-based processes and IT-based developments. We establish both an explanation of an actual process and a metamodel of rules about how to describe a process.

Defining processes

The following ideas about processes have been formed from some widely used business process engineering literature.

- Most organizations are structured in vertically functioning groups, while most processes flow horizontally.
- A process is a structured, measured set of activities designed to produce a specified output for a particular customer or market. A process is a specific ordering of work activities across time and place, with a beginning, an end and clearly defined inputs and outputs; a structure for action.
- People must agree on the way work is or should be structured.
- A process is a set of activities that, taken together, produce a result of value to a customer such as developing a new product. One way to see a process is as a collection of activities that takes one or more kinds of input and creates an output that is of value to the customer. A process is any activity or group of activities that takes an input, adds value to it and provides an output to an internal or external customer. A process is a set of linked activities that take an input and transform it to create an output. Ideally, the transformation should add value to the input and create an output that is more useful and effective to the recipient either upstream or downstream.

In general several authors agree that businesses contain a number of major business processes but disagree about how many; some say between 5 and 8, others say between 10 and 20.

Some general observations and comments about the above definitions can be made. They embody two classic views of process architecture: **structure** and **flow**.

Here structure refers to a static, architectural abstraction. That is, a system can contain one or more main processes which in turn can contain subprocesses and so on until, according to some rule, a lower-level process should not be further decomposed and is labelled a bottom-level process. This classic 'functional decomposition' propounds that processes decompose hierarchically. Traditionally they are represented by a combination of flowcharts such as data flow diagrams or information flow diagrams and corresponding structure charts.

Here flow refers to two different abstractions of system dynamics, each abstraction focusing the mind on different objects, properties and relationships.

(a) A process consists of activities or subprocesses linked together in fixed chains by data flow or material flow. The focus is on whatever flows amongst the processes. Something flows towards the system from outside, across the system boundary and is received by the first activity in the chain. The output from this activity becomes the input for the next and so on, until finally the output from the last activity flows across the boundary out of the system.

(b) A process consists of activities or subprocesses linked together in a defined work flow sequence. The focus is on the sequence

> in which activities are performed. In this view, activities are executed in some fixed sequence, each contributing to the overall process. Although information or components might flow between activities, they are not highlighted by the work flow abstraction. Processes are said to contain a set, collection or group of smaller things such as 'activities' or 'subprocesses'. No semantic difference between process, activity and task is defined, other than that these words are used to imply some level within a hierarchy.

All definitions agree that a process receives input(s) and generates output(s). However, there is no consensus about the number of inputs or outputs a single process can manage. Some authors use the singular, implying that a process is inherently functionally cohesive (which in the case of an information system, implies that the data in the single input is fully normalized) although this feature is not explicitly stated. Harrington (1991) states that: (a) processes typically have several inputs and outputs; (b) there are normally one or two 'primary' inputs and outputs; and (c) there are normally several 'secondary' inputs and outputs. Technically, this is an important point because the number and properties of inputs and outputs will indicate whether the process is functionally cohesive or needs further analysis. Harrington's definition implies that a business process is what traditional analysis calls 'top level'. Such a process would need further analysis and decomposition in order to become buildable.

The two traditional views of processes are heavily dependent on: (1) **structured decompositions** of allegedly independent business functions or applications; and (2) a notion of **input–process–output**. The former asserts that processes decompose hierarchically into subprocesses. The latter asserts that processes receive inputs, transform them into outputs which become the input to the next process and so on in a strictly defined fixed, repetitive sequence. This is the notion of **process flow**. Business process re-engineering goes some way towards reconciling these disparate views by asserting that business processes operate orthogonally to business functions, or departments. For example, a major process in manufacturing and trading companies is order fulfilment. The individual components of an order-fulfilment process are normally assigned to different business functions.

A more varied view of process flow is that of the process chain, wherein work activities are performed in fixed sequences. Harrington drives some way towards the root of the problem, but is encumbered with inadequate tools. The solution is far more profound than merely having to uproot whole business functions or departments; it depends on understanding what business 'functions' and business 'activities' are. We really need to get rid of the notion of fixed sequences of activities. However well an organization's formal procedures are documented, and however much resource is poured into corporate training plans, workers will always find 'other' ways of performing jobs more comfortably, or more efficiently. When unexpected events occur, such as sickness, absence, key staff leaving, fire or bombs, businesses have to find other ways of doing work outside of the default sequence of controlled behaviour. Apart from the really dramatic and infrequent events mentioned, real human businesses simply do not work in strict, documented sequences. How many organizations' managers rush staff through a dress rehearsal in the last days before the BS5750 auditors arrive, simply because the business really doesn't operate according to its documented fixed processing sequences! Day by day, or hour by hour, employees thread elementary tasks together in whatever sequence seems appropriate to get an overall job done within the constraints of a given set of conditions. Those conditions may be changed, sometimes predictably, sometimes unpredictably. The key to systems design is: (a) identifying elementary business 'activities' to the right level of granularity; (b) understanding which business 'processes' need to make use of which elementary activities; and (c) understanding which business functions 'own' which business processes.

Figure 5.1, which with slight changes can be applied to computer or human systems, summarizes these principles.

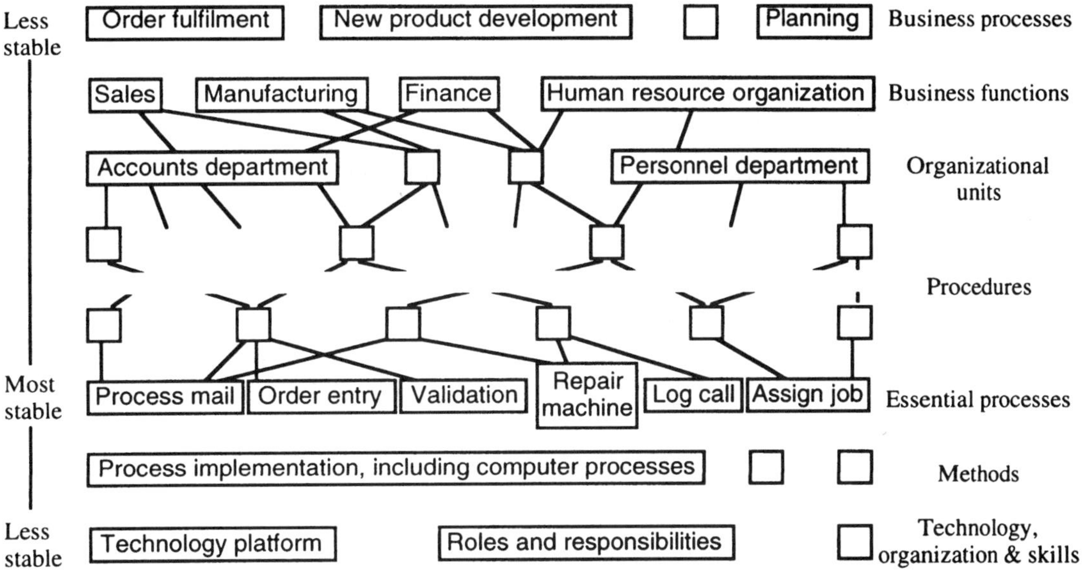

FIGURE 5.1 Organization and process – stable and changing processes.

In the lower centre of Figure 5.1, **essential processes** represents the collection of basic processes that an organization depends on independently of its organizational structure. Examples include all activities involving customers, products and services, contracts, suppliers, and so forth.

An essential process consists of: (a) a collection of resources, including data; and (b) the collection of essential actions and operations on the resources to convert its inputs into its outputs.

These low-level processes are called **essential** because they will continue to exist in some form over a relatively long time regardless of how, or how many times, the organization reorganizes itself. In a business such processes are vital although meaningless until placed into some low-level workflow context, represented in the diagram by procedures. For example in a study by Geoffrey Darnton of a financial institution there were 3000 procedures and more than 15 000 essential or elementary processes. Each procedure was a response to some event which could be represented by a process chain[†]. Many of these essential processes are also **elementary** because it is not particularly useful to decompose them any further.

The essential processes are stable

The essential business processes, such as answering a telephone query from a customer and perhaps using an elementary computer process to answer it, are relatively more **stable** than higher-level business processes or methods of technical implementation. This is because the essential processes must be done in some way irrespective of which organizational function is responsible. Indeed, they may even survive the organization itself, or be capable of being subcontracted out to a different organization. Implementation is less stable than the logical elementary process itself, because the methods and technology used to support or implement such a process may be evolving all the time.

For example, a low-level process is the entry of a new sales order. From a business perspective, a process is required to bring each sales order into existence. From a technical perspective, a process is also required to bring each order line into existence. The properties and behaviour of Create-order-line will contribute to the success or failure of Create-sales-order. To create the near-elementary business process Create-sales-order, Anna could thread together several elementary computer processes. These would need processes such as the following, with some illustrative attributes in parentheses:

```
Create-order-header(Order-no, Date, …),
  Read-customer(Cu-no, Cu-address, …),
  Calculate-creditworthiness(Cu-no,
  Credit-available), Read-inventory(Product-no,
  Quantity-in-stock), Create-order-line(Order-no,
  Product-no, Quantity-ordered, Price),
  Update-inventory (Stock-available,
  Stock-allocated), Update-customer
  (Credit-available).
```

Similarly, each other procedure or process box knits together a collection of elementary computer processes that are selected and executed sequentially or iteratively. What is selected and how they are sequenced or iterated will be determined by the external conditions occurring at each instance. So, a **procedure** in Figure 5.1 could be defined as a collection of elementary activities selected and executed iteratively or in sequence depending on certain conditions, to perform some action that is meaningful to the business. The smallest, **elementary business process** is a process that performs one life cycle step of one business object, not being meaningfully decomposed further.

In database systems, an **elementary business process** equates with one iteration of an **elementary business transaction**, such as 'Create Sales Order', 'Book Hotel Accommodation' or 'Book Airline Ticket'. The next level up could be a submenu; or it could be running a program, or it could be a higher level transaction such as 'Book Holiday', which makes use of subtransactions such as 'Book Hotel Accommodation' and 'Book Airline Ticket'.

Near-elementary computer processes could represent transactions on one database or several cooperating databases. In a manual system, the equivalent of near-elementary computer processes may be performed by one clerk, several clerks in the same office or several clerks in different companies.

Near the top of Figure 5.1, the main business processes, business functions and business departments tend to be relatively unstable. They are prone to being reorganized every few months or years, producing undesirable effects on the use of computers to support business processes. Structured-decomposition techniques yield a collection of information systems which are designed to support the work of separate business functions and departments, instead of business processes that span business functions. Specifications tend to address the requirements and issues of these top two levels as they are at some particular time, resulting in two effects.

1. Elementary business processes and their more elementary activities are usually designed to satisfy the temporary requirements of a business entity that itself has a relatively short life cycle. When departments have been replaced or reorganized, their successors often cannot make use of the elementary business processes and operations that were designed to manage events and conditions in a different organizational context.
2. The process of designing essential business processes and more elementary objects that are persistent across long expanses of time, and can serve volatile requirements, many of them currently unknown and unpredictable, is difficult. It requires a combination of organizational and highly technical skills. The technical skills include: (a) skills specific to the implementation platform of hardware, software, work study and methods improvement; and (b) platform-independent knowledge, education and business engineering skills.

The natural languages and diagrams of current business process re-engineering are targeted at managers who, generally, do *not* have the technical skills to do the supporting detailed analysis and design work in practice. Traditional structured systems analysis and design methods are targeted at the technicians but do not provide the appropriate notations to express the sheer number and complexity of objects, processes, properties and relationships found throughout the breadth and depth of today's business organizations.

Much of the focus of current BPR popular and professional literature is biased towards achieving a competitive edge by cutting costs, improving leadtime, satisfying downstream customer demand, and so forth. Important and successful as this is, we would like to see the current trends in business process engineering supplemented with formal techniques, languages and tools that ensure the following. (a) Simple language and interfaces exist to enable managers and technicians alike to define their system structure, behaviour, dynamics, resourcing, objectives, problems and solutions. (b) There are formal, precise and cost effective semi-automated consistency and completeness checks throughout an entire system model. (c) Where IT is appropriate, automated generation of software and databases, taking into account both business objectives and hardware and network configuration, should be available. (d) Where human operations are appropriate, the availability of semi-automated generation of job descriptions and business process descriptions would help.

Such a system would provide a syntax-based system definition language, together with appropriate graphical user interfaces and language definition capabilities, so that organizations could define their own objects, properties and relationships as deemed appropriate.

Chapters 6 and some later chapters explain several analysis and design techniques that can help further understanding of what a process is. The section starting p. 146 presents a worked example.

Business processes and information systems

What are the main differences between business processes and information systems? One key theme of this book is that many of the techniques that have been used to analyse information systems can be used to help with the analysis of business processes (Figure 5.2). This section takes a more detailed look at the applicability of various techniques.

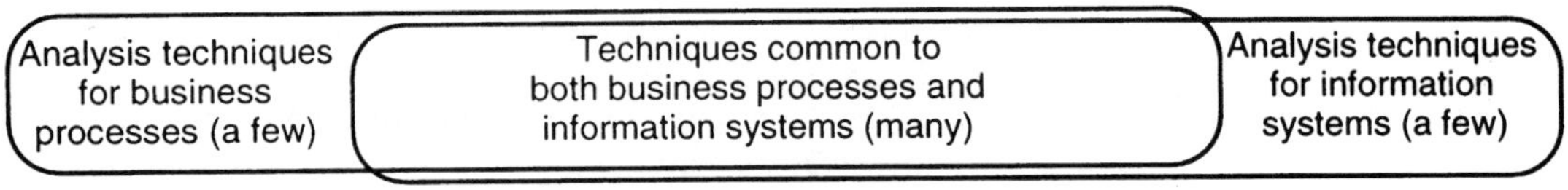

FIGURE 5.2 Analysis techniques for business processes and information systems.

The following questions arise from this diagram.

- Which techniques are common both to business processes and to information systems?
- Are the common techniques applied in the same way for both domains?
- Which techniques are applicable only to business processes?
- Which techniques are applicable only to information systems?

There is an additional dimension to these questions. Are the techniques being applied to describe the processes and systems, or are they being applied to rationalize in some way? We provide a basis for answering these questions.

Key concepts

Chapters 1 and 2 discussed the concepts of business process and information systems and definitions of both were proposed. Our definition of an information system (p. 79) can be called an **extended** definition because it includes people and equipment and is not restricted to computers. The concept of an information system being restricted to computers (and associated hardware and software) can be considered as a **restricted** concept of an information system.

The simplest idea of a process is that it takes various inputs, performs some kind of transformation on those inputs and generates some outputs. This is a rather classical concept found in many texts.

In the case of the restricted concept of an information system, the technology is used to accept various information inputs and transform them into different information outputs. Many common approaches to analysis show this by means of a **context diagram**, an example of which is presented in Figure 5.3.

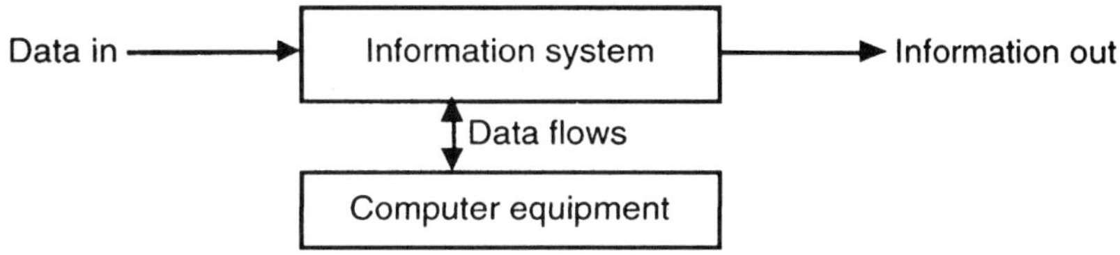

FIGURE 5.3 Restricted input–output concept of an information system.

For the extended idea of an information system other inputs, such as people and equipment, are needed in order to generate the required outputs. This is shown in Figure 5.4.

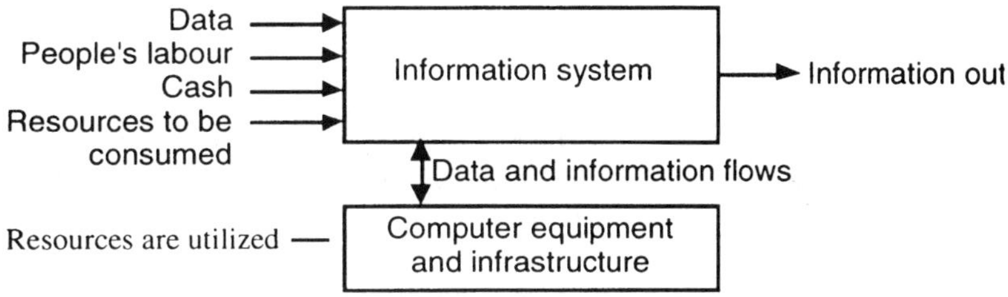

FIGURE 5.4 Extended input–output concept of an information system.

It is difficult to see why the idea of a business process at a very high level is any different from the well-established economic view of a firm or not-for-profit organization that takes various 'factor inputs', and converts those inputs into products and services.

Traditional economic factors of production can be stated as land, labour, capital and enterprise. These are very broad categories that are difficult to visualize and therefore we use a different set of **factor inputs**. We consider people's knowledge and experience (intellectual capital) as an important additional factor input, although some economists would argue that intellectual capital is included in the generic term 'enterprise'. Figure 5.5 shows our collection of factor inputs where the term infrastructure applies to the lower-level structure components that are continuously available and used in more than one application.

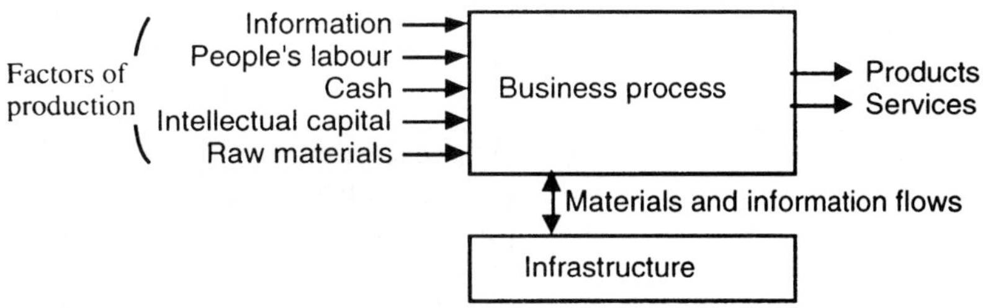

FIGURE 5.5 Input–output concept of a business process.

The distinction between our extended information system concept and the description of an input–output view of business process is very blurred. This is of some historical importance. The current preoccupation in the literature with computers tends to neglect the system context within which computers are used. When the context is considered, computers become just some of the artefacts used within the system. Therefore, the analysis of information systems puts emphasis on information but the analysis of business processes needs to take a broader view.

For information systems, there are always choices over the way the system is implemented. For example, a personnel information system could be implemented using supporting IT in different ways:

- a card-index file with employee information kept on one card per employee;
- filing cabinets with employee files and summary sheets to help with payroll processing;
- a simple computer application with employee records and a feeder file to the payroll and accounting systems;
- a full database management system managed by a server that is connected into a complex enterprise-wide set of computer systems.

The analysis of business processes should include not only analysis of information, but also subjects such as cost accounting, to deal with cash; and organizational behaviour, to deal with the people aspects. The analysis of the different ways that business processes can be arranged requires an understanding of matters such as **factor substitutability**, that is how the same outputs can be produced using different combinations of factor inputs, and operations management to show how the processes are operated in practice. This means that traditional techniques of systems analysis and operational research are very useful for the rationalization of business processes.

In recent years there has been a distinct trend towards applying traditional software engineering (= CASE) tools to the problem of business process engineering. The need for such tools to support cost accounting and operations research is discussed in Chapter 10.

A worked example

Idris plays the role of having ideas. Anna creates the generalizations

Process identified, named

Underlying principles

Suppose in an organization Idris has an idea for a new or improved business process. We will act out how he and Anna discuss it and how they document their findings.

Idris says the process is to be called 'New product line added'. Anna is at this stage not sure whether this corresponds to a process, an event, a system or to something else. Anna and Idris need to discuss it. They have in their minds the following principles:

- **What does it do**? A process or system normally supports purposeful behaviour. So they need to understand the purposes and ensure that these are implemented. **Purposeful** implies keeping in mind some intention, aim or objective to be achieved at the end. Whereas Idris and Anna are discussing the purpose, the eventual work will be done by George, and he may or may not have the same view of the purpose of his actions as Idris and Anna did when they were devising the process or system.

- **What does it do it to**? A process or system normally manipulates appropriate objects according to certain operations. So they need to understand and document the objects and operations.
- **How does it interact with the real world**? People carrying out a process interact with other people in many ways. Computer systems that perform processes and manipulate representations of reality of a universe of discourse interact with people in many ways. So these interactions need to be understood and represented.
- **How should we best work to create understanding of it**? Idris and Anna want it documented so others can understand it and do further work. Parts of the eventual process or system may be automated. The term information system does not imply whether or not something is automated. It is usually better for Idris and Anna initially to concentrate on creating an understanding of the process, system, or whatever; and leave until later exactly what parts may be automated.
- **How should we represent it**? Idris and Anna aim to create a representation of some facts that describe a process or system. The representation may be in the form of diagrams or text. For every possible diagram it is possible to create text that carries the same meaning. At this stage they are not concerned with whether or not the diagrams or text are held in a computer or written on paper. They want suitable representations to communicate the meaning. Of course, in addition to diagrams and text, information about processes and systems may be stored in computer databases for processing by computers rather than people.

When does what happen?

Idris and Anna start to discuss this process named 'New product line added'. They may make progress either by discussing *what happens under what conditions*, or by discussing the *context*. It does not matter which route they take. We illustrate both, first what happens, and then in the next subsection (p. 153) the context.

Begin to explain the process

Anna asks an open-ended question, prompting Idris to explain as he thinks appropriate. Idris says, after some thought and discussion, that there are really two processes: 'Identify the product' and 'Create a new product record'. Idris says these processes have to be done when a 'New product line is to be added'. At this stage it is perhaps not clear whether this means one or both these processes. Anna and Idris realize that 'New product line *is to be* added' is not quite the same as the original name.

Idris says that 'New product line is to be added' means that a new product line has already been created in the factory, its details will be known and the corresponding information is to be added to the data in the information system that George uses. So it seems to be an event. The meaning is that: it happens when a new product line has been created and the details are known, and when the event happens appropriate information should be added to the IS. Idris says adding this information to the IS involves the two processes: 'Identify the product' and 'Create a new product record'. When this event happens the two processes may start.

Anna may prompt for further clarification. Perhaps Idris says that when it is known that the event has happened either or both processes should start.

Anna thinks of generalizations

Anna forms, or has already formed, in her mind some generalizations and abstractions about processes. We illustrate these to you as we continue the story, though Anna might or might not say them to Idris. We put Anna's thoughts in a different font to help you distinguish them from other text.

Event may trigger processes

Anna thinks: An event may trigger a process or processes. Each of these processes (or a combination of them) may or should or must start when the event occurs. Here 'when ...' means 'as soon as reasonably possible after ...'

The term 'may' here allows none or one or several to be triggered. So Anna's generalizations mean the following are allowed in Idris's specification. A named event may trigger any one or more of several named processes or none at all. And each named process may or may not have some corresponding named events that trigger it.

Equivalents of Anna's generalizations

Anna also thinks of equivalent forms of her generalizations. The equivalents may, for example, be the opposite way round, interchanging subject and object and choosing a suitable new verb. Anna thinks:

- Equivalently, a process may be triggered by an event. This means it may be triggered by any of several events.

The equivalent form may be just an alternative wording. Or it may add to or clarify the meaning in the *opposite direction*, from process to event.

We continue the story of Idris and Anna to enable us to explain more points to you.

Anna asks Idris to say more about the first process. Idris says 'Identify the product' could involve any of several other processes, depending on what the situation was. If there is a new product line to be added, then George would create a new product record. If an existing product line is being discontinued then George would delete the data corresponding to that product record.

Delete data or date stamp and keep it

Anna is not too happy about that. She thinks that the data about a discontinued product perhaps should be *kept but marked* in some way to indicate that the product line was discontinued, in case the data will be needed later – perhaps for accounts or auditing or as history. The marking could be achieved by creating associated data that represented the old and new status and the date and time of the change from one to the other.

Anna asks Idris if a new product could really be just a small change to an existing product. Idris says that that could happen. So if the product line identified is to be changed, then the existing product details should be displayed or printed for George, and he should then create a new record corresponding to the changed product. George may either allow the record corresponding to the existing product to continue, or mark the record corresponding to the existing line as discontinued. That is how George would see it and think of it.

Conditions

Idris and Anna agree that what George would do depends on various conditions. If some condition is true then George does one thing, if some other condition arises then he does something else.

Anna thinks about the generalizations:

- A process may cause a condition to become true (or false).
- Equivalently, a condition may be made true (or false) by a process.
- A condition becoming true (or false) may trigger a process.
- Equivalently, a process may be triggered by a condition becoming true (or false).

Again the equivalent assertions are rewordings that have the same meanings as others, but are the other way round and perhaps convey extra information. The term 'may' here again allows none or one or several. For example, a named condition may be made true by any one or more of several named processes. Each named condition may have some corresponding named processes that cause it to become true. Each named condition has other corresponding named processes that are triggered when it becomes true.

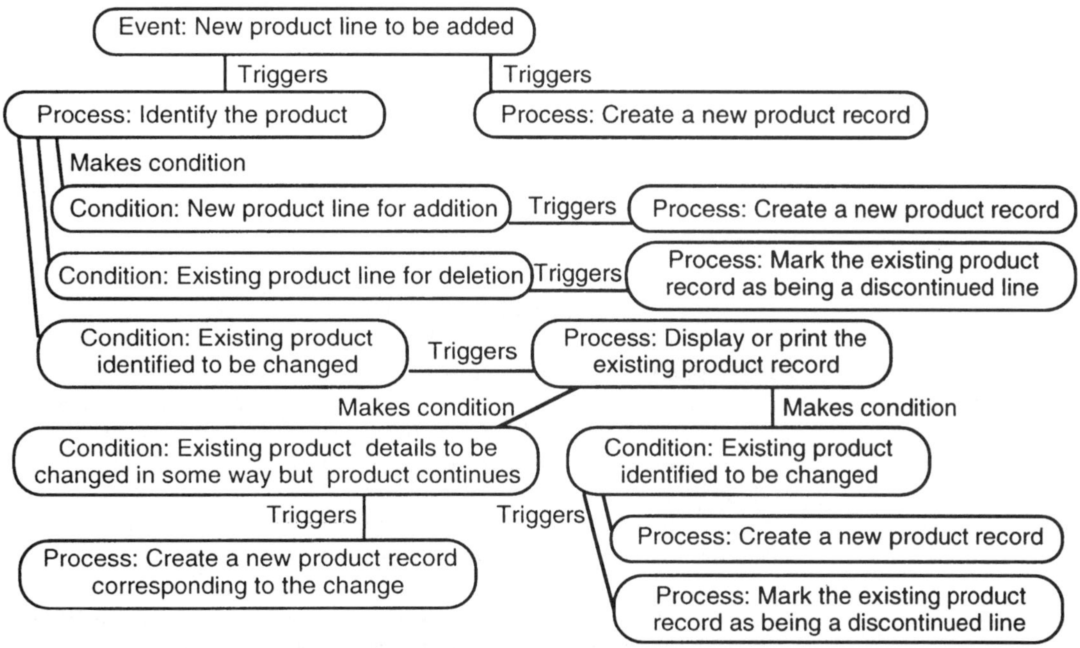

FIGURE 5.6 (a) Example of event, process, condition chain.

Event–process–condition chain

Sometimes it is easier to see the essence of the logic from a diagram. Here we have events, processes and conditions. Anna and Idris drew a

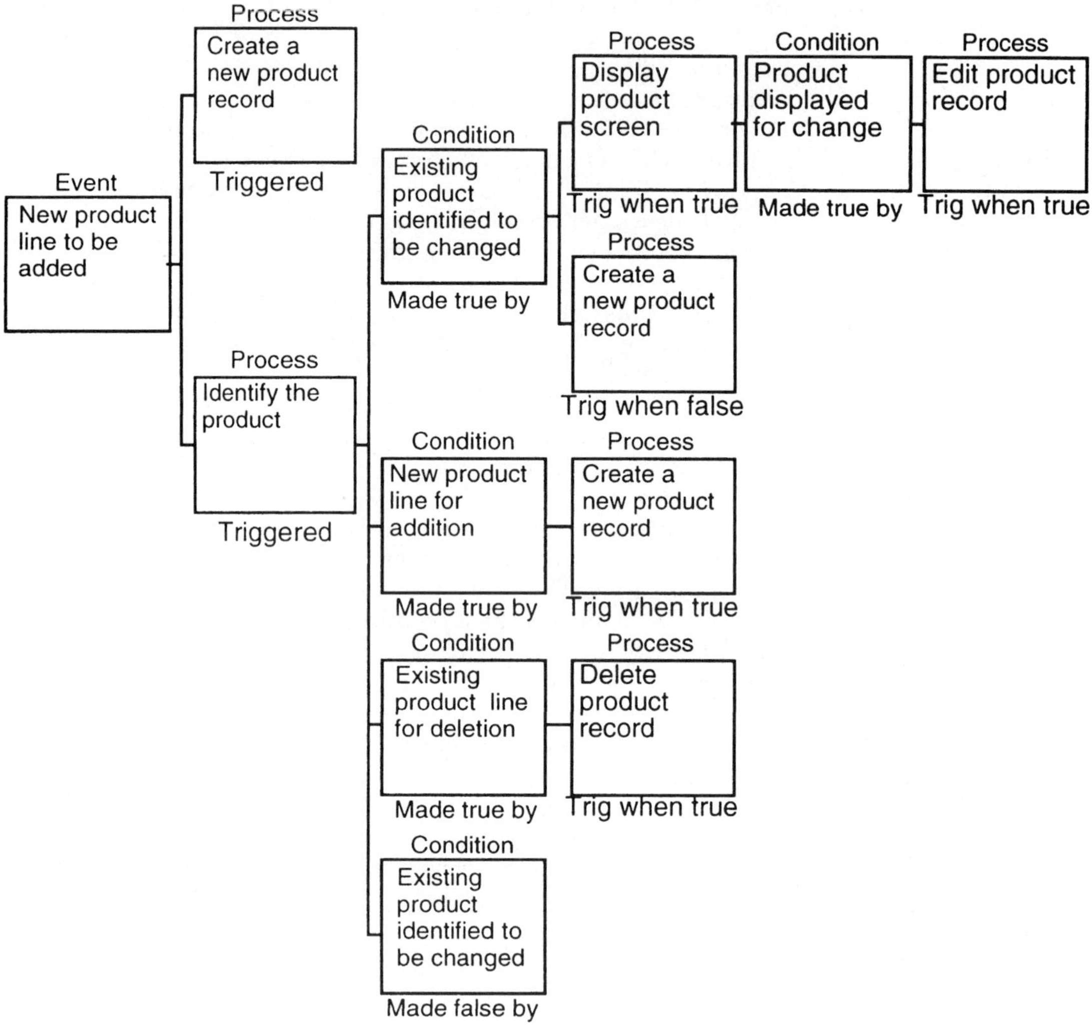

FIGURE 5.6 (b)
Computer-produced representation.

diagram of what they had decided. Our version here has been tidied up to give Figure 5.6 (a) which shows the structure of a collection of events, conditions and processes, and how they are associated through what triggers what. Figure 5.6 (b) is the equivalent diagram generated by a software package. The type of box is shown by a word above the box. The relationship between the box to the left and the current box is described below the box.

Tree structure or network structure

Some named boxes appear more than once and the whole has a tree structure starting from the root event. Alternatively the structure might have been shown as a network, with only one appearance of each named box. The lines showing associations might become longer and perhaps have to cross and the resultant whole might seem either easier or more difficult to draw and to follow. Before Anna and Idris can decide whether boxes should be merged as in a network, they must think about and discuss whether the various boxes that have the same name really are the same. Maybe there are slight differences that have not yet been discussed.

Computer-processable representations

As the discussions continue, more and more detail is added. Soon the whole may cover many pages of paper. Something arising later may refer back to and supplement or change something said earlier. Anna and Idris may realize that they have problems managing their representations of what they have discussed. If Anna and Idris talk to several other staff from different departments they may get further information that may seem inconsistent. Soon Anna and Idris will think of holding the whole in a computer.

For simplicity, we shall create for you representations mainly as sentences of text. Sophisticated software can hold such text assertions and from them create diagrams such as Figure 5.6 (b). Here the specification above is written in a computer-processable form as text assertions. Part of it is as follows, using a different font to help you distinguish it. The names of object types that occur in the organization are shown here with an initial capital to enable you to distinguish them from reserved words of the language.

Synonym means alternative name

```
The event New_product_line_to_be_added triggers
  the processes Identify_the_product and
  Create_a_new_product_record.
The process Identify_the_product makes true some
  or all of the conditions
  New_product_line_for_addition,
  Existing_product_line_for_deletion, and
  Existing_product_identified_to_be_changed.
The condition New_product_line_for_addition
  triggers the Create_a_new_product_record
  process.
New_product_line_to_be_added is synonym for
  New_product_line_added.
```

In the example text assertions, we have used an underline character instead of a space to avoid having embedded spaces in names. Many computer languages do not allow embedded spaces in names, as it enables the programming of the parsing to be simpler. An alternative is to have an initial capital letter for each word and run the words together, e.g. NewProductLineToBeAdded. The processable text has other features that we explain below.

Exercise 5.1

(i) Does Figure 5.6 (a) carry all the information in our text description that preceded the diagram? Suppose a programmer were given just the diagram, would it be equivalent to being given the text?

(ii) Would the computer-processable form of the specification carry all the information in our text description? Suppose a programmer were given just the computer-processable form, would that be equivalent to being given the text? Would it be equivalent to the diagram?

(iii) Suggest two ways that Idris and Anna might continue.

(i) The diagram is not as informative as the text which includes some points not shown in the diagram. In general, a diagram is often better for getting a first impression but text is usually also needed to explain more fully.

(ii) The computer-processable form could be made equivalent to the text or the diagram, particularly if it is allowed to include strings of characters such as could be held in a word-processing package and where the software did not have to attempt to parse such strings. If this were not allowed then the software package might only permit certain kinds of sentences which might not include all those needed to represent everything that Idris and Anna discussed.

(iii) One way that Idris and Anna might continue is to discuss the context, as we said at the start of the story above. This will lead to other associated processes and other kinds of objects.

An alternative way to continue is to investigate something that is unclear in the discussion so far, such as what is really meant by 'Identify the product', or whether the several occurrences of the process 'Create a new product record' are or are not identical.

Generally Idris and Anna may widen the discussion to associated objects (including other processes) or obtain further knowledge about the existing objects. Both ways may be needed, and they may be interleaved.

So far, we have given a dialogue between Idris and Anna while trying to understand the basic operations following on from the event which occurs because of the need to create a new product line, and have shown a computer-processable form of text assertions and diagrams.

Sources of information

We move on to some other points for you. The meaning of 'Identify the product' is unclear. Anna asks Idris about it, remembering that George will eventually have to do it and that if it is partly a computer process then a programmer will be required to implement the facilities for the automated part of it.

Suppose Idris is uncertain. He says 'Identify the product' might mean that a manager or someone decides the name or description of the new product. If all products have different identification codes then someone somewhere must create and allocate such codes, and keep records to ensure that the same code is never allocated twice. If so, who does this? If the identification code contains coded characters then the meanings of these should be known to the person doing the allocation. If so, who specifies these meanings? Who can provide the details?

If George needs to enter a description of a product into the information system, who creates that description? Does George? Or does he get it from someone else? How is such a description decided? Who agrees it? Deciding the description for a new product may involve staff from sales and marketing. Perhaps George will consult with appropriate people to ensure the best wording is created for inclusion in brochures. Perhaps Idris and Anna will discuss these questions with various people. How will Idris and Anna know who to talk to? How can they be sure they have spoken to everyone to whom they should? How can they be sure who all the stakeholders are?

Such questions apply not only to every process, but also to every event and every condition. That sounds, potentially, like excessive effort at analysis and understanding. In fact, analysts and process engineers learn very rapidly to capture much of this kind of background material quickly and efficiently as they proceed with their work.

From Figures 5.6 (a) and (b), 'Identify the product' may seem to imply finding out which of several conditions applies. George will perhaps receive and create information about a new product and will decide how it is related to past and existing products. Maybe he will also receive information about existing products and decide what to do. Typically, he will conduct a computer-based search of data about existing and past products to decide how to associate a new product to them. So he will identify the nearest existing or discontinued past product. He may or may not know the identification codes and, if not, the programmer will need to provide appropriate search facilities using only the data that George has.

The process 'Identify the product' presumably has some as yet hidden previous actions which Idris and Anna should discuss and understand. For example, by the time that the information reaches George surely other people will have designed and built prototype products. Maybe production and marketing will be being scheduled, so where will knowledge about these aspects already be held? Should George's process come much earlier in the overall flow from initial idea to launched product? Should information about a possible new or modified existing product be captured as soon as knowledge about it is created, long before manufacturing starts? If so, who typically creates such knowledge and in what processes?

As Idris and Anna discuss these possibilities they may realize that their diagram is far from complete, that other events and conditions may occur, that the logic is far more complicated, that they need to understand the wider context, and that they need to talk to George, Graham and other people before deciding anything.

Context diagram

Suppose Idris and Anna discuss the context. Idris says that the organization needs a far better inventory control system and these processes form part of the proposed new system. After a discussion (that we omit for brevity), they agree that the inventory control system will receive various requests for information from various sources and will be required to send appropriate information to various destinations.

For the moment Idris and Anna assume that the inventory control system will always hold all knowledge needed, and they ignore how that is achieved. Their discussion yields a context diagram such as that in Figure 5.7.

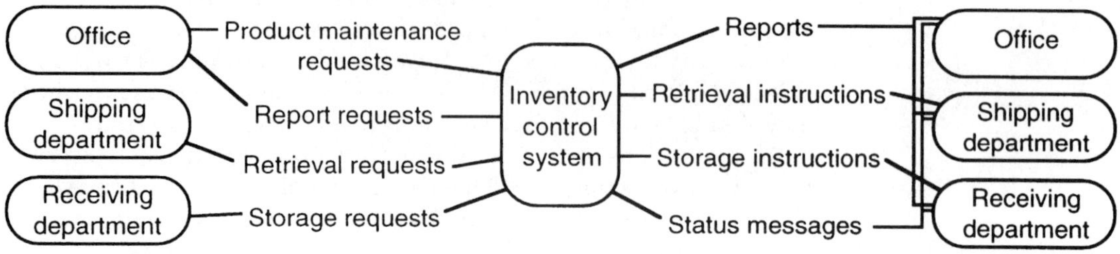

FIGURE 5.7
Inventory control system context diagram.

This can similarly be written in a computer-processable text. Here is a part. The third assertion is equivalent to the first two:

```
The interface Office generates as input
  Product_maintenance_request.
The Inventory_control_system process receives
  the Product_maintenance_request.
The input Product_maintenance_request is
  generated by the Office interface and received
  by the Inventory_control_system process.
The output Storage_instructions are generated by
  the Inventory_control_system process and
  received by the Receiving_department interface.
```

In the following sections, we build up some additional features of processes to extend the information that has been examined so far.

Processors

Usually a process is performed by a processor or several processors such as a particular person or group of people, or by parts of a computer system, or by a communication system or by a combination of these. Some processes, however, do not need a processor at all.

In the inventory control system example:

```
An Order_clerk performs: the Order_entry
  process, the Order_update process, and the
  Print_order process.
The Order_update and the Order_entry processes
  are performed by the Order_clerk.
The Order_processing_program performs the
  Order_entry process, Order_update process,
  Update_order_tables process, and the
  Print_order process.
```

These example assertions do not imply anything about the sequence in which a processor performs the processes. They only associate particular process and processor pairs. The second example assertion is equivalent to part of the first.

As in the third assertion, it is sometimes convenient to say that a process is done by a particular program or within part of a program. This regards the processor as being the part of the program or software responsible for controlling the process. The full meaning is that the process is done by the computer processing unit under the control of that program when it is run.

Anna thinks of generalizations:

- A process may be performed by a processor, meaning none, one or more processors.
- A processor may perform several processes.
- A process may exist without a processor that performs it.
- A processor may exist without a process that it performs.

Decision-making processes

Sometimes the main outcome of a process is a decision. Within a decision-making process, George typically receives information from internal and external data sources, analyses it, creates a recommendation and then makes the decision. The possible roles of a processor in a decision process include contributing to any or all of: obtaining information and data; providing expertise; suggesting and evaluating alternatives; assessing feasibility; computing some optimum subject to various constraints; forming predictions and recommendations with appropriate reasoning and justification; making the decision; and communicating the outcome, consequences and reasoning in appropriate forms to others.

Responsibility

A particular person may be responsible for a process. This could mean either that the person is responsible for ensuring that the process is done appropriately and correctly every time it should be done, or that the person is responsible for defining the process. For example:

```
The senior_order_clerk is responsible for: the
  order_entry process, the order_update process,
  and the print_order process.
```

Anna generalizes this:

- A person may be responsible for defining a process.
- A person may be responsible for operating a process.

For example:

```
The Sales_manager and the Accountant are
  responsible_definers for Order_entry process,
  Order_update process, and Print_order process.
```

Data used in processes

A data activity interaction table shows the relationships between named types of data as rows, and named activities or processes as columns. Omitting the extensive discussions between Idris and others to specify these, part of one resulting table is Table 5.1. The named types of data in the rows are not necessarily elementary data items that are not decomposable, they may be complex data structures.

Data ↓ / *Activity or process →*	7 Auto_storage_location_selection	8 Find_best_retrieval_location	9 Find_best_storage_location	10 Generate_administrative_report	11 Generate_operational_report	12 Manual_storage_location_selection	13 Product_retrieval	14 Product_reporting	15 Select_retrieval_location
21 Automatic_storage_request_data	RE								
22 Retrieval_instructions_data		DG					DG		D
23 Retrieval_validity_message		D					DG		
24 Valid_retrieval_request_data		RE					E		
25 Administrative_report_data				DG				D	
26 Stock_status_report_data				DG					
27 End_of_fiscal_year_report_data				RE					
28 Administrative_report_request_data				RE					
29 Product_file_data	E		E	RE	RE		IU	RE	
30 Operational_report_data	E		E		DO			D	

TABLE 5.1
Example data-activity interaction for inventory control system

In the data activity interaction table each entry may be any sensible combination of one or more of:

E = the activity/ process employs (= uses) that data; the data is employed by (= used by) the activity/ process
M, U = the activity/ process maintains, updates the data; the data is maintained, updated (= modified, changed) by the activity/ process
D, C = the activity/ process derives/ creates the data (or part of it); data is derived/ created by the activity/ process
R, I = data is received, input to be employed/ used in the activity/ process – this includes input to a system from a source or an interface with something external to that system
G, O = data is generated by/ output from the activity/ process – including messages generated and output to an external place through an interface.

Further alternatives include: selecting, sorting, archiving, destroying, referencing, adding data to a set of data and removing data from a set of data.

Exercise 5.2

(i) Ignoring the further alternatives, give a consistency or completeness rule involving the letters above and meaning that each named data somehow has a way of coming into existence and a way of being used.
(ii) Should there be a corresponding completeness and consistency rule that means that each named data has a way of ceasing to exist? If so, what is the rule? If not, explain why not.

(i) In a full table that includes all processes, each data row should have one or more entities that create that data, e.g. D, C, R or I; and somewhere that it is usefully used, e.g. E, G or O.
(ii) At first sight you might think that there should be a way of terminating the existence of each kind of data. The data may be destroyed by accident, or when someone decides it will never be needed in the future, or when the cost of keeping it is not worthwhile, or when the organization ceases to exist. In the UK, income tax data should be kept for about seven years, as the authorities do not usually want to reopen files from earlier years.

Alternatively, you may initially think of data as a representation of reality. With that idea, once a real situation has occurred, the data representing that situation and the corresponding time period is a correct representation for ever. So the data could continue to exist for ever. For example, think of a photograph of some past situation with the date written on the back. The photo can continue to exist.

Both these points of view are valid.

Security

Only certain processors are authorized to perform particular processes. Anna generalizes this as follows:

- A processor may be authorized to perform a process.
- A process may have a processor authorized to perform it.

In each case several processors may be authorized to perform a particular process, and several processes may be authorized to be performed by a particular processor. Also each processor may be authorized only to do a particular process at a particular computer or terminal to a mainframe system and each process may be authorized only to be performed at a particular terminal.

In the Inventory control system the authorizations are as in Table 5.2 which shows for each processor what processes are authorized.

Processor	Permitted processes	
Controller	Create new product record	
General manager	Add to storage model	
Operator	Auto storage location selection	Manual storage location selection
	Delete product record	Reduce storage model
	Determine retrieval type	Select retrieval location auto
	Determine storage type	Select retrieval location manual
	Display product screen	Update product file
	Edit product record	Update audit file retrieval
	Generate administrative report	Update audit file
	Generate operational reports	Update product file retrieval
	Identify product	Validate retrieval request
	Identify report type	Validate storage request
Stock labour	Display product screen	Manual storage location selection

TABLE 5.2
Which processes each processor is authorized to perform

Specifications of processes

The most common significant deliverable from an analysis is a document such as a process specification. So we need gradually to explain how to devise forms and tables as part of such documents. The forms and tables should have the right structures to ensure that Idris and Anna are guided to collect and think about the relevant kinds of facts and details to include.

The document should have the right balance between audience, detail and purpose. Analysis is not the same as writing a process specification.

Process identification form

Figure 5.8 shows a form that Idris and Anna can fill in with certain details of some process that they are just starting to analyse, discuss and specify. It may be a business process or a process concerning information or both.

Self check

Please spend some time reviewing what you have read and doing the questions below.

Objectives

After reading this chapter you should be able to:

- understand the key issues in defining what a process is;
- create process specifications using the features explained so far, together called Level I;
- undertake appropriate analysis of processes involving process

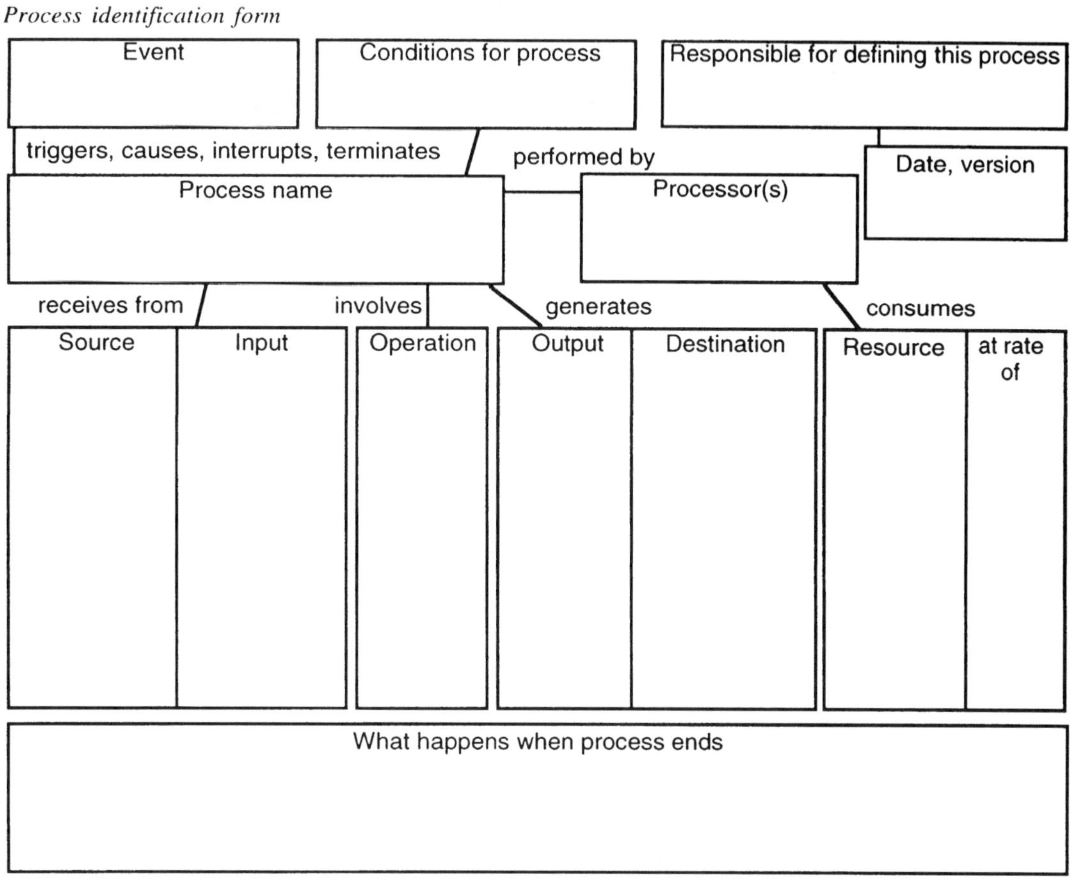

FIGURE 5.8
Process identification form.

identification, event–process–condition chain, event triggering processes, context diagram, processor, decision-making, responsibility, activity–data interaction, security and other features;

- fill in a form corresponding to various aspects of processes for a real situation;
- explain generalizations and rules about all the above aspects of process specifications, and define for an organization an appropriate schema for describing processes.

Questions

5.1 Draw a diagram showing your opinion of the stability of various business actions. Include about 10 to 15 terms like business functions, invoicing, takeover, production scheduling, organizational structure and answering an enquiry about a bill.

5.2 Draw a diagram showing your opinion about the stability of various IT and computing operations aspects. Include about 10 to 15 terms such as features and functions of packages, program and data structures, IT hardware, user interfaces.

5.3 (i) Try filling in a Process form like Figure 5.8 for a particular process of the Inventory control system, Identify the product.

5.3 (ii) What does doing this exercise suggest about the preceding text, and probably about typical similar real situations?

5.4 Make a list of all the nouns that you think might appear in Anna's generalizations. In practice the list is open ended – in different situations different terms would be needed.

6 Analysing and describing processes

The previous chapter explained various ways of defining processes and in this chapter, these original ideas are taken forward. The idea of a Level I process description has been introduced and more formality is added here by deriving a **metamodel** from that Level I description.

The idea of a metamodel is then extended to show how the model can be used to derive a set of possible completeness and consistency standards. Such standards can be used to check an indeterminate number of instances of the metamodel or parts of the metamodel.

We extend the Level I Description to what we call a Level II Process Description. We explain that and give corresponding metamodels.

Following on from the metamodelling and completeness and consistency sections, we go to more traditional aspects of process descriptions by describing the basic elements of information flow diagrams and data analysis.

Additional techniques for describing processes, data and other objects are added later in the book.

Simple metamodels

A metamodel can be seen as either (i) a model of a model or, (ii) a higher level of model.

We explain a metamodel as an object–property–relationship model. This technique was pioneered at the University of Michigan, and developed there over a period of many years in a research project that started in 1968.

Object–Property–Relationship (OPR) modelling is similar to entity–relationship–attribute (ERA) modelling. The main difference is that OPR models can be considered as metamodels of ERA models (and others).

OPR modelling requires the identification of:

- objects – the 'things' involved in the system or situation being examined or analysed;
- relationships – the connections between the various objects;
- properties – i.e. of the objects (and, in some cases, the relationships);

- statements highly formal, structured sentences made up using identified objects and relationships – such sentences should be understandable and meaningful to anyone involved in the system (certainly those sentences relating to high-level aspects of the system);
- text – the sources of all the various objects, properties, and relationships defined in the metamodel.

This idea of a metamodel can be explained in a simple way using the Level I process description developed in the previous chapter. Look back at the Process identification form in Fig. 5.8.

Exercise 6.1

Before proceeding, it will be useful if you attempt the following.

(i) Make a list of the names of the objects that are identified in order to fill in one of those forms.
(ii) Select simple verbs that could be used to describe relationships between the different objects.
(iii) When identifying the different objects, you may have found yourself wanting to qualify some of the objects – such qualifications are probably properties. So make a list of any properties you wanted to identify.

We work through this form and build up a metamodel from it in the text below.

Objects

Perhaps the first object to identify is the process itself; this is indicated on the form by 'process name'.

Working from top to bottom, and left to right, the other objects are: event; condition; processor; source; input; operation; output; destination; resource. This means that we have identified 10 objects.

The most ambiguous part is at the bottom of the form where there should be an explanation of what happens when the process ends. There are different ways in which this could be modelled, each of which depends on the effect of the process. For example: another process could be invoked; conditions could be set; certain results of the process could be treated as events; control could be returned to another invoking process. However, the objects identified in thinking this through are the same as the objects we have already identified (process, condition, event), so for the moment we will consider that our list of identified objects is now complete.

Another possible source of ambiguity arises from having two different objects identified as source and destination. Clearly the process will interact with various external entities to account for the process inputs and outputs. It could be perfectly reasonable for an analyst to argue that only one object, such as external interface, is really all that is needed. The result of such a position is that only 9 objects are needed rather than 10.

It should be noted that all the objects identified are in fact nouns.

Relationships

Identifying the objects indicated by such a form was reasonably easy; identifying relationships is not so straightforward, and often requires arbitrary selection between different possible words.

One relationship is clear from the form: triggers – an event triggers a process. Other possible relationships can be inferred from the juxtapositions on the form.

Condition has been linked to process by means of a line, therefore some kind of relationship is likely to be implied. There are many possible relationships between condition and process. Here are some, where {... | ...} denotes taking one alternative:

- process runs subject to the state of the condition(s);
- process triggered on condition(s) becoming {true | false};
- condition is changed by process;
- condition is made {true | false} by process;
- condition becoming {true | false} terminates process;
- condition becoming {true | false} interrupts process;
- process uses condition to {derive | maintain | update} {entity | attribute value | relationship}.

A processor is a person or mechanism that runs the process. Therefore a suitable relationship is something such as Processor performs Process.

There are several possible relationships between source, input and process. For example, an analyst could decide that a source supplies | generates input(s). The process could receive the input(s).

A similar pattern can be used for process, output and destination: a process generates output(s); a destination receives | obtains the output.

There are many possible relationships between the process, resources and operations. Clearly the operations describe how inputs are used to derive outputs. The operation describes how different resources are used.

What are the possible relationships between process and operation? An analyst could say that a process consists of operations, or that a process performs operations.

During and at the end of a process, possible relationships include: a process triggers another process; process causes an event; process makes condition(s) true or false; process changes condition.

We must emphasize that the examples we have given are illustrative only. If you tried Exercise 6.1 and came up with different words for the relationships, they may have been correct also. For example, we initially identified only the trigger relationships between event and process, but others may have identified other possible relationships such as interrupts and terminates.

It should be noted that all the relationships are expressed as verbs. So far in the examples the verbs are all in the active voice. In practice, every relationship has at least one **reverse** relationship and that is expressed by converting a verb into the passive. For example, we started by stating that event(s) trigger process; the reverse relationship is that a process is triggered by event(s).

Properties

In identifying objects, it may be desired to qualify some of the nouns. For example, perhaps resources are classified as consumable (used, destroyed, or changed completely by the operation of the process) or non-consumable (used by the process, but still available for use by other processes or invocations of the same process after a process has been completed). Materials are usually regarded as consumed but tools are not.

It may be desired to qualify inputs by the type of resource (cash, people, information, equipment); and outputs by the type of result (products, goods, services, information flows, knowledge).

Sources and destinations could be classified as foreign or national. They may be interfaces between systems and external objects. Operations could be classified as manufacturing, clerical, managerial, and so forth.

The simplest way to envisage properties is to consider them as adjectives that qualify the corresponding nouns.

Statements

A 'good' OPR model can be represented by a series of simple statements that should be reasonably understandable by someone who knows something about the system being modelled. Frequently OPR statements are understandable to those who have not been involved with the system before. For example:

```
Event E1 Triggers Process P1. Process P1
  Triggered On Condition C1 Becoming True.
  Operation O1 Consumes Resources R1, R2. Process
  P1 Uses Inputs I1, I2, I3 To Produce Outputs
  O1, O2. Process P1 On Termination Triggers
  Process P3. Source S1 Supplies Input I1, I2.
```

The analyst should produce a complete set of statements for all required combinations of objects and relationships. This complete set of statements constitutes a modelling language.

Text

The idea of text is to account for all the source material used by the analyst when defining a modelling language. The analyst is likely to have used different sources such as memos, reports, diagrams and interviews. These can be grouped into separate pieces of information. Each piece can then be associated with the corresponding object and relationship definitions.

Source material for the modelling is usually accounted for by the addition of an extra relationship such as 'text is', 'memo is', or 'source is'. To do this requires defining a new object such as memo, text or source. This also means that every piece of source material should also be identified by a unique name. This imposes quite a discipline on Idris and Anna, but that discipline is frequently rewarded with a very good understanding of the material being analysed.

For example, if the Level I Process Identification Form is treated as source material, a source could be defined as PI_Form. Then every defined object can have an additional relationship added to say 'Source is PI_Form'.

More advanced points

So far, most of the statements derived from the sample form are **2-part relationships**. This means that there are two objects connected by one verb, e.g. Event Triggers Process. There was one case of a 3-part relationship: Process Uses Inputs to Derive Outputs – three objects, two connected verbs. Some people would call this verb structure a compound verb.

Many cases of analysis for information systems show how relationships are usually broken down into 2-part relationships. It is beyond the scope of this book to discuss the problems of technology further, but we will simply make the observation that the vast majority of commercially available database management systems are suited primarily to representing 2-part relationships. Representing n-part relationships in the most widely used database management systems is very difficult and frequently leads to serious problems of analysis, design and performance. It will be noticed that the vast majority of texts about data analysis and database design have an implicit assumption that most relationships are 2-part. How to deal with n-part relationships is explained in Chapter 11.

In the analysis of business processes, it is our experience that n-part relationships (that is relationships with n objects, and n-1 verbs – or a verb compounded with n-1 components) occur very frequently. This is probably because the level of abstraction when analysing business processes is much higher than the level of abstraction when analysing for information systems; there seems to be a loose relationship between the number of parts in relationships and the level of abstraction. This result is not surprising, because at high levels of abstraction the analyst's job includes breaking down objects into smaller objects and simpler structures.

Whenever the analyst encounters n-part relationships, it is part of the analysis task to test the relationships to see if they can be broken down into simpler combinations of objects and relationships. We will give two examples to illustrate this point.

The first example concerns part of a university system. There are courses. Lecturers teach certain courses. Courses have booklists, so books are used to support courses. The problem is whether this situation requires one 3-part relationship (course–lecturer–book) or can it be broken down into three 2-part relationships (course–lecturer, course–book, lecturer–book). The two possibilities are represented diagrammatically in Figure 6.1.

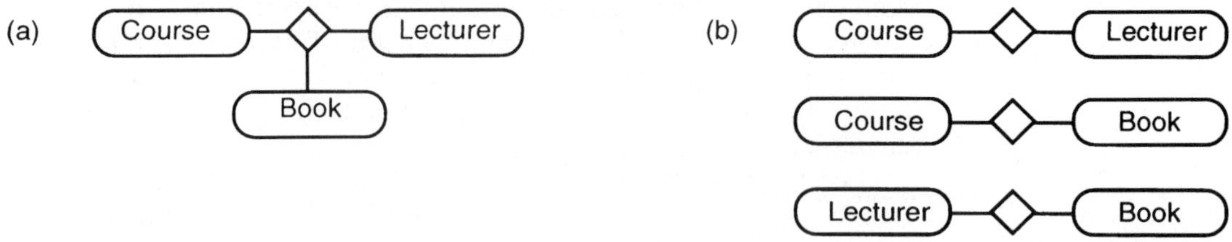

FIGURE 6.1
Courses, lecturers, and books.

The answer to this problem does not lie in the structure of the objects and relationships itself. It lies in the business rules relating to the process and these lie outside the OPR structure – but additional objects and relationships should be added by the analyst to account for all relevant business rules.

There are several plausible rules governing this relationship. One rule could be that a panel defines the books to be used for a course and that every lecturer should use the recommended book list. That rule means that lecturer and book are independent of each other because it is not necessary to know the name of the lecturer to know which books will be used for the course. In this case, the 3-part relationship can be broken down into two 2-part relationships, course–book, and course–lecturer (lecturer–book is not needed).

A different rule could be that booklists are advisory only and that lecturers are free to amend them as they see fit. The consequence of such a rule is that lecturer and book are no longer independent. A student enrolled on a course will not know which books to buy without knowing the name of the lecturer. In this case, the 3-part relationship cannot be broken down into simpler 2-part relationships.

The second advanced example concerns analysis for the design of distributable systems and security requirements. Geoffrey Darnton was involved a few years ago in the definition of a method for the design of distributable applications. This need arose because none of the standard ISD methods addressed how to undertake analysis and design to support distributed information systems. At the same time it was necessary also to understand how to produce more formal models of security requirements.

The essence of the final models produced resulted in two 5-part relationships. The objects concerned were:

- logical user – the type of system or process user, for example data-entry clerk, sales person, district manager, lecturer;
- logical location – the kinds of locations decided to implement the organizational units of the business, for example warehouse, manufacturing plant, logistics centre, headquarters office, sales office, training centre;
- function or process – the activity performed, e.g. order entry, manufacturing, training;
- resources – all the resources used by the function or process, e.g. in an information system all the data needed by the system, and for a business process all the resources required;

- constraints – special characteristics that apply to the system, for example performance requirements and consistency constraints.

The only difference between the 5-part relationship to model a distributed system, and the 5-part relationship for a security requirement was in the verbs used in the statements for the relationships, in other respecs the objects and relationships were identical.

For example, the 5-part relationship statement for a distributed system is:

```
User U1 at Location L1 Performs Function F1
  using Resources R1 depending on Constraints C1
```

The only difference in this statement required to model security requirements was the addition of the word 'may':

```
User U1 at Location L1 may Perform Function F1
  using Resources R1 depending on Constraints C1
```

Handling a 5-part relationship is not easy. In Geoffrey Darnton's work this 5-part relationship was decomposed as follows. Where a function is treated independently of the resources required in any place it is only necessary to know the function, how to implement it is then a local decision. This reduces the 5-part relationship to one 4-part and one 2-part relationship. Further simplification can take place where the business processes are re-engineered so that certain parts (logical users or logical locations) specialise in particular functions.

As with the course–lecturer–book example, simplification of the distributed system case depends on the business rules and cannot be derived merely by rearranging the 5-part relationship to suit the analyst!

Chapter 11 gives an advanced discussion of data modelling analysis. Often process engineers do not appreciate initially the value of in-depth data analysis skills because they are more concerned with business processes than information systems. The need for a process engineer to have a good understanding of data analysis arises not because of a need to perform data analysis *per se* (although frequently a business process engineer does need data analysis capability because information is one of the key business process resources), but because the same techniques are very useful in analysing an OPR model and deciding when a structure can be simplified and when it cannot.

This section has based metamodelling on OPR. There are other techniques that have not been addressed, but which may be needed in different circumstances. For example, a business process that needs to be repeated frequently and in many places, may need the application of queuing theory to understand the characteristics of the services to be provided by the process. We do not cover statistical and operational research techniques in this book.

Another advanced point concerns the components of a system that are more stable. In the previous chapter, we pointed out that essential processes are generally more stable than higher-level processes. For many components, the data and other resource structures are also more stable than the ways in which they are organized.

Model representations

An OPR model is a network of objects and relationships. Traditionally, it can be represented either graphically or linguistically.

A graphical representation is suitable for simple models where it is necessary to convey a visual image of the objects and relationships. A graphical version of the OPR metamodel for the Level I form is shown in Figure 6.2.

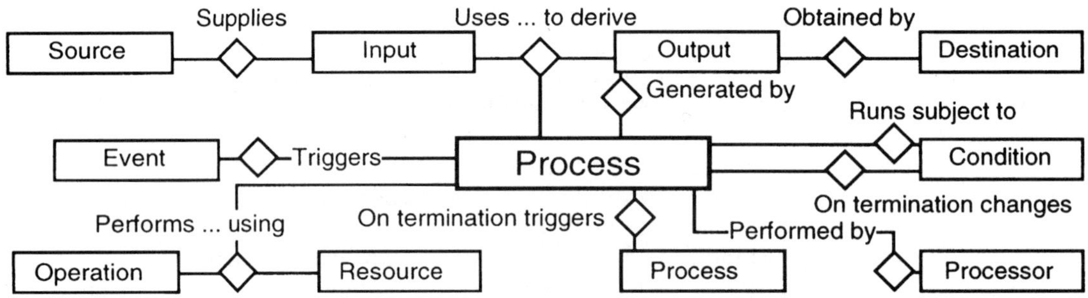

FIGURE 6.2
Process Level I metamodel – graphical.

Graphical representations are really only suitable for simple models or high-level abstractions. When there is a great deal of detail (for example it is Geoffrey Darnton's experience that modelling a 'real' business may require in the order of 15 000 to 30 000 processes) pictorial representations are unsuitable and impossible to check manually.

However, when a model of processes becomes more complex the linguistic forms of representation can be stored in a database, and thus there are no real limits on the number of processes and connections between processes that can be stored and examined.

A linguistic form of the Level I Process Identification Form is shown in Figure 6.3.

Define Process P1
  Triggered by Event1
  Runs when Cond1 is true
  Receives Input1
  Generates Output1
  Uses Input2 to derive Output2
  Performs Oper1 using Resc1
  Performed by Prcr1
  On termination triggers Proc2
  On termination changes Cond2
Define Event Event1
Define Condition Cond1, Cond2
Define Input Input1, Input2, Input3
Define Source Srce1
  Supplies Input3
Define Output Output1, Output2
Define Destination Dest1
  Obtains Output1
Define Operation Oper1
Define Resource Resc1
Define Processor Prcr1
Define Process Proc2

FIGURE 6.3
Process Level I metamodel – linguistic.

In practice, where no database management system is available to store and process a large number of process descriptions, it is still likely to be useful to the analyst to store process descriptions using the form illustrated in the previous chapter. It is our experience that the discipline introduced by using these forms is well worth the effort. In the course of training a large number of people, our experience is that there is usually agreement that the information collected on such a form is really a minimal set of the information that should be known about any process – that is why it is called a Level I form! However, it is surprising how frequently when Geoffrey Darnton audits more discursive process descriptions, it is difficult to extract this minimal set of process description information, and the analysts who wrote the text descriptions have had to go back and collect further information to complete this minimal set.

Completeness and consistency checks introduced

When the analyst has completed the development of a metamodel, it is likely that the model will be used to represent and analyse a large number of facts about business processes or information system requirements.

The analyst should be sure that the metamodel captures sufficient information for the purpose in hand. For example, if the purpose of analysis is to produce a high-level workflow model of a business process showing a sequence of lower level processes, then the amount of rigour in the metamodel is likely to be very small.

Exercise 6.2

Stop for a moment and try to produce a metamodel for the simple process flow chart shown in Figure 6.4. This simple flowchart is typical of the kind of illustration used in several key business process engineering books.

FIGURE 6.4
Simple process flow chart.

Hopefully, producing a metamodel for such a flow chart was not too difficult. A sample answer is shown in Figure 6.5.

Clearly the metamodel for such a flow chart is simpler than the metamodel for our Level I form. The simple flow chart is suitable for conveying a high-level idea of a workflow process whereas the form is more suitable for collecting slightly more detailed information about individual processes. In other words the purposes of the representations are different.

At another extreme, if the purpose is to collect and represent enough information to support the generation of source code for an information system, then the metamodel for the functional and design specifications is very complex. Similarly, if the target system is a substantial part of a business to be implemented by organizational units, management structures, information systems and other kinds of

FIGURE 6.5
Simple process flow chart - metamodel.

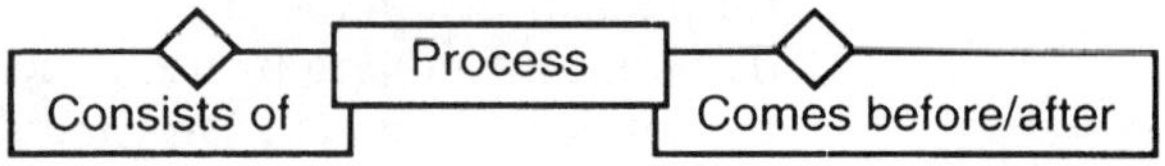

system, then the underlying necessary metamodel is even more complex.

Use of a metamodel means using that model to analyse a collection of information. Every metamodel is also a set of implied completeness and consistency requirements. For example, the metamodel developed earlier from the Level I form means that it would not be correct to make a statement such as 'input triggers process'; that would be inconsistent with the model. The availability of an input could perhaps be modelled as an event or condition and they could lead to triggering a process. For this reason the analyst needs to be sure about what kinds of statements will be considered as correct or not. In terms of completeness, it is probably reasonable to say that every process should be capable of being triggered by something (otherwise it would never run) and should have at least one input and output. The analyst may decide that it is not necessary for every process to have conditions associated with it.

The analyst should develop an explicit set of **completeness and consistency standards**. These standards provide a benchmark for the analyst to know whether analysis has been completed, and a sense in which it can be considered as consistent.

Using the Level I Form, here is a set of possible completeness and consistency standards:

- every process must be triggered by an event, change in a condition or another process;
- every process must have at least one input;
- every process must produce at least one output;
- the operation of every process in terms of the transformation of input(s) into output(s) must be stated;
- the sources of all information used to create the process definition must be indicated;
- the effect of the process on other system components must be stated;
- every condition must affect at least one process;
- every event must be handled by at least one process;
- every process with no related conditions should be checked to see if there should be any such conditions;
- every process should have a processor.

Such a list of completeness and consistency standards provides the analyst with a good basis for checking process descriptions to a **Level I** Form degree of analysis.

Strategy study metamodelling illustration

Business process engineering normally takes place in a context of some kind of strategy study. Strategy studies are usually performed in the context of senior management deliberations with the results captured by some combination of workshops and interviews. Various frameworks are in extensive use by consultants who facilitate strategy formulation work. Strategy studies are usually represented by documentation that has a combination of text and diagrams. Sometimes, workshop results are represented by large 'rich pictures' that present some schematic view of the future or desired state of the company.

Common techniques and frameworks used to support strategy studies are:

- identification of the strategic business unit (SBU) – this is usually the part of the company which is the subject of the strategy study (it is relatively rare to see a strategy study carried out for a whole company or conglomeration);
- definition of the mission and objectives of the SBU – statements about the overall goal of the SBU and what it wants to achieve over an identified period of time;
- identification of factors that are critical either for the success (critical success factors, CSFs) or failure (critical failure factors, CFFs) of the SBU;
- identification of the internal strengths and weaknesses (SW) and external opportunities and threats (OT) for the SBU – called either a SWOT or TOWS analysis, depending on which source you read;
- definition of strategies for the SBU.

There is considerable variation in the literature about what such terms actually mean. However, the business process engineer is often faced with the task of how to take the results of a strategy study and engineer an appropriate set of business processes to implement the strategies. The information system engineer is usually required to define how to implement information systems that will support the strategic, managerial and operational needs of the SBU(s).

The process engineer should produce a metamodel that represents the objects and relationships used in the course of the strategy study. In an ideal situation, such a metamodel will have been developed in conjunction with the consultants who are going to facilitate the study, so that information is collected that already stands some chance of meeting a known set of completeness and consistency standards. Frequently, little such work is done before or after strategy studies.

The rest of this section provides a simple illustration of how a metamodel, and hence a set of completeness and consistency checks, can be built up to support the process engineering work that should follow from a strategy study.

The identification of objects for the techniques listed is not too difficult. The list would look something like this: mission, objective, critical factor, strength, weakness, opportunity, threat, SBU, organizational unit, competitor, external situation, strategy, metric.

The relationships are, as usual, more difficult to construct (and more arbitrary) than the objects. This is because there is less help in standard texts about a network of desired interconnections between these objects. Each technique has been developed somewhat in isolation, so it is the consultant and process engineer who must link them together in some useful way. Here are some possible ways to construct relationships for a strategy formulation metamodel.

- For mission and objectives of the SBU, an appropriate relationship is something like 'SBU exists to fulfil mission'; between SBU and objective it is something like 'SBU pursues objective'.
- The strengths and weaknesses relate to either the SBU or some other internal organizational unit. SBU or organizational unit displays strength or weakness.
- Opportunities and threats are from external competitors or market situations. External situation presents opportunity or threat.
- Critical factors relate to the context for achieving objectives. CSF must be satisfied to achieve objective, CFF will cause failure of objective.
- Strategies are designed to deal with critical factors and SWOTs. Strategy deals with critical factor, strategy realises strength or opportunity, strategy overcomes weakness or threat.
- Metrics are needed to know if the objectives are on target, and the analyst may wish to associate metrics with many other objects. Metrics apply to objectives.

These relationships are simple and have been included to provide an example of the technique. In practice, there will be a more complex set of relationships and objects in the strategy formulation metamodel. A simple illustration of this metamodel is shown in Figure 6.6.

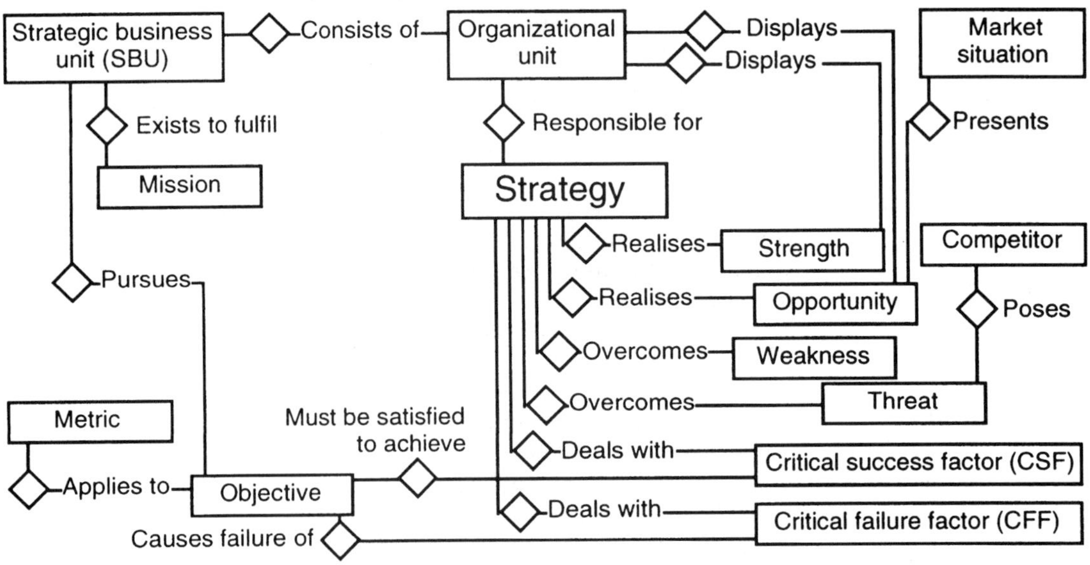

FIGURE 6.6
Simple strategy formulation metamodel.

Level II process descriptions

We can almost hear the concerns of many readers as they have proceeded this far – the range of objects and relationships is too restricted and the analyst wants to say much more about processes.

The Level I Form was intended to be a high-level summary of some key process information. It is really intended to produce stand alone process descriptions. Some information is available on the form about what happens when the process ends, but that deals with connections between one process and another.

In practice there are several ways in which an analyst usually wishes to extend an understanding of processes.

- A process may be part of a larger process, or a process could be broken down into smaller processes – this is to do with the structure and interrelationships of processes.
- Processes usually take part in some kind of workflow, process chain, or sequence – process chains may be defined by some procedures that have been laid down, or they may not be known until an event occurs which must be handled by a sequence of processes.
- It is necessary to know the frequency of a process. Information system design is affected by the number of times a process happens.

Thus a Level II process description places each process in a broader context, and the corresponding description is expanded to provide the necessary information. The extra information is handled by adding some more relationships.

- ... happens ... times per ... This adds the necessary frequency information. It requires a new object, Unit, to provide units for the process frequency. The same construction can be attached to all other objects.
- ... subparts are ...; ... consists of ... These provide structural information about decomposition and consolidation of processes.
- ... occurs before | after ... depending on ... This provides the necessary sequencing information, and the context within which particular sequences occur.

Clearly, there are many more possible ways to extend process descriptions. We have presented what we call Level I and Level II. That is as much as we can achieve within this book, except for what is in Chapter 11. When analysts collect this much information about processes, it is usually far more than is collected by more discursive methods.

Extended process metamodel

A Level II process description clearly adds more information to the metamodel.

Exercise 6.3

Before reading further, attempt to take the metamodel shown in Figure 6.2 and amend it by adding new objects and relationships to bring it to Level II.

One possible solution is shown in Figure 6.7.

The practitioner will find it useful to design a new form that can be used to collect process descriptions to this Level II. The basic contents of such a form are shown in Figure 6.8.

Further completeness and consistency checks

The extension of process descriptions to Level II also means that a more extensive set of completeness and consistency checks can be implemented (and of course should be implemented after initial process description work has been carried out).

Sample additional completeness and consistency checks are:

- every process should have frequency information associated with it;
- inputs, outputs, and events should have frequency information associated with them;
- top-level processes should have a consists_of relationship, but not a part_of relationship;
- all processes should be in comes_before and comes_after relationships, except for the first and last processes in process chains.

This approach of adding new completeness and consistency checks with each extension of the metamodel is an important aspect of analysis for process engineers.

Information flow diagrams and data flow diagrams

In this section and the next we explain information flow diagrams, data flow diagrams and some associated points; and entity–attribute–relationship diagrams. These were gently introduced in Chapter 2. Here we explain in more detail so that you should be able to use them in straightforward situations, and we give enough for you to follow the approaches in Chapter 7 which use them. In Chapters 9 and 11 we explain more about these and other kinds of diagrams.

Information flow diagrams vs Data flow diagrams

Draw IFDs not DFDs

We suggest that drawing information flow diagrams (IFD), as opposed to data flow diagrams (DFD), is preferable at the stage of trying to develop rule-free conceptual specifications of requirements. Data flow diagrams have representations of data stores, physical data flows and other design details that are not wanted while establishing the real needs. So we do not recommend data flow diagrams as such and believe it is far better to concentrate on information flow diagrams, as we have been teaching since the mid 1970s.

The main difference between them is illustrated as follows. Suppose a person A sends three copies of a document to B, who keeps one and sends two copies to C, who keeps one and sends the last copy to D. The IFD shows three flows from A, one to each of B, C and D. The DFD shows a data flow from A to B, another flow from B to C and another from C to D. The DFD would also show where the various copies are stored. DFDs show the logical or physical data stores, such as filing cabinets of papers, or their computer equivalents. IFDs do not show these stores since they may be changed or designed later to suit the information uses.

Why create IFDs?

Creating information flow diagrams encourages Idris and Anna to think about and show what information is required where in the organization or by whom, and for what purposes. They concentrate on who needs to know what, and why; and on who generates what, and why.

Those purposes are not concerned with physical copies or methods of storing the data. Drawing IFDs reduces the tendency to draw the **existing** data flows, which tends to make people concentrate too much on which documents (and even copies) flow where.

IFDs and DFDs are very common, probably the most common form of diagram used by some analysts. Anna, Idris and George create such diagrams in an attempt to help explain one part of how George handles information and data, and how the data is handled, such as in associated processes including automated processes. They are also used for showing proposed future systems.

IFD example

Figure 6.9 shows an example of an information flow diagram. The diagram is a network structure with boxes representing processes, people or systems as the nodes, and arrowed lines showing flows of information between them. Soft box shapes are used for the internal processes, people and systems. A different shape, such as a square or a square with a shadow, is used for organizations, systems, people and processes that are external to the systems and processes currently being analysed.

The example should convey the idea of processes operating on information or data. Data is received and processed, and further data is thereby generated as information that flows to somewhere else. An IFD also conveys the idea of a process receiving information from other processes, systems and people; and generating information that flows to others.

An IFD does not show knowledge or data that is held at the nodes and therefore it is not complete in the sense of showing all knowledge or data.

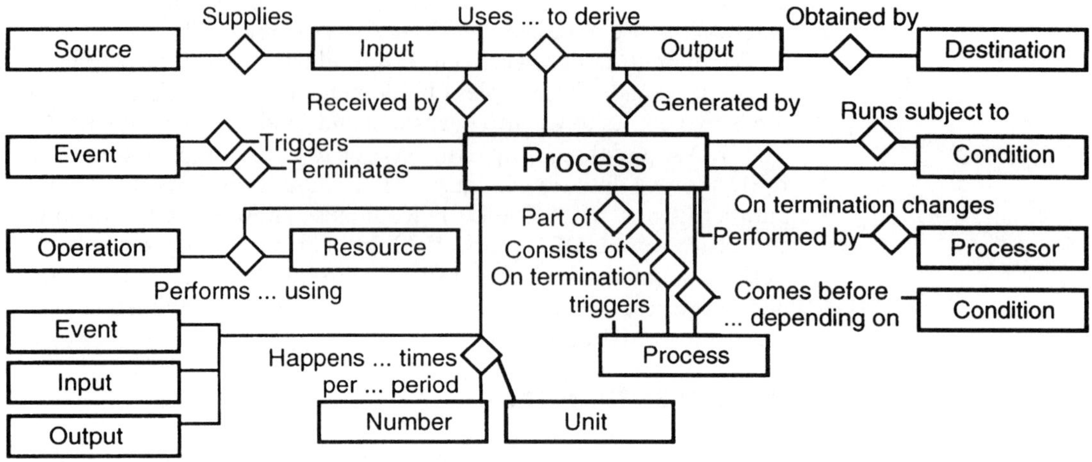

FIGURE 6.7
Level II process description metamodel.

Define Process P1
- Triggered by Event1
- Runs when Cond1 is true
- Receives Input1
- Generates Output1
- Uses Input2 to derive Output2
- Performs Oper1 using Resc1
- Performed by Prcr1
- On termination triggers Proc2
- On termination changes Cond2
- Happens N1 times per Unit1
- Part of Proc3
- Consists of Proc4, Proc5
- Comes before Proc2 depending on Cond3
- Comes after Proc6 depending on Cond4

Define Event Event1
- Happens N2 times per Unit2

Define Condition Cond1, Cond2, Cond3, Cond4
Define Input Input1, Input2, Input3
Define Input Input1
- Happens N3 times per Unit3

Define Source Srce1
- Supplies Input3

Define Output Output1, Output2
Define Output Output1
- Happens N4 times per Unit 4

Define Destination Dest1
- Obtains Output1

Define Operation Oper1
Define Resource Resc1
Define Processor Prcr1
Define Process Proc2, Proc3, Proc4, Proc5, Proc6
Define Unit Unit1, Unit2, Unit3, Unit4

FIGURE 6.8
Level II process description metamodel – linguistic.

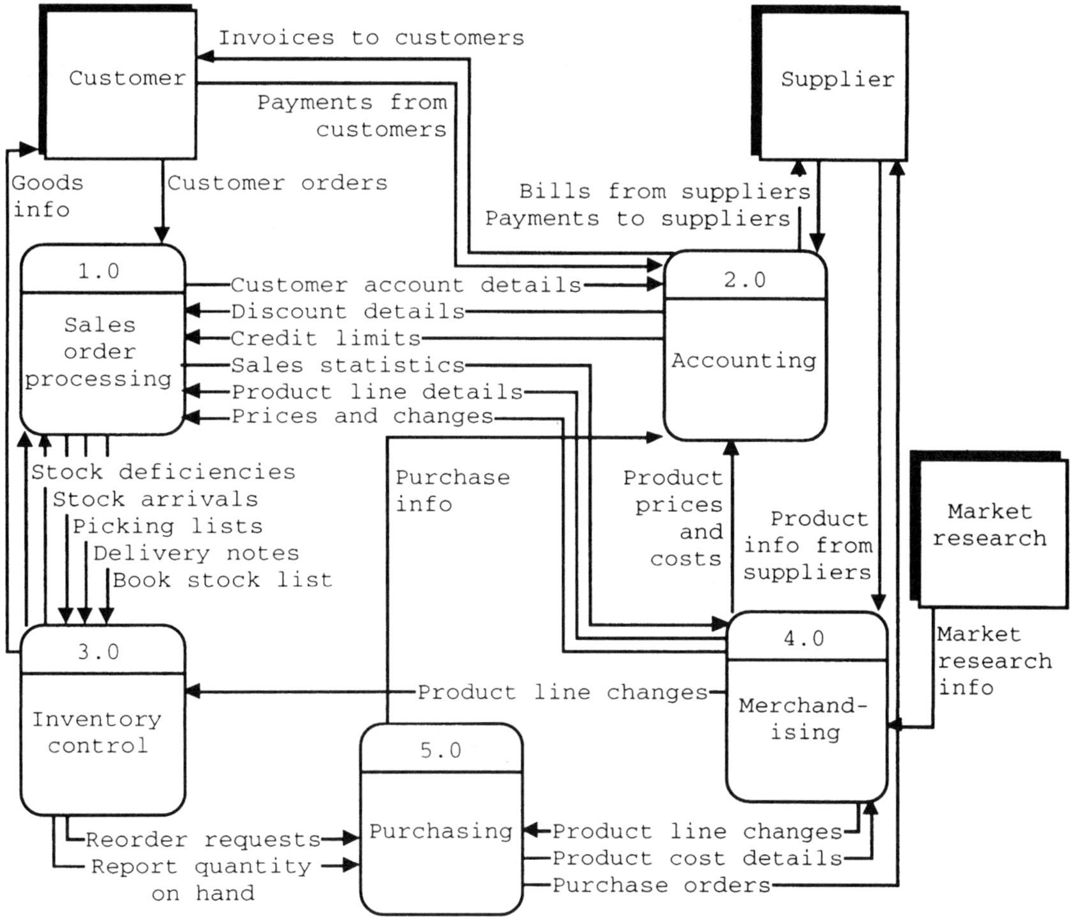

FIGURE 6.9
Example of an information-flow diagram.

> **Exercise 6.4**
>
> Imagine describing that diagram in words. Do not try to write the description, just think how long would it be. How long would it take three or four people to create such a diagram?

Count the boxes and flows – about 35. So at least 35 sentences or paragraphs will be needed. If getting agreement on the details of each box and flow and describing it takes on average 20 minutes, this diagram would take over ten hours. In practice it would take far longer, as those involved would have to check many details with other colleagues in other sections. The process of creating that diagram correctly would spread over several days, and even then people might occasionally improve it over later months. The hand drawings created during the discussions would become untidy from alterations and additions, and there would be problems of the physical layout on the paper to reduce confusing features such as lines crossing and added items being squashed into a remaining small area. Figure 6.9 here has gone through many iterations. Creating the final versions of each such diagram takes an hour or two even after the logic has been agreed and frozen.

Introduction to data flow diagrams

We need to introduce various aspects of such diagrams and of how Anna creates them. Some of the aspects also apply to data flow diagrams and in some cases there are minor differences between IFDs and DFDs. So we summarise DFDs next to make it easier to understand the explanations that apply to both.

A DFD is a similar to an IFD. It models a system in terms of named but otherwise unspecified processes that transform inputs into outputs, and it concentrates on the flows of data between these processes. A **data flow diagram** is a network representation of a system to show sources and destinations of data, logical processes, data stores and flows between them. There are four basic classes of objects in a DFD.

- **Process**: a process transforms incoming data flows into outgoing data flows. In DFDs, processes should always have the characteristic of being completely described by their inputs and outputs. They are transformations specified by what inputs are valid and what outputs are correspondingly produced.
- **Data store**: a temporary repository of data such as a file in a filing cabinet or in a computer.
- **External entity**, **data source** or **data destination**: a person or organization, lying outside the context of the system of current interest, that is an originator or receiver of system data. This usually implies an interface at the boundary of the system being drawn, and data flowing into or out of the system.
- **Data flow**: a pipeline through which flow packets of data having known components. The bi-directional nature of the communication channel is not shown. Usually in DFDs the control information, such as how often or under what circumstances the data flow happens, is omitted and not even given in accompanying text.

Information flow diagrams differ by not showing data stores, and by showing the logical flow of information rather than the physical flow of data, as explained above. We explain the DFD notations and give an example later, to avoid breaking the flow here.

Creating process diagrams and information flow diagrams

Processes may be decomposed into subprocesses, and many diagrams drawn to show increasing detail. The whole can be done with diagrams that show processes decomposed into subprocesses, and either IFDs or DFDs, or a mixture. We mention where Anna's actions for DFDs differ from those for IFDs.

Figure 6.10 shows (slightly wrongly) the expected structure of a finished set of process diagrams, information flow diagrams and data flow diagrams. Each box here represents a diagram and perhaps some associated description, typically a page in length.

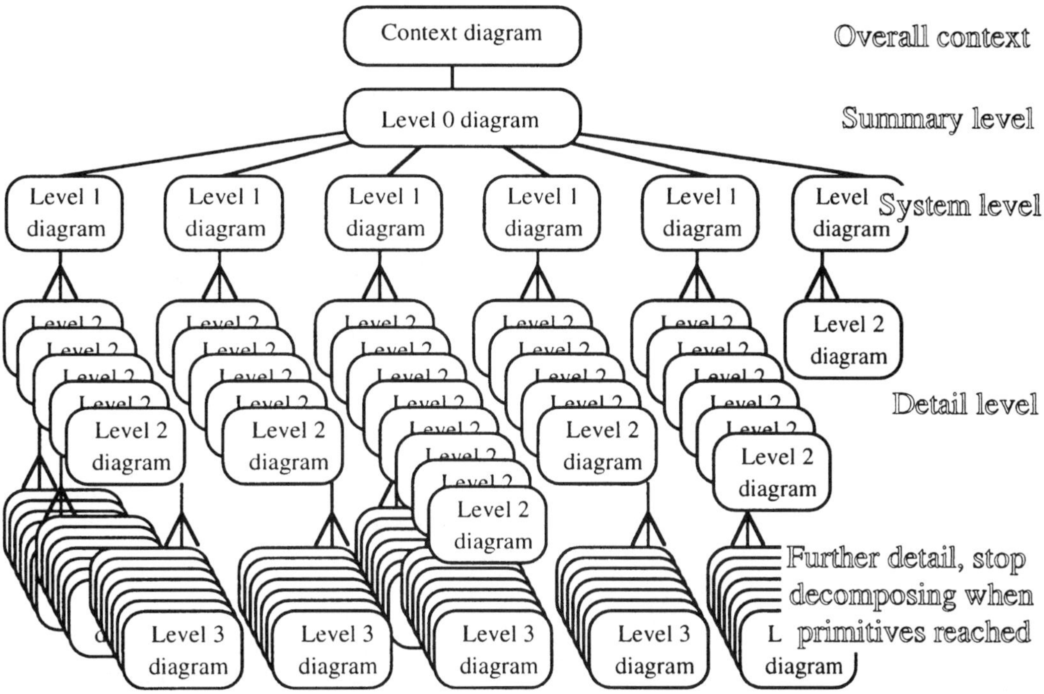

FIGURE 6.10
A tree structure of DFDs: a network would be better.

The lines represent how individual diagrams at different levels are related. The diagram is wrong because in practice the structure should be a network in which some lower level boxes relate to more than one higher box. Also the people involved rarely create all the diagrams as it is too tedious and usually not worthwhile. The trick is to create enough for the current and future purposes. It may be useful to have a one-page specification of each process envisaged in a future system and roughly the same amount of detail, such as one page, for every box, whether high level or low level.

We explain next how these diagrams are created, and particularly the levelling and balancing between diagrams which helps completeness and consistency.

Context diagram

A context diagram shows the system as one major process, and gives it a name. The diagram specifies the boundaries of the system and shows the key external players. **External** here is interpreted relative to the system currently under discussion. A key player here is not necessarily a person, e.g. it can be a part of an organization or even a part of a computer system.

A context diagram may also correspond to a business function which then gives a collection of diagrams at different levels, as in Figure 6.10, showing the subprocesses and substructures within the business function. We explain this later (pp. 272–5).

Developing a context diagram

Steps for context diagram

To develop a context diagram the following steps are needed.

1. Draw a single **process symbol** that represents 'the system', and name it.
2. Find out about all the **inputs** (or all the main ones) that flow across the boundary into the system from the external environment. Give each a name and draw it in appropriately.
3. Find out about all the **outputs** (or all the main ones) that flow across the boundary from the system into the external environment, naming and drawing each similarly.
4. Find out about all or all the main **external entities** that generate system inputs and receive system outputs. These are regarded as **interfaces** in the environment. Name and draw them.

Some proprietary ISD methods prescribe that context diagrams should show only one major input and one major output of the system. This can be very misleading and lead to omissions and errors that are costly to rectify later.

Level 0 IFD/DFD

This identifies the key internal players and how they interact. At this level a key player can be a function, a department, or a system. Figure 6.9 is an example on a Level 0 IFD.

Developing a Level 0 IFD/DFD

Steps to develop Level 0 DFD

Several prescribed methods exist for developing a Level 0 IFD/DFD. The simplest method is described here as two steps.

1. Create an IFD/DFD showing and using the system's major internal players as processes. Whereas the context diagram showed the whole system as a single process, the Level 0 diagram will show the top-level processes internal to the system; these are likely to be departments, business functions or major areas.

2. Add any new processes, flows or data stores as needed. Data stores are only needed in DFDs.

Guidelines

The guidelines for those two steps are:

- Each information/data flow on the context diagram must be included on the Level 0 diagram.
- Each external entity on the context diagram must be included on the Level 0 diagram.

Lower-level IFDs/DFDs

Different proprietary ISD methods suggest using between two and an unlimited number of levels in order to show greater detail. How far it is necessary to decompose depends very much on the purpose of the information/data flow diagrams. Where the decomposition is to include the internal workings of each process it will be necessary to decompose until functional primitives have been reached or discovered.

Functional primitives (= process primitives) are processes that are so simple and well understood that they need no further decomposition. They may be very simple operations, assumed to correspond to simple human operations or programmable procedures.

Chapter 11 explains normalized entity

> A **functional primitive** is a process that satisfies one or more of the following. (a) It can be defined by an explicit calculable mathematical function. (b) It is a transformation process that produces one output. (c) It performs precisely one life cycle step for one normalized entity occurrence, e.g. creation, change of an attribute or data item value, deletion. (d) It can be done by a table look-up. (e) It can be done as an algorithm, a programmable procedure that will always terminate within a finite time. (f) It may use values of data that correspond to the current state of the system, e.g. data of a current incomplete transaction.

Developing lower-level IFDs/DFDs

Steps to develop lower IFDs/DFDs

The basic steps are as follows.

1. Decompose each Level 0 process into several **subprocesses** and name them.
2. Find out about and name any new intermediate data stores and data flows needed to connect the new subprocesses (see guidelines below).
3. Number the new subprocesses, e.g. 2.1, 2.2 ..., and name them appropriately.

Guidelines

The guidelines for the above are:

- Balance the diagram so that incoming and outgoing information/data flows correspond with those of the parent process. This is explained below (pp. 183–5).
- Include or place each data store in the highest-level IFD/DFD that has more than one process using it.
- Include the data store in all the corresponding lower-level IFDs/DFDs where it is used. It may be used either by a single process or by a distinct group of related processes.

Common misconceptions about IFDs/DFDs

One common misconception is that there is **only one** correct decomposition for any given problem. In practice problem specifications can be represented in more than one way and so different people will produce different IFDs/DFDs for the same problem. Some people wrongly think that all problems can be decomposed in this way. Some wrongly think that those problems that can be decomposed will do so into a hierarchy, i.e. a tree structure. In practice most real problems that can be decomposed actually do so into a network structure.

Levelling

IFDs/DFDs have two principles for completeness and consistency: levelling and balancing.

Levelling is the process of decomposing and refining an IFD/DFD so as to meet certain commonly used but imprecise guidelines. The top level gives the context diagram although some people include the summary level, Level 0. The middle levels cover the system in more detail. The bottom level should be the functional primitives.

Levelling guidelines

There are no clear cut rules for how far a decomposition should be taken but here are some commonly used **guidelines**.

- Have from 5 to 9 process boxes per diagram.
- Keep expanding and subdividing process boxes until the specification of each process can be described on one page. Keep expanding until the bottom level contains functional primitive processes only, e.g. a single output data flow, called **functionally cohesive**.
- Separate all processes into either work processes or control processes, distinguishing between them. **Control processes** make decisions about other things. Flows of control data carry the decision information to other processes to control them.
- Processes that are grouped should involve closely related responses.
- Hide local data stores wherever possible, i.e. where a data store is only used within a single lower-level process do not show it even in the diagram for that process.
- Let data be the guide for decomposition. For example, if a process has a large number of inputs and outputs, one

decomposition strategy could be to encapsulate the processing of each input and output in a separate process box. The aggregated processing on all of the intermediate inputs can be confined to a central process, which derives the intermediate outputs. Obviously the central process may require further decomposition.

- Every data item entering or leaving a high-level process box should be accounted for in the lower-level decompositions.

This process of decomposing and refining an IFD/DFD so that the result fits the above rules and guidelines is known as **levelling**. The whole is performed by working with types of processes and types of data. In the implemented system there will be many similar occurrences of each type of box, particularly of the lower-level boxes.

Balancing

We explain balancing by continuing the previous example. Figure 6.11 shows what must be included to balance the Sales-order-processing box from Figure 6.9.

FIGURE 6.11
The set of items that must be included to balance the SOP box.

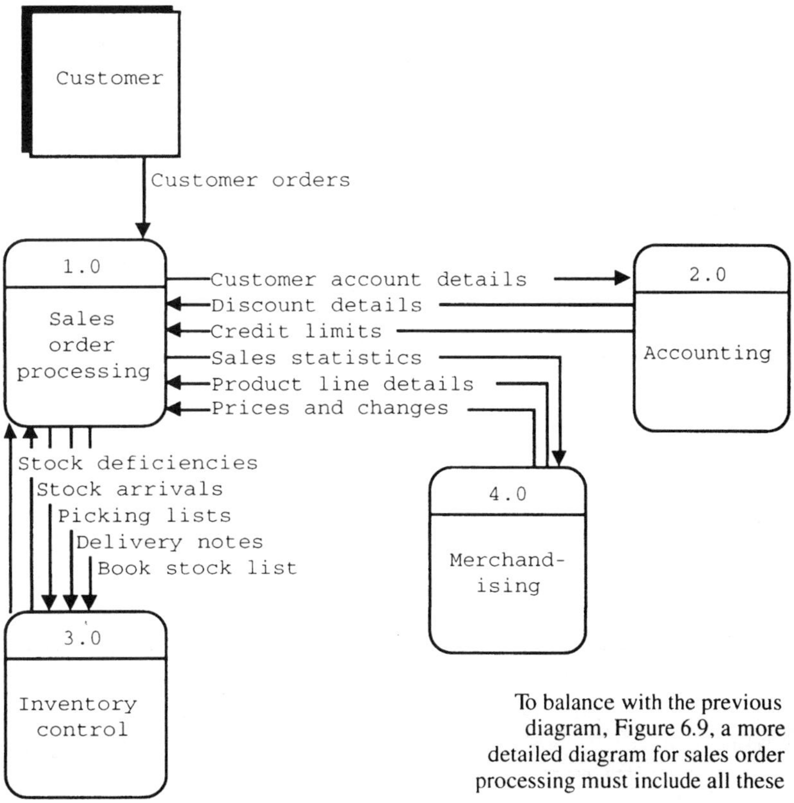

Exercise 6.5

Compare Figure 6.11 with Figure 6.9. What is the rule for what is included in Figure 6.11 and why?

Balancing rule

The rule for balancing is that the lower-level diagram includes the 1.0 box from the upper-level diagram, all the lines representing flows into and out of that box, and all the boxes thus reached. Ensuring this gives consistency and may help correctness.

Figure 6.12 shows a more detailed level diagram for Sales order processing.

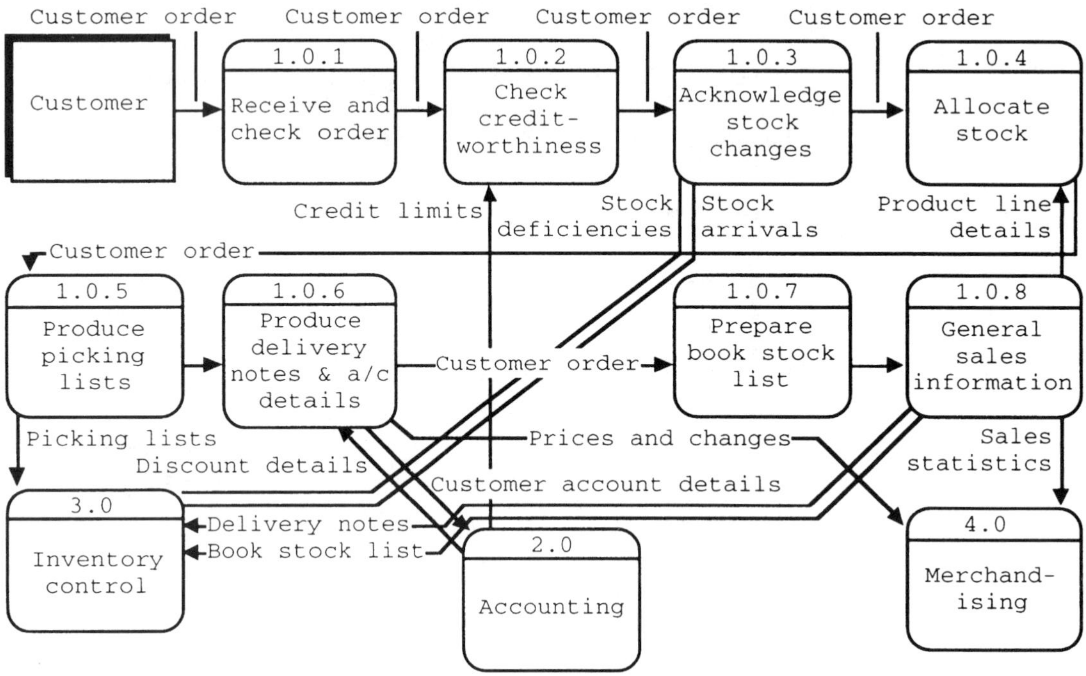

FIGURE 6.12
Example Sales order processing sublevel.

Exercise 6.6

Does Figure 6.12 correctly balance? Is it satisfactory? Say why or why not.

In principle this balances because the information/data flows into and out of the upper diagram box 1.0 of Figure 6.9 as shown in Figure 6.11 match those in the lower-level diagram, Figure 6.12. However Figure 6.12 cannot be fully satisfactory as some of its boxes, such as 1.0.1 and 1.0.7, have exactly the same output as their input and so appear not to do anything useful. Actually far more detail is needed of all the sublevel boxes and flows.

Further checking and merging of diagrams

During IFD/DFD levelling, decomposition errors may occur. In practice, different analysts working in different areas of a system may produce diagrams with different amounts of detail.

Merging DFDs and IFDs

Later, all the diagrams will have to be fitted together, sometimes called **merging**. Then some of the earlier errors and inconsistencies will appear and iteration to rectify them may be needed.

In practice the creation of IFDs/DFDs tends to be a combination of top-down† decomposition and bottom-up† synthesis. Whenever checking a first attempt at top-down decomposition, or assembling IFDs/DFDs from several sources, or both, further balancing is usually needed.

How to check flows

The data flowing into a parent process should be equivalent to the net data flowing into the processes in the child data flow diagrams. Similarly the data flowing from that parent process should be equivalent to the net data flowing from the child processes. 'Net' here means ignoring the internal flows of the child diagrams.

Understanding IFDs, levelling and balancing as above is likely to be more useful than the further details of DFDs explained below. Nevertheless, we give these details of DFDs for completeness.

Data flow diagrams notation

Unfortunately several notations are in use for DFDs. Some authors created new or slightly different forms as an improvement or for marketing reasons to distinguish their technique from previous techniques. Figure 6.13 shows some DFD notations for the four basic classes of objects we introduced earlier. To avoid lines crossing, people may draw the same box two or more times; they may indicate this physical duplication by a diagonal bar near a top corner of an external entity box or process box, and by a double vertical bar at the left end of a data store.

In data flow diagrams, the four basic classes of objects are represented by four symbols.

- **External entity**, **data source** or **destination:** this usually implies an interface at the boundary of the system being drawn, and data flowing into or out of the system. The source or destination is represented by a box (Yourdon), or double square (Gane and Sarson). The presence of a bar across one corner indicates that the interface is duplicated elsewhere – i.e. the same logical box also appears somewhere else on the diagram, it has been physically drawn twice (or even more times).

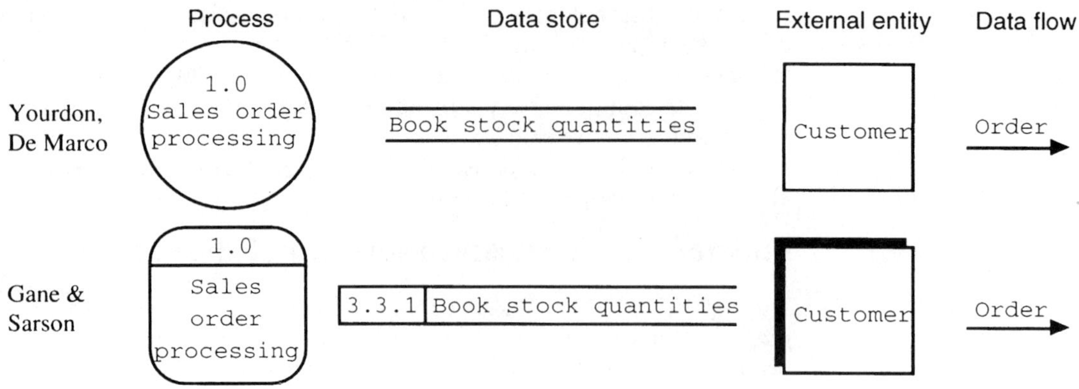

FIGURE 6.13 Different DFD notations from Yourdon, and from Gane & Sarson.

- **Process**: this is represented by a rounded rectangle (Gane and Sarson), circle (Yourdon), oval (SADT) or square (some others).
- **Data store**: this is represented by a pair of horizontal straight lines with the file's name (Yourdon) and a rectangle open at right (Gane and Sarson), in each case with the file's name. The presence of duplicate stores on the same diagram is shown by a vertical bar, per duplicate, at the closed end of the rectangle. This means that a particular data store has been drawn at more than one place on the diagram for convenience of drawing.
- **Data flow**: this is represented by a named line and arrowhead. Usually the control information, such as how often or under what circumstances the data flow happens, is omitted and not even given in accompanying text.

Features of and comments on data flow diagrams

Authors of the techniques say a finished set of data flow diagrams should present a top-down decomposition picture. By **top-down** they mean starting with high-level business functions and their corresponding main high-level processes and flows and then decomposing them into lower-level diagrams, adding further secondary flows on the way. Consequently, many authors and analysts (in our opinion wrongly) say the approach to construction of data flow diagrams should use top-down methods – starting from a high-level process box with an input and an output, and gradually breaking that into many component parts; and continuing until elementary processes and flows are reached.

Other people recommend **bottom-up** meaning that the elementary processes and flows should be indicated first, and more complicated and higher-level processes and flows built up by indicating and defining appropriate combinations of those already defined; and in the higher diagrams indicating only summaries to avoid clutter.

Another alternative is **middle-out**, which starts from something easily clustered and visualised such as one or a few middle-level processes and flows; and then develops upwards and downwards.

In practice, a combination of top-down, bottom-up and middle-out is usually needed and far more satisfactory. This means the perceived boundary and other details can evolve during the analysis, rather than being fixed, perhaps erroneously, by the initial choice of top box.

The process of decomposition is central to the creation of IFDs/DFDs. A single process is exploded and decomposed into constituent processes. Data flowing into and out of the process may also be decomposed. The result of each decomposition is called a **level**.

IFDs/DFDs are not capable of representing behaviour, i.e. system dynamics – not even the sequence of execution. The lack of representation of system dynamics knowledge is a classic deficiency of traditional structured techniques that use DFDs.

The DFD technique presents a situation from the viewpoint of the data rather than from the viewpoint of any organization or person. Unfortunately, however, the data stores are not stable in the long term. DFDs are not good cognitive models for two reasons. Firstly, they are incomplete. They often represent the consensus view of a group of people who started but usually did not continue far enough. Others might find the DFD difficult to understand and use effectively. They may disagree with the DFD, regarding it as incomplete and not helping communication and further understanding of the business processes. Secondly, the DFD usually has built into it details of current hardware, software and application structures – such as data stores representing current computer files, databases or manual files. It also shows flows corresponding to current document flows instead of the underlying flows and use of information produced by the processes.

In their pure form, DFDs do not show behaviour, dynamics, security, distribution, cardinality, optionality, retention, loops, mutual exclusivity and certain other pieces of information. They do not show the data's structure. What to include – the choices of processes, external entities and the system boundary – is arbitrary.

As a DFD grows it may need continual redrawing; and layout, clarity, and minimal crossing of lines becomes difficult and time consuming. Subdivision into many diagrams is usually recommended, leading to multiple drawing of similar boxes. Generally people do not create complete sets of DFDs, only high-level summary diagrams. The effort to create complete sets is far too tedious in realistically complex situations, and not usually worthwhile. The DFDs that are created do *not* significantly help designers and programmers in the later programming and implementation work.

The hidden agenda in creating DFDs may be to get user representatives involved in creating some kind of high-level descriptions of requirements, out of which will come a lot of other detail that should help design and implementation of something acceptable. The work may also conceal training analysts and creating human cooperation between the managers, user representatives and analysts. It gives them somewhere to start.

Common environment coupling

Sometimes several processes or subsystems may share an external source (or more rarely an external destination). For example, several clerks may use the same files in a filing cabinet for different processes, and similarly several clerks may use shared data in a computer system for different kinds of transactions. **Common environment coupling** means input from an external system interface is shown on the DFD as flowing directly to a datastore within the target system. This means that both the interface and the target system must have an understanding of the datastore's structure. Better practice is to provide a process within the target system to receive the external data. Then if the data format or communication protocol changes, only the receiving process need be changed.

In this chapter we have concentrated on a limited collection of ways of analysing and describing processes. Later, in Chapters 9 and 11, we explain further techniques and more about ways of decomposing business functions, processes and associated information.

Data analysis

Several conceptual model abstractions, including entities, attributes and relationships were explained in the section on simple modelling (pp. 59–62). Here we extend that beginning and remind you about entities and state the underlying assumptions about the data types being stable. We gradually build up to more realistic complex examples and show various notations. Further aspects which complete the description of how to perform data analysis are explained in Chapter 11.

To remind you, an **entity** is an object that a user such as George handles in an IS, whether IT-based or not. An **attribute** is a property that further describes the entity. **Relationships** may exist between pairs of entities. Usually Anna seeks **types of** entities, types of attributes and types of relationships, e.g. Employee, Surname, Is-contained-in, just as she does for processes and behaviour. Each named type corresponds to many **occurrences**, e.g. 'Smith'. The words 'type of' may be omitted where the meaning is clear.

The underlying **assumptions** are the following.

- The structures of the data types and information will endure and not change as often as processes and behaviour. The data may be held in databases and shared between many users, where this is likely to be worthwhile, e.g. for large organizations, and DBMS and relational database software packages permit this. The corresponding physical structures may be changed easily, without any reprogramming, if the patterns of use of processes or behaviours change in the future. Some software packages provide the facilities.
- By suitable techniques the entity types, attribute types and relationship types can be analysed and documented as conceptual data models.
- By further techniques to be explained in Chapter 11 these are then transformed into logical models such as suitable database structures that should rarely need to be changed in future years.

Data analysis products

At some time during the analysis of most types of system, Anna must start to discover entities, attributes, and relationships in order to build a conceptual data model.

Synonyms and homonyms

Different staff in different departments may use different **synonym** names for the same data types. Also in different departments the same name may be used with two different meanings, as **homonyms**. Anna will note and accept these synonyms and homonyms, and use the appropriate local name for the person she is talking to. She will however carefully ensure that her understanding of any synonyms and homonyms is correct.

Analysis of text

One way of looking for candidate entities, attributes and relationships is to analyse appropriate texts or oral conversations related to the area being analysed. Simple textual analysis is illustrated in Exercise 6.6.

In the analysis of textual information it can be seen that nouns, adjectives and verbs may correspond quite well to entities, attributes and relationships, respectively. Deciding whether a noun is an entity or an attribute of another entity is often arbitrary to begin with. From the example in Exercise 6.6, is 'skill' an attribute of 'engineer' or is it an entity in its own right? Similarly 'model' is clearly an entity but may it also be an attribute of 'engineer' denoting their skill? Is skill a euphemism for model? One strategy for this kind of problem is to start by considering cases such as 'skill' as entities. This can be revised as necessary when more information is known about the analysis area.

It is interesting to notice that a **data analyst** sees verbs as data structures, usually relationships between entities. But a **process analyst** sees verbs as processes that become coded as program modules. These are two very different perspectives.

Elementary data analysis example

The following example text, written in an artificial style, is analysed below.

Exercise 6.7

Before looking at the solution overleaf, highlight or mark the text to identify separately the nouns that are probably entities, their properties that are probably attributes and the verbs giving associations between pairs of entity types that are probably relationships. Use singular names even where the text is plural.

'The Rocket-Chip Computer Company designs and manufactures several models of computer (RC789, RC890 ...). Their engineers, who each have name, address, and telephone number, are qualified to repair several different models. Each model requires a different toolkit. RC's customers may each own several computers. The customer can be visited by any available engineer with the right skills – and by more than one engineer on any one day, at the appointment time.'

See Table 6.1.

Entities	*Attributes*	*Relationships*
Rocket-Chip Computer Company	Model of computer	Company designs models
Computer	Name	Company manufactures models
Model	Address	Engineer is qualified
Engineer	Telephone number	Engineer can repair models
Toolkit	Qualified	Model requires toolkit
Customer	Available	Company has customers
Skill	Right skills	Customer owns computers
Visit	Appointment time	Customer visited by engineers
Day		Visit on day at time

TABLE 6.1
Example of start of EAR data analysis

The initial decision as to whether something is an entity or not is arbitrary. Later, as analysis continues, some attributes or relationships may become new entities, e.g. qualification, time.

Data analysis notation

The aim is to show entity types, relationship types, attribute types, functional dependencies, preferred identifiers, candidate identifiers and normalized structures.

In the following we drop the term 'types' for brevity, although usually the names correspond to such classes.

Entities and relationships

Figure 6.14 shows a selection of notation styles for relationship lines in entity–relationship diagrams. Further notations that combine these have also been used. For example each of the kinds of line can be combined with each of the three shapes of box – soft with rounded corners, hexagon and parallelogram. Most people conventionally keep and use a rectangular box shape for logical or physical models.

Two entity types and a relationship type. Each customer places (may place) many orders, each order must be placed by one customer. A customer may exist without any related orders..

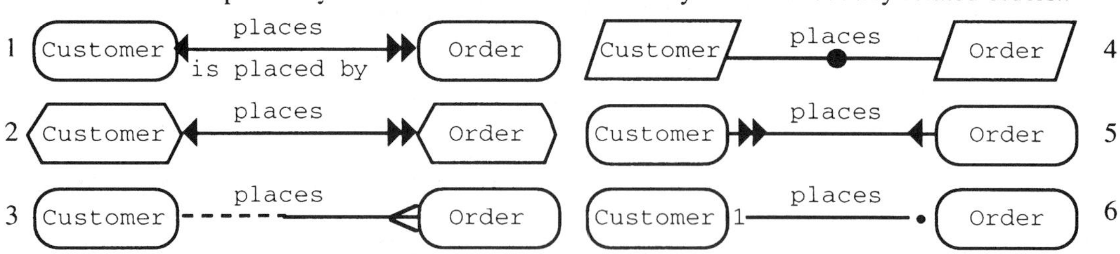

FIGURE 6.14
Various notations for conceptual entity–relationship diagrams.

In Figure 6.14 each relationship has two entities, these are known as **2-part relationships**. It is possible to have relationships between n entities, but such are usually replaced with 2-part relationships and an intermediate entity. This should not be confused with n-part relations, which means a table-like relation with n attributes. We do not agree with restricting conceptual ER diagrams to 2-part relationships, which is a logical-model restriction of many DBMS software packages. We explain this further in Chapter 11.

Figure 6.14 also shows various conventions for showing the **degree of a relationship**, one-to-many, and so on.

The various notations in Figure 6.14 are the result of several pressures. Authors introduced new features and improved on previous notations in order to gain acceptance of, and market for, their proprietary methods, and sometimes to distinguish them from previous ones that they regarded as not fully satisfactory. Technology changed; certain plastic stencil shapes were available in the late 1970s and early 1980s and then, more recently, wordprocessing and graphic packages became available so that people wanted notations which such packages could handle easily. Software packages for use as development tools forced their users to use their given representations.

Exercise 6.8

Which of the six notations allow gradual development in that the people discussing a diagram can draw a line between two entities to show a relationship before knowing its degree, adding arrowheads later?

Which notations allow the diagram to distinguish to-one, meaning to exactly one; from to-none-or-one, meaning optional?

Notations 1, 2, 5, and 6 have the advantage that a line can be drawn between the two entities when it becomes known that there is a relationship, and the symbols for to-one or to-many can be added later when known.

Notation 3 uses a dotted line for optionally-to-one, and a solid line without any other symbol for to-one. Notation 6 allows the creator to write 0-or-1 or anything else against the end of the relationship line. A slight variant of Notation 6 is to continue the line to touch the box, and to write the detail alongside the end of the line.

Figure 6.15 shows the notations for logical model relationships.

FIGURE 6.15
Notations for logical data models.

The following are logical models for the same, e.g. to fit a network DBMS with record types and set types.

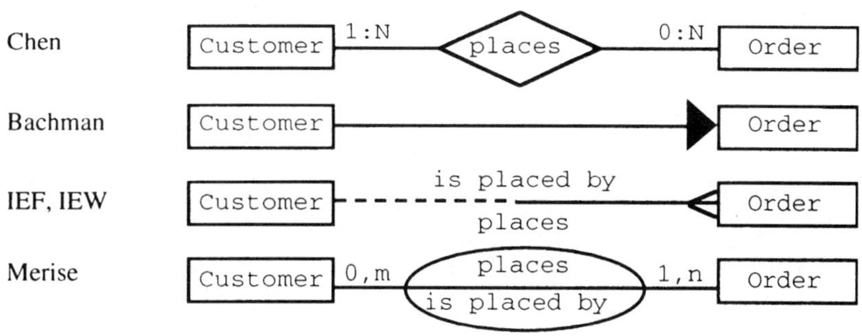

Attributes

Figure 6.16 shows four diagrammatic notations for showing attributes and how they are associated.

Attributes may be drawn to show their grouping into entities or their functional dependencies. We say B is **functionally dependent** on A if each A occurrence has a single corresponding B occurrence, in the same way as mathematical functions.

Figure 6.16 shows four alternatives, all with identifiers underlined where known, and entity names in upper case. The third notation shows only functional dependencies between attributes. The first and fourth show one-to-many relationships between Supplier and Quotation. The second notation is useful during development of the diagram, allowing name boxes anywhere on the paper to be joined, and allowing arrows to be added later as further knowledge is acquired. For example we have underlined Supplier#; but not the identifier for Quotation, as that is assumed not to have been decided at that stage. The neat fourth notation arrangement allows each attribute to appear once anywhere on the paper, yet also allows relationships to be shown; it unifies the to-one aspect of a relationship with the to-one aspect of a functional dependency and shows them both in exactly the same way as a similar arrowed line leaving the identifier attribute.

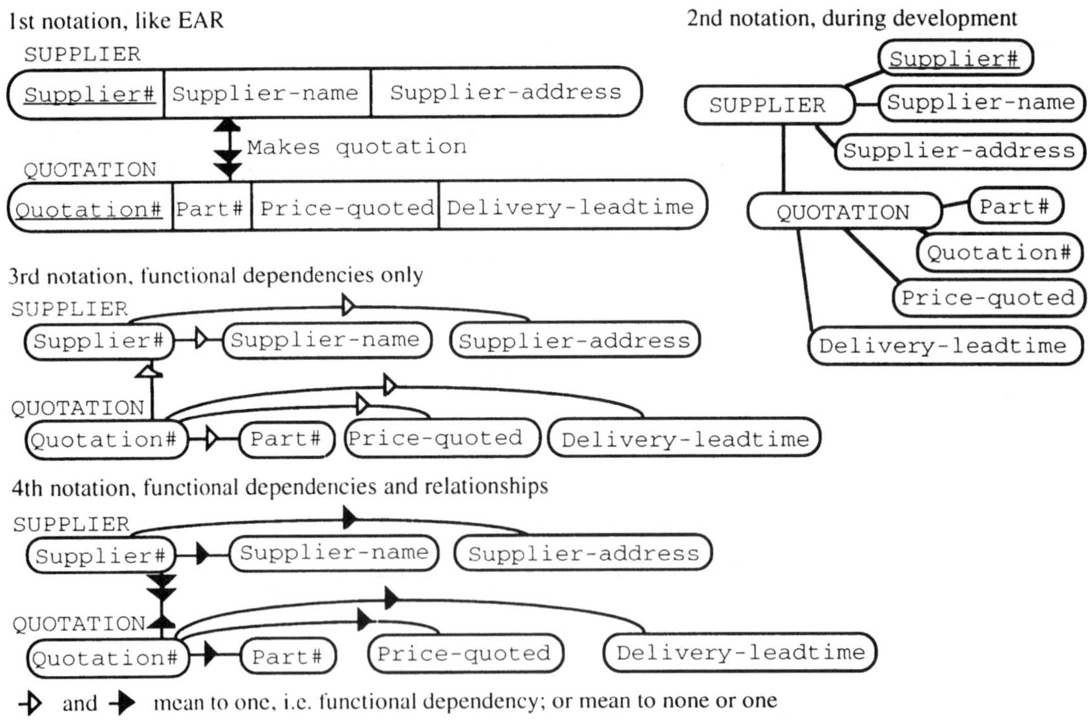

FIGURE 6.16
Some notations for showing attributes.

These notations can be extended to allow for **compound attributes** as identifiers. One way is to draw an outer box round the two or more attributes that form such an identifier.

It is sometimes easier to draw the second, third and fourth notations without the boxes round the attribute names, although in the third and fourth notations having a box round the identifier helps to associate it to the entity name above it. These notations can occasionally usefully be combined, and diagrams started in one notation can evolve into another.

Working with attributes, Anna may sometimes clarify things by introducing a group of attributes as an extra bubble, like a compound identifier, and by having other attributes each functionally dependent on the group.

Entity–attribute–relationship diagram example

> **Exercise 6.9**
>
> This exercise is easy at the start and gradually develops complexity so the later parts need more thought. Draw a suitable diagram to correspond to the following description.
>
> A Supplier has a supplier-no, name and address. The supplier is sent orders. Each order has a date-of-order, delivery-date and contains several line items. Each line item is for a quantity-ordered of a particular part, so the line is identified by the order and the part. The line has a line-item cost. The order thus has a total cost. Each part has a part-name, part details and a quantity on hand. Sometimes there are quotations. A supplier makes a quotation, which is for one part. The quotation has a quotation number and the part number, and gives a price and a delivery leadtime. There is never more than one quotation from a supplier for a particular part on a particular date, so on a telephone call these can be used to identify the quotation.
>
> Comment on the accuracy of the wording.

FIGURE 6.17 Example EAR diagram.

Figure 6.17 shows a simple entity–attribute–relationship diagram in a form that also shows candidate identifiers and functional dependencies.

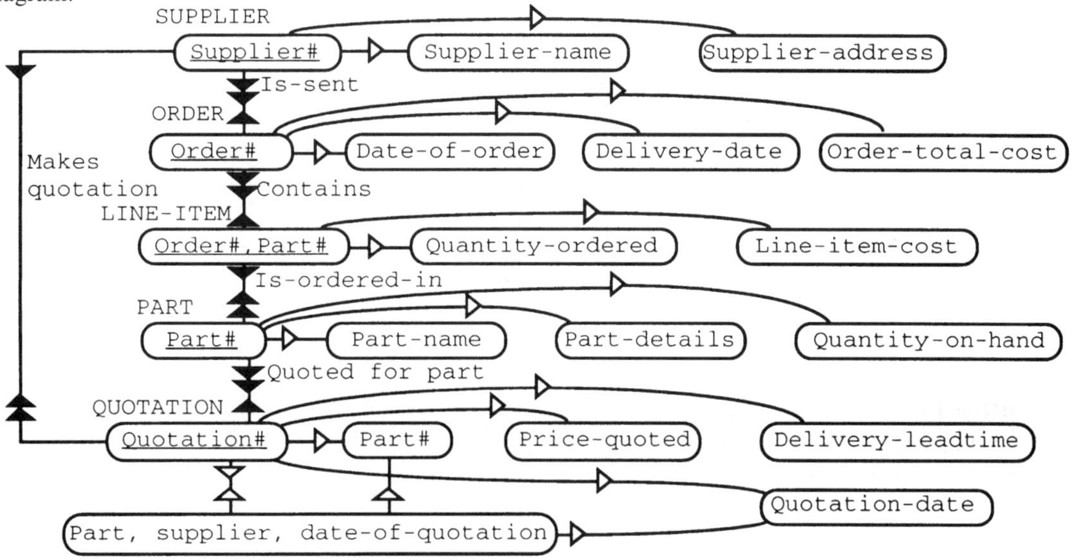

It is based on the fourth notation above. Note the alternative candidate identifiers near the bottom. This has similarities to the layout of our solution to the questions on trains at the end of Chapter 11. The exercise wording is satisfactory, except that the pedantic would spot that the term identify in the last sentence should be indicate, meaning select the right one, as the identifier is assumed not known or not stated on the telephone call. The wording uses slight variations such as no and number, and abbreviations and omissions where the context allows. We intended it to be unambiguous, although corresponding descriptions in real situations rarely are.

Exercise 6.10

Draw the result as an EAR diagram. Will any knowledge that was in our text description be lost? What, if any, is the advantage as a conceptual data model?

Figure 6.18 shows the EAR diagram. This does not show the various alternative candidate identifiers, but its advantages include being easier to understand initially as a conceptual data model. We have chosen to show the one-to-many relationships as in the fourth notation from Figure 6.16.

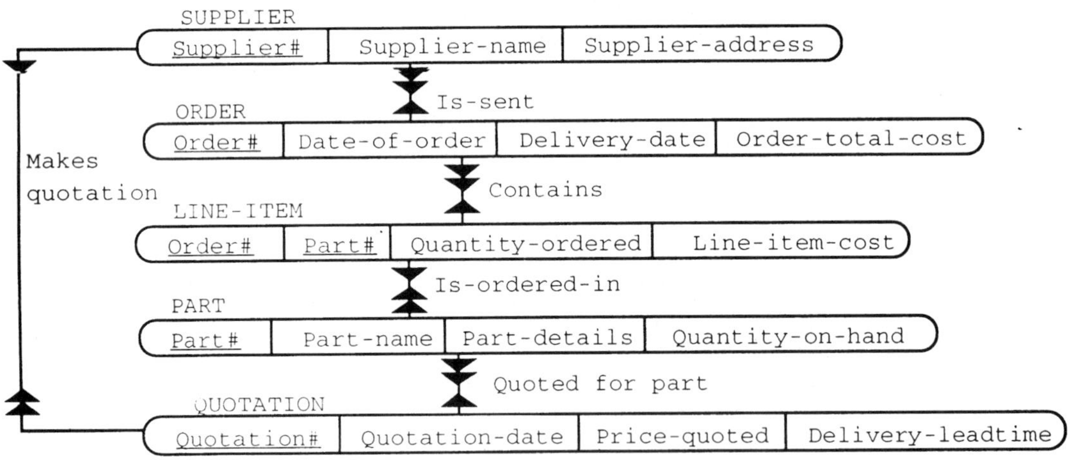

FIGURE 6.18
An EAR diagram example using a slight variant of a widely used notation.

The amount of detail in any process description is determined by the expected combination of purpose and audience. Generally, more detail is required the nearer the engineer is to the implementation of processes. Managers can often manage with very brief summary descriptions.

This chapter has discussed two levels of detail for process descriptions. The creation of a corresponding metamodel has been shown. Completeness and consistency standards are derived from the metamodel of a descriptive or analytical technique. Our approach to analysis has been through the application of completeness and consistency standards.

More traditional information flow and data flow conventions have been introduced, as well as the basics of data analysis.

Self check

Please spend some time reviewing what you have read and doing the questions below.

Objectives

After reading this chapter you should be able to:

- work with simple metamodels, particularly with object–property–relationship metamodels;
- explain what kinds of objects appear in OPR modelling, and work with rules corresponding to relationships in OPR;
- make correct decisions to model rules that might appear to need 3-part relationships in EAR models;
- work with linguistic forms of models;
- handle completeness and consistency as related to descriptions of processes and data;
- work with a simple process flow chart and its corresponding metamodel;
- work with a metamodel of a strategic business unit and associated objects;
- create and handle IFDs and DFDs, and explain the differences between them and which is preferable in simple situations;
- explain and work with a collection of levels and appropriate diagrams such as a context diagram, a Level 0 diagram and lower-level diagrams; apply levelling and balancing; and define a functional primitive;
- create EAR diagrams in realistically complicated situations, analysing text and using various notations of different ISD methods.

Questions

6.1 Suppose a programmer received Anna's information/data flow diagram corresponding to part of a requirement for part of a business process. (i) Fill in Table 6.2 to state which parts of the IFD/DFD would help the programmer with the various program components. (ii) What is the wider message about the usefulness of IFDs/DFDs?

Information from DFD	*Program component*
	Declaration
	Transformation
	Control structure
	Environmental message

TABLE 6.2
Table for Question 6.1

6.2 In principle each business activity such as a business function or a business process may be decomposed into perhaps several subactivities/ subfunctions/ subprocesses. This may be continued until further decomposition is not worthwhile.

Continuing our Inventory-control example, Table 6.3 shows the processes.

```
Inventory_control_system
  Product_storage
    Add_to_storage_model
    Find_the_best_storage_location
      Auto_storage_location_selection
      Determine_storage_type
      Manual_storage_location_selection
    Update_audit_file
    Update_product_file
    Validate_storage_request
  Product_retrieval
    Find_best_retrieval_location
      Determine_retrieval_type
      Select_retrieval_location_auto
    Reduce_storage_model
```
(continued in other column)

```
    Update_audit_file_retrieval
    Valid_retrieval_request
    Update_product_file_retrieval
  Product_maintenance
    Create_new_product_record
    Delete_product_record
    Display_product_screen
    Edit_product_record
    Identify_product
  Reporting
    Generate_administrative_report
    Generate_operational_reports
    Identify_report_type
  Find_high_volume_stock
  Stock_rollover
```

TABLE 6.3
Inventory-control processes

(i) How many levels of functional decomposition does this represent?

(ii) In what other ways could the information conveyed to you in Table 6.3 be expressed in writing?

6.3 Produce a metamodel for the components of a data flow diagram.

7 Approaches

The team of people such as Idris and Anna, asked by their senior management to work on improvements to the business, face issues other than those in earlier chapters such as how to describe and analyse processes. In this chapter we start to explain some of these other issues.

One that shows itself in many ways is how Idris, Anna and others decide what to do next. What is most important? Which aspects of a business process or an IS should be discussed first or next? How can priorities be decided? Why?

They can look for knowledge about how people in other organizations make such decisions. In one sense you may be doing this in reading this book.

In Chapter 3 we gave a reductionist way of working in which people decide the overall long-term aims, objectives, critical success factors, gaps in performance, strategy, tactics, projects, processes and operations – including development and provision activities such as analysis, design and the implementation of facilities for improved business processes and ISs; work on all these items being interleaved. This list is a suggestion of how planning and making improvements might be structured. Later items in the list are assumed to depend on, or flow from, decisions about earlier items. However, the early items need information about later items, such as the feasibility of alternatives, so we recommend that the whole be iterative and interleaved.

Somewhere about the middle of any such list, Idris, Anna, colleagues and managers have to get down to detailed work on particular suggestions for changes and improvements. We use the term **approach** to mean some broad-brush way that they might use to decide their priorities and how they might make underlying assumptions about what is likely to be important and what is likely to succeed. We explain various approaches later in this chapter.

We recommend what we term a **contingency** approach. By this we mean that the people involved should choose the way of working and do the amount of work that best seem to fit the current situation. Small and fairly static organizations should not need to be continually planning business systems and ISs that are not changing significantly. Where a business system or IS seems to need improvement, they should do the right amount of research and planning to achieve the optimum benefits and improvements for the amount of research and planning involved. Similarly, they should choose the way of working – approach, method, technique, tool or combination of these – that best seems to fit the situation. They should get colleagues' opinions as to what to do. They should discuss and decide what degree of change is needed over what timescale, and what amount of planning and resource expenditure is likely to be most worthwhile. Further aspects of contingency are explained in Chapter 12, combining ideas from this and later chapters.

We recommend that the whole is **iterative** and **interleaved**. By iterative we mean cycling through all activities several times, making some progress in each cycle. By interleaving we mean overlapping activities rather than doing them sequentially. The combined effect tends to provide some benefits to the system user in terms of improved performance at an early stage and better final system performance because of the useful feedback that each cycle provides to subsequent ones. Our experiences suggest that most people prefer gradual changes and improvements rather than big changes, and business processes similarly are usually changed gradually, by continually making fairly small changes, not huge and risky leaps.

Human issues may determine the success or failure

Many approaches have been tried in various organizations and situations. Some have succeeded, others have not. Evidence of what does succeed under what conditions and in what situations is difficult to acquire. The reasons for success or failure may involve: people's personalities, hidden agendas, education, skills, behaviour patterns and culture; the features of the organization such as size, industry sector, country, products and services; the availability of resources; the timescales, pressures, environment and external constraints; and the kinds of business process changes or IS developments proposed.

Where, after years of work by a team of people, something turns out to be unsatisfactory, people may blame the team, its managers during the project or those who set up the team and project. People may say its terms of reference were not quite right, or there were changes to the requirements, the environment, the law, the intended benefits, the resources or the priorities. Perhaps new technology meant that some design and specification changes had to be introduced during the project. Human nature being as it is, no person or group would take responsibility for the failure. If the original managers had moved on, they would not regard themselves as the cause. Many things will have changed during the project life and each one could be said to be a contributory reason. People may politely blame 'the system' afterwards, but the **human issues** are usually more important than the technical ones in determining success or failure.

The terms bounded and unbounded can also be applied to **approaches** and **methods**. For **bounded** approaches and methods the resources and timescale can be specified in advance, and human feelings are somewhat irrelevant. In **unbounded** approaches and methods the whole aim is seen as getting people to work together so that a solution or compromise will evolve, and attempting to estimate the resources and timescale should not be considered.

Kinds of issues: requirements, provision, soft issues

The issues and problems in improving business processes and ISs include the following.

- The **requirements**: both what they are and how to find out what they are, especially longer-term requirements, bearing in mind uncertainties of future policy, environment and so on.
- The **provision**: how to decide about, develop, provide and manage the new processes and other facilities, including new ISs.
- The **soft** and **unbounded** aspects of assumptions and approaches to the whole, and their management.
- **Inadequate resources** and **allocated times**: so that compromises are needed, the desired work is not achievable, worthwhile solutions might not be found and the available staff might not achieve anything satisfactory.
- **Inadequate knowledge and available information**: about any aspect of any problem, so the problem is not fully formulated and the optimum solution is missed. Similarly, inadequate education and training, including a lack of understanding of approaches, methods, techniques and tools, may cause a waste of resources and failure because the problem is tackled in the wrong way.

The methods recommended for tackling such problems are essentially empirical – vaguely based on hunch and experience. A few authors have tried to formulate a general problem-solving method. They have generally tried to form appropriate abstractions from their experiences of problems in their field of speciality. These abstractions have then been expressed in ways such as steps to be done in sequence, even for soft situations.

The tripartite assumption

Before explaining the various approaches, we discuss a hidden assumption.

There is a tripartite assumption that **everything relevant could be specified and modelled in terms of processes, data, and behaviour**. For over 30 years many analysts and designers have used models, techniques and methods assuming this, but never stating it explicitly. Here **processes** covers business functions and operations, and in practice usually only the lower-level and computer-based processes. **Data** covers what the processes operate on, its structure and which data is the input and the output of each process. **Behaviour** covers system dynamics – when do the processes happen, how often, what events trigger which processes, and under what conditions can processes start and finish.

Behaviour often ignored

Furthermore, until the mid 1980s, analysts working towards MIS components concentrated mainly on data and processes, omitting system dynamics, while those working towards machine control systems concentrated on dynamics, input and output. In MIS components there is a risk of an assumption that the users would handle behaviour at the time of use – running the right processes at the right time. So rules about the behaviour were not analysed or recorded, and had little or no effect on the programs and data for the computer systems. Many MIS components ran in batch mode so dynamics were less important. For many process control situations, data is essentially irrelevant.

Defects of the tripartite assumption

The tripartite assumption misses many other aspects – some of which are critical to success and acceptability.

Exercise 7.1

List some issues that need thought and may need to be specified for the development of a business process or an ISD, but that are not specified under processes, data and behaviour.

The tripartite assumption misses how to specify issues such as the following.

- Human issues; non-IT based parts of business systems; responsibilities such as who is responsible for what, who is authorized to do what, and who controls the access to, and use of, what data and processes.
- The desired levels of quality, accuracy, precision, integrity, consistency, correct operation, completeness, ownership and privacy; and the mechanisms for ensuring these are provided – e.g. checks, security, backup, recovery and auditing.
- The organization's long-term objectives, its strategy, survival, culture, management style and methods; changes to all of these; and how the ISs match them.
- The desirability of **flexibility**, such as ease of major changes later to cope with mergers and reorganizations and of evolution to cope with changes in external factors, cultures and legislation, personnel policies, taxation, accounting rules, and with changes in boom, recession, inflation, and turbulent environments. Flexibility may be achieved by features such as modularity, ease of changing hardware, software, and human–computer interfaces, normalized data structures, data independence, and particularly ease of changing the business processes, such as changes to rules about the rules in the models.

- How critical to the organization are the business systems and ISs, for example if they ceased to work what would happen; and how organizational strategy and objectives such as long-term improvements to products and services may depend on the business systems and ISs.

These issues have to be covered by some hidden agendas that ensure the continual appropriateness of the ISs to the organization's business and top strategies. Managers should think about how much work should be devoted towards these issues, as well as how much towards the business modelling and implementation of processes and facilities.

Combining types of analysis

Most approaches involve some recommended way of carrying out the analysis of requirements and processes. To simplify explanations later, we first explain that the various kinds of analysis described in Chapter 2 (pp. 71–3) can be combined. With our **contingency** approach we recommend that Idris and Anna should use these in any combination, alternating between them appropriately.

People, such as analysts and the authors of various approaches, have differed as to the extent an analyst should **concentrate on process analysis or data analysis or both**. All three have been successful, even though they omit behaviour – although we recognize that some authors include system dynamics in process analysis. The alternatives have underlying assumptions as we explain later under the various approaches in this chapter and in Chapter 9 (pp. 261–3).

Some analysts promote a mainly **process analysis** and **functional analysis** approach – believing user representatives can describe and specify their actions in terms of what they do and hence the information they need – better than they can describe the types of information as such.

Other analysts believe that the deep inherent structure of the types of data will remain almost unchanged through organizational changes in which processes and actions change. Hence they promote **data analysis**.

Combining these there are other analysts who say carry out both data and process analysis for completeness and as a check.

Requirements analysis, investigating what are the problems of current systems and finding out the requirements for improvements is another approach. In interviewing, managers or user representatives are encouraged to explain the problems and requirements without emphasizing data or processes. For example, the issue may hinge on a need to do an existing process faster or more frequently; or to have more staff doing larger volumes of work; or to improve privacy, security or integrity.

There are those who want to analyse **existing systems** in order to determine, understand and document what currently happens and its difficulties, or to gain training.

In our view not one of the above is satisfactory by itself. Each lacks the systems dynamics element from behaviour analysis, the knowledge of how often what occurs and under what circumstances, and who is responsible for what, when. They also usually constrain Idris and others to relatively minor improvements, and discourage lateral thinking of major changes even though such major changes may be achieved gradually. The hidden basis for such approaches is that the organization cannot justify doing the other kinds of work, or that the staff available do not have the right skills.

Summary of available approaches

Table 7.1 gives a summary of certain approaches. Further details of each, including some advantages and disadvantages, are given in the following text. There are few research findings to justify the claims made by proposers of the approaches, but disproving their worth is also difficult to substantiate.

Waterfall approach	Have a project plan with say six predefined phases/stages; each is finished and signed off by managers before the next starts. Fits subcontracting. Widely used in large organizations in the past. Mistakes in products of early stages are not found till later stages. It had been applied to many disciplines before being partly discredited, and then changed into different approaches to software engineering.
Interleaving and gradual development	Gradually change, with many small changes; not trying to do any large piece of work such as all the analysis, design or implementation at a time; interleave the activities, not having predefined stages and milestones.
Structured approach	Structured analysis, design and programming.
Systems approach	Systems are not purely technical, they interface with human and manual procedures. The system boundaries also change over time.
Planning approach	People try to plan it right, this being cheaper than building it wrong.
Data analysis approach	Concentrate on the long-term inherently stable types of data and implement systems with independence to allow easily changing the less stable structures, processes and systems.
Prototyping approach	Prototypes may be discardable or gradually developed into final systems. Continual tests and comments help.
Product set approach	Suppliers aim to develop and sell general-purpose software packages. The packages may have facilities to tailor them to fit requirements.
Socio-technical approach	Aim to get the human relations right as well as the technical aspects.
Participative approach	Get the end users involved in the discussions, planning, analysis and design; then the whole is likely to be correct and accepted by the users.
Automated tools and software engineering approach	Software tools to help the development of complex software for organizations' applications have gradually been created and are marketed by certain suppliers.

TABLE 7.1
Summary of various approaches

Not one of these approaches is widely agreed as a complete and satisfactory solution and some people have therefore attempted to combine the 'good' features of different approaches. However, the choice of what is 'good' is very subjective and people have different opinions. What is 'good' to be used and applied in one situation may not be good in another – it may depend on the circumstances.

Forming your own opinion on approaches

For each approach that we describe, you should feel free to form your own judgement as to whether or not, or to what extent, you agree with each point. You may think of examples from your own experiences. You may decide whether or not those examples were successful and appropriate. You should know whether your organization, or your area of it, does or does not use that approach, and why. You might consider whether in your opinion it should become a recommended or enforced standard – perhaps within a project, a country, an organization, customers, suppliers or world-wide. Or you may think that flexibility by not standardizing may be preferable. We discuss that further in Chapter 12.

Waterfall approach

We explain the most widely-used approach, the **waterfall approach**, first. In the past this has been used extensively in large organizations for the technical aspects of projects, but has since become tarnished. If you understand its activities and how they should be related, you should be able to explain and make decisions about when to use and when not to use its phases. Also, since many projects need these activities, with an understanding of how they are related you should be able to manage projects with similar activities.

The key waterfall approach point is to have predefined **phases** (= **stages**), where each phase must be **completed before the next phase starts**. Each phase delivers something to the next, just as each stage of a sequence of lakes and waterfalls delivers water from a higher level to a lower level. The successive deliverables should get nearer to the required final implemented working information system, except that the review and maintenance phase represents hidden ongoing improvements during use. However, a waterfall approach may permit feedback and iteration.

The waterfall approach specifies several **phases** for an IS project – usually about six. Typical names are: Feasibility Study, System Investigation, System Analysis, System Design, Implementation, Review and Maintenance. Sometimes the term System becomes Systems, e.g. Systems Analysis.

This was the traditional approach of the 1960s, 1970s and early 1980s, although the terms 'method' and 'approach' were not then used with their current meanings. It had a big impact on data processing in the 1970s and early 1980s. It was then widely regarded as 'good', and still is by some people. Even in 1994 we have heard of some large organizations that still use predefined, non-overlapping phases.

The six phases are together referred to by various names such as: **Software life cycle**, **Traditional systems analysis**, **Systems development life cycle**, and others. Most of these terms are misleading. The phases do not cover all the life of a piece of software or an information system or a business system. Traditional systems analysis is confusing since it includes Systems Analysis as one of its phases. Systems development life cycle implies an information system's life cycle, but it does not cover all the activities such as understanding business objectives and strategy.

Waterfall approach – an example

An ISD project in a large business was done in six non-overlapping stages as depicted in Figure 7.1. The six stages were **sequential** and each stage had to be signed off as completed satisfactorily before the next stage started.

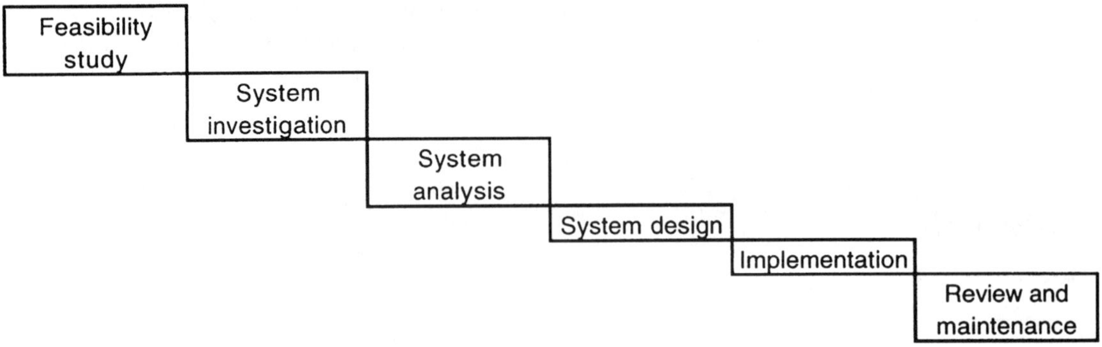

FIGURE 7.1
Phases of an example waterfall approach.

The development was assumed to be bounded and contract-driven – hidden assumptions. Managers assumed that each stage could be completed correctly within its resources and timescale and could have different contractors who were paid at sign-off. The only knowledge carried forward from one stage to the next was that contained in the formal products, as the stages had different teams from different contractors. In order to make a profit, each contractor had to complete his stage within the allocated resources and time. It was this factor that determined the amount of detail in the documents produced at each stage rather than, as it should have been, the needs of the subsequent stages. Not surprisingly, the project was unsuccessful. The tendency to operate the waterfall approach in this way is one of its weaknesses.

Stages, tasks, and products of a waterfall

The different waterfall phases produce various deliverables, as Table 7.2 shows. Each deliverable is a different kind of system description, i.e. an abstraction for certain purposes. Each phase, except the first and last, transforms the deliverable from the previous phase into a new deliverable that is handed on to the next phase. Table 7.3 gives the claimed advantages of the waterfall approach.

Several disadvantages have been experienced with the waterfall approach. Unambitious systems were produced, typically limited by the available technology and centralized management style.

Figure 7.2 shows how the Waterfall approach was usually only

***Stage**, and main activities*	*What the stage produces, the main deliverables*
Feasibility Study	
• Observe current system (in outline) • Decide requirements (in outline) • Suggest alternative solutions: evaluate technical and human aspects, costs, benefits • Recommend solution	• An outline of what is needed • Cost-benefit analysis • Report to management, verbal presentation • Decision
System Investigation	
• Document the current business functions and processes; how they are physically done; are the functional requirements achieved? problems? • What processes, data; information flows; inputs, outputs, files, records are used?	• A model of the current physical system, including: broad current system flowcharts, organization reporting structure chart, specification of the current system as physical documents and which flows where, interaction grid charts such as events and processes
Systems Analysis (= analysis of the current system)	
• Analyse in greater detail the underlying logic of the current system, problems, methods, growth, reasons • Understand in some detail the requirements, and what can/cannot change	• A logical model of the current system, i.e. a description of it with increasing detail of the required business system; its data, processes, information flows; and interactions such as what process uses/produces what data and what event triggers what process how often • A requirements specification
Systems Design	
• Design the computer-oriented and manual parts of the future system • Design a better logical model, to fit better the new requirements	• The proposed design, as a logical model of the new system; how data is to be captured, inputs, outputs, who it will go to; the processes as specifications for programs, files, records, data formats; and backup and recovery processes
Implementation (= construction, testing, installing, cutover)	
• Programming, program testing; computer system testing where data shared; manual procedures, training • Install new system; produce its documentation; deliver it; parallel running of old and new; cutover/transition; and discontinue old system	• A workable new physical system replacing the old system; its documentation; and experience that it works
Review and Maintenance	
• Does new system fully meet requirements? • What improvements, further changes perhaps desirable? • Do the work to improve the physical system	• Suggestions for further work • Slightly improved system every now and then

TABLE 7.2
Stages, main activities, and products of a waterfall or traditional structured analysis and design

applied to the lower-level business operations, and did not provide an information system that was useful to the managers.

The hidden reasons may have been that providing computer-based ISs to help with routine operations would be cost effective and acceptable to managers, but automating any of their decision making would be less acceptable. A decision support system would also be more difficult to analyse and program. The waterfall control ensured that only what had been analysed and accepted at one stage was taken on to the next. Certain managers could block developments that might adversely affect their jobs, and do so without their hidden veto being noticed.

Table 7.4 shows the unsatisfactory result in a typical organization in the 1980s and thus why, in some organizations, the waterfall

The claimed **advantages** for the waterfall approach include:

- **Improved discipline**, visibility and control. It was claimed to be an improvement on anything previously used, because previous methods mixed analysis, design, and implementation unsystematically. The waterfall had definable distinct **phases** and subphases, and allowed application of **project management techniques.**
- The waterfall assumed **computerization** of clerical operational tasks would be an improvement. Savings from such improvements were often achieved.
- The managers assumed that the **project team had little knowledge of the business**. The waterfall approach **seemed suitable** for relatively untrained analysts, designers, especially computer programmers, mathematicians and others with little understanding of the business, its objectives, plans and functions. It also seemed suitable for user representatives with little understanding of computers or programming.

TABLE 7.3
Claimed advantages of the waterfall approach

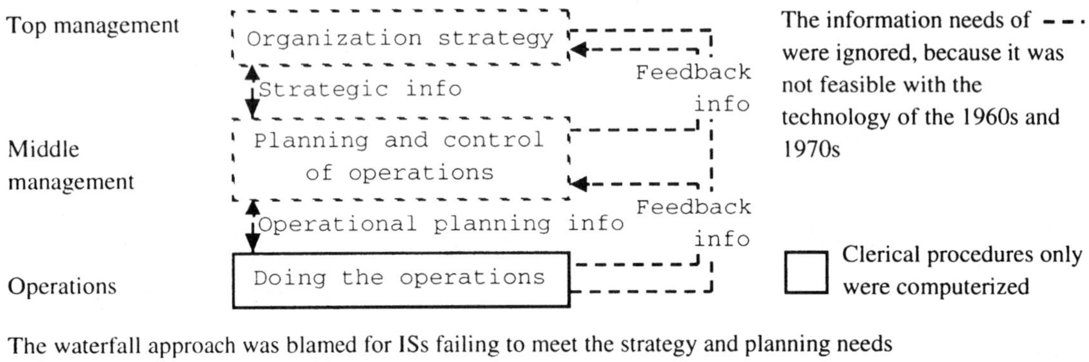

FIGURE 7.2
Criticism of the waterfall approach – only clerical operations.

approach is nowadays regarded as discredited. It was satisfactory for meeting contractual requirements but it was, and is, *not* an effective way of producing good software, ISs and business systems.

Many people paid lip service to the waterfall approach but added their own improvements and so many variants have been created.

Interleaving and gradual development

We recommend that, instead of the rigid phase demarcation of the waterfall approach, actions should be interleaved and products developed gradually. This interleaving, by starting later activities before earlier ones have been completely finished, allows feedback from the former to influence the latter. It enables potentially difficult tasks to be tackled earlier than might otherwise be the case so that their feasibility can be quantified in time to modify the early phases. So we need to kill the sequential myth.

Sequential myth

The half-truth that collections of actions are always or usually best done sequentially needs killing. Some authors have for years pushed the view that activities should be completed in turn so that each delivers well-formed products that provide a correct input to the next before it can start.

- The Waterfall process was document-intensive. For every hour spent on construction, two were spent on meetings and documentation. At a stage sign-off the managers responsible often did not know that its products to be handed to the next stage would later be found unsatisfactory, e.g. incomplete and inconsistent.
- With long timescales for each stage and for the whole, both developers and managers had often moved on to some other job before the effects of their work or of the waterfall approach became apparent at some much later stage. Detailed **knowledge** acquired at an early stage by one person could become **lost** before it was needed at a later stage by their successor, who would also find the effects of earlier errors.
- So, despite the sign-offs, at an advanced stage or at the Review and Maintenance stage managers and users gradually recognized that the whole was out of control and far from satisfactory. Sometimes the implemented ISs were abandoned – huge wastes of costs and elapsed time. Politically, people said the original requirements had been superseded, and further work was needed. Reviews became overloaded. Eventually most systems reached and remained in the phase of needing continual huge maintenance. IS users and managers were continually dissatisfied.
- So the whole six stages started again. The whole approach was thus iterative, when viewed afterwards with a sufficiently long-term view over many years. But people did not recognize that at the time. The waterfall lifecycle repeated from generation to generation of an IS, usually with different people being responsible.

TABLE 7.4
Typical experiences of using the waterfall approach

However, most good analysts and programmers do not work that way. They successively refine. They usually create many drafts and prototypes of the deliverable products with increasing refinement, and their development actions are overlapped – not sequential. They assess the feasibility of each later action before expending too much work on any early action that might later be found to be wasted. They gradually get each part right. They also gradually get the structure of the whole right in increasing detail.

With parts of many actions interleaved and with products developing on an evolutionary basis, it becomes difficult to control the work because it is difficult to represent in plans, and because normal project management methods, including PERT, are not suitable. However, dealing with this by regarding every activity as non-overlapping is an unrealistic simplification

During the early activities of large projects it is impossible to think of and specify all details. The best achievable is to have a first pass at the later activities brought forward to overlap the early stages. This really is the key to success.

Spiral Model

In an effort to solve some of the difficulties of the Waterfall Approach while still conserving its useful features, alternatives have been produced. The Spiral Model was one such result and Figure 7.3 shows an example. The actions of a hypothetical project start from the centre and go outwards and clockwise. The cycle of plan, do, review goes clockwise starting from the lower left and going round. The development actions are interleaved and iterative, the interleaving going round and the gradual development going outwards with time.

This model is a cyclic process rather than a linear one. In it the requirements evolve in parallel with the developing architecture and the understanding of what is feasible and cost effective. This enables the model to accommodate re-use and prototyping much more easily.

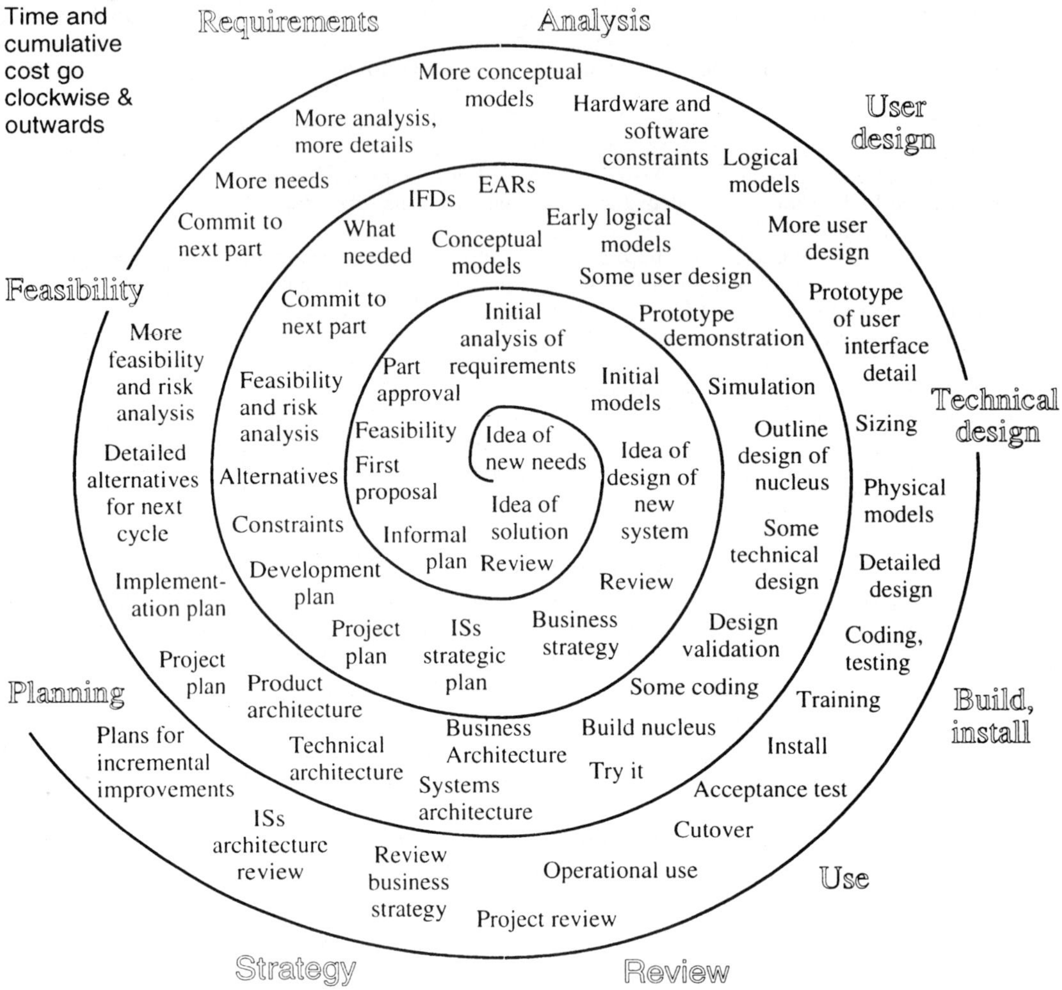

FIGURE 7.3
A possible spiral model of an information system development.

The terms in Figure 7.3 are not intended to be definitive. Many variants can convey the same meaning – that planning, analysis, design and building continue cyclically in interleaved form and in increasing detail. Feasibility, reviews and management continually also interleave as appropriate. Feasibility – costs, benefits, risk analysis – can be done at any stage for any action, for any part or for the whole. In one sense the cycle of an action goes once round, starting near the bottom of one of the spirals with planning, and then clockwise round to review. Subcycles may be interleaved and nested.

The spiral model, combined with incremental development, may be an improvement over some of the waterfall problems.

Figure 7.4 shows an alternative with overlapping, feedback and two extra phases. The **Idea phase** is for identifying market opportunities. New requirements are fed back to the Idea phase to suggest the equivalent of that phase for the next project or for improvements to the current product. The **Advanced development phase** gives understanding of the amount of work involved. Generally this phase is not performed for commercial systems.

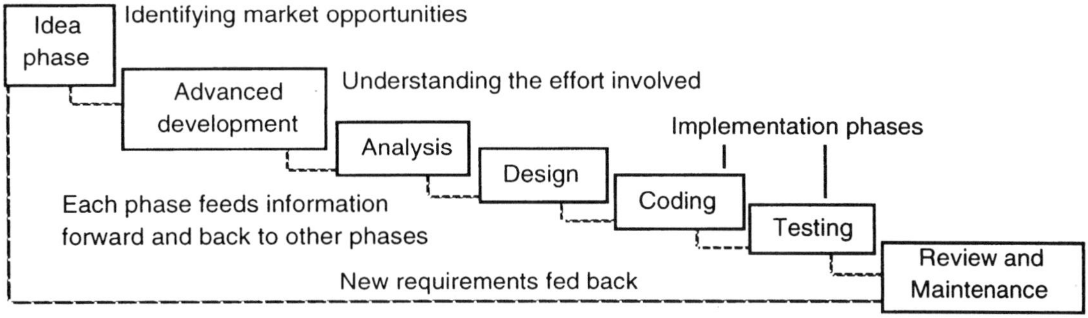

FIGURE 7.4
An alternative.

Structured approach

A Structured approach to developing software is very common and has some useful points. It recommends developing several models, some with the hidden reason of giving training. The decomposition of a process into subprocesses corresponding to programmable structures involving similar subprocess is encouraged. This decomposition is mathematically sound but is only applicable to single sequential processes such as algorithms. It is not applicable to cases where many people and systems are all doing things concurrently. The structured approach is oriented to analysing the output from processes, leading to developed computer systems that mirror clerically produced documents and that have built-in constraints that inhibit subsequent major improvements. Integration of horizontal information flows into a unified system is difficult where different areas have been decomposed separately into incompatible substructures, just as the branches of a tree cannot share a group of leaves. Worse, the approach also concentrates on the least stable aspects of the business systems and so leads to computer systems that are most likely to need change as these less stable parts of the business change.

So we recommend that you should understand which of the structured approach advantages and disadvantages depend on which of its features, so that in some new situation in the future you may use the appropriate features but avoid difficulties. You may even be able to make recommendations to others.

Connotations of structured

The term **Structured** has several connotations which apply both to the structured approach and to structured methods and techniques used within that approach. We group them into four.

Firstly, the early structured approaches were based on **functional decomposition**, meaning the analysis of business functions and their breakdown into levels. This created documents that were used to get the user's agreement. The documents were data flow diagrams, decision trees, decision tables, data structure diagrams, and structured-English descriptions of processes.

Four sets of such documents are typical, as seen in Table 7.5, and so a second connotation of the word structured is producing all those versions of processes.

Thirdly, structured approaches were based on allowing processes to be decomposed three ways, which corresponded to the available structures in programming languages. Each specified and decomposable process had to be broken down into some combination of:

- two or more sequential processes, statement; statement ...;
- conditions and corresponding processes for each, if ... then ... else ...; | case ...;
- loops with repetitions, and slight changes each time, do ... until | while ...; | for ... do ... .

Up to about 1987 these structured approaches concentrated on processes and essentially ignored specifying any data structures except insofar as data was needed in processes.

Fourthly, the structured approaches had the management of the development work structured in predefined activities. The documents produced were monitored by walk throughs – e.g. peer group monitoring. The whole was managed by regular, scheduled, but not too frequent, management meetings. Project control expected milestones at major stages to be achieved by prespecified dates, like the waterfall, but these were often not satisfactorily estimated and usually not achieved.

- **Current physical model**, being a specification of the existing system including its actual data representations, its actual forms. Doing this model assumes user representatives and managers are unwilling to work with a draft new logical model early in the project because they know or suspect that the analyst does not know how the business works. They are assumed to be unable to help develop an abstract model of something new. They may need the education of developing and seeing a current physical model. They may be frightened by new technology, both not understanding it and perhaps fearing their jobs. So doing this model is hidden training for everyone!
- **Current logical model**, being a specification of the existing system as it would be if computer hardware and software were to run as fast as need be, with no storage capacity limit, no breakdowns, no errors. This meaning of **logical** is one kind of abstraction from a physical model.
- **New logical model**, being a logical model of a desired future system, with relatively few changes. Transforming a current logical model into a new logical model was believed to be not much work, as most of the current logical model would be unchanged in the new logical model. This (wrongly) assumes the new system will be a slightly more computerized version of the current system.
- **New physical model**, being a physical model designed to be equivalent to the new logical model. The boundary of what is automated might be different from the current physical model, e.g. some things that were manual in the current physical model to be done by computer.

TABLE 7.5
Traditional structured analysis advocated and emphasized the sequential development of four models, with hidden training and assumptions

People in many projects believed the assumptions and reasons for the four models were mostly correct. However, by their second or third project, some managers regarded analysis as a waste of time as the real productive work was perceived to be programming. Analysis of the current system was regarded as of dubious benefit because it would be superseded. The idea that more work on planning and on obtaining a good understanding of the requirements might save lots of useless coding, was often not accepted. On the other hand, in some big projects so much time and work was spent on analysis to create these four models that the project never resulted in the productive use of a developed IT-based IS. Years of work were wasted.

Structured techniques – disadvantages

One disadvantage of the structured approach is how it led to **output-oriented analysis and design**, building into the design the operations and data to produce current paperwork more efficiently. This unsatisfactory and inflexible effect arises from the following. Analysts first find out what documents are being produced and then what processes will produce them. The designers assume that these processes will correspond to the programs needed and they design the programs on this basis. The analysts and designers also find out and discuss what files need to be held as static data in the computers and in filing cabinets, and what inputs are needed as data to the computers. We comment that this is initially analysing only the output, then also analysing only stored data and input, which may not lead to useful specifications of flexible business systems, processes and ISs.

Output-oriented analysis and design can lead to troubles later, rather like the inflexible waterfall. When further needs arise one finds that only the previously agreed, new logical model processes are available. The data for some further need might not be available in a form and structure that allows for easy extension of the processes.

As with the waterfall, the developers and current management are blamed. The backlog of requests for improvements grows. By the time the item on the backlog is programmed, tested and available to users they have long since found some other way of coping, or the need has passed. Hence users and managers give up making suggestions for improvements, believing that they will never happen in time to be useful. So the invisible backlog grows and the planners are unable to estimate correctly.

Other disadvantages include the wasted work in analysing the current methods, the way that the method builds current constraints into the design for the future, and the fact that the method only allows decomposable processes. In combination, these severely constrain ideas for future business processes. Omitting to analyse data that might be shared between processes tends to discourage any ideas and suggestions such as horizontal integration and cooperation between different departments, sections, areas and functions. Business systems cannot be integrated. Each will tend to have its own processes and will not share data with others. More widely, the whole structured approach concentrates only on computer based processes and so prevents fresh ideas emerging for the ways that the staff might conduct the business.

The structured techniques have several disadvantages. Diagrams are arbitrary, overcrowded and biased towards oversimplifying for human understanding, and are therefore not a truthful representation of a business system. The graphical orientation means that some concepts are not easily represented, e.g. the sequence of processing in data flow diagrams. Documents that have diagrams cannot be accurately checked by hand for completeness and consistency. Automated checking does not fulfil all the criteria, for example CASE tools commonly perform checks associated with diagram conventions such as the identification of balancing problems between levels of a data flow diagram, but automated checking cannot help with the checking of business rules.

The real world cannot be represented correctly as a set of

hierarchical structures in levels. Difficulties arise in identifying the infrastructure, for example components common to several business areas, because these typically belong to different branches of the decomposition into levels. Structured techniques do not naturally facilitate reusability of specifications and processes, although procedures that help this may be added to the structured techniques. Distributability and concurrency are not the natural outcome of structured design. Decomposition into levels can lead to stovepiped design of IT applications and business processes. **Stovepiped** here means that each of these applications and processes will be biased to its business function and so they will not be well integrated. Many definitions and implementations of the same business data objects, such as customer and price information and processes using them, will coexist. The business systems and ISs are then more tightly locked into the current organizational reporting structure and so business flexibility is severely restricted. It then takes too long to change the business systems and ISs to match changes in the business, and the full potential benefits from using IT are not realized. The multiple near-duplicates of work and program code give increased maintenance difficulties and costs.

Up to the 1970s, computer systems usually comprised one machine. Nowadays, organizations have many machines and care is needed if structured techniques are used in circumstances where many processes can occur concurrently, perhaps with many people and processors. Processes that can be done in parallel have other properties beyond the three-way decomposition of single processes.

Structured techniques are inadequate where organizational growth is rapid or the structure is complex, unstable or dynamic. System dynamics and behaviour are missing and distributed systems are not recognized and supported. Functional decomposition is unsatisfactory and completeness and consistency are weak and cannot be checked.

Structured approaches and their associated techniques, for example functional decomposition, tend to concentrate on business functions. This is the **least stable** layer of the business, as indicated in Figure 5.1. This is the most serious criticism of structured approaches. Benefits may best be gained if the starting point for the approach to systems development is one of greatest stability, e.g. the essential processes and their data types.

Structured techniques – advantages

The claimed advantages of structured techniques are: simple approach, quick to learn, widely known, and widely used. Also some principles that have emerged from structured techniques are valuable development aids. The method can help where the problem area is simple, stable and understood, providing a disciplined approach with standardized communications. The three-way decomposition of processes is mathematically sound for programming purposes, but care is needed as it is only applicable to single algorithmic processes, not to instances where many people and systems do things concurrently.

Systems approach

In the Systems approach the organization and its various relevant parts are regarded as systems and subsystems, with the features given in Chapter 1.

Features of organizations viewed as systems and subsystems

The systems approach is based on General Systems Theory (GST). By this theory people attempt to understand the nature of complex systems and of isomorphic systems.

Isomorphic systems means two or more systems that behave in essentially the same way, appearing to have corresponding parts and structure. For example, people in different organizations, departments or areas who perform corresponding processes when answering telephone calls are working isomorphic systems. Some kind of one-to-one correspondence exists: this kind of process here corresponds to that kind of process there, this kind of event here to that kind of event there, and so on.

In GST, organizations are viewed as open systems – not closed, not self-contained, and with parts. An **open system** either has a boundary whose position is not well defined, or interacts with its environment in ways that cannot be ignored, or both. It influences its environment and is influenced by it. The **environment** is whatever is external to (= outside) the boundary.

By contrast a **closed system** is viewed as having a precise boundary and not interacting with what is outside the boundary

The socio-technical approach

The socio-technical approach aims to produce work systems that are both technically efficient and appropriate to the social systems with which they interact, leading to high job satisfaction. As in the action-oriented view of systems, organizations are viewed as the products, actions and interactions of people who pursue purposes of their own. People are the actors.

We shall not discuss these variants further and instead will explain the systems approach as applied to business systems and information systems.

Organizations viewed as systems

When viewing organizations as systems, people should look at the organization as a whole, as an open system. They should be aware of the environment and of its possible changes such as reorganization, strategy and policy changes arising from external factors. Understanding an organization is a complex task.

Business systems and ISs are typical subsystems of an organization and so may be similarly open. In them an interface is usually a channel through which flow appropriate resources, data, products, energy, tools, people, messages and information. The boundary of an IS may be difficult to identify and usually does not correspond to a physical boundary. Each subsystem is usually part of much larger systems, e.g. part of an IS is a subsystem of an invoicing system which is part of a financial system which itself is part of a business. For business systems and ISs to be successful the developers need to understand the larger systems with which they will interact.

The organization is thus viewed as systems which transform inputs – people, money, materials, other resources and information – into outputs – goods, products, services, information and knowledge. It does this with suitable internal regulation controlled by information. A business needs to control both itself and its information and an information system helps to provide that control. Thus each piece of information that is generated and received should be relevant to some purpose and be capable of affecting a decision or action. Information has value and hence can affect an organization's profitability.

The systems approach may be used in situations that are soft and not well defined and with no clear method of solution. Resolving such problems requires multi-disciplinary teams with a variety of expertise – not all computer-oriented. People have differing views of all the factors, features and aspects, so part of the problem is how to bring all the appropriate people together to discuss and hopefully agree the issues and methods of solution. People should not assume that every business problem needs an IT-based solution and should appreciate that whatever solution is chosen it could cause changes to structures, procedures, attitudes and environments. The organization is viewed as behaving and taking actions to adapt in order to fulfil its needs, aims, goals and objectives. So that is what should guide the selection and specification of its business processes and its ISs. The systems way of thinking should not lead to stovepiped applications and processes.

Planning approach

A Planning approach stresses the planning involved in developing business systems and ISs. This counteracts any tendency to piecemeal implementation and takes an organization-wide view. Top management involvement and support are vital to ensure good planning so that management needs and the organization's objectives are met directly by the business and information systems.

The planning approach includes strategic planning as explained in Chapter 3, concerned with finding out, assessing and documenting the organizational strategic objectives, and their consequences at more detailed levels in order to produce not just a business plan, but business system strategic plans, ISs strategic plans and tactical plans for each business system and IS. These lead to project plans. Such planning will not lead to an IS for each business function since the plans should show that the various business systems and ISs together cover the many business functions.

Each business system project and each IS project should be as cost-effective as other projects – they bid in the same way as other projects in internal competition for management support, decisions and resources. Hence people develop the strategy, plans and tactics for each system, avoiding the waste which occurs when extensive development has been done without planning and is found to be useless.

Independence of the business plans from computer applications and data structures means that, in theory, organizational strategy and plans can change without corresponding reprogramming or restructuring of databases. In practice, however, this has generally not been achieved.

Information architecture approach

The aim of an information architecture approach is to represent what goes on in an enterprise, e.g. its business, its systems, its techniques and its products, in several independent layers for ease of understanding and future evolution.

Motivation for information architecture

Information systems tend to be locked in to an enterprise's organizational structure, giving stovepiped development, and a large amount of management effort is required to resolve inconsistencies. An enterprise is faced with complex components in a fast changing environment and these cannot be synchronized among themselves because the enterprise *does not have the necessary control.* An information architecture can provide an enterprise with the ability to manage the consequences of the rapidly changing environment.

What is an information architecture

Information architecture is an approach to finding out the information requirements for an enterprise. It tries to give a framework for defining a high-level picture of a desired future state and identifying how the current systems should move towards it. It gives a collection of principles, components, processes and building blocks which together should give a complete information infrastructure to meet the information needs of an enterprise

Information architecture concept

The concept of information architecture is that when change occurs on one layer the other layers are isolated from the need to change as a result. There should be a measure of functional cohesion between them, but each can evolve iteratively and each layer can be built up simultaneously. Security aspects of information systems run throughout the four layers. An architecture (business, systems, technical or product) created for a specific business area is known as an **occurrence**.

An information architecture example

An example of information architecture consists of four layers, each of which has a separate purpose. They are: business architecture; systems architecture; technical architecture; and product architecture.

Business architecture

Business architecture is a model of business functionality and information requirements. It is a framework of statements that are stable over time, for example business principles, and establishes a clear understanding of the nature of the enterprise and its main objectives and activities. It provides a top-level framework within which information systems, organizational units and other kinds of system can be placed in context with their interrelationships clearly understood.

Systems architecture

Systems architecture is strategic. It indicates the ISs required to support the business and results in guidelines, direction and blueprints of desired future business states. It indicates components, component–component interfaces and component–environment interfaces. It is a major input to project planning and project commencement. The goals are investment planning, project definition and resource efficiency.

Technical architecture

Technical architecture gives a classification of information processing activity – as transactional, reference, management reporting or office environments. This indicates product-independent building blocks for each kind of system and includes design principles which can be applied to achieve certain goals, flexibility, distributability and reconfigurability.

Product architecture

Product architecture gives a set of products and software components to implement the technical architecture which is then used by projects in the building of information systems. It considers aspects such as horizontal integration across multiple platforms and the consistency of user interfaces.

Data analysis approach

A data analysis approach concentrates on data types and structures. It assumes these to be more stable than the continually evolving processes and operations.

The original hidden agenda was the availability of database management systems after the mid 1970s. The emphasis fell on developing a data model, usually an EAR model, as diagrams and text that represented the main features of an overall specification of the data requirements. This was independent of rules of any particular hardware or software packages. So neither Anna nor Idris should say 'It must be like that to fit the computer software or hardware'.

The process of transferring an idea of a requirement from Idris's mind to diagrams and text is informal. Idris is usually helped by discussion with colleagues, analysts and designers. Use of EAR modelling techniques grew in the late 1970s and 1980s. The structures were usually expressed as diagrams and text involving entities with attributes and relationships between the entities. Processes were not ignored, they were specified and entity life histories analysed. But at the analysis stage it was not necessarily implied whether a process would be done by people or be programmed. How the Georges or the computers used the various kinds of data, in what combinations in what processes, was analysed. Specifications included system dynamics, such as how often and in what situations the various entities, attributes and relationships were used; and how many of each would occur. All these contributed to understanding the patterns of use. The whole could then be checked for completeness and consistency.

Afterwards the team were able to develop a data model matching hardware and software constraints such as a chosen DBMS or relational database. Then they could develop a physical database specification aiming for effective performance for the patterns of use. The implemented database would have a variety of application programs to provide users with views corresponding to the actions needed, but integrated by the centrally coordinated consistency and control arrangements. Independence features to allow for easy changes of processes and entity life histories in the future without reprogramming are important.

Some proprietary ISD methods and products have merged data analysis methods with structured techniques, combining features of this approach with a variant of the structured approach.

Prototyping approach

The main features of prototyping were derived from engineering practices. Prototypes were developed for demonstration, experiments, trials and testing and used to get future users' comments. Such comments provide feedback to modify the specification and design giving the advantages of a gradual and interleaved development of specification, design and trial use. Prototyping gives David and Peter a feeling for what they are developing and gives the Georges a feeling for what they will be provided with. It makes them feel involved and able to influence the end result.

Prototypes are useful where the problem and solution have parts that are unclear, and in situations where the cost of failure is high. This includes circumstances where software affects the control of other expensive systems and must not have errors.

Prototyping can be applied in two ways. One is to develop a discardable prototype that is not intended to be part of the final implemented system. Special prototyping software, by which demonstrations can be given and changes easily made, could be used but the final product might not run efficiently or have the right facilities for a production system. The other way is to develop a product that is not discarded but intended to evolve into the final system. Good analysts and programmers usually excel at this evolution.

These two ways can be combined, starting with the first alternative then reprogramming what is thus agreed to give a more effective version of the nucleus of the final system, and using that to build the final product. Prototypes are not usually built as a matter of course in software engineering but can provide benefits although sometimes the traditional contractual relationship between customer and supplier may become more complex and need careful drafting. This is especially so where the customer's staff (i.e. the users) are contributing to the supplier's system validation.

Prototyping is also seen as a means of achieving rapid application development.

Product set approach

A product set approach is where a company drives its IT strategy by putting in a set of products, e.g. software products bought off the shelf. To a degree, some suppliers try to produce a set of software and hardware products to meet almost every need. The supplier develops a software package aiming for many sales. Organizations buy it to reduce development work since a package approach should be cheaper than corresponding individual development by each enterprise.

A package may have facilities to customize it. For example it may have parameters that the installer or user can set in order to tailor the software to particular needs. The tailoring may be sophisticated, with many optional facilities and features and there could even be a special language for it. Development and programming of the package then becomes a task only achievable by a team of specialists. A package ought to be reliable and well documented so that users do not need to seek help although they want the supplier to stay in business just in case the need arises.

The supplier also wants to continue in business and therefore continues development of better versions which will be released down the years. The product approach may therefore result in tying an enterprise to a particular supplier and package. Issues of standards can arise in order to allow collections of packages to be integrated. On the other hand, some packages may be completely incompatible and difficult to integrate later.

Participative approach

A participative approach aims to get all the right people involved and committed, and hence ensure that the right products are produced. It may be combined with other approaches.

In the past many managers and users of computer-based systems felt resentment at systems analysts, who were seen as expert technically but as not listening at a human behavioural level. Systems analysts were seen as driving each IS development – separately from the users and managers' viewpoints. To avoid this, the participative approach requires that Gwen, Graham and George are involved and participate at each step that is relevant to their own work and responsibilities. Mutual trust and cooperation then grow as a result. With better communication between them and with Anna and David, they should relate happily to the developed new business processes and the changed ISs. Participation should prevent those situations where systems fail because of human problems, even though the features are technically correct. It should avoid the problem of people fearing computers, they should instead find the equipment simple to use, consistent and flexible. Human–computer interfaces and satisfaction should improve with the resulting feeling of ownership meaning that people will not try to beat the system, sabotage it, cause it to lose things or blame it for delays and failures. This all contributes to job satisfaction.

Participation should be consultative and representative in order to aim for a consensus acceptable to all.

One possible problem is that fragmentation of user groups can occur. The process may be manipulated through a biased selection of participants or by telling staff to participate in a certain way or suffer the consequences. Specialists may feel resentment as their skilled work is being undertaken by unskilled people. Managers and other staff may also feel resentment as what they consider to be their real job is being hampered by demands to participate in the development of new business processes or computer systems. Developments and provisions of improved business systems and ISs will be delayed. Making quick decisions becomes more difficult, depending on the number of staff involved.

Automated tools and software engineering approach

An automated tools approach was initially aimed at semi-automating program construction. Nowadays it aims to automate as much as possible, including documentation during analysis and design. It also gives higher productivity and more nearly correct products through the semi-automated checking of completeness and consistency. Different proprietary products combine in different ways software engineering, formal methods of specifying requirements and implementation coding, structured techniques, and data analysis as explained below.

Software-engineering approach

The need for software engineering (SE) originated from the recognition of increasing program complexity, the need for fewer software errors and growing software development backlog and maintenance problems. Better methods of producing software were needed so that the developer could get more code correct at the first attempt, and be better at coding complex cases with tens of thousands of lines of code. It was considered that engineering methods should be used with special computer software being developed to aid and semi-automate the development of IT-based ISs. Languages with mathematically sound features should be used at all steps of converting requirements into IT-based systems.

Software engineering implies applying the principles of good engineering practice and its management to software development. Validation and verification need to be applied to all of the technical actions of software development. Good notation and facilities are required to describe, represent and handle the details of requirements, design and implementation during all the various actions of an IS development. This can be assisted by computer-based tools but these take many people many years to develop, may be complex to learn to use and need to achieve enough sales to recoup the outlay.

The problems include the difficulties of languages, how to represent models and specifications and the difficulties of specifying rules for translating from possibly soft specifications into hard program code. The objectives of SE include improving program design and correctness. This includes making the correctness of the translation and of the resultant program partly provable, based on mathematical theorems, and leads to the need for mathematical constructs that cause many people difficulty. Software engineering has not yet evolved sufficiently to handle easily and well the semantics of requirements.

Table 7.6 gives features of CASE tools. **CASE** means Computer Aided Software Engineering, and is a software package that helps the creation of program code starting from some high-level specification..

- Language-sensitive editors, operating systems and checking systems are provided.
- Easier coding, editing, testing, debugging is an aim.
- Semi-automatic assembly of lowest level box codings into structures that match the structure of the higher boxes.
- Higher levels of specification and decomposition are formulated in ways that are codable later – i.e. the structures of the upper boxes translate into corresponding program code and data structures.
- They assume that users' requirements can be so structured and specified.
- They concentrate on software and its production, i.e. the technically complex part, not the whole of IS development, provision and use.
- Some commercially available (but complex and expensive) tools can hold details of: business planning, analysis, design and software construction.

TABLE 7.6
Features of CASE tools

Most CASE tools are one of a kind, for example specific to a proprietary ISD method. These are known as methods workbenches and they semi-automate the creation of program code. They usually lack facilities for computerized completeness and consistency checking of the features of specifications and of program code.

Reverse engineering means translating one level of abstraction (such as pre-existing programmed code) back into a higher level (such as a specification of the requirements that it satisfies). Then the specification could be changed and the corresponding new code generated. This has many technical and semantic difficulties. Most tools do not provide it.

Some proprietary ISD tools have been developed further into integrated programming support environments that aim to provide total coverage of what is needed by software developers. This may include allowing different development styles, having project and program management tools and handling documentation production all in an integrated way. Table 7.7 shows some of the issues.

- Automated components are expensive to develop because they need so many features.
- Choices about manual components are needed – how to balance between which components to automate in the tool and which remain for the analyst/implementor to do manually.
- In the next few years integration of products for CASE and IPSEs will be a continuing problem and a potentially large market opportunity.
- Current tools are oriented to single programmer use, not concurrent use by teams.
- Current tools are incompatible. They cannot be merged, and once a project has been started using a particular tool it is impossible to change to another tool. Occasionally suppliers of such tools drop out.

TABLE 7.7
Some issues about CASE tools

Formal methods approach

In formal methods, **formal** means expressed mathematically, using mathematical sets, properties, rules and notations. The resultant specifications may be unreadable by non-specialists whereupon user participation is difficult and people become alienated. However, high quality and productivity can be achieved from expressing what is required completely and formally so that semi-automated translation into the corresponding design and code is highly productive. The ability to provide partial proof of the correctness of the translation and code, as a result of using only mathematically sound procedures and processes with the correct properties, saves a lot of work.

However some aspects of requirements cannot yet be handled in this way, and many aspects of ISs cannot either. Formal methods can only deal with algorithmic processes.

In principle, formal methods should be more valuable for large complex systems – too large for one person or team to know fully. Where the whole is regarded as a collection of parts that are essentially independent, each part may be discussed and specified separately. If each part, including its interfaces to other parts, is specified formally, then hopefully formal methods and appropriate automated tools can ensure the successful integration of the whole.

What can be automated

Many software development tasks are repetitive and rule-based, implying a possible candidate for automation. However, opportunities for this are constrained by the need for human decisions, control and checking. This leads to semi-automation as explained below.

Some technology, including the integration of, and interfaces with, earlier computer systems has improved. The high cost of some tools limits what developers do and complexity can become an issue. For example, some people cannot cope with or understand the multiplicity of features, with the result that many are only used by a small fraction of users.

Issues of management understanding and acceptability, such as fitting in with the ISs strategy, may limit what can be automated. People want enough control to be able to change strategies, tactics and processes.

Standards, such as to what extent should tools and interfaces be standardized, may limit automation. Standards are desirable when a part of a system is changed, because then the standard interface specifications and independence features save the need for changes and maintenance to other parts. Standardizing too early, however, can impede subsequent technical improvements, unless a new standard is created.

We distinguish automated from semi-automated. **Semi-automated** means needing human decisions, control and checking, where the software tool helps a person but does not do everything automatically. Some people use the term **automated** where the correct term should be semi-automated.

Table 7.8 shows the gradual automation and semi-automation of software development.

- Compilers for programming languages, linking and loading the code.
- Report program generators.
- Interpretive languages plus operating environment, e.g. BASIC.
- Operating systems, multiprogramming, spooling, filing, version control.
- Database management, shared data, multiple use, security, integrity, query languages, independence features. Systems holding descriptions such as a dictionary, graphics packages.
- Online user environments such as windows, online use, networks, communications, terminals, desktop computer systems and software, laptop systems.

TABLE 7.8
Automation of software development since about 1958

Self check

Please spend some time reviewing what you have read and doing the questions below.

Objectives

After reading this chapter you should be able to:

- participate usefully in discussions about alternative approaches to business processes, developments and ways of tacking the analysis of complex requirements involving many people and many problems;
- explain the advantages and disadvantages of having phases, and of the alternative of interleaving and gradual development;
- explain the main features of the various approaches that we have covered, including forming opinions about their advantages and disadvantages;
- discuss the assumption that everything is describable as processes, data and behaviour so that these are the only things that need be considered and planned for.

Questions

7.1 Which approaches aim to have Idris and Anna create representations of requirements in forms that Idris or other staff can understand, so they can check and comment on them?

7.2 Explain in one sentence and give examples of: hard problems, soft problems, hard approaches and methods, soft approaches and methods, bounded and unbounded approaches.

7.3 Suppose a manager said 'The issues of IS development, maintenance and use are made extra complicated by **soft** aspects – human factors and uncertainty'. Explain at least six kinds of such issues, perhaps based on your experiences and your organization.

7.4 Explain the differences between a hard and a soft definition of the term **information system**, and of the term **ISD method**.

7.5 In a **prototyping approach**, Anna and David develop a

prototype and improve it in the light of comments from George and Graham. In a **waterfall approach** Gwen insists that Mark arranges a series of separate stages and Anna must finish each stage before starting the next, giving well-defined milestones for project control. Where is each of these two approaches on the hard–soft spectrum?

7.6 In the examples of process, data and behaviour models in earlier chapters we assumed that a person such as Idris specified what was required and we showed how a diagram or text could represent it. What soft aspect does this omit? Do Anna's generalizations in Chapter 5 cover this omission? Is there an underlying assumption, and if so what is it? Or what should be done?

7.7 Explain the connotations of the term logical.

7.8 Traditional structured analysis recommended that four models should be developed. What were the reasons? Are the reasons still appropriate? Are the models still appropriate in suitable situations?

7.9 Summarize the underlying assumptions of conceptual data models as in the data analysis approach, and the main consequences.

8 Business and information systems principles

To aid understanding and communication, Idris, Anna and others form ideas such as models, diagrams and descriptions. These involve abstractions, generalizations and rules. They also have some underlying principles about their methods of working, for example how a specialist helps a client to solve a problem. They make assumptions about George and his colleagues and about how they will use the systems, tools and facilities available to them.

So we need to explain to you some principles underlying such abstractions and methods of working. We begin with some points about people's behaviour and actions, and widen these to other actors. These points are fundamental to the way people think of and work with the many physical and mental concepts that form the basis of business systems and ISs, and which we explain next. Later we deal with problem handling, how clients get help from specialists and make some generalizations about the scope of ISs and ISs as tools and systems, illustrating ways that help and ways in which things may go wrong. From a managerial and technical viewpoint the various models used and actions taken during the provision of an IS need to have certain properties both to satisfy human issues and to yield satisfactory systems.

People can act

People vary in their concern as to how their actions and behaviour are seen and interpreted by others. Some people, **concerned with impact**, choose actions that they hope will have a desirable impact on certain others to whom an action may be expected or unexpected, and seem reasonable or unreasonable. Other people may have different views. An action, and the way it is done, may to a greater or lesser extent fit the **culture** and expectations of a group or organization. Some people try to conform, keep a low profile and do as they think others want or expect them to.

People's needs

Sometimes a person's actions are aimed towards a reward, such as a payment, happiness or some goal or purpose. People's goals range from basic needs to the altruistic: basic physiological needs – breathing, food, drink, warmth, sleep, comfort; safety needs – the artefacts and environment for life; belonging needs – love, companionship, partners, groups with similar interests; esteem needs – recognition, status, respect of others; and self-actuation needs – personal development, achievement of potential.

How well a person performs an action can depend on training, education, practice, experience and knowledge.

An action need not be done by a person – it could occur just by the passage of time, or be done by equipment, an animal or a system. Hence some people use the term actor, being wider than person. An actor's actions may be triggered by receipt of information, a thought, the result of a process, or the occurrence of a particular time, event or situation. In some instances below, the term **actor** may encompass an information system or a business system.

Actors need ways of communicating effectively to others in order to cooperate, to achieve their needs and to guide others' actions. Experiences may be difficult to communicate. ISs can receive and hold representations of a part of the real world, create appropriate information about it and send it to other actors in the form of messages about situations, plans and actions. Computer-based and automatic systems follow rules and processes that are ultimately algorithmic, but may appear to hold and use knowledge appropriately. This permits the wide accumulation and selective use of collective knowledge and many individual experiences in ways that were not feasible with any previous technology or with face-to-face communication. Actors can exploit information.

Physical and mental basic concepts

People assume that a physical universe exists, has existed in the past and will continue to exist, and that a selected part of it is currently relevant to some issue. Each person has a mental image, but no one really knows if different people's mental images are the same. Things that exist in the universe can be represented both in a mental image and by other real objects, as descriptions or as information transmitted in the form of communications.

Forming a concept

Forming concepts or ideas is a way that people try to understand the world. A concept is something conceived, a general notion formed, initially in someone's mind. The process usually involves intellectual action involving memory and receiving information through the senses. A thought can be discussed with others and gradually refined. A definition, an explanation of something or a plan may emerge. With other people's contributions a concept may become more easily explained and recorded, and memory aids may be added. If the concept is widely accepted examples will abound. People will learn to apply the concept in routine situations and perhaps in new ones. Some will also analyse it and synthesize it with associated concepts. Richer concepts give increased ability to discuss the world's complexities. Much of business and information system development involves forming concepts to describe requirements, plans, designs and processes. To be accepted, an idea might need to be presented in an appropriate way, and that might be difficult. Sometimes, in order to communicate something, one needs to take the listener or reader through the same reasoning and sequence as on a previous occasion. Most ideas are relatively minor improvements to something that already exists.

Having an idea does not imply acting on it or communicating it to others. Other people cannot access directly the idea in the person's mind. Brain scans for information retrieval are impossible with current technology! If an **actor** does not communicate an idea to others then the others cannot know of the idea in that actor's mind. An idea may or may not be appropriate as judged by that person or by others. Generally it is not an offence to *think* of a naughty idea or an illegal action. What is illegal is to *commit* the illegal act or to plan to do so.

Abstractions

For effective communication people create abstractions. These give new units of communication such as new terms, abbreviations, phrases, pictures and symbols. When a new idea is created, the tendency in our culture and language is to use an existing word that has a fairly similar meaning. Thus words acquire many meanings – homonyms. When explaining well known things, some people think that using a common word instead of the correct term makes for easier understanding. But most people have learnt many thousands of words and can easily learn more. People educated enough to deal with business can learn the correct terms, and usually prefer them.

Sometimes multiple meanings confuse. A few people create new terms to give a marketable distinction. A new term may become a vogue expression and then be misunderstood by others to whom it has perhaps not been fully explained, leading to it perhaps becoming discredited as its disadvantages become known.

In describing business and information systems and requirements, people use many abstractions, some of which are given in Figure 1.4.

Abstractions involving objects and properties include the following:

- **Existence** – e.g. a physical or abstract entity or an idea exists.
- **Indication** – e.g. indicating which object is of interest by referring to some property that indicates it uniquely within its context. This leads to names and identifiers.
- **Symbol** – a unit of communication, e.g. part of a fact or property that cannot be meaningfully subdivided, such as a word or name.
- **Attribute** and **value (attribute–value pair)** – e.g. a role name and a value such as Date-of-birth and 1 July 1987. Many kinds of attributes are useful. These include: physical properties such as length, time, mass, density, speed, direction; scientific and technical properties; adjectives such as the colour green; measurable quantities; abstract properties such as truthfulness, quality, style, performance, probability; comparisons such as

more, highest, last, numbering, sorting, sequencing; and human, social, arts and educational attributes.

- **Classification** – a relationship that groups all instances of an object into an **object class**, which can then be **named**, e.g. buildings. This is essentially a set builder form, except the property may be not explicitly stated. It leads to entity types.
- **Mapping** – **associations** and **relationships** use a rule of association between sets. The rule usually involves some property such as associating people, their places of birth and their birthdays.
- **Aggregation** – a relationship between an aggregate object class and its components, e.g. an entity type and its attributes or an employee and his/her employee-number, date-of-birth, and telephone-number. The opposite direction is known as **decomposition**, e.g. a process may decompose into subprocesses.
- **Generalization** – the relationship between a generic object class and one of its categories, e.g. person is generic of author, speaker, manager, observer. Each particular person instance may be in many categories. The opposite direction is known as **specialization**, e.g. author is a specialization of person. Alternatively, the generic is sometimes defined so that each individual occurrence must belong to the generic class, and each instance of the generic class belongs to at most one category; e.g. each vehicle is one of a car, motorbike, bus, lorry and so on, and each employee is one of manager, secretary, clerk.

Can represent

Our languages have terms for many kinds of abstractions and representations of real-world experiences and predictions. Technology provides many representations of these in various kinds of equipment. Computer and communications equipment provide transformations from one representation to another.

One's memory may hold not only a representation of past experiences, actions and future plans, but also a representation of the brain's action itself. For example, one may remember the details of when and how one thought of an idea or a possible future action, or what one was thinking about or doing when some event happened such as receiving some news or information.

Memory of past events may seem to fade and perhaps change. Presumably different people have different mental images even of the same experiences, but no one really knows.

Any signal or representation takes a certain amount of time to travel. Even the light from the paper being read takes time to reach the reader's eye, the sound from a person's voice to a receiver's ear and the signal from eye or ear to the brain. The transmission of information always takes some time although usually it is short enough to be ignored.

Strictly speaking within our current understanding of physics, different objects may have different internal clocks, affected slightly by gravitation and relative movement. For the practical purposes of transmitting representations these differences do not matter.

Objects may represent other objects. Toys and models illustrate this. The arrangement of ink on paper represents words and symbols and hence other objects. So does light and sound in reading and speech. So do electronic and magnetic patterns in IT and other equipment. So do photographs and films. Indeed in films and videos consecutive physical frames represent time sequencing.

Knowledge

Knowledge is assured belief, known, usually shared and agreed by a group of people and it may involve abstractions from experience and information. Knowledge is initially formed in a person's mind and the initiator usually communicates it to others, which involves creating a representation.

The knowledge may be of a single instance, such as a straightforward representation of some single past situation, event and/or action – for example a full moon occurred on 15 April 1995. Or it may be some **assertion** covering several occurrences such as Anna's generalizations in Chapter 5.

Knowledge may be about the relevant real world or some fictional or hypothetical situation such as a universe of discourse. The knowledge may be held as a representation in a person's mind, or in a form for communication which can be stored. Knowledge is thus seen as a representation of some past experience or thought about the world or some hypothetical situation. Many individual items of knowledge are usually abstracted into knowledge that is a generalization or abstraction based on experience or observation of several similar objects or situations.

A rule may be not completely correct. It may have unstated exceptions – perhaps because not enough situations have been observed. The rule may be sufficiently near correct to be usefully applicable in several similar situations. The rule may be useful in trying to predict, as in the expected result of a proposed plan and action. The rule may be useful in certain situations – to act more quickly and skilfully, to achieve a desired result or to short-cut details.

People may make similar but different assertions, e.g. during proposals about a business process. Conceptual models ought to allow representation of the knowledge of who made which assertion and when. In principle, every piece of information or knowledge is an assertion created by a particular **actor** at a particular time, and the association back to the originator and the circumstances might be useful occasionally. Few information systems allow the systematic storage and processing of data about the origination of information and knowledge. It is often not feasible and usually not worthwhile, although some systems keep it for auditing and backtracking.

Different **actors**, or the same actor at different times, may make contradictory assertions, even about specifying business requirements. Few systems for handling such specifications have facilities for multiple contradictory assertions to be held systematically and resolved later.

Wisdom means not only having knowledge, but making

appropriate use of it in situations that need judgement and perhaps speculation. Wisdom implies more than routine ability.

Universe

Everyone has in their mind an idea of the universe, with greater detail about the parts they have experienced. Part of the universe may represent something about some other part, or the state of some other part at some earlier time, or a plan.

Scientists generally agree on various laws that are general rules about the universe, or part of it under certain simplifying realistic assumptions. Often such rules can be used and applied to explain collections of observations, and to make predictions. Many computer systems have various such rules programmed for users to apply in their work. Representing such rules and knowledge in computer systems is useful where there is widespread agreement on their applicability. Otherwise users may disagree over soft issues such as the validity and interpretation of predictions.

People's views of the validity of information obtained from an IS are tempered by their personal experiences, their interpretation of what they have heard from other sources and their assessment of those sources. For example, most people expect a bus or train to run roughly to the timetable, being information received from an information system, but would be surprised if it ran exactly to time.

Time

Times associated with an abstraction

In handling abstractions some people have difficulties over the treatment of time. You may find it helpful to distinguish the kinds of **time** in the manner shown in Table 8.1.

Where a system handles a representation of an object, there are many associated times:

- The instant a system was implemented, e.g. the start of the system's ability to hold a representation of something or do a process.
- A real object's duration, e.g. the period during which a particular object or association existed or will exist. Here object may be anything, including processes and actions; and existed may mean occurred or took place. Each differing assertion or opinion about something is a separate object here.
- The instant when the corresponding relevant modelling abstraction was created as a representation, when an actor thought of something.
- The instant when information was created about the object, e.g. a message is passed into an IS or a business system.
- The instant when information about the object is passed out of the system, and received by another actor.
- The instant when it is decided that the knowledge should never be needed again, or not needed after some particular future time, giving a time when stored data about the object can be discarded, and a later time when the stored data about the object is discarded.

TABLE 8.1
Times that may be associated with an object

Actions have times associated with them. Generally an activity may have a planned interval such as a week, with its start and finish dates and events; and corresponding actual dates recorded when it takes place. The action itself may take far less than the interval period to complete, allowing for interruptions and breaks.

Computer held data has associated times such as the times when it was transferred from one area to another or when some other operation was performed – such as being transmitted, printed, archived, retrieved, copied, deleted or recovered. Where change does not result in a new version, or where only the current situation is represented, times are associated with when it was revised. Sometimes for simplicity, a period of time is modelled as the instant of its completion.

Several times may be chained. At the moment that to you is 'now' you are reading this sentence. You may now recall a time such as at school when you were told of some historical event of an even earlier time. This chains three time instances or periods. Similarly, for imagining and planning some future situation, several times may arise including the interval when the planning is being thought out and the imagined future times of various future events.

Problems arise in simple systems and models where the sequence of actions and events in the model is not the same as in reality. For example, with postal delays information can reach a person or system in a different sequence from that in which it originated. A customer could send a payment for a telephoned order before that order has been internally created and represented in an organization's IS, or an insurance claim may be received before the premium. Systems need ways to cope with this and to distinguish attempted fraud from genuine situations.

Can only access things currently available

People can only access things that exist at the time of the access, and where the person has an available means of access, such as a communication channel for receiving the information. Access is controlled by privacy principles, security mechanisms and integrity.

Privacy is a moral right of individuals and organizations that includes ensuring that certain information should not be disclosed to the unauthorized or misused. Information made available for one purpose should not be used for a different one. The individual or organization may determine what is disclosed to whom, when and for what purpose. This implies a decision to be made at the time of each request for information – whether to supply it or not. ISs need such facilities. The law may be very similar to this moral right but vary from it in detail, and from one country to another, so that relying solely on the law is not satisfactory. **Security** is provided by mechanisms, features and processes that help to ensure privacy by preventing unauthorized access to, use of or disclosure of information, knowledge, data, processes and resources. These include keys and locks, secret personal identifiers and passwords, authorization and validation procedures, and shredding documents.

Integrity implies that all processes and information flows should match the universe of discourse correctly, and be consistent. If the processes needed to yield the correct information cannot be completed, then to ensure integrity the IS should say so, and not give out-of-date or possibly wrong information.

Access to information that was created in the past implies some form of storage memory. Where people recall something from memory they must have stored some mental image of it from the time when information about it was first received (modified since then by any subsequent new information relating to it). Similarly when information from a system is required, the relevant data must have been stored since the moment when it was first created. The data might be held in many different representations during the period, whether in IT-based systems or not.

Can change

Everything can change with time. At different times a person might have many different mental images of an object, as it was originally or as it might become, and also the object itself might change with time. Computer systems themselves also change gradually – with improvements being continually added.

Can select

People can select real-world objects, including information, according to some criterion, such as whether or not each object is relevant to some purpose. In practice they select a **universe of discourse** and then select objects within that context. The selection may be as actual reality; or may be as envisaged under some plan, assumption, proposal or hypothesis; or a combination. This implies an ability to distinguish and to indicate objects and representations of objects.

The criterion used to select what is relevant is arbitrary but has to be limiting. For example two or more objects can be associated together to form a new association. This abstract association is another object. The number of ways that further such associations can be created may grow to a very large number or be without limit. So in practice each person limits the selection of those that they consider as relevant by including only the more limited number that satisfy a particular criterion. Hence they never have infinite numbers of actual objects.

Similarly a computer system has a limited, though maybe very large, number of locations that can store data, i.e. it has a finite number of possible states. So the number of objects about which it can store facts or knowledge is finite, and the design of a computer-based information system has to include a criterion that limits the number of objects in the real world that it represents. There has to be some way that limits the number of ways in which objects can be associated to create distinguished further new objects.

In practice the selection criterion may limit the number of objects to a number that corresponds to the user's needs. The time taken to create data, communication channel capacity, resources available and cost-effectiveness will each impose a limit.

In discussions leading to design decisions, different people may suggest different boundaries for what is or is not included. Eventually some selection criteria are chosen, though the system may be implemented in a way that allows expansion later. People may differ in their opinions of what may or may not seem reasonable.

Another factor affecting selection criteria arises from the nature of computer storage. There are several kinds of storage ranging from very fast access which is expensive and so of limited size, mass storage on-line which although slower is cheaper and therefore available in large capacity, and off-line bulk storage which is useful for archiving and occasions when access measured in perhaps tens of minutes is acceptable. For economy reasons, data should be deleted if unlikely to be required again. It is not feasible to store everything for ever, although becoming more so as technology evolves. In principle, criteria are required for discarding data but in practice most people are somewhat haphazard, particularly where the long-term storage costs are small or possibly because they just do not know the real cost of storage.

Selection is done at the planning stage and there is the inevitable problem of deciding how much time and resources to devote to it. Enough needs to be done to avoid later problems as prevention is far better than cure. However, as an organization's activities proceed, there will be many possible alternatives of which only one actually happens, although knowledge of hypothetical alternatives is needed to sensibly answer what-if questions. This can lead to an enormous planning load and careful selection and judgement are needed to strike a realistic balance. Fortunately, specialists gradually develop a feel for such judgement from experience.

As technology has developed it has become advantageous to simulate and evaluate alternatives using an IT-based IS in the planning stage and thus pressures have grown for ISs with facilities to simulate and evaluate alternatives and help selection. For example, the rules of stock control, production planning and scheduling, and transport and other mathematical optimisations have long since been programmed. These principles of planning, evaluating alternatives and selecting apply to the development of the business, including its strategy, tactics, products and services; and also to the development and provision of its ISs.

Communicating

People need to **communicate** for several reasons: to convey commands, information, education, skills, knowledge and wisdom to others so they can be in a position to act appropriately. By discussion people develop ideas, concepts and plans, and get feedback and evaluation of past situations and actions. As part of a long-term process they pass knowledge on as education and preserve knowledge. Human desires motivate social interaction, establish and maintain human relationships and indicate the desirable kinds of communication.

Actors verify agreement of the meaning of the language and symbols used and establish a communication scheme within which it is possible to attempt to communicate some desired deeper meaning. At a surface level they establish, maintain or break contact and generally control the deeper communication – including sequencing, structure, timing and interruptions.

Effective communication may involve frequent interaction and feedback from listener to speaker or receiver to sender. Difficulties arise in a situation where continual fast feedback is impossible, for example where each message has to be in writing without any other contact between the parties. While the sender is creating the words, the receiver cannot interrupt for clarification or amendment. The receiver may become frustrated because the message from the sender contains too much or too little detail, explanation or justification. The sender has to decide on style, form, language and sequence and these may not be appropriate for the receiver. The sender may be frustrated and uncertain what to say, e.g. what words to use, through lack of knowledge of the receiver's culture and hence of what style would be most acceptable. Similarly, some communication may need to be slow for its effectiveness.

Where there are many receivers, the sender has to create a method of broadcasting such as a document, notice, timetable, directory or report. The readers have varying prior knowledge of the context and therefore might become frustrated in different ways by the amount of detail or seeming lack of it. A reader may find the content does not include the information required in a form that can be found and used for the reader's purpose.

Information systems, regarded as senders and receivers of messages to and from users, can also experience the above difficulties. The style and skeleton of each communication has to be inbuilt in advance, being programmed at the time the IS is developed or selected from preprogrammed alternatives either at the time of installation or at the time of use. Many difficulties thus arise, sometimes giving misunderstandings.

Problem handling

How a specialist helps a person or an organization, and how a system helps a client, customer or user to solve problems, have some common principles which we explain gradually below. Here are some examples of getting help with a problem.

- How an IS helps a user involves the ways they each interact, and the ways that together they achieve solutions to some business problems.
- An IS may be viewed as a tool shared between many people as its users, clients and customers. Each interacts with it – providing information to it and receiving information from it. Each person may have different objectives and purposes. Various people may have different problems and need appropriate help.
- External clients want enterprises to provide solutions to their problems as products and services, such as tools and expertise. Suppliers may want help with logistics problems.
- Within an enterprise a particular business system may be providing others such as customers with products and services, and in some sense solving their problems.
- Managers may need improvements to business systems or ISs to cater for current or expected future problems.

All these kinds of situations have similar principles concerning the ways a client gets help from a specialist. The specialist may solve the client's problem, or provide a tool or system that the client uses for future similar problems. We gradually explain the underlying roles, actions and sequencing. The tool may be an IS or a business system or an improvement to such. A system may play the role of the specialist. The client with a problem may be a user of an IS, a manager, the whole enterprise or an external client or customer.

Problems are often nested or chained. Claire is a client wanting something from George. George needs an IS. Mark arranges for Anna and Idris to help with the analysis of George's problem, for David to develop the IS facilities and for Peter to provide them. George needs help with problems using the IS and so gets help from Isobel. George has other problems and obtains products and services from other business systems within the enterprise. George combines all of these to solve Claire's problem. Gwen and Graham have problems managing the whole and they want help improving it.

Methods of tackling a problem

In order to describe the various roles and actions involved in a typical complex case, we gradually build up the whole from simpler situations. For clarity we use singular terms in our descriptions such as problem, client, specialist, user, information system and action, which should generally be interpreted as including corresponding plurals and even consultants or organizations.

Specialist helps client with recognized solvable problem

Suppose a client has a solvable problem and is to get help from a specialist to solve it. We take **Claire** as the client, customer, or someone in a part of the organization with a problem, or even as representing the whole organization with the problem of needing improvements to itself. **Sophie** is the specialist providing help and may represent a whole organization, or a business system or IS within it, or a person such as Anna, David, Peter or Isobel, or a consultant, or a subcontractor.

First assume that Claire already recognizes the problem and understands it well in her mind. As a simple example, think of the client as having a one-off requirement for a product, a service, expert advice, knowledge or information, and of the specialist as a provider who knows the solution. With the problem recognized, their actions and roles may then be seen from Table 8.2, ignoring various aspects discussed later.

In this and later similar diagrams, our convention is that **time sequencing** goes to the right where entries start on the same horizontal level. Otherwise time sequencing goes downwards to the next horizontal line at which an entry starts. So the sequence of the lower

Situation	*Client's role*	*Roles involving both*	*Specialist's role*
1 A problem exists.	2 The client, C, recognises the problem. C describes it, e.g. writes it down; or knows that he/she could describe it. C knows that a specialist, S, exists.	3 The client, C, hands over the description of the problem, so the specialist, S, understands it. They agree S is to solve it.	4 S does the work to solve the problem. S obtains the answer. Maybe S checks the method of solution and answer.
5 Problem solved. Answer can be made available.	8 C knows that the problem is solved. C knows the answer, and may understand the method of solution.	7 S hands over to C the information that the problem is solved. S may tell C the answer, and may explain the solution to C.	6 S knows that the problem is solved, and knows the answer.
	9 C arranges that the answer is applied to the business.		

TABLE 8.2
Roles of client and specialist for solving a problem

entries in Table 8.2 is 5, 6, 7, 8, 9. We have numbered them here, but in some subsequent tables we have no numbers and rely solely on the layout.

Varying terms of reference

Various cases may arise:

(a) The specialist does the whole job and applies the solution to the problem, which may be part of something wider. Once the client has asked the specialist to do the work, the client only wants to be told it has all been done. Table 8.2 is this simple case. The specialist has to tell the client that the problem has been solved otherwise the client would not know.
(b) The specialist supplies the answer to the client. The client then uses it or applies it in the appropriate wider situation.
(c) The specialist provides the essential core of the solution leaving the client to do a minor part of the work. From the core of the solution the client can create the full answer and apply it to the actual wider situation.
(d) The specialist provides a one-off tool or method that the specialist or client then uses to solve the one current problem. The tool may be such that it can only be applied to the one problem and might not be useful ever again.
(e) The specialist partly trains the client in the required skill and hands over a tool or method so that the client can solve not only the current problem but also similar problems without again needing a similar amount of work from the specialist.
(f) A mixture of these. For example, different parts of the whole problem and solution are treated differently. Or the specialist and client may work together on certain parts with other parts done by one of them without involving the other.

Next we gradually build up to the more general case (e), where the tool may be suitable for later similar problems.

Specialist provides tool for one-off problem

Exercise 8.1

Draw up a table for case (d), where Sophie the specialist produces a tool for Claire the client to use once. If you have difficulty please just read on.

See Table 8.3.

Situation	*Client's role*	*Roles involving both*	*Specialist's role*
1 A problem exists.	2 C recognises the problem and describes it.	3 C hands over the description of the problem, so the specialist understands it. They agree that S will produce a tool for C to apply.	4 S does the work to produce a tool that can be used to solve the problem.
5 A tool exists.		6 S hands over the tool, maybe demonstrating it and training C to use it.	
	7 C receives the tool. C knows how to apply it		
	8 C applies the tool.		
9 Problem solved.	10 C knows that the problem is solved		

TABLE 8.3
Actions for a client with a specialist that provides a tool

In Table 8.3, the specialist does not know whether or not the client applied the tool and solved the problem. Claire should tell Sophie, as an extra step, so that Sophie gets feedback and thanks.

Mixture of cases

Generally the problem situation may require a **mixture of cases**, e.g. the client and specialist together applying the tool or both helping or there may be parts of the problem done each way. We summarize this in Table 8.4.

Exercise 8.2

List some features of the ways that Claire and Sophie talk so as to communicate the required information effectively.

Situation	Client's role	Roles involving both	Specialist's role
1 A problem exists.	2 C recognizes the problem and describes it. C recognizes that there may be similar problems in the future.	3 C hands over the description of the problem, so the specialist understands it. They agree which cases apply to which parts of the whole, e.g. S is to create a tool for a certain part of the whole.	4 S does some work, creating tools and/or methods for appropriate parts.
5 A tool exists.		6 S explains and hands over to C the tools and methods, so C understands how to use them. S and C together apply them to the problem and do the rest of the work to solve the problem.	
7 The problem is solved.	9 C applies the answer as appropriate.	8 Both know that the problem is solved.	
10 Subsequent similar problems.	11 C solves these, building up experience of the tool and the business.	12 C gives feedback to S on the suitability of the whole process, including how good the tools or methods are, and whether the right parts are handled by the tools and methods. Maybe they think some aspects of the whole could be improved, so a new problem, to devise improvements, now exists.	13 S may think of and make improvements to the tool.

TABLE 8.4
Actions where a tool suitable for several problems is provided

In practice **effective communications** between the client and specialist involve a combination of the following.

- Descriptions, each being a representation of part of the required deep meaning. The meaning may be expressed using models and symbols.
- Explanations, e.g. to explain and agree the meaning of a particular symbol or part of a model.
- Continual replies and gestures to confirm understanding, to indicate partial understanding or to ask questions.
- Surface communications to establish appropriate contact and context, to deal with the communication systems used (e.g. telephone, mail, protocols), to interrupt, and so on. There may be several kinds of these.

Mental processes and mental images

In practice Claire and Sophie also have mental processes. For example, when Claire recognizes the problem, she forms an idea of the problem as a mental image in her mind. She then describes this to Sophie, usually orally or with diagrams and Sophie forms her own mental images and begins to think ahead.

Then the above case (a) expands as in Table 8.5. The descriptions are needed for effective communication since, for example, Sophie cannot directly access what is in Claire's mind.

If the client has or expects to have many similar problems, then the specialist may produce a more generalized tool that the client can apply to each such problem when it arises.

Situation	*Client process, senses*	*Client mental state*	*Client process, e.g. writing, speech*	*Client and specialist*	*Specialist process, senses*	*Specialist mental state*	*Specialist process, e.g. writing, speech*	*Specialist action, mental or manual*
1 A problem exists.	2 C recognizes problem.	3 Idea in C's mind of problem.	4 C describes problem.	5 C hands over description of problem.	6 S receives information of problem.	7 Idea in S's mind of problem.		8 S invents idea of doing solution.
						9 Idea in S's mind of doing solution.		10 S does the solution, solves the problem.
11 Problem solved.					12 S recognizes that the problem is solved.	13 Idea in S's mind that the problem is solved	14 S describes that the problem is solved.	
				15 Handover of statement that problem solved.				
	16 C receives information that problem solved.	17 Idea in C's mind that problem known to be solved.						

TABLE 8.5
Actions and mental images for Case (a) where the specialist does the whole

Exercise 8.3

Create a table for the situation where Claire will have many similar problems and Sophie produces a suitable tool.

Table 8.6 gives the solution.

Agree proposal before doing the work

If additionally the specialist is to devise and agree a proposed method of solution before doing the actual work of solving or building the tool, then the following are added at the appropriate stages. Claire and Sophie may have to arrange the budget and other resources, and get management approval, as in Table 8.7.

Situation	*Client's role*	*Client's thinking*	*Roles involving both*	*Specialist's thinking, writing, speech*	*Specialist's role*
1 Partly predictable future.	2 Recognise that many problems are expected to arise.	3 Think out a mental image of the possible problems and of having help from a specialist.	4 Agree a description of a generalization covering all such problems.	5 Think out a method of solution using a general tool, including how C will use it.	6 Develop the general tool.
7 General tool created by S.	10 C understands the tool and how to apply it appropriately to various different kinds of problems.	11 C can think of recognizing appropriate problems and using the tool in the future.	8 S describes the general tool to C, and how to apply it in different problem situations. C is trained.	9 S envisages C using the appropriate methods and tools for future problems.	
12 Later, a problem exists.	13 C recognizes the problem and knows how to select the appropriate method and tool.	14 C can envisage solving it before actually doing so.			
16 That problem is solved.	15 C solves the problem using the correct tools and methods.				

TABLE 8.6
Actions where several problems need a generalized tool

Situation	*Client's role*	*Client's thinking*	*Roles involving both*	*Specialist's thinking, writing, speech*	*Specialist's role*
				1 Think of a method.	2 Devise a method of solving the problem, e.g. a tool, but don't make it yet.
			4 Agree the proposed tool and method.	3 Describe the proposed tool and method.	
				5 Plan the work of making the tool.	6 Do the work.

TABLE 8.7
Actions for agreeing a proposal before doing the work

Examples of other scenarios follow.

- While solving George's current problem Isobel uses the computer for some subprocess or calculation. In principle, George need not know whether Isobel used a computer to do arithmetic, sorting or any other operation.
- Isobel helps George to solve a problem. This short-term view assumes the IS is available but cannot be improved during the time available. George is a client of Isobel's service.
- George uses the computer system itself to get help. Computers are programmed to respond to help requests with text explanations of their facilities, and to give error messages at attempts to do something which is not allowed.
- Peter helps George to solve a problem. In this medium-term view Peter and George will discuss a class of related problems and Peter will provide George with a system or an improvement. Then George will use it to solve actual problems.
- Anna and others help the whole organization to improve its business processes. In this long-term view Anna and managers discuss the organization's strategy and plans, aiming to improve the ways of solving the enterprise's problems.

In all the above any action can be done gradually with increasing refinement of its products. Also generally, any **action can be started** as soon as a first draft of its prerequisite products is available. For example, as soon as Claire has a partial idea of a problem she can start to describe it to Sophie, who may start to imagine the solution.

From here on we shall omit the mental images, the actions of recognizing situations, forming ideas, and describing them for communication, defining who applies a tool, whether the specialist hands back a tool or actually solves the problem, and all repetitions. Without further explanation we also omit how the structures above are extended to deal with several problems, several clients, several specialists, teams and management coordination.

The above essentially applies to the range of problem situations given near the beginning of this section. It also applies to short-term problem handling such as getting help about the facilities of an IS; medium-term problems of improvements to ISs such as a user wanting a computer system with straightforward software for a well-understood routine business application; and longer-term issues such as the complexities of devising new business processes, innovations and improvements. In practice in a large organization all of the above may be happening concurrently.

Scope of information systems

Information exploitation, not just ISs and IT

Much of the information handled by an enterprise is not IT-based. Upper management information such as corporate plans are usually held in people's minds, memos and notes of meetings, and not in an IT system. Very low-level operational information, particularly short-term information such as phone messages and reminders, is not usually handled by IT.

Many reasons justify such current common sense. A lot of planning, strategy and tactics is argued out, discussed and decided in meetings. The issues are so wide-reaching and diverse that IT-based systems could not meaningfully handle the variety of information, thoughts and interactions. Face-to-face meetings provide a social interaction that may help create friendship and trust in ways that cannot be achieved through IT-based information. Some kinds of information cannot be effectively handled by IT. This includes routine enquiries such as progress chasing, giving warnings of delays, asking whether minor changes to agreed plans would be acceptable and seeking the consequences of IT-based problems. The wisdom and knowledge required for certain kinds of situations cannot be modelled and handled in current computers.

In some situations other technologies are far more appropriate than IT-based systems, e.g. telephone, radio, television, newspaper. In some situations it may not be feasible to transmit the required data representing information and knowledge, e.g. for security and privacy reasons, or for technical or cost reasons. Cultural considerations limit what is acceptable. Word-processing and electronic mail can help in passing information as messages and reports, but are currently too limited – not having facilities for processing the meaning.

Information is wider than ISs, IT and computers

Information and knowledge in its totality is wider than ISs, which themselves are wider than IT, which is wider than computer-based information systems, as shown in Figure 8.1.

FIGURE 8.1 Information and ISs are wider than IT and computers.

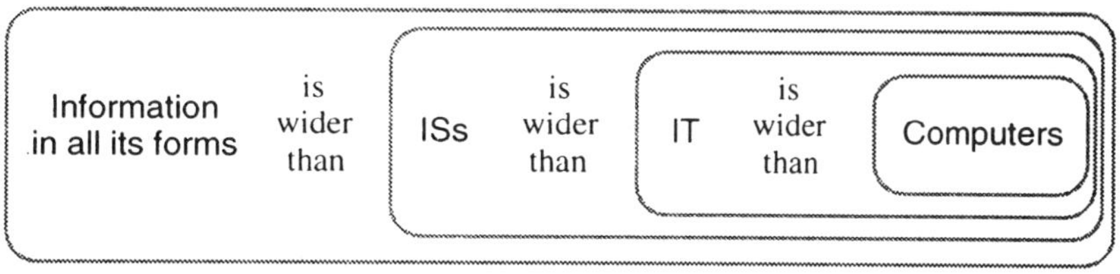

Most proprietary ISD methods assume that an organization's problem has a computer-based solution. This ignores the issues above that are wider than can be conveniently solved by IT. Figure 8.2 shows the failing.

FIGURE 8.2 Don't always assume computers needed.

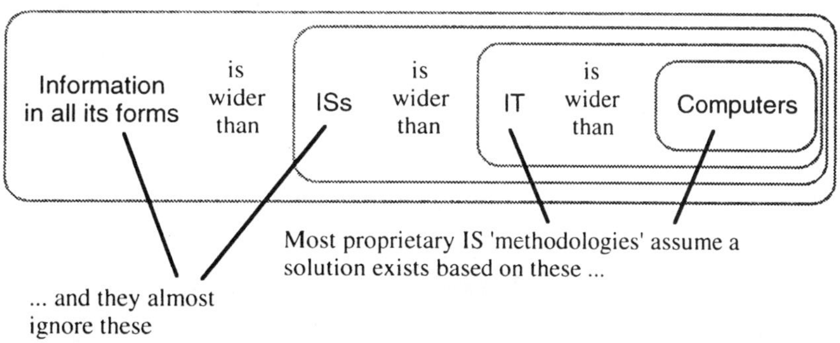

Essentially they assume in a hidden way that the people involved have already broadly identified a problem that is narrow enough to be likely to have an IT-based solution, and that non-IT aspects are relatively unimportant.

Almost all published literature in this field ignores the non-IT aspects of information and its handling. It misses how to deal with and manage information in its totality, and how to manage non-IT based information and its handling.

How getting help may go wrong

Often life is not so simple. People do not have the education and skills to handle everything and do not behave as others expect or hope. They have hidden agendas. They do not trust others, do not believe that others can deliver and cannot cope with complex situations so that they try to manage them by making simplifications and procedures that in fact make things worse. They cannot choose appropriately where the problems are messy and not fully understood.

These behavioural issues often have profound effects on projects which are greater than the effects of computer technology. We give some examples here from real life, but concealing the identities of the people involved.

Case 1

A family shop in the UK Midlands, with husband and wife employing four other staff, had a problem. They thought a computer system would solve it. As clients (C), they consulted a specialist (S) and explained the problem. They agreed a contract. S was to provide a tool. S did provide a software package and an appropriate computer. Then C explained more about the problem and this meant that the facilities of the package had to be changed. This cycle was repeated. S realized that this would not have happened if C had explained the whole problem initially. The clients, C, however, could not form the whole problem in their minds and had no previous significant knowledge of computers. They perhaps did not believe that S could create a package for the whole problem if it were explained fully at the start. It seemed big to them and so they wrongly presumed that it would seem too big to S as well.

The result was that both C and S were dissatisfied. S initially responded to requests for further features by providing them free, then eventually stopped. S felt underpaid. C did not get a good package covering all requirements, so they eventually felt they had not got good value for their money. They were stuck because S refused to help any more, and no other software house could be found to continue or maintain S's package.

Eventually C had to buy a different computer and software from a another supplier who moved into the market as a competitor to S.

Case 2

In another situation the client was a small engineering firm, making custom-designed products each of which typically needed a small amount of design for a particular customer. There are many similar engineering firms in the world. The client wanted a software package for a part of this design work and asked a specialist small consultancy for help. The specialist thought of creating a package that could perhaps be sold to many engineering firms and so developed a far more general package than the client needed. It took longer than expected to develop and the client found that it had features that were unnecessary. For example, using it required many unnecessary keystrokes to select between unwanted options. The client was dissatisfied. The specialist then had to adjust it to try to satisfy the client in order to avoid creating a bad reputation which could have harmed future sales. The specialist thus had to do more work than expected to develop the software.

Case 3

A scientist who could program asked Richard Maddison how to program double-length arithmetic. Richard told him. Two weeks later the client asked Richard about evaluating determinants. At that stage Richard asked why. The scientist said he had six equations in six unknowns to solve. Richard knew there was a standard program for solving such equations. The scientist had wasted two weeks programming a mathematically poor way of solving equations and doing it double length. The two weeks work and all the previous advice was irrelevant and wasted. The lesson is that when asking for help state the problem in its original form and context as it might well have a known method of solution, and do not create some derived problem out of context which might be irrelevant. However, the scientist didn't spot the wider lesson. Four weeks later he contacted Richard again explaining the whole wider problem, of which solving many sets of six equations was only a part. Richard knew of a more general optimization procedure that had been programmed and that essentially catered for and solved the whole original scientific problem. The scientist had wasted six weeks.

Mental, conceptual, logical and physical models

We need to explain certain principles that build on combinations of the above abstractions and lead to building a sequence of models and artefacts that have certain desirable and theoretically provable properties. We have introduced earlier in Chapter 6 some desirable properties concerning knowledge, information, data and representations.

Next, facilities need to be provided with certain other desirable properties which start from assertions made by managers and staff, and with ideas from people like Idris. Eventually these have to be formed into things that staff such as George can use to help the business. So the Georges need better tools, such as improved ISs, and better ways of working, such as better processes.

We introduce **Peter**, who provides the Georges with everything needed – tools, equipment, resources, ISs, procedures, methods and training. We consider Peter's view. He wants whatever he provides to fit optimally with the organization's, and George's, needs and requirements. But Peter, being within the organization, is a part of it and realizes that the overall objective is to optimize the whole, not just his part or what he provides. He incurs costs in creating whatever he provides and to avoid failures and waste these costs must include finding out about what is required. This should include the costs of teams including Anna and others, and the cost of the time of managers and people like Idris. In some organizations certain costs, such as managers' time, are not always allocated and charged to the development of improved business processes and/or ISs, but that is either because the existing accounting systems cannot cope with it or because it would not be worthwhile to do so. It is simpler to regard managers' time as an overhead and save the costs of trying to allocate it more exactly.

Peter is also concerned that the artefacts and procedures he produces fit the needs. But as the whole is so complex, the work is done in various kinds of activities each of which produces products for use in later ones.

The approaches explained earlier discussed how the choice of such activities might be made, and whether they should be in distinct phases or overlapped for the gradual iterative development of the products. Whichever of these is used, there will be a sequence of intermediate products many of which will be representations of the needs or other aspects of the organization. Peter wants the sequence of intermediate products to have the right properties so that the last product of the sequence, the tool and way for George to work, match the requirement.

Therefore you need to understand some principles and properties of the intermediate products in a typical sequence. The principles apply whether Peter will be providing better business processes for the Georges, tools such as improved ISs or a combination of these.

During the development of a business process or an information system, the types of knowledge that exist in the relevant part of the organization are represented in several intermediate forms before the final design and implementation. Some of this knowledge is in the form of abstractions and generalizations about the business, its environment, strategy, products and services. Other knowledge is abstractions and generalizations about what George will do. Some of each of these kinds of knowledge will be represented as data and information occurrences available to George, some will be in his head and some can finally be stored as data within a computer system that he uses.

Figure 8.3 shows a typical sequence of intermediate forms. Each box corresponds to several models, e.g. different people's views of parts of the whole. This is an expanded form of Figures 2.11 (p. 68) and 2.12 (p. 70).

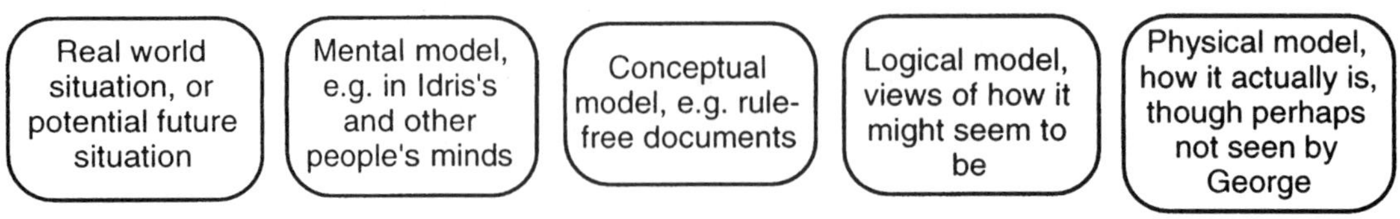

FIGURE 8.3
A simplified sequence of intermediate products.

The real-world-situation box represents the types of processes and knowledge as they actually exist or as they will exist. This not only corresponds to things within the organization but is widened to the relevant part of the real world, including outside organizations. The other boxes represent different *models* of the process and knowledge.

All these play important roles in the creation of new processes or an IS with perhaps databases or spreadsheets.

The stages of analysis and design of a new process or a computer-based information system involve several models, as introduced earlier. In summary, the conceptual model represents those kinds of knowledge about the real world that are relevant to particular processes such as George's. A conceptual data model is used in two ways. It describes knowledge, information and data representing real-world situations so that it can be discussed with other people. And it forms a starting point for the construction of a logical model.

The **logical model** is a detailed representation, based on the conceptual model, and is created by the application of formal modelling techniques and notations. A logical *data* model for a database management software package is commonly known as a schema. Its structure can be described and coded for use in computer systems.

George's view, his manager Graham's view and the administrator's views of the implemented processes and/or systems are also **logical** models. Different views are called local logical models.

The **physical model** takes into account the facilities and constraints of the implementation tools available – e.g. the database management system, the spreadsheet package, library and infrastructure hardware. In the case of a business process it will take into account constraints on how George can work, such as the limitations of telephones for communication. It would imply that certain kinds of knowledge were held on paper in files. The physical model will also include technical design details that need not be known to the Georges or the managers.

In practice there are far more intermediate models. These include the discussions at, and minutes of, meetings about business strategy, objectives, plans, quality and performance. They include the discussions between team members, and the mental abstractions thus formed. They include training George. Within computer systems they include programs and data, and the code produced by compilers and by linking for loading and execution.

Some authors have used different terms from our use of conceptual, logical, and physical.

Peter sees the processes by which the various intermediate models are created from earlier ones as a chain summarized in Figure 8.4.

From Peter's viewpoint, the early representations are soft, indefinite and incomplete and cannot be made complete. But the product to be delivered, be it a new process or an IS, obviously has to be far more definite and complete. So the transformations represented by the lower boxes in Figure 8.4 have to transform the indefinite and incomplete into the definite and complete. Therein lies a central difficulty.

Self check

Please spend a few minutes reviewing what you have read and answering the questions below.

Objectives

After reading this chapter you should be able to:

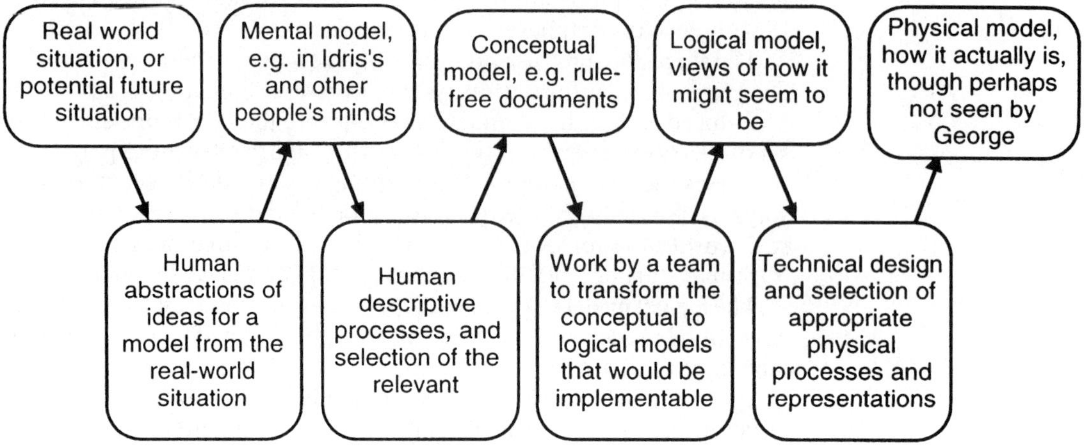

FIGURE 8.4
A chain of processes to produce the various models.

- explain and use where appropriate various physical and mental abstractions, representations and concepts about the universe, time, access, selection, communicating;
- explain and apply general principles of how clients and specialists work together in various situations to solve problems, create tools and systems, and to agree proposals for them;
- explain how information is wider than ISs and IT, and the disadvantage of ISD methods that assume that an organization with a problem must need an IT system or improvement to an IT system;
- appreciate that getting help may go wrong, e.g. if a client or specialist supplier has a hidden objective or if the real problem is not understood and communicated;
- explain the need for and work with various models that gradually translate requirements into systems.

Questions

We have not provided questions that test understanding of this chapter alone. Instead, the following questions are based on your own organization and combine ideas from several chapters. You may do them individually or in a group discussion. We suggest you write down your answers before looking at ours.

8.1 (i) Describe and justify the main business functions of your organization.

(ii) Taking account of your answer to part (i), what are the most important areas of your organization where computer systems and IT are or should be used to provide information for your organization's management, and explain why?

(iii) Does your area of the organization use an IT-supported information system? What organizational functions does or should that information system cover? Give reasons. If your area of the organization does not use an IT-based IS, then say why it does not.

(iv) If major IS or business system developments were needed, which approach or approaches would be appropriate and why?

(v) Suppose your organization as a whole needs changes to business systems and ISs and its managers need specialist help. Draw up a table summarizing the main steps and roles when the client is the whole organization, a major part of it or a manager such as Mark, and the specialist corresponds to the information systems providers who provide a new tool and/or system for others to use.

8.2 (i) Explain the main products or services of your organization. How have these changed in the last ten years, say, and how might they change in the future?

(ii) Imagine how the future needs of your organization might change in some way. Describe briefly the existing arrangements and the likely change.

8.3 Here we examine a possible IS structure using simple analysis methods and diagrams. Think of your organization as a system with a small number of major subsystems. You are presumably familiar with the subsystems that involve your area. Presumably also these subsystems have subsubsystems.

(i) Draw a system map showing your organization subdivided into its major subsystems; and show the subsubsystems of at least one of these. Try to show at least eight subsystems and/or subsubsystems. In a system map, subsystems should be drawn inside the relevant system, and each should be named. Show the main interfaces by making the inner boxes either touch or have a line joining them.

(ii) List the main data items that flow between some subsystems and/or subsubsystems, and for each item of data say which subsystems it flows between. Think of the structure and layout of the answer.

(iii) Draw an information flow diagram showing your area's subsystems and some other areas, and give a name to each of the main information flows between them. Show each system or area as a box, and each flow as a named line with an arrowhead.

(iv) Which of the subsystems and areas are mainly involved with computers or with a communications network?

(v) Describe what broad types of data are input to your area of your organization and your part of its information system, and the data output from it. Perhaps you can draw an input–output diagram for your area of the organization. This should have a named box representing the area, and inputs as named arrowed lines flowing in on the left and outputs similarly on the right.

(vi) How does your area of your organization ensure that data held in a computer system is accurate, up-to-date and consistent?

8.4 (i) List some data items that arc handled within your area and that can be specified precisely in terms of range of allowed values and format. Are some of them identifiers? Are some used as indicators to select relevant occurrences?

(ii) List some data items that can be defined with limited precision, in that their length, format and perhaps structure can vary from case to case, with your area having no control over those variations. For each data item say why it fits here and not in (i) or (iii).

(iii) List some data items that cannot have a standard format and length. Comment briefly as in (ii).

(iv) From your earlier answers list some information and data that mainly flows vertically rather than horizontally.

9 Phases, methods, activities and techniques

Many proprietary ISD methods have somewhat similar phases, sometimes with different names and with different recommendations to developers. We explain these commonly used phases. They have prerequisites and should deliver products that are descriptions of the target system. These system descriptions have various purposes as they are aimed at different audiences.

Each phase has its main activities, its purpose and its products. Proprietary ISD methods generally do not cover all the phases, tending to deal only with the more important ones. Some methods have assumptions about the kind of systems likely to be needed and the probable skills of the developers, and also assume that data will be structured, that single processor computer systems will be used and that time sequencing will not be a problem.

In Chapter 6 completeness and consistency were explained from the view of the processes, data and metalevel rules. In this chapter we explain other aspects as related to methods and techniques. We create a table of completeness and consistency ideas between metalevel object types and system description aspects.

In Chapter 4 we explained points of control. Here we give techniques to analyse and describe them, and more generally to describe real-time systems. Performance measurements and external-value metrics may be viewed as measures of the satisfactoriness and stability of the control mechanisms. To describe the target system needs control flow diagrams, levelling, balancing, process specifications and control specifications which include decision tables and state-transition diagrams. So we explain those together with various other techniques which are widely used.

Phases

Many ISD methods envisage the whole project as done in phases. Although we consider it valuable to do this you should realise that this does not mean that each phase must be done in isolation. As explained in Chapter 7, overlapping phases and allowing activities from one phase to be interleaved with activities of the next can provide useful feedback and reduce errors.

We give our explanation of the features of phases first, then describe the various phases.

Phases common to many ISD methods

Most proprietary ISD methods do not cover all phases and they differ in the terms used. Typical names of phases are (where semicolons separate groups of related phases and/or alternatives): Planning, Business Strategic Planning, Information Systems Strategic Planning, Information Systems Tactical Planning, Information System Project Planning, Feasibility study; Analysis, Understanding requirements; Design, User design, Technical design; Construction, Building, Implementation, Testing; Installation, Training, Deployment, Cutover; Operation, Use, Maintenance; Minor upgrade, Migration, Decommissioning, Retirement.

Features of a phase

As explained in Chapter 4, a phase has **prerequisites**, needed before it can start. It produces **deliverables**. The actions done during the phase are **activities**, tasks and operations. In the phases before construction most deliverables are some form of **system description**. Each phase translates this from one form to another, adding more detail until the whole working system is produced. Usually a phase ends with the delivery of some document or major product.

System descriptions

In approaches and proprietary ISD methods that have phases, the deliverables at the end of each phase have various **purposes**. Some are for project approval and control but most are system descriptions. They are for different **audiences**. If a description is intended for many audiences it may not contain the appropriate amount of detail that each one requires. The descriptions give different **perspectives**, with different underlying **assumptions**, e.g. a functional specification should be hardware and software independent; but a design specification depends on chosen hardware and software. They have different **scope**, covering the existing or the proposed new system.

Expectations about what descriptions are needed for what purposes, what intended audience and about the perspective and scope should be discussed and balanced to make good use of time and resources.

The system descriptions should be in increasing agreement and detail with what is wanted and finally built. Agreement and correctness should be proportional to the total work done at the stage reached.

An initial document will be a crude system description giving an **outline of what is needed**, mainly aimed for management acceptability.

Next there will often be a **specification of the current system**, which will be in broad brush terms because of limited time and resources, and which doesn't fully specify the current system anyway. Its hidden purpose might be to give practice and training to those involved, so they are more likely to get the corresponding descriptions of the new system correct.

A **requirements specification** will *not* attempt to specify all the essential and desirable features of any new system. Many details will be left for later choice – to be made by designer, programmer and installer – because the people involved cannot think the details through.

A **proposed design** may seem to be intended to be complete, but will really be a compromise in order to be manageable. Designers have no way of checking self-consistency and no way of nicely representing actions, processes and procedures that change things dynamically. They cannot ensure that there will be no problems of timing and speed when the system is built.

The corresponding **implemented system** is described by actual coding, programs and data. Often the coding is like a private language invented by the programmer for describing certain rules and operations. The programs and data are unlikely to be correct or to work first time and many minor changes and improvements will be needed. Most of these will be discovered by testing but some might not appear until demonstrations and early use, as other people will expect different things from what the programmer coded. Many details are thought of and designed at this stage. The testing may be incomplete and not fully systematic and so the system may contain undetected bugs needing later correction.

Its **documentation** may be slightly incomplete or incorrect and only a summary of what was programmed and installed. Those involved may have lost interest in completing a tedious task after the system seems to be working. The documentation may be insufficient for future maintainers and developers, who are likely to be different people.

Early phases and their activities

Analysis phase

Analysis activities include gathering information from many sources – interviews, documents, questions and questionnaires. The objective is to perform 'analysis' and to understand and document particular aspects of requirements and systems, such as for a particular area, in sufficient detail for the next activities and within the resources and time planned. It may sound odd to suggest that analysis should involve performing 'analysis', however our experience in recent years is that many tools and techniques that are labelled analysis actually do very little analysis.

In Figure 9.1 no sequencing between the kinds of analysis is implied. They can be done concurrently or sequentially, and incrementally. The various kinds of analysis were explained in Chapter 2 under *Analysis methods and skills* and in Chapter 7 under the various *Approaches*, and are revised in a question at the end of this chapter.

FIGURE 9.1
Kinds of activities in an analysis phase and their interleaving.

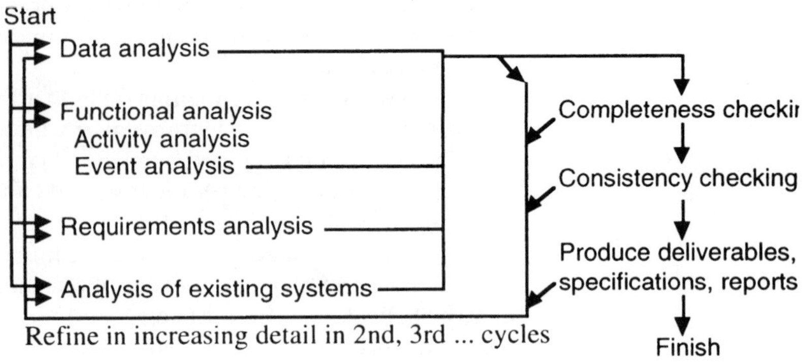

A list of analysis activities and products is given in Table 9.1.

Requirements-oriented analysis activities	*Analysis products*	*Management–oriented analysis activities*
• Data analysis	• Progress and exception report	• Broad requirements analysis
• Functional analysis	• Functional specifications	• Risk analysis
– Activity analysis	• Function charts	• Project approval
– Event analysis	• Conceptual data models	• Contract negotiation
• Requirements analysis	• EAR diagrams	• Proposal preparation
• Analysis of existing systems	• Existence conditions	• Internal project commitments
• Completeness checking	• Information-flow diagrams (and DFDs)	• Preliminary project planning
• Consistency checking		
• Production of reports	• Other data–function mapping models	*Analysis phase end products:*
• Production of functional specifications	• Business function models	• Requirements specification
• Production of management reports	• Requirements report	• Design proposal
• Functional specification preparation	• Functional specification	• Contract
		• Project plan

TABLE 9.1
Possible activities and products of an analysis phase

Many techniques are available but each is capable of creating a representation of only part of an information need or a business process. Many have hidden assumptions (e.g. that the target system will be IT-based, or IT-based and not distributed, or IT-based and using a network, or likely to need a particular kind of design of software or hardware). These assumptions are not widely understood. The interaction of one technique with another is either not well defined or non-existent, e.g. how data stores in a data flow diagram (DFD) relate to entities derived from other techniques. This particular issue is eased by creating the data model first then using its entity names as the basis of data store names.

To use a technique satisfactorily an analyst needs to know the principles supported by the technique, and also where it is incomplete, i.e. the principles that are not supported. The analyst also has to know what knowledge needs to be supplied from the analysis products to the later phases.

Perspectives on analysis problems Throughout the whole development Anna and others need to understand project constraints and features: complexity, size, costs, benefits, resources, timescales, human issues, priorities, urgency and politics.

An analyst needs to understand the **role of analysis** and why the analysis activity is being performed. Different audiences seem to want different things, so the analyst should judge what is required and in how much detail. For example, senior managers should need only a summary whereas developers, consultants and designers need far more detail. Each deliverable has a purpose. Various application problem areas may require different facilities such as office automation or a database and transaction processing. They may want structured data or non-structured data such as free text. They may want fixed or variable formats, regular or ad-hoc reports. The physical design may have to be distributed or be centralized. It may look like a knowledge system or an expert system or a deterministic system.

These aspects may vary depending on how well or ill defined the application problems are, and the abilities of the future users.

Analysis should create understanding and the documentation of requirements to fit the needs of David and Peter in later phases. Each analysis problem needs to be viewed from several perspectives and this fact helps to determine which techniques to use.

Programs use utilities Some techniques start with the hidden assumption that the objective is to create a working application program for an existing computer system. The program will use computer infrastructure facilities such as non-procedural utilities and operating system facilities. The various facilities and the libraries of software differ between computers but the assumption is made that the facilities needed are available. There is a danger that the analysts forget what has been assumed, particularly where several specialists do different parts of the whole development.

The amount of work necessary to create a working application program depends on the quantity of application details that have to be explicitly programmed and to a lesser extent on the number of infrastructure facilities used. As more such facilities are added to computer operating systems, so the amount of work reduces.

A program contains information/ knowledge about:

- declarations, such as types of data and structures;
- transformations, such as what processes are to be done on appropriate data;
- control structures that select which subprocesses to call and execute; e.g. if ... then ... else ... ; case ...;
- surrounding environmental arrangements, such as interfaces between the system of which this program is a part and other systems, and messages across such interfaces which may be part of the input to and output from the program; also passwords, keys and security facilities;
- integrity checks that ensure that the data is valid, that appropriate preconditions are satisfied before a subprocess is executed, and that the results of a subprocess satisfy appropriate postconditions at the finish of the subprocess execution;
- relationships between parts of the system and parts of the program.

What should the analyst supply The analyst is trying to provide the programmer with enough appropriate knowledge about each of the above, having obtained limited information from other sources in completely different forms, and having partly made analysis decisions and perhaps also preliminary design decisions during the analysis work. Both the analyst and programmer want the program to be all of the following.

- Complete, covering every situation that might occur and every situation that might be wanted.
- Consistent, so that stored data and messages are kept consistent under all circumstances.
- Correct, enabling the eventual user, George, to ensure that everything modelled in the IT-based system correctly matches reality, that it changes correctly as reality changes, and that predictions will be appropriate. This means that the business rules and processes must be coded correctly in the programs, data and/or human procedures.

Figure 9.2 poses the question: can the minimum knowledge needed be collected, processed and provided by an analyst?

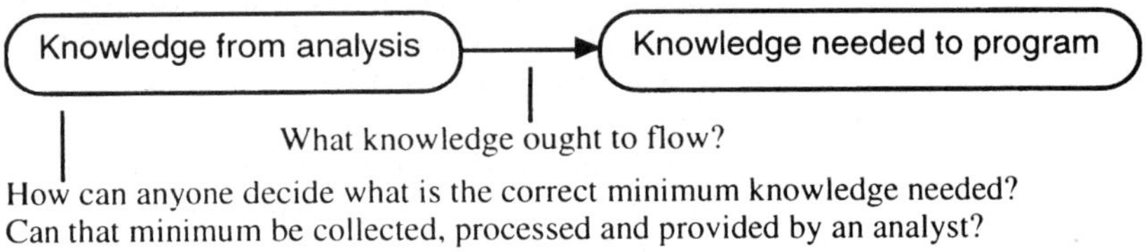

FIGURE 9.2 Can anyone decide the correct minimum knowledge needed? Can it be collected, processed and provided by an analyst?

This leads to: what is the minimum analysis work to provide enough knowledge about the requirements and business processes so that the programmer does not have to make arbitrary guesses where knowledge is missing? What kinds of analysis and what techniques are therefore needed?

Few analysts and programmers think like this although they need to understand how the implementation is done.

Independence issues arise. To what extent should the analyst bear in mind the kind of software and hardware architectures that are to be used for the IT-based parts of the IS to be provided or improved?

Exercise 9.1

Contrast the advantages of analysis being free of implementation constraints with the advantages of an analyst bearing in mind the kind of software and hardware architectures to be used.

We have emphasised the advantages of rule-free analysis in Chapter 2, including the fact that thinking of new business processes is not constrained by existing technology, that it makes it possible for George and Graham, who need not understand all the technical details, to participate, and the many consequences that result. A further advantage emerges here, that Anna's specification of requirements will be independent of the current software and hardware details. So if in a few months or years different hardware and software with different details becomes available, her analysis will still be correct. At that time it should then be fairly easy to evaluate the costs and benefits of changing to new hardware or software.

If on the other hand Anna's specifications have details of the current hardware and software built into them, it will be more difficult to disentangle them at the future date. At that time further changes to business processes will seem to be much harder although the work Anna needs to do now is reduced. This method also simplifies the work of specifying to the programmer what changes to the current system are to be implemented. So the choice is between a short-term reduction in the current work with potentially bigger problems in the future, and more work now with less risk in the future.

With improvements in software and hardware, the roles of analysis, design, programming, building, installation and evolution are increasingly all being done by the same person. So that person needs a variety of skills in order to acquire knowledge of what is required and to design, implement and document all of it.

No attempt at a complete and consistent specification of the whole is made, since to create such on paper would be too difficult. Ultimately the specification of the processes and features of an IT-based system evolve as the detailed implementation progresses.

Design phase

The analysis and design phases often overlap since some design actions need to be done to give feedback to analysis actions.

Different proprietary ISD methods use the terms analysis and design in different ways and so they may appear to contain different activities. To some people the functional specification is a deliverable from the analysis phase whereas to others it is a deliverable from the design phase. This is seen in Table 9.2. Some practitioners separate the design phase into user design and technical design, as explained below.

Design phase activities	*Design phase products*
• Systems design specification preparation	• System design specification
• Acceptance test specification preparation	• Acceptance test specification
• Contract negotiation	• Implementation proposal
• Prototyping	• Project plan
• Internal project set up	• Support contract and plan
• Proposal preparation	
• Project planning	

TABLE 9.2
Possible activities and products of a design phase

User design phase We separate design into user design (UD) and technical design (TD). **User design** consists of the activities that create design features that the user sees. Some people call these activities logical design although that term is also used with other meanings by various people as we explained in Chapters 2 and 7. Others use the term **cognitive model**, which means a description of the system as users will see it, conveying a very good idea of how the system will behave. The actions of the user design phase may be as Figure 9.3 depicts.

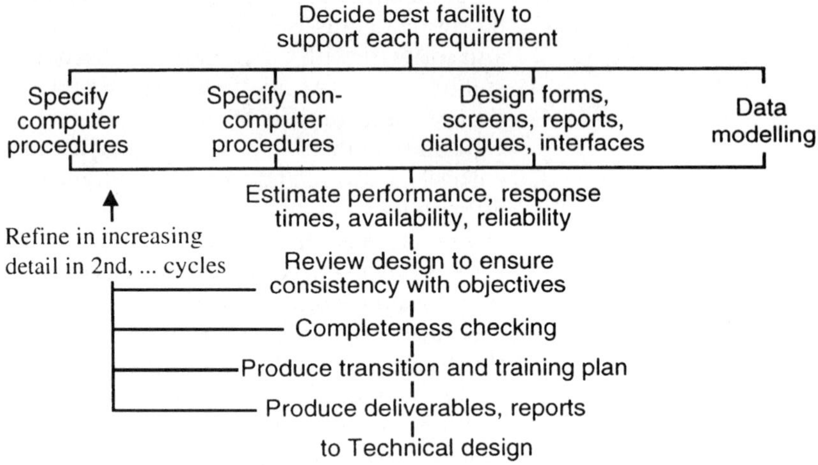

FIGURE 9.3
Possible activities of user design.

Technical design phase **Technical design** is more concerned with features that are mostly hidden from the user, except for the fact that they may have a major effect on the efficiency, speed and performance of the target system. For example, they include details of which kinds of pointers and indexes to provide in database and other data structures. More pointers and index entries mean more computer processing to create and maintain the data occurrences at each change, but give faster searches and retrievals. The decisions are complex compromises. The physical design may need minor changes when the patterns of use change significantly. Figure 9.4 shows these activities.

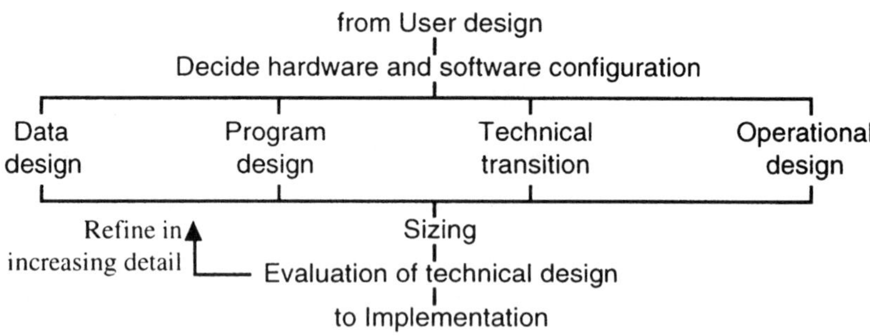

FIGURE 9.4
Possible activities of technical design.

Later-phase activities

The following phases and activities generally occur in the later stages of developing and providing an information system: construction; testing; deployment; training of users and those who help them; operations and maintenance. Associated aspects include documentation; configuration management; version control; and dictionary issues.

Construction

Correctness and quality are important, particularly the need to construct software that is free from bugs, conforms to the design specification and is also easy for others to understand and alter later. Surprisingly some programmers who have only learnt software and computer systems at college or university are not as good at programming reliably as those who did some hardware or engineering.

Many **languages** are available. Choose an appropriate one and conform to its standards and interfaces. Many software packages have their own internal language for specifying the differences in the current application from the package defaults.

Non-procedural utilities provide a software environment – for example editor, operating system facilities, database management system (DBMS), communications, network facilities and human–computer interfaces. Managers may help the builders' morale by having up-to-date tools for them. This should increase the likelihood of them getting it right first time.

Coding methods and standards should unify structures of names, descriptions, versions, styles and the use of dictionary techniques. One should conform to *de juro* standards where they exist, otherwise to *de facto* standards.

Prototyping, by getting user representatives to participate as details are gradually added, should help to ensure that the system is acceptable.

Program **modularity** means arranging the code in suitable independent blocks. Nowadays operating systems have automatic facilities for version control of files, linking software modules and linking software to hardware.

Testing

Ideally, testing should include testing the design on paper before it is implemented in terms of hardware and software but this is not yet practicable. There are few automated tools available to help and no good methods other than building prototypes. The size and complexity of IS means that it is impracticable to test every aspect and confidence that the complete system does what is wanted therefore has to be provided by very comprehensive testing at module and submodule level.

Testing techniques include blackbox, whitebox, regression, and boundary value analysis. For example, during the testing of a computer system with various inputs and outputs: blackbox tries various inputs and observes the corresponding outputs; whitebox involves monitoring internal signals and intermediate data values obtained during calculations but not normally output; regression means subdividing anything suspicious and testing each part, and boundary-value analysis tests the cases leading to maxima and minima of attributes such as working at high and low temperatures and handling extreme data values or very large tables.

Generally one cannot fully test equipment behaviour that depends on accurate timing, e.g. keeping up with fast input, and the timing of communications. One cannot test in advance issues such as the ability to handle within a limited time a volume of randomly initiated messages. One can sometimes perform simulations or statistical calculations to estimate whether the proposed system design will work as regards timing, but that does not guarantee successful operation later.

Generally one should separate the testing environment from the operational one. Keeping test programs and test data logically separate from those in use for the real business operations avoids many difficulties. Administrators should arrange clean and auditable handover procedures for changing the operational facilities.

Deployment

Deployment involves **organizational readiness** and the orderly **transition** from the old system to the new. Each place where equipment is to be installed must be ready, especially as it may have to be installed and brought into use without work being significantly interrupted. Timing the installation of equipment may be very important, e.g. doing so over a particular weekend in order to minimize disruption to the business. User **training** should be timed to fit, finishing just before live use, with further training as new people come into posts in the future. **Handover** needs to be carefully planned. From some moment the staff will be using the new system instead of the old. In large organizations with many sites and locations, agreement is needed on who can **authorize** whom to do what at each local office. The way this is monitored and controlled should be decided explicitly.

Operations

Operations means the routine control of systems and is an area where proprietary ISD methods are generally weak. Identifying a common operational infrastructure may be done through generating a product architecture. Operational procedures should include backups, privacy, security, integrity, correctness and up-to-date agreement between reality and the information stored in the ISs; logging of critical actions for auditing purposes, and monitoring the performance of various parts of the systems. Administrators may also have to ensure application-specific procedures such as database backups and recovery. Rollback can undo an error immediately after it has occurred and roll forward can restore data from an appropriate dump copy of the data, made at some past time when its integrity was satisfactory, and apply subsequent transactions to it.

Maintenance

In addition to preventive and corrective actions, maintenance nowadays includes minor enhancements to the existing hardware and software, and bug fixing. Some enhancements arise from business, organization and technological changes, and some from the availability of new products on the market. Some of this maintenance really consists of planned improvements and has repercussions on analysis and design. The way that the analysis and design are performed can reduce the impact of environmental change and reduce the future need for maintenance support. Systematic administrative procedures for initiating, controlling and recording changes are desirable.

Minor upgrades, migration, decommissioning and retirement of ISs and business systems involve planning, parallel operations during changeover to different systems, archiving and support. When an IS or business system reaches the end of its useful life, its replacement or removal should occur in a planned way. This involves making decisions during the changeover to a new system such as whether to keep the old system during a transition period and perhaps for some further time as a fallback in case the new system runs into difficulties, whether and when to scrap it, and how to transfer or archive the old contents.

Documentation

Documentation serves several purposes and audiences. These include the users of systems; those who have to give help and advice when users need help; those who have to maintain the systems; and operations staff who have to control the system and its use and who may have to carry out fairly rare processes to recover systems that have failed unexpectedly. These various people ideally would like different kinds and styles of documentation to match their knowledge and different needs.

Not many standards exist for the documentation of deliverables from the software development process. Perhaps the most cohesive publicly available documentation standards in the software engineering sphere are from the IEEE. Authors should think of form, accessibility, purpose and audience for each standard.

Configuration management

In a **static** configuration the logical arrangement and interconnections between parts cannot be changed during use. In a **dynamic** configuration, a new computer can be added to a network without resorting to shutting down the entire network, and new software can be installed during use. Software distributability needs control; it is better to have all copies of shared packages administered centrally through a network. Any user who wants to use a particular package gets access to it through a network that links his/her computer to the one holding that software, and the facilities ensure that not more than, say, five users may use it concurrently if that number is the limit of the licence. Client and server processing arrangements are well understood and widely used. Software has become internationalized and transmitted to many countries. Some packages allow local keyboard and spelling dictionary variations, and some packages have been arranged to allow input and output in various languages, so clerks in different countries may use their local language.

Configuration management is concerned with ensuring adequate mechanisms for the control of hardware and software, so that changes cannot be introduced unapproved and undocumented. This covers planning, identification of items to be subject to configuration control, carrying out this control and conducting audits to verify that controls have been correctly applied. Configuration control becomes necessary when a system can exist in many different variants, either because large numbers are sold and each has particular variations (e.g. local keyboard and spelling dictionary variations, input and output in local language) or because there are many changes over its lifetime. It comes into being during the design stage and the point in time when the design has become sufficiently well defined and stable to be able to document it (and when the discipline and costs that control imposes can be accepted), and continues to the end of the life of the system.

When in place, configuration management ensures that a proposed change is not incorporated until:

- it has been fully tested at module level;
- system level testing has been repeated to verify compatibility;
- repercussions on interfaces to other parts that have not been changed have been assessed and any uncertain areas explored;
- it has been ascertained that the change does not contravene the basis on which the system was accepted at handover, e.g. safety, maintenance policy, test results training policy;
- system documentation changes have been produced;
- software licence rules have been complied with;
- a responsible authority has given approval.

Version control Version control means that the software packages automatically ensure that the appropriate versions of each product, data, program, compiler, executable code and subsystem, are used – without the developer or user having to think about it. This aids project management and automatic control of documents, sources and executables.

Data dictionary issues

Various terms have been used for the centrally held descriptions of an IS – **dictionary**, **encyclopaedia** and **repository**. The contents are data describing all the objects relating to the system, including system representations, documents, processes, data and behaviour; dates and responsibilities; the OPR and metamodels; and the histories of everything from creation to use.

Passive means that the interface between the encyclopaedia and the implemented system involves manual procedures, so the dictionary may be not up to date. **Active** means that the data in the dictionary is fully integrated with the implemented system, so the system actually refers to the entries whenever it needs to during use, reducing problems of consistency and completeness. **Static** means that each person has a copy of appropriate entries, just as a person may refer to a copy of a book. **Dynamic** means that people use the dictionary system through online facilities.

The ideal is to incorporate system representation, documents and data into a single active dynamic system. The dictionary need not be centralized, though for most CASE tools it usually is, and multi-user dictionaries are needed to aid project management. The required coordination is not easy. While CASE tools may help in detecting inconsistencies, they cannot automate the solution. Most tools are directed at a single developer, not the team or organization.

Methods

Assumptions and properties of ISD methods

Methods of developing and providing business and information systems often have assumptions, some of which might be hidden while others might be mutually incompatible or contradictory. Many methods assume that an IT-based system, or a major change to one, is needed and hence the work required is to carry out the consequent analysis, design and implementation. Most methods do not have explanations of how different approaches, treatment and techniques may be needed in different application circumstances, e.g. how developing an accounting and stock control system differs from developing a robotics system or a knowledge system.

Method assumptions

Some methods assume only **structured data**, such as tables, forms, records, lists and collections of data items with values. A large amount of information is not so structured, for example diagrams, graphics, voice and free text, and few methods help with the structuring of these.

Methods may assume that the real-world has **single sequential processing** or that the target system will be a **single processor** computer system. Assuming that only one process, transaction or operation occurs at any instant is sometimes too simplistic. In life, although at each second a person may appear to be doing only one thing, over a longer period he/she may be interleaving many activities. Interrupted to answer the phone and receive a message, he/she then continues the previous activity while also dealing with the phone message. Every day many things can be interleaved in an almost indescribable way and the methods of modelling should handle this. Many methods were originally developed from work in the 1970s and 1980s creating central mainframe systems, such as large database systems with many users at terminals, for the routine operations of large organizations. Where parts of a method assume a single processor computer system, those parts cannot help in a large organization or situation that is likely to need distributed systems, networks of interconnected computers and client-server systems, such as those more recently available.

Methods usually assume the correct **time sequencing** of transactions. One might assume that information will always reach a computer system in the same sequence as the corresponding real processes and events happened but this would be unwise. For example, building a system which assumes that data about the creation or renewal of an insurance policy will always reach the computer before information about an incident that might give rise to a claim, could lead to rejection of the claim information. Postal delays do occur, and telephone calls can be made before incoming mail has been processed.

Some methods assume the developers have, or lack, particular skills; so the method is arranged to use the assumed skills or provide opportunity for training. Methods typically assume knowledge of languages like Cobol, Pascal, C, and/or C++, but not logic-programming languages such as Prolog even though some processes can be expressed in Prolog more curtly. Modelling the current situation as a method of hidden training is well known.

Some methods have been extended and changed as weaknesses or inapplicability surfaced. Extra phases such as a strategy phase and/or feasibility study were added during the 1980s. Real-time extensions to structured techniques were added to the steps and techniques to model control and points of control, in about 1986. Object-oriented features have been added to some languages and methods in the late 1980s and early 1990s.

Hidden assumptions may help choice

Different types of system have different characteristics, particularly among the commercial applications of computers. Knowledge of these characteristics can be used to determine an appropriate choice of methods, techniques and tools, bearing in mind their hidden assumptions. Table 9.3 shows some possible technical features of different types of commercial system, and corresponding relevant database products.

Commercial system	*Features*	*Database and software package systems*
Transaction processing	Record oriented, high volume, complex structures, many relationships	DBMS, several available
Office automation	Large amount of unstructured data, text, mail, reports, some spreadsheets	Wordprocessing, Email, many packages available
Management reporting, MIS, Reference, register of equipment, budgeting	Simple fixed-structure reports; simple view structures, table oriented	Relational database, spreadsheet
Data analysis, e.g. of sales data by region	Ad hoc queries, statistical arithmetic, aggregation of huge volumes	Query language, various packages available

TABLE 9.3
Features of commercial applications and databases

If the long-term strategies are correct then providers and developers can use them to look at methods and select the most appropriate whilst being aware of their hidden assumptions.

In Table 9.4 you may prefer to cover up the assumptions in the right column whilst thinking about the strategies, revealing the right column as appropriate.

Method strategy	*Philosophy assumptions*
Analyse each business function by partitioning it into more and more detail, i.e. structured decomposition.	The organization needs an IS to help with its business *functions* (not viewing the whole organization).
Look for the information types that correspond to the fundamentals of the business. This gives entity types, relationships, attributes.	The inherent nature of the organization will endure (no takeovers, mergers, diversification, changes).
Concentrate on data analysis more than process analysis.	The activities, methods of working, will evolve. Responsibilities may change. New processes, procedures may come, new information uses, new query types, but data remains essentially the same.
Divide the organization into areas, for example, corresponding to business functions. Analyse each area in turn. Merge the models; or gradually extend the first area model into neighbouring areas.	A *large* organization must be tackled gradually (as a whole is impossible).
Acquire and implement traditional methods of structured analysis and structured design.	Distributed systems are not relevant; data consistency between systems is not an issue; code reusability is not an important objective.
Use graphical analysis and design tools.	Graphical representations exist for most aspects of an IS description; users like graphics (gets pretty pictures, interfaces; but may miss the needed functionality).

TABLE 9.4
Examples of hidden asumptions and philosophies

Scope of proprietary ISD methods

Figure 9.5 shows our beliefs about which phases some proprietary ISD methods cover. It partly conveys whether a method is data or process oriented but can only be used to compare methods very

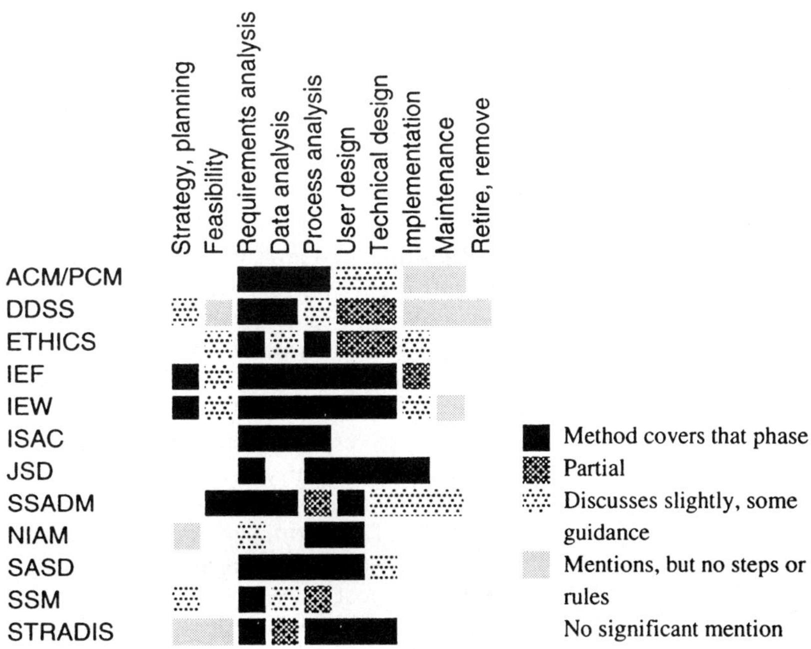

FIGURE 9.5
Scopes of certain proprietary ISD methods, in 1980s.

loosely. Many details of techniques are subsumed and there may be small discrepancies between this diagram, which is our opinion of the scopes, and what the method authors or marketing staff claim. If so we apologize.

Methods differ depending on whether they were developed for complicated situations in large organizations, or for small organizations or just a small part of a large organization. The former cannot be scaled down conveniently and the latter cannot be scaled up easily.

Real-time issues and methods

We explain the nature of control and define real-time systems. These lead on to the Ward–Mellor and Hartley–Pirbhai techniques developed during the mid-1980s.

In Chapter 4 we explained about **points of control**. In one sense a business organizational unit is a point of control. The more operational business processes may be more stable than the organizational structure and points of control that currently control them. Middle and higher management may be reorganized into a different reporting structure. David perhaps ought to provide flexible systems to aid control, including facilities to change the system easily at some unexpected future reorganization of the less stable parts. Rarely, however, will such information be known. Idris and Anna need ways of expressing points of control as diagrams and text in conceptual models.

> A **real-time system** involves two systems, which are usually independent . The timing of events in one system depends on (or satisfies restrictions determined by) the timing of signals and messages from the other system. Within a determined time the first system has to act on and/or respond to input messages from the second, otherwise something unsatisfactory

Real-time systems are most easily illustrated by examples such as aircraft flight control systems and industrial process control. They also occur in business, where a business system can sometimes be thought of as performing on a real-time basis, with the need to respond within a defined time. In cycles such as those in Figures 4.10 and 4.11 (pp. 132–3), managers and other staff must on occasion so respond to information requiring control decisions. Business operations must so respond to messages from a customer. The information systems must provide for the transmission and handling of such time-critical information. Reliability and integrity must be ensured, so that no time-critical information flow is delayed or lost.

Real-time issues include the modelling of time and relative timing, sequencing, the triggering of control signals, synchronization, frequency and stability.

Stability

A system is in **equilibrium** if in some sense the values of the relevant attributes are not changing. A system may oscillate like a pendulum about an equilibrium point, and may or may not converge towards it. With several variables you can visualize more complex patterns, such as two-dimensional curves around the equilibrium position, and motions such as the earth round the sun and the moon round the earth.

An equilibrium may be stable or unstable. If a system is disturbed from a **stable** state it will tend to return towards it, as a boat, disturbed by waves, pitches and rolls around a stable floating position. If a system is disturbed from an **unstable** state it will not return unaided.

A business system regarded in this way has to be stable or to oscillate in acceptable ways around a desired state. This desired state is usually stable. The people and points of control have to arrange that the central position is whatever is the optimum for the business objectives, strategy, tactics and plans; and must also ensure that the operational variations from that position are acceptably small. The average central position and the variations can be observed as values of performance measurements and external-value metrics.

Techniques

Completeness and consistency techniques

Some ideas of completeness and consistency were explained in Chapter 6, related there to metamodel rules. Various commonly used approaches and methods have already been explained so we can now consider a different view of completeness and consistency, related to approaches, methods and techniques.

At any stage in the development of an information system, a particular piece of work should have a sense of 'completeness' in order that the people doing the work know when the job is finished. For example, when some analysis or modelling has been performed the resulting products should possess the property of being consistent, and also the property of not being inconsistent, although there are certain exceptions to both of these.

One of the most important tools for a professional analyst is the set of completeness and consistency standards which are to be applied as the analysis and modelling work proceeds.

Most current CASE tools do not provide a comprehensive set of such checks. The work of specifying and programming the rules is huge, and to some extent they will vary from one organization to another, so attempting to build them all into CASE tools is hardly practicable.

We give some simple techniques for checking completeness and consistency. We apologize that we occasionally refer to techniques explained later, but we think it preferable to have all these checks together for reference.

Some checks for consistency and completeness

Decision tables should be such that the entries should cover all conditions. More widely, procedures, processes and programs should do something sensible in every situation. This can include alerting the appropriate person – not every rare case needs to have an automated process.

An **entity life cycle** represents the complete history of an entity occurrence. In entity life cycles, for each data object all primitive operations should be accounted for, e.g. there should be ways that each can be created, used and cease to exist, so that representations may be either deleted or archived.

More deeply, each possible **fact** in the universe of discourse should have appropriate ways in which its history can evolve. So representations of the creation of the fact and associated attribute-value pairs need to be handled. Consistency with other associated facts may need to be checked. When the fact changes or evolves or ceases to be relevant, further representations need to be handled. Most facts have associated time periods during which they are true or believed true by a particular person or system.

Within each procedure where data is being created or its status altered, there should be ways that the user can undo minor errors, and ways that the user can confirm what has been done up to that point in terms of making a complete transaction. Sometimes several associated facts have to be created simultaneously for consistency – half a transaction is not sensible. Database software packages have facilities for ensuring such consistency and for undoing half-done transactions, but simpler packages often do not.

In state-transition diagrams all possible states should be covered. Every state should have a way in which it can be reached correctly, and ways by which appropriate other states can be reached later from it. Where the logic is equivalent to tokens flowing between nodes, the logic of the various kinds of tokens and nodes should not only allow and represent the various situations, but also should not allow combinations that could not occur in practice. Some care is needed here, as information may reach an information system in a different sequence from that in which the corresponding actual situations and events occurred or became known. The state-transition diagrams, the models and the ISs should allow for this.

Formal description languages can provide certain limited but useful kinds of automated checking. These may have to be supplemented by many kinds of checks done by developers.

Completeness and consistency ideas can be applied to an action. For example, was the action completely finished, was all of it done, or was part of it omitted, or was part skimped? Was the action done consistently, or were different parts done using different attitudes or criteria? As part of the review and control evaluation of the action, should its completeness and consistency be evaluated?

For a product, questions such as the following may be asked. Is the product complete or are parts missing? Is the product self-consistent; are there (perhaps standard) consistency checks for this kind of product; have these checks been done? If the product has many parts, are all the parts present, as expected for completeness? Are all parts correctly related to each other, e.g. consistent with each other and the whole? As part of the review and control of the project of which this product is part, have the appropriate (standard) completeness and consistency checks on this product been done?

For a project, in principle one may apply the above to all the actions and products of the project. Mostly this is done mentally while looking at prototypes, documents and reports.

For an IS as a delivered product, one may ask: does it completely provide all the features and facilities needed? Were the specified features and facilities complete and consistent? Do they fully meet the relevant needs, strategy, tactics and objectives of the organization?

In a sequence of products that gradually transform a requirement to a new process or IS, Anna and David may ask: is each product, such as a system description, **complete** enough for the next activities? This is the essence of **completeness**. Are all representations and statements about the system **consistent** with each other? This is the essence of **consistency**.

Analysts use many partial representations of system requirements in the course of their analysis. The totality of all the various documents and products used by Anna and Idris and others should display internal consistency. For example, if an analyst uses information flow diagrams, input–output diagrams, entity relationship diagrams and others, they should be consistent with each other. Consistency does *not* necessarily imply **correctness**, meaning agreement with the universe of discourse (UOD). Consistency can be established in many arbitrary ways. It should be tested with the aid of a set of consistency standards. Correctness means ensuring that information about everything in the UOD is correctly transmitted to the IS.

Exercise 9.2

To what extent are the following reasonable checks that Idris and Anna should think through during the development of models and at other steps during the development of a business or information system?

(a) The allowed sequencing of processes should be known, such as that process A comes before B which comes before C; these cannot be overlapped.
(b) Opportunities for overlap are identified, e.g. to what extent actions can be done concurrently or in parallel, how the starting and finishing events are related, and whether each can be interrupted.
(c) Every process can be triggered by at least one event that is external to it.
(d) Every possible combination of inputs can be handled by a process that receives those inputs.
(e) Each required business rule is represented in the system descriptions.

Checks (a) and (b) are both part of the rules about relative timing of process occurrences, such as what may happen at the same time as what, or what may happen after what. Such sequencing rules should be picked up during analysis. A PERT package should detect circular-activity errors, such as A before B and B before C and C before A. But more complicated errors in a conceptual model description are more difficult to spot and less likely to occur. Generally the conceptual and logical modelling of time is a problem. Many people fail to specify completely how actions and pairs of actions are time related. Cases include: one has to finish before the other starts, as FS in PERT; they may overlap in various ways; they can be done independently; and one may be interrupted while the other is done. Diagram conventions to show all of this are weak or absent, and the set of theoretical possibilities is not widely understood.

Check (c) is a rule that Anna carries as an OPR abstraction. A process occurrence cannot trigger that occurrence itself, although it can trigger another occurrence of the process, as in recursion.

Check (d) is essentially correct, but rare inputs may just cause the process to produce an exception report or a warning message for action by someone.

Check (e) is sensible. In the same way as each fact about the UOD should be capable of being handled, so should each rule. Chapters 5 and 6 gave some examples, and the data analysis section of Chapter 11 gives more examples.

Demonstrable representation of business rules is vital. Each information system implies a set of business rules and these must represent the actual business rules. For example, if a system holding employee information uses the employee badge number as the key to access information about employees, the implied business rules are that each badge number must be unique and the relevant badge number will be known to anyone wanting information. Does this reflect the business rule in the real world? Usually not, as occasionally someone will want to access information about an employee without knowing the badge number. Think of the difficulties if anyone wanting an employee's telephone extension number had to quote the employee's badge number to the system that holds the phone numbers.

Analysts cannot perform analysis without a set of business rules, and completeness and consistency checking should involve the checking of any assumptions that have been made. For example, one may assume that employee or badge number uniquely identifies a person – however, in some large companies that has not always been true!

Table 9.5 indicates some other completeness and consistency ideas.

Completeness and consistency of structured methods

Structured methods have completeness and consistency checking activities between creating the diagrams and entering them into the data dictionary. The methods do not cover or are not applicable to business analysis, business planning, infrastructure, audit controls, project management, standards, construction of the final information system, testing, maintenance and retirement.

Aspect → *Object ↓*	*Process*	*Data*	*Behaviour, system dynamics, control*	*Other, responsibilities, environment*
Attributes, attribute-value pairs, entities, relationships	Created, used, in processes,	Related to other data, normalized, functional dependencies, EAR diagrams	How often created, used, volume, pattern of use, volatility	Responsible person asserts that valid for a certain time; maybe conflicting opinions and assertions
Condition, event	Triggers process, made true by process, changed by process, decision table shows which process goes	May affect validity and appropriateness of data, entity life history, how is the right data occurrence selected/ found	Condition changed by event, how often does condition/ event happen, causes, decisions	Who is responsible for action when condition occurs, how important, how urgent, response time, approvals
Input, output across interface	Received by process, generated by process, how used in process, information-flow diagrams	Contributes to data occurrences, how is it identified	How often, volume, how is it controlled, accuracy, precision	Who is responsible, who uses the information, why needed, privacy, security, integrity, consistency
Processor	Performs process, has role	Described by data	How is processor controlled, how does it make decisions, workload	Responsibility for what, reporting structure, quality of performance
Resource	Used as tool or consumed, leads to cost accounting	Described by data	How its use is controlled, organizational behaviour	Needs to be acquired, unit of measure
Time	When process occurs, when allowed, how long process takes	Duration of validity of data, interval it corresponds to	Allow or not allow objects to be out of sequence, interrupted, late, early	Priorities, time units, frequency of various regular objects, recovery

TABLE 9.5
Some ideas for completeness and consistency checks

Structured techniques include: data flow diagrams, structured functional decomposition† of business functions, structure charts†, transform and transaction analysis†, structured natural language† and pseudocode†, data dictionaries, data analysis and decision tables†. The last three of these were developed in the 1970s or earlier, independently of structured analysis.

Complete ISD methods encompass techniques, phases and management, all within an overall rationale, as opposed to just being collections of techniques.

Ward–Mellor techniques

The Ward–Mellor techniques are a collection of diagrams, notations, rules and recommendations for how to analyse and design real-time systems. These can be applied to analysing the control of business systems and the use of information systems where other systems are controlled.

They acknowledge that different real-time systems require very different life cycles and so the choice of life cycle is left to the developer. They recommend the development of an 'essential model' and an 'implementation model' within the chosen life cycle. The models 'do not constitute a system development methodology'. Ward–Mellor models are a general scheme for real-time systems development, emphasizing processes and control and covering analysis and design. They place greater emphasis on the role of data modelling than the Hartley–Pirbhai techniques, which we explain later.

The Ward–Mellor techniques to be used by Anna and David include:

- combined data and control flow diagrams, based on Yourdon;
- state-transition diagrams† for each control process;
- entity-relationship diagrams;
- process specifications;
- structure charts†.

Figure 9.6 shows the various types of objects and relationships to be used by Anna, Idris and David to show the flows and effects of control. These were originally proposed as additions to data flow diagrams.

FIGURE 9.6
Ward–Mellor notation for analysis of real-time systems.

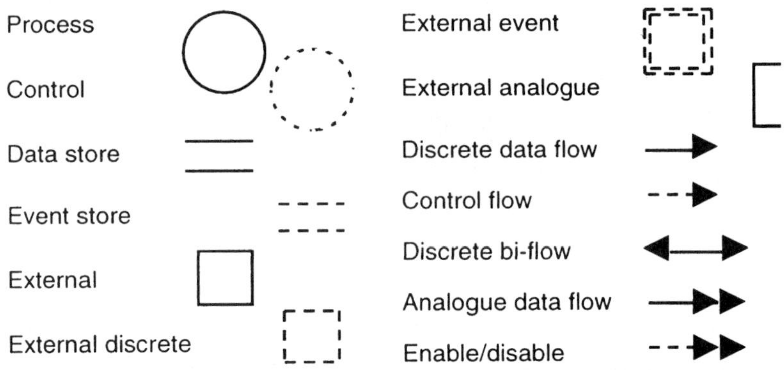

Figure 9.7 shows an example of the notation in use. Here the control box 2.1 receives a signal that selects the main or the auxiliary engine, and it sends appropriate signals to boxes 2.4 and 2.5. Box 2.4 also receives other control signals such as Main on/off and thus sends appropriate control signals to the main engine. Box 2.5 is similar.

The full semantics of Figure 9.7 are unclear without an accompanying state-transition diagram to show the various states and the ways that the controls and the system being controlled can change from one state to another.

Hartley–Pirbhai techniques

For real-time system specifications Hartley and Pirbhai suggest the use of the following.

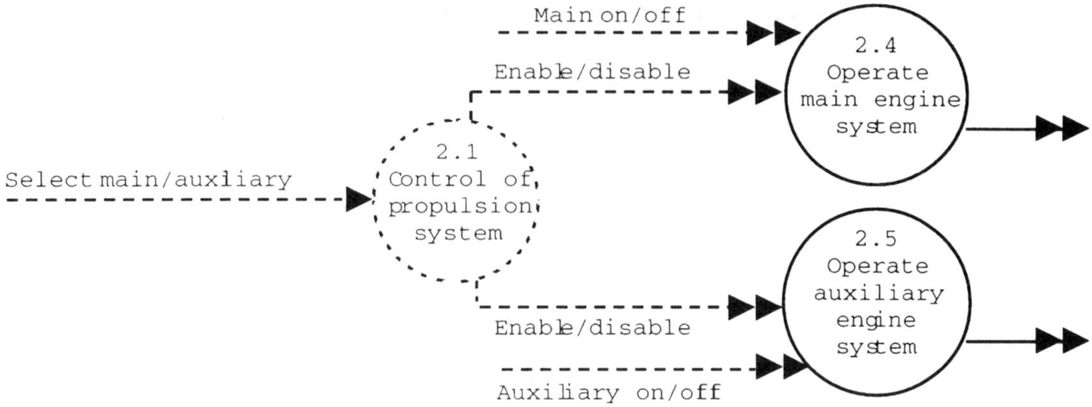

FIGURE 9.7
Example of use of Ward–Mellor notation.

- **data flow diagrams** (DFD) and **context diagrams**;
- **control flow diagrams** (CFD) – an adaptation of DFDs where the control flow and process information is held on a separate diagram called a control flow diagram (CFD), and where for every DFD there is a corresponding CFD;
- levelling and balancing concepts;
- **process specifications** (PSPEC) using structured English, explained later;
- **control specifications** (CSPEC), which may use decision tables, state-transition diagrams† and matrices, explained later;
- **timing specifications** – where necessary;
- **encyclopaedia** – holding data and control flow definitions, as explained earlier (p. 260).

The Hartley–Pirbhai deliverables are a system requirements model, being a form of systems specification; and a system architecture model, being hardware and software systems architecture.

The scope and emphasis of the technique is on the process and control aspects of analysis and design. It supports and uses iterative development to produce its deliverable items. The need for a data model in some cases is acknowledged, but there is very little emphasis on this in the method as it is reasonably argued that not every real-time system needs requirements modelling from all the three aspects of process, control and data.

Figure 9.8 shows the Hartley–Pirbhai notation. This is not identical to that of Ward–Mellor, and the deliverables take a somewhat different format.

FIGURE 9.8
Hartley–Pirbhai notation for analysis of real-time systems.

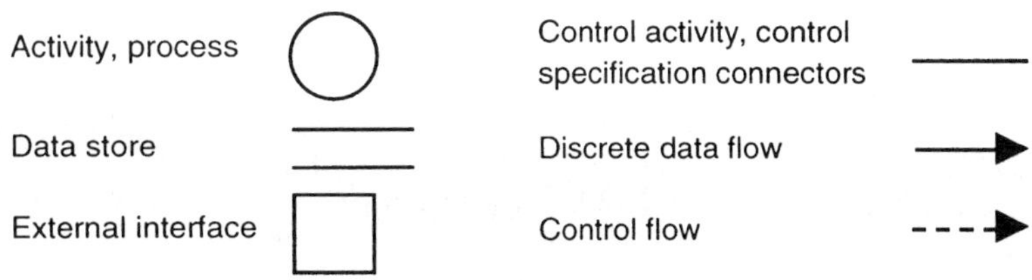

Functional decomposition

Functional decomposition is a top-down analysis technique for progressively decomposing a business function into its major constituents. The top-level process is taken as the business function or equivalent business system itself. The diagrams produced are sometimes called **process diagrams** or action diagrams. Management reporting structures may be shown by similar diagrams. No information/data flows or controls are shown.

It progressively decomposes each business function into its constituent business processes, and each process into subprocesses, until functional primitives are reached at the bottom of the tree or network. It highlights and illustrates the following relationships, which are usually said to be hierarchical but may be networks: the reporting structure of the business functions, e.g. organization has suborganization; a business function consists of processes; a process consists of subprocesses; an organization uses processes; and a process uses a subprocess.

It does not usually show the execution sequence of modules or processes. These may be recorded separately either graphically, using a hierarchically structured chart; or non-graphically, using a simple indented list; or using structure charts as described in the next section.

Functional decomposition example

Figure 9.9 shows the structure of business functions and processes by a tree-structured diagram.

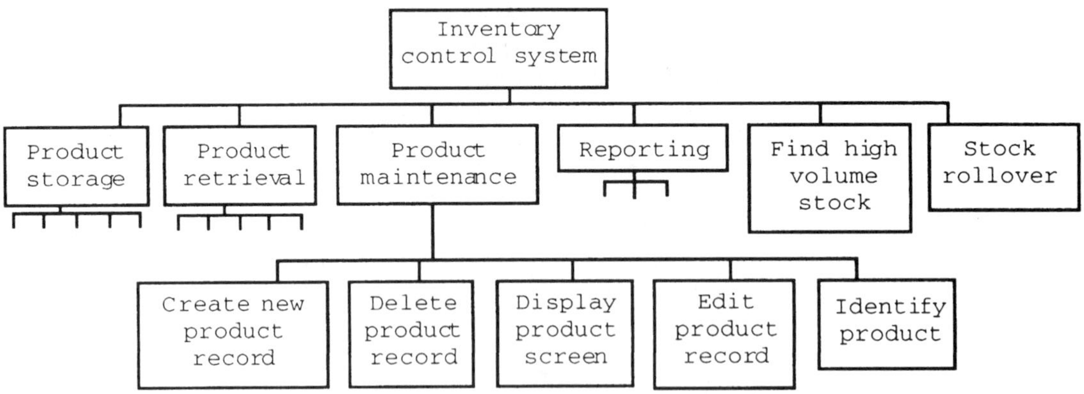

FIGURE 9.9 Example of a functional-decomposition diagram.

Structure of subprocesses, but no sequencing implied

Table 6.3 shows the structure of processes by nested indentation. The functional decomposition may appear to indicate the sequence of subprocesses, like a piece of program code, however *no* such sequencing is implied.

Exercise 9.3

What is the fundamental logical error in such tree-structured functional decomposition?

Generally business functions are not a tree structure. They are a network, since a low-level function may form part of more than one higher-level function. However at the upper levels the structure usually is a tree. People's discussions and diagrams often oversimplify and the functional decomposition is not continued further than about two sublevels. So the fact that the branches would come together at even lower levels is not recognized.

Comments on functional decomposition

Functional decomposition gives a useful summary of the business functions of a system and their decomposition into components but it omits behaviour.

Functional decomposition is an important feature of some software packages, capable of creating code for simple functions, but with no control mechanisms. The assumption is that the programmer can add the control information later. In practice the eventual user, George, will usually have to apply the controls mentally when using the software.

Avoid top-down decomposition and hence stovepiped function-based application packages

Top-down decomposition encourages **stovepiped** applications. Analysts produce specifications that match existing functions, instead of the more desirable business process oriented analysis. Then the provider selects a software package that matches that (undesirable) functional specification, and tailors it to fit the detailed functional needs by suitable use of the options in the package. Most such available software packages are biased towards business functions – e.g. marketing, sales, accounting, personnel, manufacturing – so several such packages are needed. These packages generally cannot be integrated and therefore integrating all of the data is impossible. Hence allowing a user to view an appropriate selection from that data regarded as a whole is impossible.

Such stovepiped separate systems make it much more difficult for managers and operational staff to take a business systems view. They encourage manufacturing for stock rather than to order, and make it difficult to reduce the leadtime from order to delivery. They prevent a sales person who answers a phone call from a potential customer from having a computer screen that could show when something could be manufactured. Similarly other business processes cannot be integrated, with consequent inefficiencies, poor management, poor decisions and poor services to customers and suppliers.

Other examples of undesirable effects include inhibiting: identification of those customers using certain products who are likely to be customers for some other product – with the aim of providing better targeting of what is otherwise junk mail and wasted advertising; better integration of manufacturing with engineering design and development; faster new-product development, manufacture and marketing; better logistics and relations with suppliers; faster receipts and payments and better cash flows; less paperwork and better procedures; and innovatively combining such examples.

This leads to difficulty in both identifying and showing the **reusability** of lower-level process descriptions. Thus not only can analysis and design activity be duplicated between projects but also code generation is duplicated. Different teams working in different business areas will produce different code with different structures and different names for variables, parameters and procedures. This leads to implemented systems that cannot easily be merged at some later stage, even though they have common subprocesses and procedure logic. This increases software maintenance difficulties and cost.

Techniques associated with functional decomposition include common environment coupling, transform and transaction analysis†, and state transition diagrams†, which we explain later.

Structure charts

Structure charts are similar to functional decomposition but also show behaviour and the modular structure of a system. Indicators on structure charts, as in Figure 9.10, show the following aspects.

- Pre-existing modules; control information distinguished from other data; and passing procedure parameters.
- Doing each of several subprocesses once and in a specified order, called **sequence**. Sequence may be shown by left-to-right and/or downwards layout.
- Doing several subprocesses each once and where they do not interact, e.g. no one subprocess uses any result from any other. They can then be done in **parallel**, each independently on a separate processor. If only one processor is available the equivalent to doing them in parallel, perhaps interleaving the work by doing a little of each in turn, is called **concurrent** operation.
- Doing the same subprocess (or programmed procedure) several times with slightly different data, e.g. once for each line on an order, called **repetition**. A repeating loop may be shown by a directed arc cutting across the structural lines that fan out from a module.
- Doing the same process several times with increasing precision, called **iteration**, to gradually get nearer to some optimum. Finding a square root by trial and error and improved estimating is an example. Trial discounted cash flow calculations to find the required rate of return are similar.
- **Cardinality**, how many times a process is done.
- **Selection**, mutual exclusivity, doing one or the other.
- Doing some combination from a set of subprocesses, depending on the current situation. Doing exactly one from

several is called **case**. The structure If … then … else … is similar but allows only two alternatives.

- Either doing a subprocess once or not doing it, called **optional**. Optional may be shown by a diamond.

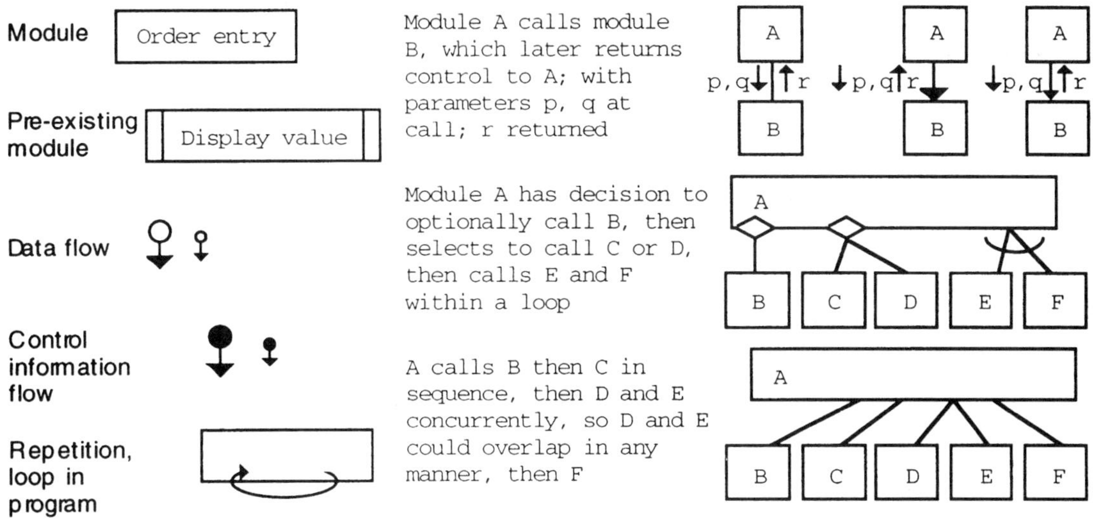

FIGURE 9.10
Structure chart notation.

Exercise 9.4

Do the above possibilities cover all possible ways in which processes may be related as regards doing them in turn? Do you know of other notations?

The notation is not complete. PERT allows SS, SF, FS, FF. Other notations include {a | b | c} for selection, which means do exactly one process from these; and [a | b | c] for optional, which means do none or one of these.

The example structure chart in Figure 9.11 illustrates the use of the notation. In this figure some minor data and control flows are omitted.

The assumption is that a clerk will initiate the order entry computer process when an incoming order is received by phone or as an order on paper. In some organizations the process may also be initiated by an electronic message from a customer's computer system.

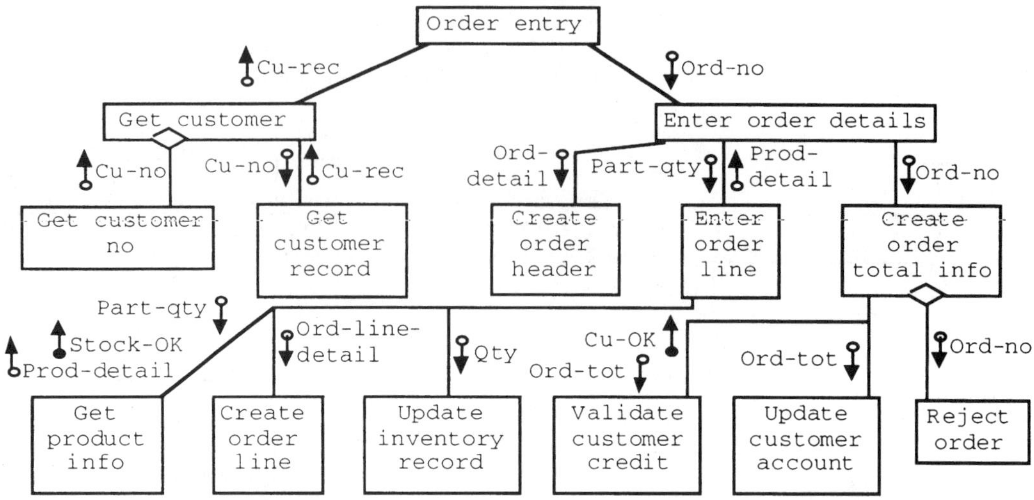

FIGURE 9.11
Example of a structure chart.

State-transition diagram

Figure 9.12 shows a state-transition notation using rectangles for states. Some notations use circles.

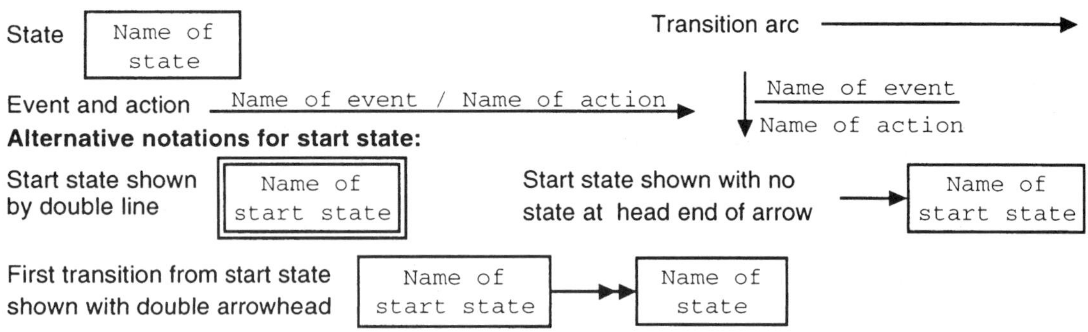

FIGURE 9.12
State-transition diagram notation.

State-transition diagrams capture information about state changes within a system. In this notation the states are enclosed in rectangles. The transitions to the next state are represented by the arrows and an associated input–output pair. This means that on receiving a certain input then the associated output is generated. After performing the output the machine is in the next state.

Figure 9.13 shows an example state-transition diagram for a two-speed ceiling fan.

The example is a logical rather than a physical model. This is because two accelerating states are shown, but only one decelerating state. Whether the final implementation of each will require one or two decelerating states will depend upon the selection of appropriate control mechanisms, after which the decision can be taken and the model changed to give a correct physical model.

It is neither possible nor desirable to use a state-transition diagram in isolation, it must be supported by other techniques such as control specifications.

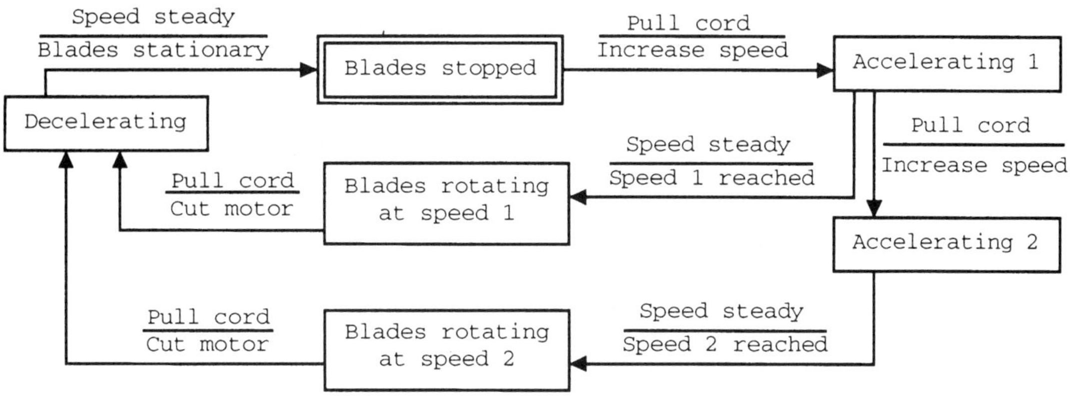

FIGURE 9.13
State-transition diagram example for a fan.

> **Exercise 9.5**
>
> The logic of the diagram allows the user to pull the cord twice before speed 1 is reached to accelerate to speed 2. Is the logic fully satisfactory? What would be needed if there were, say, ten speeds?

The logic is not satisfactory as after speed 1 has been reached it is not possible to increase the speed to speed 2.

To expand this form of diagram to ten speeds and draw it in full would be tedious. Notations for new kinds of substructures such as to increase the speed by one increment, and perhaps by five increments, and to decrease it similarly, are required. Such a substructure could then be drawn and described once as an object with properties that Obadiah, who is **object-oriented**, would enjoy. Even with just two speeds Obadiah would want to unify the properties of the two accelerating boxes, speed steady arrows, and blades-rotating-at-speed boxes; and not show two sets.

Structured natural language and pseudocode

Structured natural language and pseudocode are used for describing programmable processes. The difference between them is only a matter of how much they are program oriented. Programmers need written specifications where the programming is done by a different person from the analyst and designer, such as when programming is subcontracted. Some people recommend that designers should not overspecify, but should leave some common sense and fun for the programmer. Sometimes writing the specification in detail, subcontracting the task and explaining it to the implementor may take nearly as long as to code it.

Claimed advantages include: readily understandable to a systems designer, precise, conversion to a program is easy, concise and can be written quickly. Disadvantages include: no guarantee of correctness and it takes time to build up the skills for effective use.

Figure 9.14 shows another style of pseudocode.

```
find Customer_record with Customer_no = Customer_no of Order
if New_customer then print New_account_application_form
  else do while Order_lines_for_order
    find Product_record with Product_no = Product_no of Order_line
    if Available_stock of Product is less than Quantity of Order_line
      then call Create_back_order
      else call Create_picking_list_line;
        call Update_available_stock; call Update_order_total
    end_while
if Order_total greater than Customer.available_credit
  then rollback; print Customer_order_rejection_notification
  else call Update_customer_balance;
    call Update_customer_credit;
    call Trigger_shipment.
```

FIGURE 9.14
An example of pseudocode.

Exercise 9.6

Ignoring minor errors of syntax in Figure 9.14, think whether the specification of the process is sensible or could be improved.

The specification is not really sensible. A better logic would be to calculate first the value of the order and check the customer creditworthiness and available credit. Second, when it is known that the order will not be rejected later, allocate stock and do the picking, invoicing and accounting.

The principle recommended here is to check all sensible preconditions before starting a procedure, rather than starting and then perhaps having to undo later, which is usually harder to specify and program correctly.

Pseudocode is untestable. Minor inconsistencies and lack of syntax are tolerated and some are left in this example. Ultimately those involved should allow whatever constructs help effective communication, unambiguous specification and understanding.

Decision tables

The structure of each decision logic within a process may be represented by a decision table. A process may have many such tables – one for each decision point. The tree or table shows which actions are to be taken at each occurrence of its one decision point. But many decisions are not best communicated that way.

Any number of criteria for the decisions may be represented in a decision table, although this will obviously increase the complexity and may make the combination of circumstances leading to particular actions seem less clear. The intention, however, is to clarify the logic – especially in complicated cases.

Table 9.6 shows a single decision tree for selecting programmes for a washing machine. Notice the size and complexity.

To interpret the table for a particular situation, start at the top left and find the relevant conditions, then move to the right and find a column with the appropriate combination of Yes and No, then downwards to the lower right, then left to the action needed.

Condition																		
Machine washable	Y	Y	Y	Y	Y	Y	Y	Y	Y	Y	Y	Y	Y	Y	Y	Y	Y	Y
Coloured								Y	Y	Y	Y							
White	Y	Y				Y	Y											
Colourfast at 60°C			Y	Y	Y							N	N	N				
Silk/printed																	Y	
Acetate																	Y	
Acrylic															Y			
Cotton	Y		Y							Y		Y						Y
Linen		Y		Y									Y					
Polyester/cotton							Y		Y									
Nylon						Y		Y										
Viscose					Y						Y			Y				
Wool																Y		
Colours not fast at 40°C																	Y	
Capable of being boiled																		Y
Special finish e.g.·drip dry	N	N	N	N	N					Y	Y							Y
Heavy soil	(see note in the text)																	
Decision																		
Wash temp. 70°C, 85°C	Y	Y																Y
Wash temp. 50°C, 60°C			Y	Y	Y	Y	Y											
Wash temp. 40°C, 50°C								Y	Y	Y	Y							
Wash temp. 30°C, 40°C												Y	Y	Y	Y	Y		
Wash temp. 25°C, 30°C																	Y	
Spin 1000rpm	Y	Y										Y	Y	Y				
Spin 800rpm			Y	Y	Y											Y		
Spin 600rpm						Y	Y	Y	Y	Y	Y				Y			
Spin 500rpm																	Y	Y

TABLE 9.6
A decision table showing the main operation for a washing machine

Complexity

Tables of this size are difficult to create and to understand fully. The accompanying 'note in the text' is that in the first five decision rows the higher wash temperature of each pair is to be used for heavy soil, otherwise the lower temperature is to be selected. This rule would double the number of columns and split each wash temperature row into two. Such a rule is easier to express in words as a note. If expressed as a full-sized table the object oriented aspect of the rule would be lost. Indeed the table already contains groups of similar entries such as a group of Ys, which presumably indicates some rules that could correspond to objects.

Completeness

A decision table is a powerful technique to check that a proposed system specification allows for **any** combination of conditions.

Sometimes the logic of a decision can be explained in a table or in other layouts in ways that are easier for non-specialists to grasp. Table 9.7, for a hypothetical machine with seven machine settings and two buttons, is nearly equivalent to the decision table, and much simpler.

Garment	*Symbol*	*Machine setting*	*Machine temp °C*	*Spin speed*
White cotton, white linen, boilable cotton; but not special finishes such as drip dry. For drip-dry non-white cotton press low spin		1	70 or 85	1000 or 500
Colourfast at 60° cotton, linen or viscose; but not special finishes. For white nylon, white polyester/cotton without special finishes press low spin		2	50 or 60	800 or 600
Coloured nylon or polyester/cotton; and cotton or viscose with special finishes		4	40 or 50	600
Cotton, linen or viscose & colourfast at 40°C but not at 60°C		5	30 or 40	1000
Acrylics, acetate, or triacetate, including mixtures with wool; also polyester/wool blends		6	30 or 40	600
Wool mixed with other fibres; also silk that is not acetate		7	30 or 40	500
Pure wool. For printed silk and/or acetate press low spin.		8	25 or 30	800 or 500

TABLE 9.7
Garment table as an alternative way of describing the machine's use

Exercise 9.7

What is the identifier in our garment table? What are the other candidate keys? Why does it seem so much simpler than its decision table equivalent? Do the tables contain exactly the same information?

To the reader of the table the row identifier is the symbol column. The machine setting column is also a candidate key, and is the feature that selects rows from the designer's viewpoint. To the machine user the garment column indicates the row, and also indicates what garments may be washed together. Machine temperature and spin speed together also form a candidate key. The entries in the garment column cover the various user requirements, and for each there is only one corresponding row. Some details of our hypothetical machine are based on an actual washing machine in the UK. In our design the user has to rotate a knob to the wash symbol, press a button if heavy wash is required, and then press another for certain low-spin garments.

The garment table seems simple because all the values in a row are associated with that row's symbol and machine setting, as functional dependencies. The garment table contains more information than the decision table, since it explains, for example, wool mixed with other fibres and polyester/wool blends, which for simplicity we had to omit from the decision table.

Entity life cycles and life histories

The life cycle of an entity, attribute or item of data is usually regarded crudely as involving the following primitive operations: create; read; modify; delete; and archive. We regard that as unsatisfactory as the list is computer oriented whereas business activities involve other actions. The objective of entity life cycle (ELC) analysis is to ensure that the specification of an information system includes functional requirements covering all of these primitive operations on each item of data.

By contrast, an entity life history (ELH) shows how an entity (or entities) is affected by various events or activities. It shows the correct sequence for the actions or computer processes. Its objective is to show which entities are affected by which events.

In practice, the first decision an analyst will make concerns the granularity of data to be checked. For example, the checking may be against major business objects only, such as customer, product and person. However, there will often be different business rules applying to groups of data or even to single data elements themselves. For example, there may be different rules related to the reading of the salary field for an employee and the modification of the field. There may also be different rules about reading the values of many employees' salaries to calculate the average, and reading an individual salary.

The list above of primitive operations is not complete. In practice there may be other actions on entities or data values – e.g. allowing use in statistical calculations such as counting and calculating the mean and standard deviation but not reading, and the interactions on p. 156–7.

Entity life cycle analysis is a technique, and one that can be extended to analyse in greater detail by taking a different point of view. For each entity (and where appropriate attribute, relationship, event, information flow, action, ...), answers to questions such as the following are researched and documented. How can the need for an entity occurrence arise? What causes it? Where? Why? Who creates an occurrence? Who authorizes it? What approvals are needed? What conditions must apply when it is created? What conditions should apply when it is created? What conditions may apply when it is created? Are there any exceptions to the answers to the above? Rare cases? What conditions must/should/may apply (immediately) after it has been created? What actions are taken exceptionally if the 'should' conditions are not satisfied? Do these conditions have to continue to apply throughout the rest of its life? Similarly, for a change to occur to the entity, including it ceasing to exist, or ceasing to be relevant, or ceasing to be represented in the IS, almost all of the questions above – how? who? under what conditions? when? can apply, and be asked and answered.

Self check

Please spend some time reviewing what you have read and doing the questions below.

Objectives

After reading this chapter you should be able to do all of the following:

- explain the features of phases, name the widely used phases, justify whether to overlap them and explain the main activities and products of the various phases;
- discuss how the objectives and products of analysis should be arranged to fit the needs of others involved in later phases and activities;
- know the meaning of some terms which generally occur in the later stages of development, and appreciate their use;
- describe version control and a data dictionary, and use associated terms;
- appreciate that some proprietary ISD methods have assumptions, and be aware that sometimes assumptions may be mutually incompatible or contradictory;
- describe some completeness and consistency suggestions related to methods and techniques, and judge appropriateness;
- use appropriate techniques for modelling points of control, and model real-time systems correctly;
- explain stability of simple systems and apply the idea to business systems, performance measurements and external-value metrics;
- explain and use functional decomposition, structure charts,

state-transition diagrams, pseudocode, decision tables and entity life histories.

Questions

Some of these questions combine points from earlier chapters with the current chapter. To save space we have not included questions on some of the techniques.

9.1 Give a soft, people and management oriented explanation of what is an **information system**.

9.2 Give a hard, technically oriented explanation of what is an **information system**.

9.3 (i) Explain how the way a user gets help differs when asking a person from when using the help facilities of a computer system.

(ii) Explain what kinds of information should ideally be given by an IS to a user asking for help. Comment on the quality of this aspect of help from current computer-based ISs.

(iii) Explain the roles and actions when a user asks Isobel or an IS for help. Create a suitable table.

9.4 Classify each of the following approaches to information systems development as either hard or soft or a mixture. Look for one key feature as the basis of your choice: (a) structured approach; (b) participative approach; (c) waterfall approach; (d) conceptual modelling; (e) planning approach; (f) prototyping approach; (g) systems approach; (h) socio-technical approach; (i) automated tools such as CASE.

9.5 List some ways in which people differ in their ability to do some of the things explained in the chapter.

9.6 Comment on the assumptions in Table 9.8, which correspond to three separate organizations.

Method assumptions	*Organizational assumptions*
(a) The systems to be built will be a single system, and analysis and design done by a central team.	Distributed processing is needed because the staff are in several buildings.
(b) A common infrastructure is required to support different applications.	Individual business functions can commission the systems they need. Each business functional area has authority delegated to it to make its own investment decisions.
(c) After a system has been developed and installed, the team who did it will be available thereafter to answer users' questions, train future users, make improvements, and do the maintenance.	The management say that the developers, after their excellent development work under pressure, including foregoing holidays to produce an excellent new system on time, can now catch up with their backlog of other matters. In accordance with company personnel policy the management offer them the opportunity to attend a further training course the week after next, and they must attend as they have not attended their quota of training over the last two years and they cannot carry their training budget forward to next year.

TABLE 9.8
Example assumptions for Question 9.6

10 Cost analysis for business processes

In this chapter we explain two particular points: (a) one of the main motives for rearranging business processes is cost; (b) one element in the specification and design of information systems frequently not considered is cost. We summarize the key cost concepts so that you will appreciate the various ways of classifying and allocating costs.

There is a real professional gulf between many of those who carry out analysis for business processes (BPs) and/or information systems (ISs), and those who work in the area of accounting. Few process engineers or information system analysts are qualified accountants, and few qualified accountants have a good operational understanding of business processes and information systems.

It is not an objective in this book to prepare you for professional accounting qualifications, but to provide you with a degree of literacy for understanding costs and some of the issues concerning the role of costs in business processes and information systems. Readers who need a formal accounting background should take appropriate professional advice, education and training.

Determining how much it *really* costs to perform a business process can often produce several perfectly reasonable but different answers. This is because although a business must bear all of the costs it incurs there are several ways in which those costs can be assigned to the processes performed. We introduce the reader to the differences between traditional costing and activity based costing. This is an important discussion as many companies are exploring a change to this latter method in a belief that it will produce a more suitable understanding of costs in relationship to the processes being performed.

Recent trends in analysing business processes lead to the need for a new way of expressing costs in terms of how they can be allocated to the different stages of a business process. This is referred to as process costing, and we present the main ideas for that in this chapter.

Key cost concepts

There are many possible reasons why someone wants to measure costs. Before continuing, attempt the following exercise.

Exercise 10.1

(i) Make a list of several different reasons why cost information should be collected and classified by different categories.
(ii) List five different kinds of cost that you have heard or read about.

In doing this exercise, spend some time reflecting on the first question, which is very important for understanding the many ways in which cost accounting can be approached, before looking at the solution.

(i) There are many different reasons why cost information may be used. Possible reasons include: knowing how much it costs to make and supply a product or service; producing a profit and loss account; placing a value on stock; deciding how much to bid for a contract; monitoring a budget.
(ii) Many kinds of costs are referred to in the accounting, economics, and business literature such as: variable costs; total costs; fixed costs; marginal costs; opportunity costs; product costs; overhead costs; unexpired costs; deferred costs; activity costs; relevant costs; labour costs.

Cost information needs to be collected in some way, and then classified so that it can be used in conjunction with specific cost objectives. The **collection** of cost information involves recording cash and liabilities as the business is in progress. The **classification** of cost information poses greater complexity.

Perhaps the most important concept related to an **analysis of costs** is that of cost objective. This is the first concept that will be explained in more detail shortly. At a very simple level, cost information is needed by a business in order to know if it is making a profit, breaking even or making a loss. For other organizations that are not pursuing profit, measuring cost is still probably very important in order to know if a cost budget is being followed. Beyond these simple reasons there may be very complex cost objectives to be achieved by a cost measurement system. We will present ideas of cost objectives by reference to business processes as well as information systems.

Some costs can clearly be seen as wholly incurred for some part of a job that can be *directly* charged to the customer, such as a service engineer's time repairing a faulty machine in response to the customer's request. Other costs, such as those for the service engineer's holidays, sickness and training are costs which clearly have to be paid for by the work done but need to be shared over all jobs done in, say, a year. They are *indirect* costs and, together with all other costs in this category such as equipment, facilities, management and a multitude of others, are lumped together as the **overhead** cost and are paid for by allocating a share of them to all jobs that customers pay for. Some of the most difficult decisions about the classification of costs concern the allocation of shared costs to particular goods and services. The most common dichotomies used are to categorize costs as fixed or variable, and production or non-production. There are no standard answers. There are some professional accounting guidelines and rules (we will not be concerned with professional accounting practices in this book) that must be followed in certain cases, but great care must be taken to ensure that the cost allocation regime adopted is appropriate to the specific cost objectives being pursued. We introduce a different approach, that of classifying costs at a high level of aggregation as either product or infrastructure costs.

Deferral of costs means that each cost is associated with the periods of related *revenues* instead of just with the periods when the cost was incurred. Clearly, doing this can have a major impact on the reported costs of current production. Where cost deferral is not practised, future profits may be underestimated if part of the production cost is written off elsewhere.

Opportunity costs are concerned with the idea that the *real* cost of doing something is not just the cost of the cash consumed but also the lost benefit that could have been obtained by using the same resources in an alternative way. Thus, considering just cash resources, the cost of a process is the cost of the cash spent plus the lost interest that cash could have earned.

Two developments in cost allocation have occurred. Firstly, the usual **overhead cost allocation** involves sharing out indirect costs by some standard measure such as the number of people employed. It has been recognized that this often leads to serious distortion in statements of costs for particular goods or services. An alternative approach is **activity based costing** whereby cost drivers are identified and then costs allocated to the activities that give rise to the costs. Secondly, the recent emergence of business process engineering has led to greater interest in allocating costs across a series of interlinked processes, called **process costing**.

Cost classification and collection

The basic collection of cost information is essentially a matter of self-discipline and organization. In furtherance of a business, or the objectives of an organization, every time something is purchased, or obtained with a promise to pay, cost is incurred. The first part of cost collection is a matter of recording the costs. Failure to do this is usually a matter of records of expenditure being lost or not made available for some reason. For example, it is possible for employees not to claim business expenses for some period of time, and so there is no visibility to the business of those costs until the claims are made. Similarly, some transactions may occur without formal records at the time, in which case someone needs to make a note to ensure they are recorded.

A large organization may have many responsibility centres that are responsible for expenditure and revenue and given a budget at the beginning of a year. Where a department is only spending money, and has a budget for its expenses, a frequent way to approach managing this is to define the department as a **cost centre**. Each cost centre will have various categories of expense and as cost information is collected, it is allocated to the appropriate cost centre and classified according to the different categories, as Figure 10.1 shows.

Goods purchased	100 000			
Transport costs	3 000			
Advertising	15 000			
Cost of sales		118 000		
Salaries	30 000			
Employment taxes	3 000			
Medical insurance	300			
Perks	5 000			
Travel and subsistence	10 000			
Employee costs		48 300		
Occupancy charges	3 500			
Utilities	500			
IS costs	2 000			
Professional fees	0			
Management charges	4 800			
Miscellaneous	2 500			
Functional costs		13 300		
Total cost centre expense			179 600	
Year-to-date total expense				1 550 300
Budget for year Apr 1995-Mar 96				2 160 000
Budget to date Apr-Nov 1995				1 440 000

FIGURE 10.1
Example of cost centre report for end November 1995.

It can be seen from this example that there are several simple ways to classify costs. Some of the common categories are: employment expenses; employee travel and subsistence; property occupancy costs; utilities; goods purchased to make into final goods for sale; advertising and marketing; equipment; buildings; repairs; office supplies; postage; postage and delivery. As will be seen below, in designing a system for classifying costs it is necessary to know what the consolidated cost information will be used for.

Beyond the simple forms of classifying costs, more complex variants may be used. For example, employment costs would collect all information about wages and salaries along with other unavoidable employment expenses such as employment taxes, pensions and medical insurance. The employment expense information could then be classified further according to different types of employee. For example: people employed directly in the production and delivery of goods and services; managers; secretarial and administrative support; research and development; building and transport services.

Some costs are related directly to the production and delivery of goods and services, whereas other costs are only related indirectly because they are incurred while providing some kind of infrastructure to support the production and delivery of a range of goods and services. For example, some managers may be responsible only for a service delivery activity which could not be delivered without operations management support. Such costs could reasonably be allocated to the service itself. However, other managers might have a range of responsibilities that cannot be attributed to particular goods or services.

Beyond cost centres, the other common type of responsibility centre would be a **profit centre**. This is a centre with budget responsibility not only for costs but also for some revenue. A profit centre is interested in comparing costs with revenues to establish profitability or **margin**.

Exercise 10.2

Before reading further, write down a set of categories of cost and revenue information that might be useful for a profit centre report.

A suggested solution containing some hypothetical data is shown in Figure 10.2.

Profit centre report for November 1995

Cost		
Goods purchased	100 000	
Transportation costs	3 000	
Advertising	15 000	
Cost of sales	118 000	118 000
Salaries	30 000	
Employment taxes	3 000	
Medical insurance	300	
Perks	5 000	
Travel and subsistence	10 000	
Employee costs	48 300	48 300
Occupancy charges	3 500	
Utilities	500	
IS costs	2 000	
Professional fees	0	
Management charges	4 800	
Miscellaneous	2 500	
Function costs	13 300	13 300
Total cost centre expense		179 600
Year-to-date expense		1 550 300
Budget for year (Apr 1995-Mar 96)		2 160 000
Budget to date		1 440 000

Revenue	
Orders booked this month	420 000
Current orders delivered this month	150 000
Previous orders delivered this month	230 000
Previous orders cancelled this month	17 280
Transferred to work in progress	59 600
Miscellaneous revenue	0
Revenue forecast for year	4 320 000
Orders booked to date	2 610 500
Cancellations to date	86 400

FIGURE 10.2
Example of profit centre report for November 1995.

From Figure 10.2, you will see that in addition to the simple cost and revenue information, some more complex information has been added to illustrate the point that even though a sale has been recorded, some care needs to be exercised until it has actually been paid for – much can go wrong until then.

Exercise 10.3

Examining Figure 10.2, how near is the cost centre to meeting its targets for the year? What should managers pay particular attention to? What additional information would you like on the profit centre report to support cost centre control?

The cost centre needs to be careful for the rest of the year. Its expenses are slightly above budget, and average monthly orders booked are below forecast. The profit centre is on target to make an operational profit. The best target for reducing expense would be cost of sales as employee and functional costs are likely to be difficult to reduce in the short term. It would be nice for the profit centre report to show the total value of work in progress compared with total orders outstanding to see if inventory provides scope to reduce goods purchased. The cost centre information does not indicate any required margin contribution to help the company achieve breakeven, so although the centre will make an operating profit, there is not enough information to know if there is any margin contribution to overall company profit.

In the design of information systems related to costs, it is very important to provide mechanisms to help people to record and classify costs. The provision of timely cost information is one of the foundation stones of knowing if a business is under control or not. It is astonishing how many businesses have great difficulty in providing estimates of what a particular activity costs, or get into financial difficulty through not knowing their level of costs for some time. In the design of business processes it is important to make provision for the processes to collect and classify cost information, and then take decisions based on an analysis of the consequences of the information.

Cost objectives

One of the key concepts related to analysing costs is to identify the specific **cost objectives** to be achieved by the way costs are allocated to activities. A cost objective refers to some kind of decision or category of information required with respect to cost information. At an overall aggregate level, a key cost objective is to compare total costs with total revenue in order to know gross profit. A marketing cost objective could be to compare marketing costs with revenues to understand the level of expenditure needed for marketing. Other examples of cost objectives were provided in the answer above. Here are some examples of more complex objectives for calculating and assigning the costs of particular processes in order to compare with:

- other ways of performing the process;
- taking decisions about which processes could be done externally;
- comparing with attributable revenue to establish the **added value** of a process;
- alternatives to the process;
- budgeted costs for the process;
- comparison with competitors' costs for performing similar processes.

The following subsections continue this discussion by reference to cost objectives for business processes and information systems.

Cost objectives for business processes

A frequent question in business process engineering is 'how much does a particular process cost?' A question like that needs to be unpacked in order to decide how to classify the various costs incurred. Several ways of interpreting the question follow.

(a) What is the cost over a determined period of time, of providing a certain service? – for example, how much will it cost to provide a three-year telephone service to 10 000 people who have bought a particular product where telephone service was provided as part of the sale?
(b) What does it cost to deliver a particular professional service? – for example, how much does it cost to produce the architectural plans for a house?
(c) How much does it cost per transaction for a service to provide a transactional environment? – for example, how much does it cost to make an airline reservation? How much does it cost to enter an order?
(d) How much does it cost to provide an IS infrastructure service? – for example, how much does it cost to acquire, install, operate and maintain the computers, communications and software to support all the computer-based applications of a company?

These examples indicate very different cost objectives to be met by collecting and classifying cost information. They illustrate the difficulties faced by the analyst.

Exercise 10.4

Before continuing with the reading, try to write down some of the problems that arise from each of the questions above – do this by sketching out tables to classify costs in such a way that the problems posed by the questions could be approached.

Suggested solutions are shown in Table 10.1.

Cost objectives for information systems

As with business processes, there are many different reasons why cost information may be collected and classified with respect to information systems. Here are some examples of information system cost objectives.

(a) What are IS costs as a proportion of total costs and total revenue?
(b) Which IS costs produce the greatest efficiencies in operation?
(c) How do electronic mail costs compare with hard copy mail techniques?
(d) What is the cost-per-seat for system development, or document processing?
(e) What are the IS costs of processing an order?

Question	Cost objective	Sample cost schema
(a)	What is the cost over a determined period of time, to provide a product support telephone service?	Number of calls per period; average duration ; costs per person answering calls; useful person days per year; hours per day.
(b)	What does it cost to deliver a particular professional service?	Labour; overheads; materials.
(c)	How much does it cost per transaction for a service to provide a transactional environment?	Number of transactions; person time per transaction; machine time per transaction; fully loaded labour costs.
(d)	How much does it cost to provide an IS infrastructure service?	Equipment costs; acquisition and maintenance; operational costs; occupancy costs; communications costs; support costs; software acquisition; software development.

TABLE 10.1
Business process sample cost objectives

Exercise 10.5

Before continuing with the reading attempt to set out a table of cost information that you would collect to answer these questions (a) to (e) p. 290.

Table 10.2 sets out some sample cost schemes for these questions.

Question	Cost objective	Sample cost schema
(a)	What are IS costs as a proportion of total costs and total revenue?	Total IS costs; total costs; total revenue.
(b)	Which IS costs produce the greatest efficiencies in operation?	Metrics for IS-supported activities and inputs; IS costs apportioned by activities; estimated costs of activities without IS support; operational metrics for activities without IS support.
(c)	How do electronic mail costs compare with hard copy mail techniques?	Preparation costs; transmission costs; storage costs
(d)	What is the cost-per-seat for system development, or document processing?	Number of professionals doing system development or document processing; costs of system acquisition, deployment, and use.
(e)	What are the IS costs of processing an order?	Number of orders per period of time; IS costs per period of time.

TABLE 10.2
Information systems sample cost objectives

A major problem with estimating the 'real' costs of an activity or acquisition is that many of the costs may not be realized explicitly. A typical example of this occurs when new equipment is made available. **Explicit costs** include categories such as acquisition, installation and training costs. Implicit costs can arise from incomplete training when the normal flow of work is interrupted to deal with enquiries about the new equipment. In order to understand this, consider the following exercise.

Exercise 10.6

Make a list of the factors that need to be taken into account to estimate the costs of computer ownership and use in an organization.

Direct costs include: computer hardware, communications and other ancillary equipment; software and associated licences; installation and training costs; and maintenance contracts. **Indirect costs** include: costs of the time to become familiar with the new features and functions including time obtaining informal support from colleagues and time they give to interruptions and providing help; time spent on version control, integrity, backups, recovery and security.

Product and infrastructure costs

A key concept of cost classification is to divide costs into **variable costs** and **fixed costs**. The essential difference between these two is that variable costs have a direct relationship to the volume of output whereas fixed costs are independent of output and must be carried in any event (even if for some period the output is zero).

Figure 10.3 (a) and (b) show these.

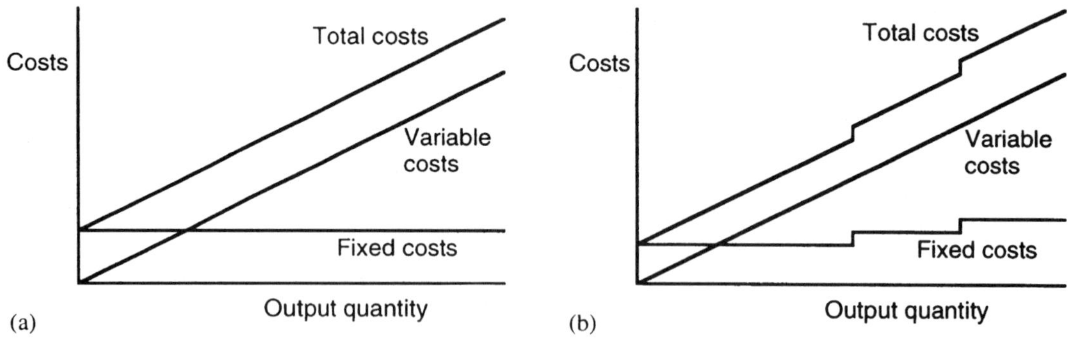

FIGURE 10.3 (a) and (b)
Variable and fixed costs.

In reality, however, the relationship between fixed and variable costs may be more complex than the example given in Figure 10.3(a). Fixed costs can only be considered as fixed for a particular period of time, or for a particular range of levels of output. For example, a particular information system configuration will have a maximum capacity for the work it can do, such as a maximum number of transactions and the IS costs will be the same within this capacity range. If new business leads to a need for more capacity, the new IS equipment and new configuration will then have fixed costs within a different range of output, as illustrated in Figure 10.3(b).

The graphs in Figure 10.3 give very simple relationships between output and cost. Economics and accounting texts give more detail.

A slight variation on fixed and variable costs is to refer to **variable costs** and **overhead costs**. Overhead costs are incurred for facilities that are used for many different goods and services, rather than being related to the volume of specific goods and services. We prefer to separate total costs into **product costs** of goods and services and **infrastructure costs**.

Product costs include materials purchased, direct labour and manufacturing overheads. Infrastructure costs include building occupancy, utilities, communications, ISs, office services and security. Other ways might allocate infrastructure costs to particular products.

Allocating overhead costs

Overhead costs were defined earlier as costs incurred to support the production and delivery of more than one good or service. Because they are effectively part of infrastructure costs, there are usually many possible ways to allocate them to the costs of delivered goods and services.

The first problem in deciding how to allocate overhead costs is to decide whether or not any attempt should be made to allocate them to the production of goods and services. This is usually more straightforward in a manufacturing system – manufacturing overheads are allocated to goods produced, whereas non-manufacturing costs are deducted from gross profit in the calculation of net profit (we will not be discussing the construction of balance sheets or income and expenditure statements). The need to do this is more apparent when it comes round to valuing stock and work in progress. Services and business processes have far less need to value stocks because there is little stock of value.

Table 10.3 shows some particular scenarios along with different ways in which the overhead costs could be allocated. These ways of allocating overhead costs are in common use.

In each of the examples shown in Table 10.3, the suggestion of a different way of allocating overheads is based on the recognition of an overall cost driver for the business, and the cost objective can be expressed in terms of metrics such as profit per person, profit per machine-hour, or profit per square metre of retail space.

Opportunity costs

The performance of a process involves the use of resources. A simple view of the cost of the process is to add up the cash costs of the resources used.

Scenario	*Usual overhead allocation mechanism*	*Example*
A service organization sells consulting services. The consultants use an infrastructure that includes building facilities, information systems, and secretarial support. There are central management services to cover human resources and finance.	Overhead per person	The various overheads are grouped into categories of expense (e.g. facilities, IS and telecom, secretarial support, HRO, finance), and the total costs in each category are divided by the number of consultants to give an average overhead cost per consultant.
A manufacturing company has extensive mass-production factories. Labour costs are only 17% of total costs. The main overheads relate to buildings and production machinery.	Overhead per machine-hour	Overheads are added together and divided by the average number of machine hours available for production. Product costs are built up from direct labour costs, material costs, and overheads obtained by multiplying the number of machine hours to produce something by the overhead rate per machine hour.
A retailing organization has a substantial amount of retail floor space and some separate office accommodation. The main direct costs of sales are the costs of buying in the products. The biggest overhead costs are rent and the cost of sales staff.	Overhead per square metre	Overheads are added together and divided by the total number of square metres of retail area. Goods are considered for sale in the shops depending on the profit per sale, number of sales per year, and area of sales space needed to handle the volume.

TABLE 10.3
Traditional overhead allocation criteria

A much more sophisticated approach to the cost of a particular process is to consider the nearest alternatives. Could the resources used for this process be used instead for a different one? Would that different process lead to higher revenue or higher added value? Could the process be done by someone else at a lower cost?

Hence the opportunity cost of a process can be measured by the alternatives foregone by opting for that process rather than by the cash cost of the process. One case of calculating opportunity cost led to the conclusion that a decision to undertake a software development inhouse was a more costly alternative to looking outside for two different reasons: (a) the equivalent functionality could have been purchased from an independent supplier for substantially less than the inhouse cost; (b) the people doing the development work could be used instead to earn revenue in a consulting role and thereby generate better cash flow.

This problem of opportunity costing explains in part why many companies arrange their activities to concentrate on **core competencies**. Undertaking processes outside this core is less efficient with respect to business objectives than using the resources for processes the company is actually better at doing.

Activity based costing

One of the reasons cited frequently for business process engineering and re-engineering is to do with achieving greater competitive advantage by more effective control of costs. This can only be done by more accurate costing to support decision making about which processes to undertake inhouse and which to subcontract.

Enterprises are becoming more extensively integrated, partly as a result of supporting information systems. One consequence of this is the increase in the size of infrastructures. Early overhead cost allocation systems were developed when non-product or non-manufacturing overheads were a relatively small proportion of total costs. Today, when knowledge work can absorb 50% of cost and most knowledge work is an overhead in some form, the allocation of costs has become a more complex problem. It is against this kind of background that activity based costing has emerged in recent years.

There is an additional reason why a recent emphasis on business processes may be more appropriate to activity based costing for the allocation of overheads. Traditional overhead allocation is based on allocating overhead costs to different departments (or responsibility centres) according to some volume-based formula (such as number of people employed, number of machine-hours, or space occupancy). Activity based costing is concerned with identifying those activities (processes) that contribute the most to the emergence of the overhead costs.

This means that the first step to implement activity based costing is to identify the activities performed, which is the same as identifying the business processes. For each activity, the resources used are determined together with their costs. As explained in Chapter 5, every process should be characterized by at least one type of event, and there may be more than one. Every process will also process inputs in response to those events. The events and inputs are the most likely **cost drivers** of the activities.

For activity based cost allocation, the work done by people whose costs are part of the overheads is classified by the activity to which it pertains. Thus the overheads are apportioned to the activities. The volumes of the events and inputs for each of the goods and services produced should be determined. The next step is to identify the cost drivers of the activities so that costs can be allocated to goods and services based on their contribution to the cost drivers.

Activity based costing is not practised universally, and accounting and management literature has debated its advantages and disadvantages. The process engineer should take note of the controversy but, ultimately, should be sure that: the main activities performed have been identified; appropriate metrics for the process/activities have been defined and data obtained for those metrics; whether the process engineer uses traditional cost allocation or activity based cost allocation, all relevant overheads must be accounted for and allocated; the cost-allocation procedures adopted should provide the most suitable information for the appropriate cost objectives.

Hence, although the process engineer is likely not to be a professional accountant, the engineer should be able to establish a set of cost objectives based on the decisions needed about the various processes and their costs. A professional accountant can always be used to help with defining the relevant collection and classification schemes, and making sure that they can be mapped to other objectives such as financial reporting requirements.

Process costing

In **process costing** (as opposed to job costing), the flow of costs follows the flow of work. In other words overheads are allocated to the processes in a process chain. As goods and services pass from one process to the next, the costs associated with the flow are brought forward into the next process.

Revenue considerations

So far revenue has been mentioned briefly. For the purposes of this book the most important consideration is that of using cost information as one basis for the rationalization of processes. We do not intend to address revenue.

The process engineer only needs to refer to revenue information where that is needed for the application of some cost objective, such as maximizing margin from a range of alternative ways of performing a process.

Self check

Objectives

After reading this chapter you should be able to:

- understand the terms in most frequent use concerning BP and IS cost accounting;
- understand the main differences between traditional costing and activity based costing;
- state a set of objectives for a classification and analysis of costs;
- identify and help with the allocation of product and infrastructure costs.

Questions

We have not provided questions that test understanding of this chapter.

11 Analysing and describing data

We need to explain to you several further principles about types of information, knowledge, data, processes and behaviour. Some of these principles have a sound mathematical basis. In this chapter we use the term **data** to correspond to a representation of facts about any combination of knowledge, information, behaviour, systems, processes or almost anything. So data structures created by analysts, programmers and/or users of ISs and correctly built on the principles will have desirable properties, which can help with correctness, completeness, consistency, ease of use and integrity – like Table 9.7 for the washing-machine. Updates to data occurrences and changes to data structures should not cause confusing difficulties where the data is structured and manipulated correctly. So the actions that are done should conform to the principles to avoid trouble. Some of these principles were researched in the 1970s and only became reasonably widely understood in the 1980s. Others researched more recently are still not widely understood.

Be warned. Some of what follows is intellectually not very easy to grasp. Some people will find parts of what follows easy and familiar and then perhaps almost suddenly meet something new. Others will find it all too difficult, and should perhaps just skim through or omit it altogether. Most people need several tens of hours of tuition to understand the majority of what follows – coupled with examples and perhaps face-to-face explanations of each concept. Usually such text would be five or ten times as many pages as we can afford here. However, many simple cases and early versions of models appear not to need all of the points explained. Those who are happy with only partial understanding, just enough for their current needs, may like to skim through what follows and use it for reference when they need it for their work.

Even in the 1990s, through lack of understanding, many users of spreadsheets create poor structures and then run into difficulties that could have been avoided. Designers of database structures have to work carefully to ensure that later users can do all the actions that they need yet cannot create inconsistent data. Similarly, creators of object oriented structures do not always get it right, and are also constrained because software packages do not provide all of the facilities needed. In each case there is a need for the skills to describe data and data structures correctly.

First we shall explain how to create entity–attribute–relationship (EAR) data models. These should be produced with constraints of particular hardware and software ignored while doing the analysis. This idea was not widely accepted before the late 1970s, but it avoids the pitfall that 'the data must be structured like that to fit the computer system ...', whether or not it matches the user's needs.

Anna may carry in the back of her mind the principles below. So if Idris proposes something that conflicts with the principles Anna can ask for clarification. Idris need not know the principles and Anna need not know the underlying mathematics. We explain the principles without using any mathematical symbols.

Purpose and form of models

The general objective is to create a data model that represents the structure of the information, data and knowledge used in relevant processes. The model should be understandable and have minimum redundancy – avoiding several representations of the same thing. It should be suitable to be used later as the basis for models needed during design, construction and use.

The organization of the business – its size, management system, objectives, strategy and its existing systems – will affect secondary aspects of the purposes of the EAR model. There are several alternative ways of creating a suitable model including the four below, aspects of which could be combined.

The first alternative is to create a **global** data model. The intention is that it will form the basis of a *model such as a schema for a database*, or an improvement to an existing schema. The main intention is to include all the kinds of data, knowledge and information handled in the organization. Some of these will be held in IT-based systems and others will not. The business processes are assumed to be likely to evolve more than the data structures (which are assumed more likely to be stable), so the analysis mainly concentrates on data, not on business functions and functional analysis.

A second alternative concentrates on **functional analysis** to identify the main business functions, which are given an order of priority. In principle each function could be analysed to create a local model but, in practice, after the first has been modelled it is simply extended to add anything needed for the subsequent functions. Different analysts may work in parallel in different business areas and combine their models as soon as convenient.

In the third alternative, various **separate** business functions and processes are analysed to indicate the various kinds of data, knowledge and information flows. The purpose is to create *separate local* models that cover the various kinds of data and processes. Each local data model may be created by gradually extending a small initial part of it. These local models should be cross-checked for consistency, otherwise difficulties may arise later in merging the many local views.

The fourth alternative assumes that only a **part** of the business is likely to be a worthwhile application of IT. The aim is, therefore, to do the minimum work for that part, which might use only spreadsheets or a particular standard package.

All these four alternatives can be modelled using entities, attributes and relationships (EAR), and they can also be modelled using normalized entity types, as described later (pp. 311 and 319). Databases, spreadsheets and object oriented structures may be used with any of the four alternatives and as implementations of either EAR or normalized entity types. This discussion is continued later (p. 318–325).

Entities

We have briefly introduced entities in Chapters 2 and 6. People like Anna think of knowledge and information as being about entities, e.g. a particular object, building, person or vehicle. In general anything can be thought of as an entity. It may be a physical object, e.g. the Eiffel Tower, or the coffee table in the lounge in Geoffrey Darnton's house on 29 June 1994. These entities are particular physical objects. We have carefully chosen examples where only *one* exists. Alternatively an entity may be intangible, e.g. 1 January 1994, a particular telephone call or the thought in your mind at a particular instant.

Idris and Anna need not have seen or experienced an entity to discuss it. Each can imagine it, forming a mental image, and each may do so slightly differently.

Usually in the real world many somewhat similar entities exist. People then have names for the set, e.g. population, customers, staff, roads, buildings, furniture or rocks. Each of these is a name for a **type of entity**, with many actual occurrences. How people choose to group objects into sets corresponding to named entity types may depend on what aspects they think are likely to be useful. Most descriptions of business processes and information requirements are explained in generalizations using the names of the entity types. For example, Idris might say: 'each customer sends in orders'. This generalization covers a thousand sentences for a thousand orders.

Data analysis involves finding out what are the relevant sets, i.e. classes of similar entities. Each is given a name, e.g. Customer. Usually **singular** names are used, with an initial capital letter. This helps Anna and others later. In discussions and text describing requirements and processes Idris and Anna may use singulars or plurals with or without an initial capital.

Entities, attributes and relationships

Data analysis also involves finding out what kinds of knowledge and information exist about each entity, e.g. each building has an address and a person or an organization owns or rents it. Here Building, Person and Organization are names of entity types. Address is the name of an attribute type because it can have a value – a string of characters. Sends in, Owns and Rents are names of relationship types.

Relationship types are normally **between entity types**, *not* between attribute types. We explain that word 'normally' below (p. 308–9), under *Choosing the initial entities or tables.*

From here on we drop the word 'type' where the context indicates that it is not needed. For example we say Building and Person are entities, Address is an attribute, and Owns is a relationship.

You may wonder how to choose whether something is an entity, an attribute or a relationship. You can spot attributes because the *occurrences have a value*. Think of an **attribute-value pair**. For example, in colour green, Colour is the name of the attribute type and Green is an occurrence. Address is a **compound attribute** (= **composite attribute**), composed of several subattributes, each being a line of characters or postcode/zipcode.

Often, in ordinary sentences the **nouns are entities** and the **verbs are relationships**. A particular occurrence of the subject of the sentence may be related through relationship occurrences to several occurrences of the object. For example, 'Each Organization may Own several Buildings', as above. Also each entity occurrence and each relationship occurrence does *not* have a simple *value* in the way that an attribute has. Each entity usually has several named attributes. For example, an entity, Customer, perhaps has attributes: name, invoice address, telephone number, delivery address, customer number, and so on.

We now go on to explain tables representing entities and attributes and return to relationships later.

Table structures corresponding to entities and attributes

Another way to represent entities and attributes is a table with several columns, as in Table 11.1. This table corresponds to packets of seeds. A typical packet has on it below the name instructions such as: 'Sow in light, well prepared soil from May to July, in rows 50 cm apart, with seeds at 10 cm spacing and 5 cm deep. Water in dry weather.' Such sentences can sometimes be converted into table structures where some attribute names might have to be invented as column headings. In some occurrences data may be missing or not specified.

Seed packet table

Name	*Preferred soil*	*Earliest UK sowing date*	*Latest UK sowing date*	*How to lay out*	*Depth to sow each seed*	*Other notes*
Dwarf French Bean Selection	Light, well prepared	May	July	In rows 50cm apart, with seeds at 10cm spacing	5cm	Water in dry weather
Forcing Chicory Apollo	Deep and rich	Late May	Mid June	In rows 50 cm apart	Not specified	Thin plants to 30cm apart

TABLE 11.1
A table with each row corresponding to an entity occurrence and its attributes

The name of the whole table is usually the name of an entity type, e.g. Seed packet. The headings of the columns are usually attributes. Each row represents an entity occurrence, a packet of seeds. The value in each cell of the table is an attribute occurrence.

For the moment we call the types of knowledge associated with an entity its **attributes**, where each has a value. We give a more precise definition later (p. 314).

The specification of Table 11.1, giving the entity/table name and the attributes is written:

```
Seed_packet(Name, Preferred soil, Earliest UK
  sowing date, Latest UK sowing date, How to lay
  out, Depth to sow each seed, Other notes).
```

Features of a table and the meanings of associations

Tables are a way of representing associations between objects such as entities and attribute values. It is useful to understand properly the underlying assumptions and structure, which are built on the properties of sets and associations. So we explain these next and gradually build up to functions and other properties that are used extensively in information systems and processes. These properties are used in later sections.

A table such as Table 11.1 represents various facts about occurrences of a single entity type. Each row is called an **entity tuple**, pronounced to rhyme with couple. It represents several facts about a single entity occurrence.

Consider the second entity tuple. The existence of the entity is represented by the occurrence in the first column of the **identifying** attribute value. This is an **attribute-value pair** – Name and Forcing Chicory Apollo. Strictly it represents an **association** between the real world seed packet and the name 'Forcing Chicory Apollo'. This is an association between a real object from the set of seed packets, and a value from a set of names. The names must be distinct. We explain the detailed properties of identifiers later, to avoid breaking the flow here.

Sets

A **set** is a well-defined collection of distinct objects, called **members** or **elements**. It may be defined either by listing all of the elements, called **tabular form** or extensive form, as in the first column of Table 11.1; or by stating a rule or a property that the members have to satisfy, called **set-builder form** or intensive form. The set-builder form would be that each element must be the name of a seed packet available from a particular supplier. When written, members of a set are enclosed in curly brackets and separated by commas, e.g. {Dwarf French Bean Selection, Forcing Chicory Apollo, ...}. **Cardinality** is used to mean the number of members in a set.

> A **set** is a well-defined collection of distinct objects, called members or elements. A set may be defined by a rule or by listing the elements. No meaning is carried by the order in which they are listed. A subset is some or all of the members.

Facts, properties of entities and associations

A **fact** is an assertion either that a particular entity occurrence exists or that a particular entity occurrence has a particular value for a particular property. Each real world **fact** is represented by the value appearing in a cell of an entity tuple row and an attribute column; each such entry is an **attribute-value pair**. A cell entry represents an association between members of two sets. For example, the occurrence of the name Forcing Chicory Apollo in the first column represents the fact that the corresponding real seed packet exists. And, for example, 'Mid June' represents the association between real Forcing Chicory Apollo seed from the set of real *Seeds*, and the value 'Mid-June' of the attribute 'Latest UK sowing date'. Alternatively and equivalently, it can be viewed as between 'Forcing Chicory Apollo' from the set of *Names* and the value 'Mid-June' of the attribute 'Latest UK sowing date'. The first view was an association between a real object and an attribute value: the second was between members of two sets of attribute values.

A **fact** is an assertion that, either implicitly or explicitly, involves an entity occurrence, the name of a property (an attribute name), the corresponding property value, and the direction of the association (to show which is the entity and which is the property). For example, 'Sue lives in London' involves the entity Sue, the property Lives in, and the value London. A fact can also be an assertion that associates several property values in a particular meaning. For example, the assertion 'Westminster and Euston are in the same city' involves two attribute-value pairs (Place – Westminster; Place – Euston) and the implied associated property (In city – Lóndon).

A **property** is a named characteristic of an entity occurrence, e.g. Name, Colour. A **property value** is an occurrence of a property of an entity, e.g. Brown. By itself such a value has no meaning, it has to be associated with a property as an **attribute** of some entity.

Next we need to explain some points about the *collections* of values that actually occur and those that could occur.

The entries in a whole column of a table such as Table 11.1 represent the whole collection of associations for that particular attribute. The values that *actually* occur in a particular column are chosen from the set of values that *could* occur. For example, married couples are associations of a male person and a female person, each from the appropriate sets of people, but not all males nor all females belong to the association.

Sometimes an association is from a set to itself. For example Reports-to is an association between employees – from the set of employees to the set of employees.

Where the sets are different, role names usually do not have to be specified explicitly since the roles played by the sets are usually obvious from the names of the sets. So usually the set names can also serve as role names.

In Table 11.1 two columns, 'Earliest UK sowing date' and 'Latest UK sowing date', have the *same* set of values that *could* occur. Each represents an association between a seed and a date, but the dates have different roles and in this case the attribute names distinguish the roles. Invoice address and delivery address associated with an order have the same feature.

In an association from the members of a set A to the members of a set B, set A is called the **domain**, and set B is called the **codomain**.

Next we distinguish and define three kinds of associations.

Simple, conditional, and complex associations

A *single* value occurs in a cell where the corresponding attribute is simple. A **simple association** between two sets A and B always has a single value in B for each occurrence in A. Exactly one member of B is associated with each member of A. This is also called **to-one**. 'Can sow in UK until' is a simple association. The definition is not concerned with whether or not the values are known. For example marital status is a simple association, even though a particular information system might or might not know the marital status of a particular person. Each person maps to one of single/married/widowed/separated/divorced.

A **conditional association** between members of two sets A and B is where, dependent on some condition, each member of set A is associated with either none or one of set B (but not more than one of set B). This is called '**to-none-or-one**'. An **optional attribute** of an entity type is similar, meaning that each entity occurrence might or might not have an associated value for the attribute, e.g. each person might or might not have a telephone number. Where an attribute is optional and conditional, for each entity occurrence either a single value of the attribute will occur or no value will occur. In Table 11.1 'Depth to sow each seed' is an optional attribute since for some seed it is not specified.

An association is called **complex** where each member of set A can be associated with *any number* (including zero) of members of set B. This is also called '**to-many**'. An example would be where each student had a collection of corresponding courses being studied. Similarly if some people have several telephone numbers that is a complex optional attribute, assuming telephone number is treated as an attribute without having Telephone as a separate entity type.

Sometimes the entries in a column may each have a substructure or may even have no predefined allowed structure or set of allowed values, e.g. the Other notes could be almost anything.

For two sets A and B, the applicability of simple, conditional and complex depend only on the associations in the direction from the members of set A to those of B. The mapping in the direction from B to A may be the same or quite different.

Sometimes two names may be given for the two directions of an association, e.g. Owns and Owned by or Reports-to and Manager-of. Where the names are derived from verbs it is sometimes convenient to use an active form and a passive form for the names in the two directions, e.g. Contains and Contained-in.

Associations can be formed from two sets, a domain and a codomain. Associations may be: simple, to-one; conditional, to-none-or-one; or complex, to-many. The association in the other direction may be different.

Cartesian products of any number of sets, and relations

The above was restricted to mappings between two sets or from a set to itself. The concepts can be extended by defining mappings between two subsets of Cartesian products of *any number* of sets. This leads to the idea of relations, which are the basis of **relational database** structures.

An **ordered pair** consists of two elements, say a and b, and is written <a, b>. For example, <Richard, Maddison> is an ordered pair consisting of a first name and a surname. The two values in an ordered pair are chosen from appropriate sets.

The **Cartesian product** of two sets A and B, written A × B, is the set of *all* ordered pairs <a, b> where a belongs to set A and b belongs to B. For example, the Cartesian product of the first names {Geoffrey, Richard} and the surnames {Darnton, Maddison} is the four ordered pairs {<Geoffrey, Darnton>, <Geoffrey, Maddison>, <Richard, Darnton>, <Richard, Maddison>}. These four *could* occur, but only two actually do occur.

The Cartesian product of several sets A, B, … E, written A × B × … E, is the set of all tuples <a, b, … e> where a belongs to A and so on. The Cartesian product of Courses × Rooms × Staff represents all possible combinations of those, e.g. all that *could* occur. The term **Product set** means the same as Cartesian product.

Where all the sets involved have a *finite* number of members, the Cartesian products will also have a finite number of members, in other words finite cardinality.

A **binary relation** of two sets A and B is a subset of the Cartesian product A × B. Typically it represents the pairs that are *actually* associated. Here binary means on *two* sets. A scatter diagram of actual heights and weights of people is a representation of a binary relation. It shows what weights occur for each height. There is only one dot for several people who all have exactly the same height and weight. A typical couple/tuple occurrence is <1.94 m, 76.9 kg>. Each couple/tuple is different.

An ordered pair can be reversed, e.g. <Maddison, Richard>. Every binary relation has a **reverse relation**, from its set B to its set A. The reverse of the above example would show what heights occur for each weight.

An **n-ary relation** extends the idea to subsets of a Cartesian product of n sets. For example a list of what kinds of car (Make, Model, Colour, Year of manufacture) are available at a dealer on a certain date is an n-ary relation. All four attributes must be specified for each tuple or car. They could be printed as a table with four columns. Such *relations* will not have repetitions. Two cars with different registration numbers but which are otherwise similar will give only one tuple. No information is carried by the order in which the tuples are printed down the page.

A **ternary relation** is based on three sets, e.g. Suppliers, Materials and Products.

A **unary relation** is based on just one set. The years between 1970 and 1990 in which snow fell in London form a unary relation; it does not matter how many times snow fell in a particular year.

By contrast a **list** is a structure in which an item may be repeated – duplicates are allowed in a list. For example, the names of the employees of a firm is a list, since two people may have the same name and thus result in a duplicate entry in the list.

> Ordered pairs have one element from each set, placed in the right order. An n-tuple is a structure with n elements in the right order and chosen from the n corresponding sets. Cartesian products consist of all possible tuples from appropriate sets. A relation is a subset of a Cartesian product. It cannot have any duplicate tuples, all are distinct. By contrast a list may have duplicates.

Functions

Functions are needed for creating correctly structured data models and for corresponding business structures. A **function** is a special kind of association between *two* sets, A and B. In a function *each* member of A is associated with *exactly one* corresponding member of B. *Every* member of A must participate. Two or more members of A may have the same member of B. A member of B may be involved none, one or more times in association occurrences. We say '*f* is a function of A into B' and write f: A → B. Again A is called the domain and B is the codomain. The members of B that participate are called the **range of the function**. For example Age is a function of/from person into years. For an occurrence we write 'Age: Mr Jones → 20' or Age(Mr Jones) = 20', and say the 'Age of Mr Jones is 20'.

The domain and codomain of a function may each be subsets of Cartesian products of any number of sets. Some of the associations in Table 11.1 are functions from the name of the seed to the attribute value – those where the attribute *must* have a value. But the relation between heights and weights, and the kinds of car relation, are not functions.

We say B is **functionally dependent on** A if there is a function from A to B. Two or more such functions need different names to distinguish them and roles may be needed.

A is **compound** if it consists of several attributes. We say that B is **fully functionally dependent** on A where values for *all* the attributes in an A occurrence are needed to determine the corresponding B occurrence. For example, Quantity-ordered is fully functionally dependent on both Order-no and Part-no; or on both Order-no and Line-no-on-order.

> A **function** is a rule that associates each member of a set A to exactly one corresponding member of B. Members of B may participate but need not do so. Sometimes a function can be represented by a set of ordered pairs, with all their first elements different.

Two functions, say *f* from A to B and *g* from B to C, can be *combined*. This creates the **product function**, also called the **composition function**. Using the function *f*, each member *a* of set A has an image *b* in set B. This *b* then has an image *c* in C, by using the function *g*. These combine to give a function from *a* to the image *c*. We write and say '*g* of *f*' or '*g* o *f*' for the product function or composition function. It means do *f* first then do *g*. For example, Age of Manager of employee means start from the employee, find the manager, then find the age of that manager. We could write 'Age of Manager of employee = Age(Manager(employee))'. This shows why *g* of *f* means do *f* first: here *f* is Manager, and *g* is Age. This example assumes every employee has a manager. This idea of product function is used extensively in information systems and business processes, usually without explicitly saying so.

The term **total function** means a function where starting from a given input or data it is possible in a finite number of human operations, and/or amount of computing, either to find the image or else to report that the input data is not a valid value in the domain. Procedures that look up values in tables and/or databases are total functions. Total functions can also apply to sets with infinitely many members, where the possible values could not all be held in a finite-sized store. For example, the area of any rectangular plot of land may be calculated by multiplying its length and width.

A **partial function** is where *some* members of set A do *not* have an image in set B. Strictly this is *not* a function as defined above. The meaning of partial function is that given some input data, within a finite time either the image will be obtained, or it will be reported that the input is in the domain but does not have an image, or else it will be reported that the input is not in the domain. If some people have passports, from person name to passport-no is a partial function.

Products of functions apply a second function to the result of the first function. Total functions are computable in a finite number of steps. Partial functions allow set A to have either none or one image, optionally, so strictly are not functions.

Time

The above was restricted to tables, data, associations, facts and knowledge that could exist at a particular instant of **time**. But marital status can change with time, new seeds can become known or created as time passes and the cars for sale change.

In order to model time dependence correctly Anna can adopt any one of three ways. In the first, any attributes that can have values which change with time have a corresponding time associated with them. So instead of a relation or table associating an Employee-no with a Name, the fuller relation in the conceptual model has Employee-no, Start-date-for-name, End-date-for-name, and Name.

Name is **fully functionally dependent** on all the first three. A new **entity tuple** is created whenever a person changes their name.

In the second way the table or stored data represents the real situation only *at a particular instant*, so the table entries never change. The table may have a time associated with it and a new table with new entries or stored data is created occasionally as time passes and the real situation changes. One such table represents the **current** situation, others represent past situations. A collection of several changes is handled together to create a new table, such as having a new holiday brochure for each year.

Care is needed if the second way is extended to a *period* of time, e.g. the whole seeds table is correct for several months of 1994 but may or may not be correct and/or complete for other years. Introducing extra columns corresponding to instants of time and/or the starts and ends of periods as in the first way, usually helps to clarify things but does lead to complications.

The third way leads to even more complications. Here the table has to be maintained so that it always represents the **current** state of knowledge of reality. Whenever the real situation changes, the appropriate information about the change must be captured and transmitted to the person or system maintaining the table, and the appropriate table entries must be altered. Information about the past is lost and cannot be so represented. Extra rules are needed about which cell entries can and cannot change and alternative futures such as various possible plans cannot be represented.

Mixing these alternative ways in different places in an information system, e.g. in different parts of a collection of databases, can lead to confusion. However, in practice they *are* frequently mixed, perhaps for efficiency. The first way is used to hold the representation of the past and possible futures, and the second way is used for holding the current situation. Extra and more complicated processes are usually needed, e.g. to convert between these different representations, and to update the past in one way and the current in another way when the current situation changes.

Further complex processes are needed if the information about real world changes can be delayed during capture and transmission to the IS. Then facts about changes reach the IS in the wrong order and extra complex features might be needed to cope with this. For example, someone may phone and arrange something tentatively, to be confirmed later. The organization's procedures are usually such that it should not be formally entered in the IT-based system until it is confirmed. The staff therefore have to keep notes of the phone call. What if further facts, dependent on the tentative agreement, arrive before the written confirmation? For example, what if someone phones to renew an insurance policy and then makes a claim before the renewal premium is received? Again, if an IT-based system allows only one address for someone, how does a clerk input a letter giving three future addresses each covering a few days or weeks? Students at home, at college, and in temporary work can easily have multiple addresses. The perceived problem is that the clerk wants to input *now* information corresponding to various real world changes that will take place at various future dates. The underlying problem is how to form the right models and processes so that every future communication is posted to the right address, allowing for the variable number of days the post is expected to take to different places.

Primitives

In the above discussion the following are **primitives**, i.e. they cannot be meaningfully decomposed into simpler ideas: entity, property, property value, relationship. The representations were developed from other primitives including: set, element/member, domain, association, role, Cartesian product, relation, list, function. The real world has many primitives in most everyday views of it, including: physical and mathematical primitives such as time, mass, distance, object and number; and properties such as distinguishable.

The terms entity type, entity set, relationship occurrence, relationship set, domain, entity attribute and relationship attribute are defined more fully below.

> Tables are constructed from rows corresponding to entity tuples. The columns correspond to attributes and are named in the column headings. The entries in each column are members of an appropriate set. Roles may be needed where two or more columns have values from the same set. Usually the left column or columns are attributes that have distinct values that identify or associate them with the corresponding real world objects. Other columns have cell entries that are values in attribute-value pairs. These other attributes may or may not be functions of the identifying column values. A table structure may be a relation or a list. Table look-up processes can be used within total and partial functions.

Choosing the initial entities or tables

When Idris and Anna choose what to have as an entity, attribute or a relationship their choices depend on their point of view. This includes their views of the likely purposes of the data, information and knowledge occurrences. They choose what to include, and which way round to include them.

For example, an organization usually does not want to store and process knowledge about the colour of each employee's eyes, or their heights. So Eye-colour and Height will not be included as attributes in an EAR data model. But Surname will be an attribute of the entity Employee. Most people think of marriage as a relationship between two persons, each person being an entity. But to a registrar the marriage certificate is an entity and the names, date and other details that are filled in are attributes.

We wrote the word 'normally' in: 'Relationship types are normally between entity types'. Our meaning is that initially Anna and Idris work in a rule-free way, so they initially allow relationships between anything. Eventually some of their initial attributes may become further entities, and some of their initial relationships may become something else. At the end of working out the whole structure, they usually finish with a structure in which each entity has some attributes, and each relationship is between entities.

Relationships may be between several entities

Some authors recommend or insist that each relationship type only involves two entity types. We do not agree for two reasons. Firstly, Idris and Anna should work in a rule-free way and not be artificially forced to create relationships only between pairs of entities. Secondly, many situations naturally need relationships between *more than two* entities.

Universities/Schools, Teachers, Courses, Books and Years could have a relationship that declares which teacher uses which books on which courses at which university/school in each term/year. Each of the entities needs to be an entity type as it has several attributes, e.g. each Book has author, title, publisher, publication date, ISBN, price and other attributes.

Another example is the need to define which maintenance engineers visit which customers to mend which makes and models of equipment.

Desirable properties of conceptual data models

The data models using entities, attributes and relationships have several desirable properties. We illustrate this by first discussing a table.

Property 1. In a table such as Table 11.1, each cell corresponds to one fact about one attribute within one entity occurrence. Each cell may have a suitable value entered in it. The structure should remain correct for ever with further occurrences of the entity being added as extra rows.

Property 2. The occurrences avoid **redundant** repetition of any fact, e.g. the preferred soil for a particular seed only appears once. There is only one place in Table 11.1 for it. This is the basis later of *avoiding inconsistencies* from structures that allow more than one place for that knowledge to be placed, and where different values could be entered in the various places.

Redundancy is not the same as duplication, i.e. having several copies. **Duplication** includes having several copies in a business system or an IS or computer for efficiency, but controlled so as to avoid inconsistency of the information produced. Duplication by photocopying and distributing the copies does not cause difficulties. Of course people are not allowed to change their individual copies and think that they have changed the master version. Essentially only one person is allowed to control the master copy.

Property 3. *All* relevant facts can be represented although only once. Every occurrence row has a place for each attribute value. The structure automatically ensures that when a new occurrence is created, there are places for all of the relevant facts.

Property 4. The whole structure can easily be extended. Anna and Idris can add further attributes as extra columns to a table.

Property 5. The different users of an information system that holds such a table can be allowed to have slightly **different views as structures**. For example, several different users could be given facilities as follows. The first is allowed to enter extra rows in a table such as Table 11.1 which then goes into the information system. A second user is allowed to read a copy of certain columns of that table, but not allowed even to know of the existence of certain other columns. A third user is allowed different headings for certain columns, e.g. the equivalent of different attribute names. A fourth user is given a view in which the left-to-right order of the columns is different. A fifth user gets a view where the rows are sorted into a different order, e.g. in order of earliest sowing date. Where people in different departments have different views or models, these are called **local** models.

Anna and Idris can think of these various user views. More importantly they may, during the analysis of requirements, talk to various people in different departments. These various people may think of such differing views and structures quite naturally and Idris and Anna should allow them to speak in these terms. Anna and other specialists should know how the various views and structures can be merged, so that each is seen as a different view of a more global whole structure.

Property 6. Table 11.1 has another desirable feature. Each row has a different value in the first column and so can be used to identify the rows, even if shown in a different sequence.

This gives the idea of an **identifying attribute**. All the values that occur are distinct and every occurrence has a value for the identifying attribute. The value of the identifier must be known or created when knowledge about the occurrence is first created, or when anything about that occurrence is first entered or stored for the first time. The value must not change thereafter, except for correcting errors. For George's convenience, the values should not be prone to mistranscription, e.g. confusingly using the letter O and the digit 0. An identifier may include coded characters, e.g. most UK vehicle registration numbers have a letter that is a code for the year of first registration. Some identifiers include a check character, often at the end, which is arranged to help detect wrong values or copying errors.

These desirable properties of tables can be extended. Not only do they apply to tables such as Table 11.1, they can be extended and applied to all appropriate entity–attribute–relationship structures. Specialists should be educated to know the details, some of which are given later (pp. 316–8).

> Identifying attributes should be chosen so that values will be known or created when information or knowledge first occurs, values will not change and mistakes in copying are unlikely.

Various alternatives and how they correspond

Practitioners should be able to create correctly structured data models. They also should be able to check the completeness and consistency of corresponding business processes.

Of the various ways of representing the structure of knowledge, data and information we concentrate on four. For clarity below we assume Anna has four colleagues, **Eric**, **Aggie**, **Nora** and **Obadiah** who specialize in these four ways.

1. **Entities, attributes and relationships** (EAR) – introduced in Chapters 2 and 5 and earlier in this chapter.
2. **Aggregates** – an intermediate alternative that has some of the good features of EAR and normalized entities.
3. **Normalized** entities – this type is explained below. Essentially a collection of normalized entity types has certain desirable features with attributes of each entity type selected to prevent redundancy, disallowing two representations of a single fact. It is like a correctly structured table in which all relevant facts can be represented once, and the whole structure can easily be extended. Local views for different people and applications can easily be derived. This forms the basis for well-structured relational databases.
4. **Object oriented** structures – these concentrate on certain aspects, particularly properties, rules and processes and on how subobjects inherit the properties, rules and processes of their parent objects, together with the consequences. For example, all attributes that are dates have a certain collection of properties, rules and corresponding processes. The ISs should provide facilities to exploit these.

Specialists should understand how to transform between these alternatives.

We concentrate below on what Anna and others should do, i.e. the skills the practitioner should be able to apply. We summarize the underlying reasons such as the desirable features but omit the underlying mathematical foundations, or express them in ways that avoid strings of mathematical symbols. Some practitioners understand how to create an entity type in third normal form (3NF, explained below) but generally most are unable to structure correctly more complex cases or to spot the business processes needed. Most real situations, however, involve these more complex cases and also need a complex collection of business processes and so we gradually build up to explaining how to do both.

The skills developed from understanding normalization are useful. They lead to an ability to ask the right questions to help clarify an initial draft model that has unsatisfactory relationships or entities. They also lead to an ability to spot what business processes need to be specified, and whether at any stage those currently specified are sufficient. Consistency and completeness checks are valuable.

The skills also lead to an ability to create correctly implementable specifications of transaction systems, management information systems, and knowledge handling information systems. They also lead to correct logical model structures, and hence to avoiding implemented ISs with certain undesirable features.

Better definitions of entities, relationships and attributes

Next we give better definitions and generalizations of some terms concerning entities, relationships, domains, and attributes. These are needed for the proper definition of keys and identifiers.

Entity occurrences having the same kind of properties are classed together into the same entity type which we call an **entity type**, or a type of entity. Each entity type is named, e.g. Employee, and an **entity set** is the collection of such entities that exist at a particular instant as, for example, the collection of employees. Entity sets are not necessarily disjoint, i.e. an entity occurrence may be a member of more than one entity set. For example, a person may belong to a set of Employees and to a set of Customers. Further points are made later, under *Reconsidering the entities*. Two sets are **disjoint** means that no element of set A belongs to set B and no element of B is in A.

A **relationship occurrence** is an association between entity occurrences. A **relationship set** is an n-ary relation on n entity sets which need not be distinct provided they are distinguished by roles or by their ordered position. A **relationship** is a named collection of relationship occurrences involving n entities belonging to the corresponding n entity sets. For example, a 3-ary/ternary relationship could be defined involving the entity types Suppliers, Materials and Products. Another could be which teachers teach which courses to which students. Previous examples in EAR structures were mostly named relationship types between *two* entity types, but this definition generalizes that to involving *any number* of entity types.

A **domain** is the set of eligible values for a property. A domain has the same features as a set, in that the values are distinct and their order is not significant. A domain should have a predicate, which is a process by which one can decide whether a given value is or is not a member.

An **entity attribute** is defined as an association from an entity set to the domain of a single attribute, or to the Cartesian product of several domains where the attribute is composed of several domains together. For example, Surname is a single attribute since each person is associated to one occurrence in the codomain of surnames. However, Date-of-birth is composed of day, month and year, and is called a **compound attribute**. **Composite attribute** means the same. Its domain is composed of the Cartesian product of the three corresponding domains – the weekdays, months and years. Each person is associated to a weekday, a month and a year. The term **aggregate attribute** in this context also means the same, composed of several parts like a date or an address. The entity–attribute *association* may be simple, conditional or complex. Surnames and Date-of-birth are simple, to-one, except for changing with time as discussed earlier.

A **relationship attribute** is defined similarly as an association from a relationship set to the domain of the attribute or to the Cartesian product of several domains. The association may be simple, conditional or complex.

Eric, Aggie and Nora each have the same first steps and guidelines. They choose or give names to all the entity types and all the attribute types, using the singular form of a noun or a noun-based phrase.

They choose meaningful relationship names. If they know that an association between two entities is from-one-to-many in a particular direction, then usually they choose the active form of a verb or phrase as the name in that direction. For one-to-one and for many-to-many relationships between two entities they choose names that suit understanding of the drawing, e.g. left to right or top to bottom. Roles are distinguished if necessary. For some relationships they may initially not know whether it is to-one or to-many in either or both directions.

Each attribute corresponds to a mapping/association from one domain to another domain. They choose names that match the roles. An attribute may be compound/composite – using Address rather than all its details simplifies the model. The details can be added and handled at a later step.

They preferably use attributes that correspond to properties that have single values. Sometimes they help understanding by creating a new entity type corresponding to a complicated attribute. Later steps explain how to deal with attributes that do not have single values.

At this first stage they are aware that the model may be unsatisfactory. The entities may be poorly chosen. Some attributes are structures such as entities or more complicated things that do not have single values. Some relationships may seem unsatisfactory and in some cases it might be unclear whether an entity and an entity property such as an attribute should reverse roles. Perhaps a relationship should become another entity. And so on.

Obadiah additionally notes where several associations involve the same set or domain, e.g. Date-of-birth and Order-date both use the domain Date. He also notes cases where compound structures have the same domains in the same underlying structure, e.g. Customer order date and address, Delivery date and address, and Purchase order date and address.

The next step is to choose an identifier for each entity type.

Keys and identifiers

An attribute that has different values for each entity occurrence is an **entity key**. The mapping between the entity set and the domain underlying this attribute is one-to-one, i.e. to-one in each direction. For example, each employee has a **unique** Employee-no, and each

Employee-no corresponds to one employee. More than one attribute may have this uniqueness property, e.g. any one of the following would fit: Employee-no, National-insurance-no, National-health-no, Passport-no – assuming all employees have passports.

This definition extends to a collection of *several* attributes that together give a **compound key**. The mapping between the entity set and the subset of the Cartesian product of the domains underlying the attributes (with appropriate roles if necessary) is one-to-one. For example, First-name, Surname and Date-of-birth together will be sufficient – assuming names are not unique and that people with the same name have different birth dates.

Sometimes the available data does not have such attributes to give an entity key and an artificial attribute may have to be created to simplify the identification of the entities.

If several alternative entity keys exist, called **candidate keys**, then one is chosen as the preferred **identifier**, also called the **primary key**. The entity identifier may be a single attribute or a compound of several attributes. Other attributes that are candidates but not chosen as the identifier can usually be modelled as though they are just other attributes that are functionally dependent on the chosen identifier.

In the draft model each entity set is then replaced by the identifier domain, also called the primary key domain. So instead of thinking about representations of real employees the modellers think of Employee-no.

Eric, Aggie, Nora and Obadiah all do the same. They decide on an identifier for each entity type, i.e. choose the preferred attribute or compound group of attributes. The chosen attributes are referred to as the **identifier**. In their subsequent steps the identifier replaces and represents the set of real entities.

This gets rid of representations of the real entities in the model. It may also help to begin to clarify attributes that were structures such as entities that do not have single values. If a new entity type is created later and created without an identifier then this step of choosing the identifier has to be done for such a new entity when it is first recognized.

Next we explain about relationship identifiers.

For a relationship set one similarly defines the idea of a relationship key. Each such key may be a single entity identifier or a compound of several as can a **relationship identifier** which means the preferred one.

Eric may, but usually does not, choose relationship identifiers and neither do the others. They are however aware of the concept, which leads to the following better definition of an attribute.

An **attribute** can thus be redefined as an association from the identifier domain to the domain of the attribute or to the Cartesian product of several domains. This applies to each of entities and relationships; for entities one maps from the identifier domain of the entity set, and for relationships one maps from the identifier domain of the relationship set.

Reconsidering the entities

Next we restate the definition of an entity more fully and explain what Eric does.

Fundamentally, anything may be considered as an entity. However, the choice of entities will depend on, and reflect the purpose of doing, the modelling as explained above, the choice of the relevant part of the real world and the expected business processes.

Therefore choosing something as an entity type implies one of the following intentions.

- Some or all of the IS users will want to collect, store and handle knowledge, data, facts and information about corresponding entity occurrences.
- Some or all of the IS users will want to start to handle and store data about an entity occurrence as soon as the value of the identifier is known; or the identifier value will be known or created as soon as the real world entity is created or becomes of interest. This implies that the IS will have a storage structure that will allow users to handle an entity occurrence initially using only the identifier value. If necessary the user may create the identifier value. The stored data representing the entity occurrence can be accessed knowing only the identifier value. Values of other attributes of the entity need not *initially* be stored.

The above two points give a restated definition of an **entity type**. In a conceptual model the appearance of a named entity type, even without any attributes or relationships, represents the existence of a class of corresponding real world entity occurrences of interest. In the storage structure the occurrence of a value of the identifier, i.e. the primary key value, represents the entity occurrence. Hereafter in this chapter we use this restated definition.

The representation of objects by entities requires an identifier to be chosen for each entity type. The identifier occurrence serves to identify rather than to represent facts about the entity. So identifiers should be chosen to be as simple and as easy to use as possible.

Replacing the entities by identifier values makes it easier to represent them in the form of diagrams or tables. If there were no identifying seed names, then Table 11.1 would need a distinguishable picture of each seed or of each packet in the first column.

We mentioned above that entities and properties may reverse their roles. A table about entity occurrences may be merged with a table about appropriate relationship occurrences.

For example, a table about packets of seeds could be merged with a table about the people who sowed them, giving a table with an extra column. The extra column will hold the identifiers of the people who sowed the seed corresponding to each row. If two people both sowed some of a particular seed packet, that would give two people's identifiers in that extra column on the row for that seed.

Alternatively a different merged table structure could be formed by starting from the people table and adding an extra column giving which seeds each person sowed. If a person sowed two seeds then both of the seed identifiers would be in the extra column on the row for that person.

This example illustrates two alternative tables both corresponding to the same information about who planted what. In the first the seed is the entity and who planted is an attribute, and in the second the person is the entity and what they planted is the attribute. Either structure is acceptable as part of a data model.

We call the model at this stage a skeleton model.

Desirable features of final data models

Further steps are needed to improve and gradually complete the data model. Some of these steps can be done in various ways, perhaps in different sequences, and perhaps in parallel.

However, practitioners need to understand the objectives – particularly the features that the final model should have, and how to achieve them. The final data model should have the following features:

1. The final data model should correspond only to *separate* well-structured facts and associations. For example, an employee's date-of-birth and date-of-starting employment are two separate facts. Each should be represented separately. It should be possible to undertake processes that use either one without accessing the other. Processes may derive information from separate facts, e.g. derive age-at-date-of-starting, but this derived fact need not be and should not be represented redundantly in the model. This principle is sometimes summarized as having **pure data model** structures. **Nora** likes to create such models.
2. The final model should behave in completely **predictable** ways, just as computer programs and their data structures behave as expected from an understanding of programming. The final model must have appropriate properties to be unambiguous. Anna and all the assistants want this.
3. A **rule-free** model should not be biased towards the rules and features of particular software packages, particular hardware, or particular modelling conventions or rules. It should not assume the use of a particular database management system, query language or spreadsheet package. It should not have assumptions, explicitly stated or hidden, about what data is held in an IT-based system and what is handled by pen and paper or other representations. All those aspects are to be dealt with at the corresponding logical modelling stage.
4. The model should be such that it can be **extended** easily. For example, if some new kinds of facts are to be added to the model then the ways in which the existing facts are represented and handled should not need any alteration. More strongly the

model should be such that Anna and her colleagues know that extensions can be made without them even having to check whether any existing parts may need adjustment.

5. **Local** models, corresponding to appropriate parts of the final whole global data model, and suitable for processes on parts of the data occurrences, need to be independently derivable. These can then be used in discussions with user representatives from different areas of the business.
6. The corresponding data model should have the right features for easy extension. This means having logical data independence, growth independence and physical data independence. **Logical data independence** means that from an implemented data model such as a schema specifying the structure of a database, several subschemas for different applications can be derived and each can be changed independently. **Growth independence** means new subschemas and new data types can be added to the implemented data model without the need for programs using the existing subschemas to be modified. **Physical data independence** means that the physical structures, e.g. of pointers and records that are the structure of the stored data, can be changed, e.g. by adding an extra kind of pointer for efficiency, without needing any modification to the application programs.
7. The final model should be easy to understand and check. In particular it should help Anna and Idris to specify a suitable and **complete** collection of appropriate business processes so that all sensible actions involving any sensible combination of the data occurrences can be achieved. It is not sufficient for users just to be able to insert, change, delete and archive, and to retrieve data satisfying a query criterion (see 8 below). Although Table 5.2 seems reasonable in a rule-free model, the full situation may be more subtle.
8. The data model should be **orthogonal** to the process model in the following sense. If any data type or structure can be processed or handled in a particular way, then all similar data types or structures can be, irrespective of the context or whatever else is also part of the situation. This means that the associations between data and processes should not be directly between entities and processes, nor between attributes and processes. Instead, from each named data type such as an attribute there is a function to a corresponding domain of allowable values, which could be named, and with appropriate properties. There is then a further association from that domain to the set of processes that can use its occurrences. If the models correctly set up this function and these associations, then if one data structure can be handled in a particular way, then all of them can. For example, if an invoice name and address can be used in a word-processor letter and printed in a particular way, then all attributes that are names and addresses can be so handled. This applies both to conceptual models and to logical models.

   This principle can be used at the conceptual modelling stage to help to indicate in one direction what are all of the processes that should be available, and in the other direction to indicate all the similar data structures that a process can handle. Obadiah should watch for these and know how to model and implement them.

Further actions by Anna and by colleagues

To achieve the above, Anna and Idris need to do certain actions to ensure that discussion occurs leading to representation in the model of various things about the business. On the other hand, Eric and the other colleagues need to do certain further steps to ensure that the models have the right features. These two sets of actions can proceed in parallel, but we have to describe them separately.

Next we explain what Anna and Idris might do. Their actions can be done in any order, possibly overlapping, and emphasis may be arranged to suit the purposes explained above.

From a skeleton data model, which may be just a model of part of the data for a particular business function, Anna and Idris may do the following.

- Further analyse and model the area covered so far, building up a skeleton that includes all the data used in that local area. The area may have several processes and the local model should include all the data for all of them. Much of the data may be used in several closely related processes. This leads to completeness such as all the attributes of an entity, domain details and rules about what values are valid. It also suggests checks and processes that should be done when data is created, accessed, and when it ceases to exist. These checks and processes interest Obadiah. The further analysis may also lead to security checks concerning which staff may do which processes. The modelling of the rules of authorization should be discussed by Idris and Anna.
- Extend gradually into adjacent business areas and other corresponding applications in a similar manner.
- Analyse a separate area of the business and develop its local model and then merge the two local models. This parallel work can save time where two separate teams of analysts and user representatives are available.
- If the local data model is well advanced but other analysis is not, then for the local area do other kinds of analysis, e.g. functional analysis, process analysis or other kinds mentioned in the section of Chapter 2 on *Analysis methods and skills*. Finding out about a process such as calculating mean and standard deviations without disclosing the actual values, as is done on census data, indicates the kinds of use and points about privacy and security. Sometimes data is selected using a **secondary key**, which means selecting all entity occurrences that have a particular value for an attribute that is *not* a primary key. This can be widened to selecting all occurrences with values within a stated range, and also combining criteria

involving several attributes. For example, select all male employees aged over 50 on a certain date, calculating each age from the stored date of birth.

- If the analysis done so far is mainly process analysis, then complement this with some data analysis and other kinds.

Next we explain what Eric and the others might do, in parallel with the above.

Further actions by Eric and colleagues

Eric and the others will want to do certain kinds of checks and other steps to ensure that the developing models have the right features and self-consistency. For example, the data model should not allow the representation of an order when there is no corresponding customer having sent it in. Also they want to avoid having two possibly inconsistent representations of the same fact – even through some chain of intermediate structures. The model should not have as separate and independent facts both a date-of-birth and age at some later date.

Eric uses representations involving entity types, relationship types, entity attributes and perhaps relationship attributes. As he improves on the skeleton model he may create extra entity types, change the relationships and improve the grouping of the attributes into the entities. This leads to a better EAR model.

Nora looks for functional dependencies, where an attribute is functionally dependent on another. These help her to group attributes better into new entities. She does not work with relationships, but instead may add an attribute to both the entities that are linked through occurrences of that attribute.

> Where Nora has (A,B,...,C,...) with an attribute C that is dependent on part A of a compound identifier {A,B}, and not fully functionally dependent on that compound identifier of the current draft entity, she creates two new entities. In the first new entity she puts the part of the original identifier A and the attribute C that is fully functionally dependent on A, giving (A,C,...). In the other new entity she puts the compound identifier A, B and the attributes that are fully functionally dependent on those two, giving (A,B,...). She gives appropriate names to the new entity types. This gives **second normal form**.

Nora has another step.

> Nora also looks for attributes that are functionally dependent on other attributes that are not the identifier. Suppose F is functionally dependent on E, and E is functionally dependent on D, and both E and F appear in a draft entity with D as identifier. Then Nora creates two new entities: (D, E) and (E, F) and gives them names. This gives **third normal form**.

Gradually after suitable steps she creates normalized entities with the right attributes in each entity. These are also called pure entities.

In Nora's model an attribute can be duplicated, i.e. appear in two entities. This corresponds to the existence of a relationship between the entities. Thus the equivalent EAR model can be created, by adding a suitable relationship wherever two entities share a duplicated attribute.

Aggie transforms the skeleton model into irreducible units called **elementary relations**. Each one is a relation and would correspond to associated occurrences of the domains underlying an appropriate group of attributes. **Irreducible** means that a relation cannot be broken down by project operations to give several smaller relations such that these smaller relations can be joined by a join operation to reconstitute the original relation.

A **project operation** means choosing certain columns of a relation and discarding the other columns to form a new relation.

A **join operation** means taking two relations and choosing a column from each relation so that the chosen columns both have the same underlying domain, usually the same attribute. Then form a new relation, the joined relation, with all the columns of both relations except that the two chosen columns become one column in the new relation. Then in the new joined relation create a tuple for each pair of rows, one from each of the original relations, that have the *same value in the chosen columns*, giving this same value in the new join relation.

It then turns out that each **elementary relation** is one of:

- a relation that is all key, i.e. all attributes are needed to give a primary key;
- an n-ary relation such that the last attribute is fully functionally dependent on all the earlier n-1 attributes, so the first n-1 attributes are the primary key; this includes a binary relation in which the second attribute is functionally dependent on the first, and a ternary relation with the last attribute fully functionally dependent on the first two, and so on.

The first kind of relation can represent entity occurrences; its structure represents in the model the entity type. All other facts can be represented in only one way in a relation of the second kind.

Both kinds are needed. For example, if student numbers are allocated sequentially then the first relation is needed to create the representation of a new student. A second relation with the student-no and the student name could not be used to represent the student until the name becomes known, and even then only assuming that all names are distinct.

Aggie then determines a minimum collection of the elementary relations. This can be done in a fairly straightforward process.

For Table 11.1 Aggie's minimum collection would be the relations:

```
(Name), (Name, Preferred soil), (Name, Earliest
  UK sowing date), (Name, Latest UK sowing date),
  (Name, How to lay out), (Name, Depth to sow
  each seed), (Name, Other notes).
```

The minimum collection is such that if used to hold the user's data then: there would never be any inconsistency in the stored data, no matter what values occur; all relevant data can be represented; and all possible meaningful information can be deduced by allowable operations and processes on the stored data. So such data can be used later for processes that were initially not even envisaged by Anna and Idris. This achieves at this data model stage the desirable features mentioned above.

Nora joins relations in her model

Where two or more relations in Aggie's minimum collection have the same identifier in their first n-1 attributes, *one might think* that these relations may be combined into a new single relation having the same first n-1 columns and then, as further columns, the last column from each such relation. The combined relation or entity type would be:

```
Seed_packet(Name, Preferred soil, Earliest UK
  sowing date, Latest UK sowing date, How to lay
  out, Depth to sow each seed, Other notes).
```

That is the same as Table 11.1.

But that joining is strictly not correct, although its equivalent is often done as a shorthand notation to give Nora's pure entity types. It is acceptable in discussions with Idris where the overriding need is to be rule-free as this allows table structures such as Table 11.1 to be created. The difficulties of such joining arise from needing to be able to represent entities before facts about them are known, and also to handle optional facts such as Table 11.1's entry `Not specified`. In Aggie's minimum collection there will not be a tuple occurrence for that seed in the relation `(Name, Depth to sow each seed)`. The earlier minimum collection, however, did provide for that optional value.

The relation that is all key represents the entity type. Other relations will only have a tuple if a corresponding fact about a non-key attribute actually occurs in the real world. Otherwise such tuples will be missing. Tuples in the minimum collection will never have void values in any cell. Some of the various relations of the minimum collection would have fewer rows than a combined table such as Table 11.1.

The model is changed to an unsatisfactory one if these minimum collection relations are replaced by the combined one. However the form of the combined one can be written down as a shorthand for those relations of the minimum collection that share the same first columns, provided people understand the real meaning.

A corresponding combined table such as Table 11.1 can also be used as part of a database structure or spreadsheet structure provided people understand and have a way of representing and handling void (= non-existent) values. In such logical models people need ways to distinguish void from unknown, known and empty/blank, and zero.

Exercise 11.1

Think of two ways of using a spreadsheet to represent how many people live in each house of several streets. Distinguish the minimum collection structure from the combined structure. Think how to calculate in each case the average number of people per house in each street.

The structure corresponding to the minimum collection has one table per street, the table name giving the street name. Each such table has a column giving each valid house number and a second column giving the number of people in that house. The tables have different numbers of rows corresponding to the different street lengths. For each table the average value in its second column is easy to calculate.

The corresponding combined table has a first column with values from 1 to the highest house number, and a named column for each street with values giving the number (possibly zero) of people at the corresponding house. But in some streets some numbers do not exist so a way of representing void is needed. These void cells have to be ignored when the column average is calculated. The problem is calculating the average of a column that includes some zero values and also some cells that are void.

In general the minimum collection, e.g. having a separate table for each street and within each table a row for each house number that exists (no voids), creates more tables but gives easier processes.

Transforming between the various models

Eric and his colleagues will produce different kinds of models. Fortunately these correspond in certain ways so that it is possible to transform between them. Anna and Idris may use any combination of the different kinds of models. Indeed with experience based on what follows, Anna may be able mentally to transform between the various kinds and thus help to guide discussions with Idris and others.

People need ways of transforming between the various model representations produced by Eric, Aggie, Nora and Obadiah. We explain these next.

In the whole collection that Aggie or Nora produces there may be two relations that both have the same attribute name amongst their attributes. If so, that indicates a relationship type between the two corresponding entity types. They are said to be associated on that attribute, or linked on that attribute. Entities can also be linked on an aggregate of two or more attributes.

The attribute appearing in two entity types or relations is called a **duplicated attribute**. Duplicated attributes in two or more such entity types indicate relationships in the equivalent EAR model. The equivalent EAR model may be constructed by thinking out the meaning of the duplicated attribute, an appropriate name for the relationship and whether it is one-to-many or has some other form.

Thus Aggie's or Nora's model can be converted to Eric's EAR model by a process that involves human thought and cannot be fully automated.

Sometimes a many-to-many relationship can best be modelled by creating an intermediate new entity type with a new relationship from each original entity type to the new one. Some people call the new entity an intersection entity type.

More generally, if an attribute appears duplicated in three or more relations in Aggie's shorthand or in Nora's pure entity types, then that indicates a relationship between three or more entity types. Some thought about the meaning will be needed. Eric may be stuck if he only allows relationships to be between exactly two entity types but he can overcome the difficulty by creating an extra entity as an intersection between the three or more, with three or more corresponding new relationships.

In the opposite direction, Eric's EAR model can be converted to Aggie's or Nora's form by adding, to either or both the entity types at the end of a relationship, the attribute associated with the relationship. This attribute will be duplicated in the resulting EAR model at that step, and some thought about meanings is needed.

After all the EAR relationships have been dealt with, and in the right sequence since sometimes a duplicated attribute of one relationship then also becomes further duplicated as another relationship is dealt with, then the resulting entity types with all the duplications shown give essentially Nora's model. Effectively the relationships have been remodelled as duplicated attributes.

Generally Eric, allowing Idris to be as rule-free as possible in discussions and diagrams, will allow representations in diagrams either with or without the duplicated attributes shown.

From Nora's form the equivalent of Aggie's model can be deduced easily, reversing the shorthand.

Associating processes with the various models

In Aggie's model each attribute in each relation has an underlying set or domain. For example, Order-date has the set name Date. These sets or domains should be named, though by default the corresponding attribute names sometimes suffice. Role names are sometimes needed.

Processes should be associated with the underlying set names rather than with the entities. Thus any process that can be done on a particular set, such as Date, can be done on all attributes that are dates. Obadiah does this. It fits in with desirable feature 8 above (p. 317).

Eric does something different, which is not always as good. For each application process involving two or more entity types Eric looks for a relationship or relationships that can be used to associate them. The entity types and these relationship types should correspond to the collections of data used together in processes such as those underlying Table 5.2. If a collection of processes can together handle an entity life history, then the collection of these associated entities and relationships should be the ones needed in the processes.

Nora does not have a satisfactory equivalent way of associating pure entity types with processes.

Internal representations and corresponding models

The **physical** model essentially specifies what attributes will have their values stored together as a unit that can easily be accessed, and how the relationships between these units will be represented. This applies whether using manual files such as paper in a filing cabinet or a database management system (DBMS) software package.

For a CODASYL-based DMBS, the physical data model structure is specified as and called a **schema**. Usually the entity types become record types and attributes become the data items in those records. The relationship types become set types, which typically associate occurrences of two record types. The software packages have the facilities for any sensible subset of the record types, data item types and set types to be made available as a subschema for an application program. The **subschema** permits the program to allow the user to access and maybe alter the record, data item and set occurrences, as appropriate to handle an entity life history and associated facts. The software should provide all the **independence** facilities needed for subsequent changes to the models and patterns of use.

For a relational database software package, the relations of Nora's or Aggie's model become the first draft logical schema of relations. In principle the same might be the structure of tables in a spreadsheet, but spreadsheet packages do not usually provide all the appropriate structure facilities, e.g. to link together entity tuples represented by rows of tables. Spreadsheets can handle single tables, but not more complicated structures such as arise in modelling the scenarios in the questions at the end of this chapter.

The designer, **David**, should arrange the physical data model so as to be consistent with the conceptual and logical models, and also arrange the storage structure to reduce the number of record accesses when a user wants to obtain or handle facts about an entity occurrence.

Optimal and well-structured storage structures

To achieve the above David needs to understand candidate keys, normalization of storage structures, optimal relations for a collection of relations or records and the implementation facilities. So we explain these next, but in fairly brief form.

An attribute K is a **candidate key** of a relation if in each tuple the value of K identifies that tuple, so that each other attribute is functionally dependent on K, and if K is compound then all of K is needed. David arranges that if a user quotes the value of a candidate key attribute then it will select the right record representing the entity occurrence. A **prime attribute** is an attribute that is part of at least one candidate key. A non-prime attribute does not participate in any candidate key.

Normalization is essentially done as in Nora's modelling above. Each relation or record type is such that the non-prime data items are fully functionally dependent on the identifier (or any candidate key), and not transitively functionally dependent through some other attribute. That gives third normal form. David separates out transitive dependencies to create new entity types.

But also David has to work with a *collection* of relations or record types. He needs to specify **optimal** relations as the model. For example, if in a manufacturing situation each part P can be made on only one machine M, and by only one employee E, and also each machine can only be operated by one employee, and there are no other dependencies, then various logical models might work. These include: {R1($\underline{P}$, M), R2($\underline{M}$, E)}; {R1($\underline{P}$, M), R3($\underline{P}$, E)}, and {R3($\underline{P}$, E), R2($\underline{M}$, E)}. At first sight any of these might work but in fact only the first will, because the others allow inconsistencies which arise because R3 represents a transitive dependency. It turns out that R1 and R2 also allow each fact to be represented only once, with no redundancy, thus also minimizing the storage space used as well as having the right properties for consistency.

David also has to watch for more complicated forms. For example, if instead of the above rules each part could be made on several machines and by several employees, then the relation R4($\underline{P}$, $\underline{M}$, $\underline{E}$) is in third normal form. But suppose there is another rule, that whenever a part can be made on a machine by any of several employees, then all those several employees and no others can make any of the parts made on that machine. The structure R4 is unsatisfactory because the existence of an association between a part and a machine cannot be stored until an employee capable of operating it exists. Also if the parts made on a particular machine cease to exist, then the association between the machine and its several employees cannot be stored. Also if an employee changes, several tuples have to be updated. These anomalies are overcome by splitting R4 into {R5(P, M) and R6(M, E)}. This is an example of fourth normal form. Additionally David only uses structures for which project and join operations give the correct effects.

> David's trick is not just to create relations or record structures in third normal form, but to create a structure for each rule such as the association between machines and employees.

We have not given a worked example of all the above, but have given two long exercises chosen to bring in the main points.
Please spend some time reviewing what you have read and doing the questions below.

Self check

Objectives

After reading this chapter you should be able to:

- contribute to analysing and describing data, particularly as

entities, attributes and relationships in complicated and typical situations;
- explain the desirable features of well-structured tables, which may help in creating well-structured collections of tables and spreadsheets;
- explain some desirable features of models, including the justification for representing each fact once, and the ability to extend and merge models that are tables or EAR structures;
- for entities and other structures choose identifiers with appropriate properties;
- handle correctly EAR representations, aggregates, normalized structures and object oriented features, and transform appropriately between representations;
- model correctly situations involving n-part relationships;
- understand the way to create appropriate logical models corresponding to conceptual models, and hence unified easy-to-use user facilities.

Questions

Instead of short questions we have provided two long exercises. They may be done individually or in a small group discussion. Try not to spoil it by looking at the solutions at the back until you have done all the questions that are based on a particular scenario. You may learn from your mistakes. The parts and questions develop gradually. Each scenario may take a couple of hours.

Manufacturing and distribution

This scenario, based on two real organizations, gives various staff views of how a manufacturing company, ABC, uses vehicles on trips to deliver its products to its customers. By interviews you have obtained the following partial views, which have been restated in a precise style.

View (a) – Trip-scheduling staff view. A date is identified as year, month, day-no. On a date there are many trips. Each trip takes place on a particular date. For each trip there is a vehicle type, e.g. 3-ton truck. This has a vehicle volume, e.g. 4 cubic metres, and a vehicle weight.

View (b) – Customer shipment view. For a customer there are many trips. Each such trip has a TripNo, and occurs on a date. Each Shipment has a ShipNo and is for a particular customer. Each customer has a different CuNo, and has a delivery address.

View (c) – Customer and product view. To each customer there are many products delivered. For each such product there are many packages. For each customer there may be one or several packages. Each package is for one customer. Each package has an identifying pack-no, and contains a quantity of a particular product which is identified by a product-no. Each package is packed on a particular date.

View (d) – Packages for trips view. A trip usually involves deliveries to many customers. Each package goes on a particular trip. Each package is numbered with a package-no. A particular package is usually delivered on a particular date and as part of a particular shipment-no. But if it is undelivered it goes on another later shipment and trip, and the staff keep records of all shipments that each package went on.

View (e) – Shipment history view. From a shipment-no the following are uniquely determined: customer-no also called CuNo, trip-no, trip-date, vehicle volume, and vehicle weight. For each such shipment-no there may be many packages, each having a package-no, also called PackNo. A package-no uniquely determines package-volume, package-weight and manufacturing-no.

View (f) – Customer view. A customer has a unique customer-no. Each customer has a name and delivery-address, but these names and addresses are not unique. Each customer may have several tel-nos.

View (g) – Manufacturing view. Each product that is manufactured has: a ProdNo, also called ManufacturingNo; a description; and a ProductGroup. A product can be made or procured by any one of several methods, these each have a different MethodNo within that product, but Method-no values may start from 1 again for each product. Each method has a leadtime from request till availability. Purchasing is a method. A particular method may need many component items with an ItemNo that typically runs from 1 to 100 for a particular method of a particular larger product; and each component indicates a quantity used of some smaller product. These smaller products are just like other products, each has a ProductNo identifier and description just like a finished product, and may have methods and components. A component indicates where a smaller product is used, called where-used.

11.1 Using Nora's way of modelling, draw up a normalized data model for the above. Discuss whether the resulting model would be appropriate for a relational database system, or what changes would be appropriate to give a data model for implementation. What about having spreadsheets?

11.2 Draw Eric's EAR data model for the company. Could it serve as a basis for a schema for a database management system software package? Each entity occurrence will have an entity life history. Staff will need to handle representations of all the associated facts during the entity life. Can the various entity life histories be catered for? Could the views of seven staff corresponding to (a) to (g) be catered for, assuming each was not allowed access to any data type not mentioned in their section of the scenario?

11.3 What would Aggie have done differently from Nora? What would be the advantages of those differences?

11.4 What extras does Obadiah notice and why, being object oriented?

11.5 Does the scenario agree with your understanding of such organizations? What changes to the scenario and models would be needed to make it fit your organization or some typical organization or future changes to such an organization?

Freight trains and wagons

The following scenario describes trains, based on British Rail and Southern Pacific. Various staff views are given in a precise style. For simplicity assume you only have to model the current situation, and not model the keeping of the history of wagon movements nor the modelling of future planned operations.

View (a) – Locomotives. There are many locomotives, each identified by a loco-no, e.g. 14625. Each loco belongs to a loco class, e.g. Class 86. All locos of a class have the same power. For each loco class there is a specified number of miles between each scheduled maintenance. Servicing can be a major service or a minor service. Each loco has a miles since last maintenance.

View (b) – Wagons and their status. A wagon has a unique wagon-id, up to ten characters, similar to road vehicle registration numbers. Its status may be loaded, empty, in maintenance, being cleaned, and so on. It is at a named location, identified by a location-id, LcnId. It is on a journey from an origin location to a destination location; except that where it is in maintenance or being cleaned both these are taken as the current location. If loaded its origin is the location where it was loaded, and its destination is where it is going to be unloaded. If empty its origin is the location where it was unloaded, and its destination is the next location where it will be loaded or where it is going for cleaning or maintenance, e.g. a maintenance workshop. If ready to leave the maintenance workshop the origin is the workshop location and the destination is either the location where it is next to be loaded or a marshalling yard location where it may wait till needed. A wagon is usually scrapped only while in a workshop.

View (c) – Wagon maintenance. There are many wagons of each wagon class, e.g. 100-ton lumber/timber low loaders. Each wagon class has a fixed mileage between each scheduled maintenance. For each wagon a record is kept of the miles till the next maintenance is due. When this gets to near zero and the wagon is empty the wagon is sent from its current location to the nearest workshop, which becomes its destination. Similarly each loco class has a miles between maintenance.

View (d) – Locations. Each location has a 5-digit identification, rather like a postcode or zipcode, a name and sometimes an abbreviation for the name. At a location there are usually many wagons. A location may have an office with staff who are responsible for both that location and some other locations nearby. Some locations do not have an office and staff. In your modelling ignore the modelling of the office and staff, but include that each location has either itself or a neighbouring location that is responsible for its wagons. A typical marshalling yard shunts and sorts wagons that have arrived on an incoming train into outgoing trains that will go to other locations.

View (e) – Geography. For every pair of locations the route miles from one to the other is known. The return miles may be the same or different, e.g. where single tracks are used only in one direction. As wagons move, their route miles value is to be added to their records, so the IS is to keep the calculated equivalents of mileometers for each wagon.

View (f) – Trains. Each train on a journey has a train-id, this headcode is shown on the front of some locos during the journey. Each train-id is only used once on any day, but the same train-id may be used for the same timetable slot on different days. Each train has a departure time and an arrival time. For simplicity ignore all intermediate stops. On a particular date a particular train may be a few minutes late departing, in which case for simplicity its expected arrival time will be calculated as the same number of minutes late. A train may have several locos and up to 100 or more wagons of mixed status and destinations. A loco and wagons can form part of more than one train during a day, but at any time can only be part of at most one train.

11.6 What might Obadiah, with an object oriented view, comment on the above before starting to model it?

11.7 Assume all the object oriented issues have been dealt with. Draw up a table similar to Table 11.2, based on discovering entities, identifiers and aggregates that are fully functionally dependent. Will this table be correctly normalized?

View	*Entity*	*Identifier*	*Functionally dependent attributes*	*Multivalued entity or attribute*
a	LocoClass	LocoClassNo	Power	Loco
...				

TABLE 11.2
Beginnings of table for Question 11.6

11.8 Derive an EAR data model as follows. Some entities and some identifiers may appear in more than one view. Mentally merge each of them into a single entity with the appropriate identifier.

Do the following leaving some space to the left, perhaps leaving about a third of the width of the paper. For every entity put its name, and put to the right of it in brackets its identifier underlined and all its attributes that are fully functionally dependent on the identifier. Put an * against each such attribute that also appears in some other entity, e.g. is a key of a foreign entity. Afterwards, use the space on the left to draw the relationships, each being between two entity types. The multivalued entities and attributes column of the table and the attributes marked * should help you to create the relationships.

11.9 This tests understanding of optimal structures and fourth normal form. Before a driver can drive a train he must be passed and authorized both for the class of locomotive and for the route. Drivers are generally authorized for a group of similar classes, e.g. all diesel locos up to 100 mph. Is this satisfactorily modelled as follows: {DriverAuthorization(StaffNo, LocoClassNo, LcnFrom, LcnTo)}?

11.10 Make a list summarizing the purposes, reasons and advantages of normalization.

12 A framework

Introducing a framework

Figure 12.1 gives an overview of the framework. The organization wants improvements and achieving them involves actions to find out what is needed, planning and decisions about how to do the work, methods of working and management of it all. Each of these aspects is unpacked to explain various details and features, which fit with and are based on experience. All these actions and their aspects, details and features, combine together to contribute to your understanding of how to do the work in a new situation.

The framework has several aspects, as in shown in Table 12.1.

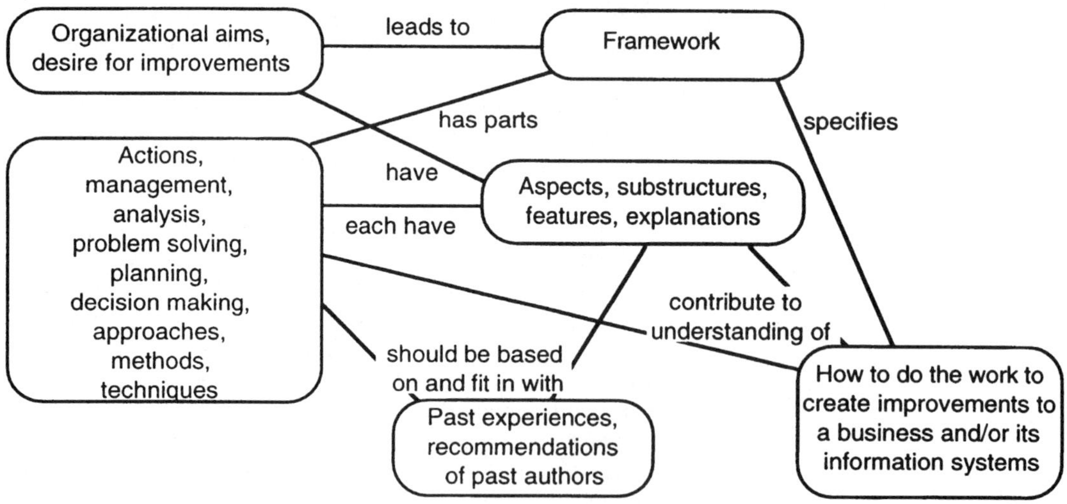

FIGURE 12.1 Overview of the framework.

We have gradually built up a framework with many strands. We separate them here for clarity and summarize each aspect.

The **aims of the organization** lead to mission statement, objectives, desired performance, gaps in current performance, long-term plans, strategy and the need for improvements.

The organization, and everyone and everything within it, are subject to internal and external forces and pressures. The people and

• The aims of the organization	• Kinds of problems
• Improvements to processes and ISs needed	• Features of objectives
• Actions, features of each action	• Short-term, medium-term and long-term cycles
• Feasibility	• Gaps between performance and desire
• Management cycle of each action	• Kinds of planning
• Management and its aspects	• How to make decisions, points of control
• The work of finding out what is required	• Management styles
• The work of creating improvements	• Human issues
• Solving problems	• Choosing a development method.

TABLE 12.1
Aspects of the framework

the state of the organization have strengths and weaknesses and the environment creates opportunities and threats leading to ways of discussing and analysing their consequences. **Improvements** are continually wanted.

The situation is continually changing. The work needs to be done sufficiently quickly to be useful and to bring increased revenue, job satisfaction, reduced costs and other benefits within an acceptable time. The work becomes so large that **teams** of people are needed. This leads to problems of team management, and to extra work coordinating the people in the team.

Each action has a cycle which involves assessing feasible ways of doing it, planning and carrying out the chosen course, monitoring what is happening and applying feedback to control events so that everything goes to plan.

Assessing the **feasibility** of an action necessitates having criteria by which to judge success. Usually there is a choice to be made between several alternatives, so criteria to choose between these are needed. Then each alternative can be evaluated against the criteria, the results compared and the best course of action chosen. This itself involves several actions. The nesting stops because the assessment of feasibility of fairly small actions is trivial and can be done mentally while on the job.

If the planning is wrong the actions and products will probably be unsatisfactory, and for large actions this will lead to considerable waste. So planning large actions, such as significant improvements to a business or to an IS, must be done in such a way as to reduce the risk of failure or unsatisfactory final products to a minimum. This means doing a lot of planning before starting the action of building the final product. **Planning** therefore becomes the focus of attention.

Actions can usually be attributed to purposes and typically produce products or services either for someone else within the organization or for someone outside. They are grouped into larger and smaller structures, for example phases such as design, development, procurement and manufacture; activities within phases such as design module XX, procure new computer; tasks within activities such as specify new computer requirement; and operations within tasks. These actions may occur in sequence or in parallel or, more usually, with partial overlapping where an action may start as soon as its prerequisites allow. For management and project control purposes, it is convenient to mark the end of phases by milestones, and to have activities starting and finishing at events. Products are generally developed gradually with continual evolution and several interim versions.

Improvements to **performance** depend in part on the resources and tools available. In the **short term**, given only the available tools and current knowledge, improving a particular level of performance by more than a few per cent is impossible. But **medium term**, with some improvements to resources, tools and methods, a greater improvement should be achievable, perhaps ten or twenty percentage points on some measurement scale. **Longer term**, using quite different processes and methods, with staff having different skills or better training, new kinds of tools, new ISs and other significant changes, major improvements may be achieved. The output might be doubled, with improved product quality and fewer errors giving major benefits. However, to achieve all this requires a lot of detailed work that requires time.

The **planning of major improvements** is so large and complex that most people usually do not know how to do all of it. Specialist teams are needed with appropriate tools and techniques.

The ways in which a **client obtains help from a specialist** to solve a problem, and the manner in which they work together where the specialist develops a tool for the client to use on future problems, needs careful examination. The ways that a user of an IS obtains help are essentially the same and the features need to be understood by developers and their managers as they get and give help during the development. They also need to be defined in the specification and design of the IS facilities, including its built-in help facilities for users. These users play the role of clients with problems and the IS has to help them solve those problems.

Management styles can impact ISs and business processes in various ways. Conversely, the changing ISs and processes can also have an impact on management styles.

Large organizations have to decide to what extent to **standardize**, and to what extent to allow staff in different departments, doing different functions or providing different business systems to have different and perhaps incompatible equipment, processes, methods and tools.

Human issues abound. People may disagree over many aspects, including priorities. People initially believe they are right and need ways of avoiding situations in which they lose face. Though these are not central to this book, the approaches used have to accommodate such issues.

Different **approaches** presume different priorities. Often the underlying reasons and assumptions have been hidden and understanding them may sometimes help toward better decisions and management of improvements. The various approaches have advantages and disadvantages.

With continual developments in management education, computer systems hardware and software, communication techniques and scientific knowledge, what is **feasible** continually changes. Judging what will be feasible a couple of years in the future is a valuable skill when making improvements and innovations.

Finally **all the above are combined** in a complex and interacting way in any real situation. So people are faced with high level choices, such as whether to make general directives for their organization, or their part of it, reducing complexity and restricting choice. For example, there could be a direction that the organization should standardize on a particular approach or method. One possibility is normally to obtain equipment only from a particular supplier, assuming that supplier will stay in business for many years to come providing compatible and satisfactorily priced equipment together with good support logistics and services. How can one know whether the chosen method is actually the best or even suitable for the organization? Even to evaluate it properly may be impossible. This issue is considered below.

Contingency and choosing a development method

The key point we will make in this section is that it is more satisfactory to adopt, deploy and evolve a *flexible* framework of methods and techniques than to adopt a single method or process to be applied to all problems of a particular kind.

The essence of **contingency** is that the action to take depends on the context and situation. A contingent approach implies that it may be unreasonable to prescribe methods and techniques *before* the context and problem are understood to some degree. One should *continually* select methods and techniques for solving a problem as one's understanding of the *context* and the details of the problem increases. One should do whatever seems likely to be worthwhile in the current situation.

The reader may well respond: 'of course the methods and techniques to be deployed depend on the problem and situation'. However, it is an unfortunate fact of life that many departments responsible for the analysis of business processes and development of information systems proceed by adopting one proprietary ISD method that is to be applied universally. Indeed, the problem may be compounded and institutionalized by the introduction of formal 'quality' programmes such as those pursued to obtain BS 5750 or ISO 9000 certification.

When analysing business processes, analysts and consultants have frequently depended on one or a few specific frameworks, for example:

- wall-charting techniques, where people create lists and diagrams on large sheets of paper and hang them up;
- workshop brainstorming sessions, where participants individually note down some ideas, then read them out in a group with no idea being rejected no matter how apparently impracticable, after which some are selected for detailed examination;
- SWOT analysis, giving four lists of ideas from which some are selected for further discussion;
- a proprietary method, such as one from a consultancy;
- competitive analysis.

A similar problem exists in the development of information systems. The systems development staff of an organization may proceed by applying a particular set of methods and techniques, such as: structured analysis and design; object oriented analysis and design; a proprietary ISD method or one from a consultancy.

The examples of methods listed above can be described as **monocultural**. By contrast a method with a *variety* of approaches suitable for different problems and contexts can be described as **multicultural**.

We are saying that generally it is not a good idea to operate by adopting a specific monocultural method or a limited range of techniques. It is usually far more satisfactory to have a framework of available methods and techniques that can be used for the variety of problem situations likely to be encountered by the organization.

Matching problems to methods

In this section we lead you gradually into issues about matching problems and methods of solution – choosing solution techniques and tools to match problems. We develop the earlier metamodelling techniques to present a simple explanation of the problems associated with prescriptive monocultural methods and disconnected collections of techniques. We use the techniques introduced in Chapter 2 and developed in Chapters 5, 6 and 11 for analysing text to develop entities and relationships.

'An organization experiences a range of problem areas.' This sentence has three nouns (organization, range, area), one adjective (problem) and one verb (experiences). Although this is typical of the way people speak and write, it is not precise. The word 'area' is meant to be conceptual, not a physical area, and 'a range of' means 'many'. The sentence first has to be expressed more clearly as: 'An organization experiences many problems.' The opposite direction has to be thought out, giving that a problem may be experienced in many organizations. These relationships can be represented as shown in Figure 12.2, where we have given a single relationship name, 'Experiences', and also for clarity given two explanatory assertions.

FIGURE 12.2 Organizations experience many problem areas.

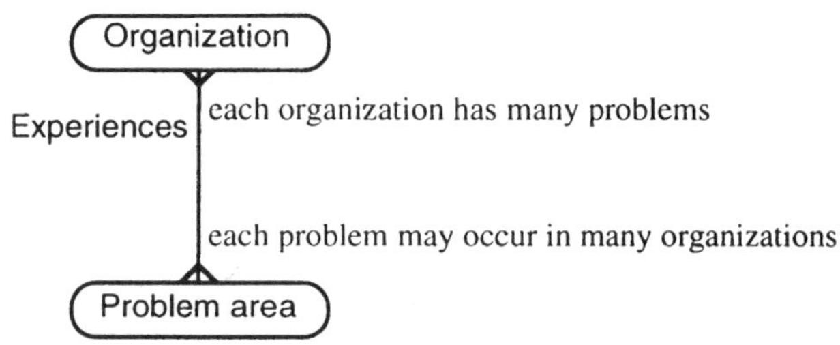

Turning to the adoption of a method, we observe that 'each method consists of several particular techniques'. Analysing that observation, there are two nouns (method, technique) and one verb-like unit of information (consists of). Therefore the corresponding objects and relationships are as shown in Figure 12.3. Again we have given a single relationship name and some assertions.

FIGURE 12.3
Each method involves many techniques.

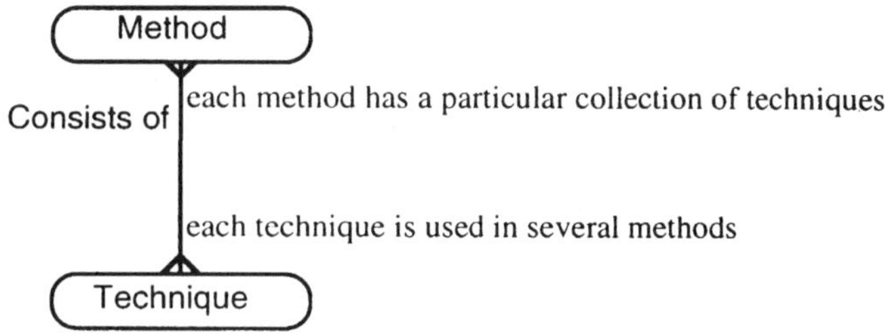

> **Exercise 12.1**
>
> It is useful to stop at this point and invite you to construct two further simple OPR (object–property–relationship) diagrams, before we continue the discussion. Sketch out simple OPR diagrams corresponding to the following two statements.
>
> (i) An organization doing analysis or development usually standardizes on one method.
> (ii) A problem area needs suitable techniques to solve it. Several techniques may be needed to solve a problem situation. A particular technique may be suitable for several problem areas.

As usual, there are several possible correct solutions and here is just one version.

The first statement, 'An organization doing analysis or development usually standardizes on one method', implies two main nouns (organization, method) and one verb-like term (standardizes on) as shown in Figure 12.4.

FIGURE 12.4
An organization standardizes on a method.

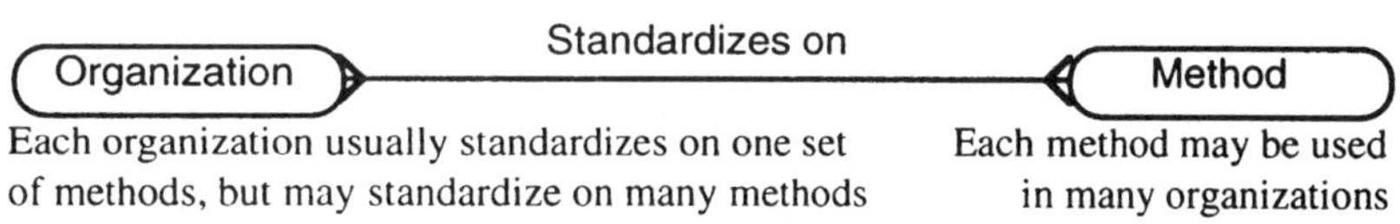

In the text of (ii) we gave several sentences, including some synonyms and further details. For this, 'A problem area needs suitable techniques to solve it. Several techniques may be needed to solve a problem situation. ...' there are also effectively two nouns (problem area, technique) and one verb (needs suitable). Figure 12.5 shows a solution.

FIGURE 12.5
Each problem area needs suitable techniques to solve it.

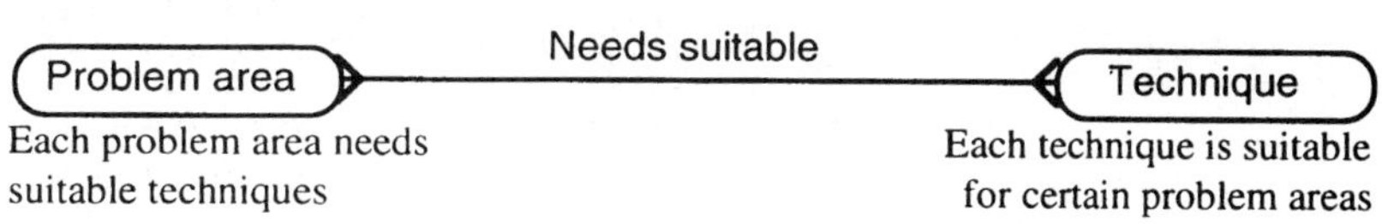

Exercise 12.2

Next we need to combine all these four simple OPR models. Therefore, before proceeding, attempt to produce a composite OPR model that combines all the four models produced so far.

One solution is as follows. Each of the objects (organization, method, problem area, technique) appears twice, each time associated with a different verb. Therefore in OPR terms, each object participates in two relationships.

A combined model is shown in Figure 12.6. Note that for each of the verbs, two relationship names have been presented, corresponding to the two previous assertions, rather than the single relationship names in the four diagrams above. This is to recognize that for every relationship there is usually a corresponding relationship in the opposite direction, sometimes called reverse.

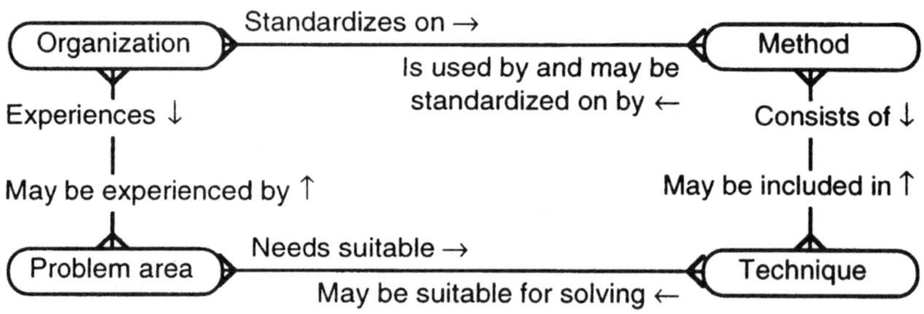

FIGURE 12.6 Relationships between organization, method, problem area, and technique; named in both directions.

When expressed in terms of verbs, the simplest way of expressing a relationship and its corresponding reflexive relationship is to use the active and passive voices of the verb. This is what has been done in Figure 12.6. The equivalent of that showing the more detailed assertions is in Figure 12.7.

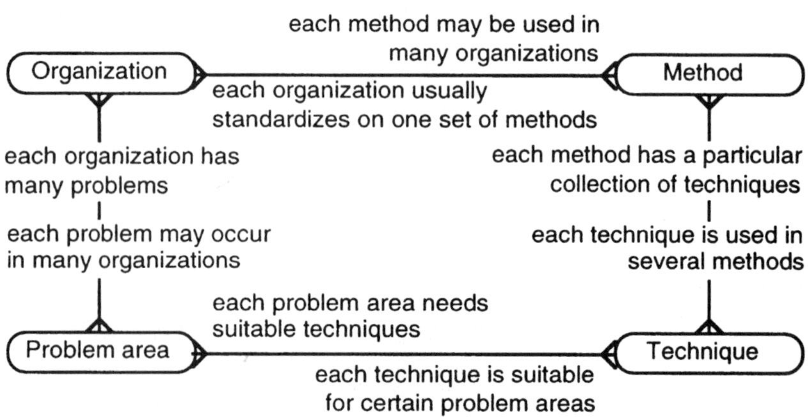

FIGURE 12.7 Relationships between organization, method, problem area and technique.

It is now possible to use this metamodel to derive some consequences that may follow from the common behaviour of business process engineering and information systems development in organizations.

Exercise 12.3

Spend a little time thinking of answers for the following two questions, before continuing with the discussion.

(i) If, in an organization, a process analysis or information system development follows the 'normal' behaviour of selecting one method and using it, which of the necessary relationships in the metamodel of Figures 12.6 and 12.7 is likely to receive the weakest implementation?

(ii) If an organization starts by considering its problems and then chooses the techniques for tackling those problems, which of the relationships in the metamodel will have the weakest implementation?

We can now discuss conclusions for these two key questions.

(i) Taking a common scenario where an organization adopts a method, clearly that method prescribes a particular collection of techniques. The collection is likely to be biased more towards those specified for the method, than towards those for the solution of the problems being faced by the organization. There is an even greater danger – the organization is likely to be faced by continual change which will alter the problems that need to be solved. If the techniques prescribed by the method evolve more slowly, then there will be a widening disparity between the method and the problems to be solved. This **method-driven approach** is unsatisfactory.

(ii) The second question leads to a different kind of difficulty with methods.

A method could be constructed artificially after selecting those techniques that are most suitable for the problem situations facing the organization. The difficulty with this is not so apparent from the diagram. Essentially, an arbitrary collection of techniques faces risks of inconsistency and incompatibility. Notations may be very different. In fact, the resulting collection of techniques is not really a 'method' in the sense defined in Chapter 1 (p. 31–2).

The final version of the diagram that we have been building up is shown in Figure 12.8. This has the arrows corresponding to the two questions (and possible corresponding answers) superimposed. It shows the **organization's dilemma**.

FIGURE 12.8
An organization's dilemma.

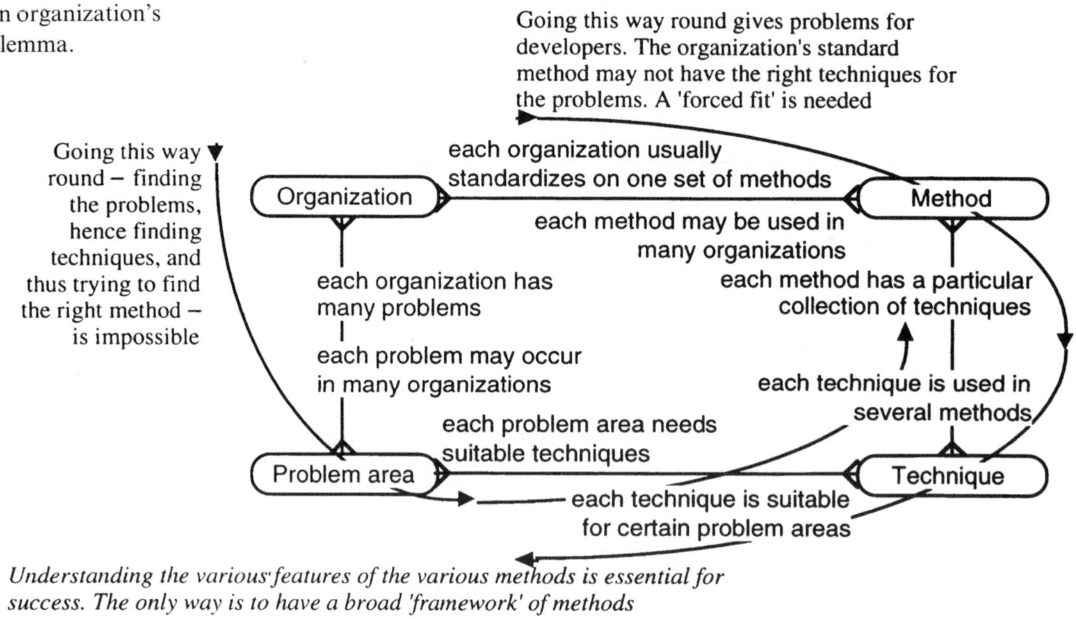

An organization cannot make ideal choices about standardizing on an existing method for analysing and improving business processes or IS development. The context is the overall need to take decisions about methods for long-term standardization. The organization might aim for some options which appear satisfactory in the medium term. We recommend a flexible contingency approach which can adapt to circumstances.

Figure 12.8 shows that an organization can have many potential problems in future years. It could select a method or a collection of techniques and direct that its staff standardize on these and subsequently find that the selected methods might not be the best, or even satisfactory, ones for the problems. And yet the organization certainly cannot evaluate its future potential problems and assess which methods might solve them more easily in advance of a decision about such standardization. In summary, there are four relationships. All are many-to-many.

- Typically an organization experiences many problem areas.
- A particular method contains a certain collection of techniques.
- Organizations usually standardize on one set of methods.
- Any particular problems will require a particular collection of techniques to deal with them appropriately.

Organizations may consider doing either of the following.

- Proceed clockwise. The organization selects a method and hence the techniques and tools inherent in that method. These then have to be made to fit the problem – an unsatisfactory solution.

- Proceed in the anti-clockwise direction. This would yield a chaotic situation and an incoherent set of techniques.

Other issues of choosing a method

Within a given method, different techniques can be used for performing various activities and producing the deliverables. The applicability of techniques to different kinds of problem needs occasional discussion among those involved in a particular organization, such as Mark, Idris, George and Anna.

The tools and techniques must be appropriate to the kinds of problem that the organization is trying to solve. As new kinds of problems arise, the organization should continually rethink and re-evaluate whether to continue the current policy or whether to expend effort reassessing and perhaps changing.

This concept applies again at the level of each information system, method and tool that the Georges use. As potential suppliers develop new versions and announce new products, often reducing prices in real terms, so Mark should continually rethink and reassess whether to consider improving the facilities and processes that the Georges use.

Indeed, whether to do this continually or to have a more systematic and major review regularly, say every two or five years, becomes a strategic policy decision. Most major organizations have regular reviews of their information system strategies and architectures. In some organizations it is such a continual and major work that some staff are essentially doing it for ever. After reviewing one area they move on to another.

The design of a method for analysing business processes and developing information systems can be considered as the design of a system. **Ashby's Law of Requisite Variety** (Ashby and Ross, 1956) may help with a very important aspect of such system design. The implications of Ashby's Law are, in lay terms, that a system should be designed to be able to handle the variety it is likely to encounter. In other words, methods should be able to work with the range of problem situations to be handled.

There is a further point that has not yet come out of the questions we have been asking. An important factor in the usefulness of various techniques is the context in which they are applied, and the techniques by themselves are usually necessary but not sufficient for a good resolution of the organization's problems. For example, six people may be given a problem to solve and a particular context (physical setting, available infrastructure, time and resource constraints, management style, and so forth). The same people with the same problem, may well produce a different outcome when faced with another context. More concretely, the result obtained by setting everyone in a formal meeting room with a specific agenda, facilitator, and time constraints is likely to differ from setting everyone in a more informal environment which is aesthetically pleasing, and in which brainstorming is encouraged as part of the process.

Applying Ashby's Law in simple terms means that what is needed is a methods framework with the following properties:

- the range of problems likely to be encountered should be stated;
- there should be enough techniques in the method to handle the problems likely to be encountered;
- these techniques should be integrated into a culturally compatible method;
- the method must evolve continually as the problems and organization evolve;
- the relationship between the application of the method and organizational context needs to be understood.

Desirable features of ISD methods and approaches

Desirably, an ISD method or approach should be able to cover:

- planning and management of information system development;
- all the development phases;
- communication with users, thought processes for 'problem solving' and decomposition, description, verification and quality assurance;
- communication of the method to developers – through courses and documents;
- evolution of the method;
- supplying support such as software tools and automated processes for developers;
- how to support integrity, consistency, validity, testing and interfacing; and constraints affecting: design, performance, efficiency, resources, costs and the flexibility of developed systems.

An ISD method should be compatible with:

- various ways of working by a team of developers;
- any size of team;
- various levels of expertise – of managers, developers and users;
- various sizes of projects and systems, mainframe, mini and personal computer;
- various cultures, management styles, environment, turbulence.

Styles of development

In many situations application development has proceeded with a hybrid of development styles. This section describes briefly various styles that were not covered earlier. Simple diagrams illustrate the sequences of tasks for the various styles of development. Where incremental refinement is allowed, the diagram gives the sequence in which actions can start, depending on prerequisites from an earlier action. Incremental refinement is assumed within actions.

Contingency

Contingency can be applied in several areas:

- selection of phases, activities, tasks and techniques;
- sequencing of phases, activities, tasks and techniques, and overlapping of them;

- starting points for business strategic planning (BSP), business process engineering and information system development (ISD);
- scope and style of development.

One essence of a framework is that the selection of methods and techniques to deal with a problem can be made in the light of an understanding about the problem and the context in which the problem arises. The result can be regarded as a project – with phases, activities, tasks and techniques – even if it is really a change to an ongoing process.

The first application of contingency arises from the need to select which phases, activities, tasks, techniques and tools could be appropriate for the job in hand. The second area is in the sequencing of those phases, activities and tasks. For example, several very different approaches could be used: waterfall, spiral, prototyping, subcontracting or incremental development. Our framework allows these approaches to be flexibly intermixed to show the possible variations in the sequences of business strategic planning (BSP), information systems strategic planning (ISSP), information system tactical planning (ISTP) and IS project planning (ISPP). In this way a life cycle is defined for each IS and each project. Figure 12.9 shows some examples.

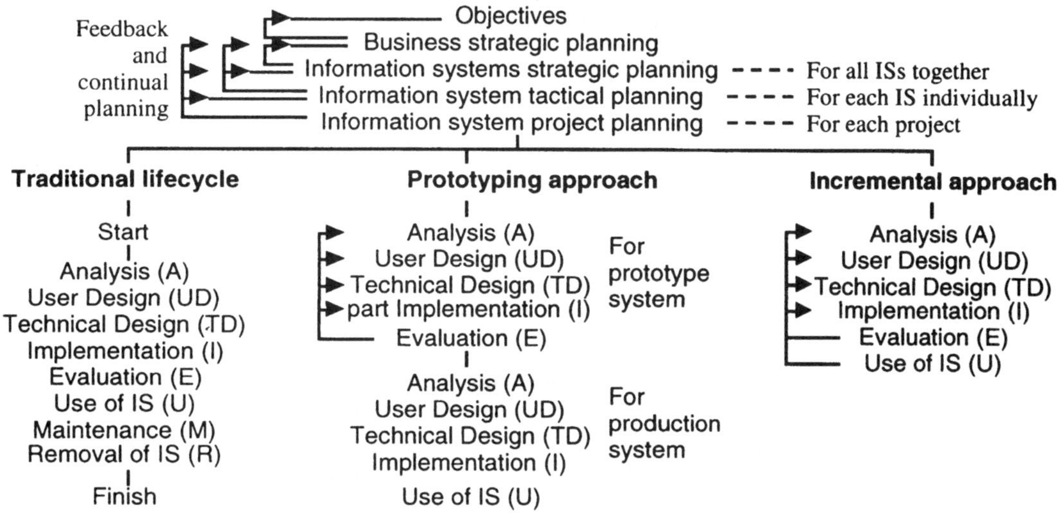

FIGURE 12.9
Methods framework – some possible project life cycles

The framework helps in matching the problem to the available models, methods, techniques and approaches – what we call **process analysis life cycle models** (PALCM). A particular problem is tackled by constructing a project life cycle by selecting from among the available PALCMs, as in Figure 12.10.

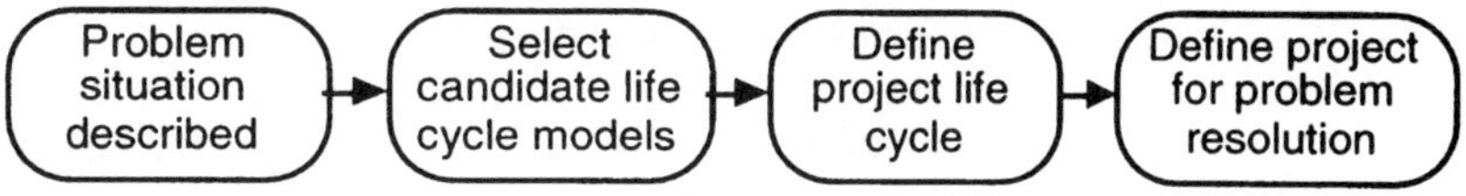

FIGURE 12.10
Process analysis life cycle selection.

A different view of this PALCM aspect of **contingency** is shown in Figure 12.11.

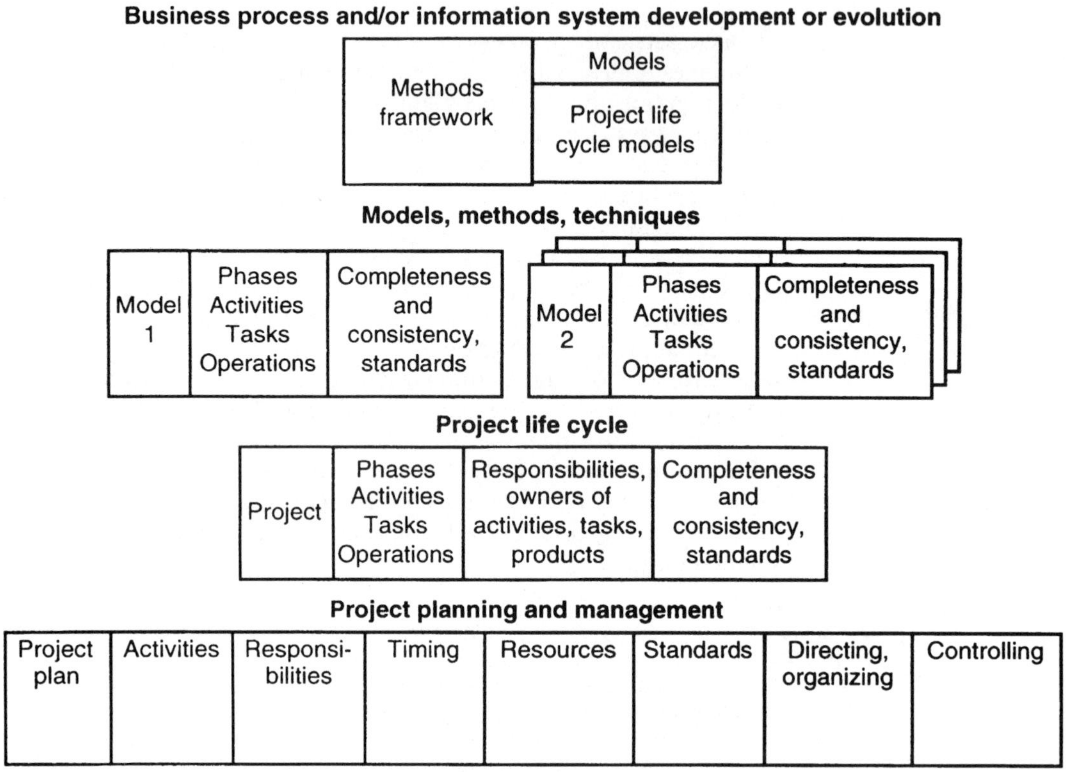

FIGURE 12.11
Basic contingency model applied.

The framework usually contains several life cycle models, methods and techniques. Each model and method has associated with it a set of completeness and consistency standards to drive the phases, activities and tasks until a desired level of completeness and consistency has been achieved. These life cycle models are compared with the problem in order to identify candidate models and one is either selected or constructed for application to the problem.

The next step is to develop the model into a project life cycle by allocating responsibilities for the various activities. Constructing a feasible project plan also requires allocation of the resources necessary for the project to be carried out.

The third aspect, the starting points for BSP and ISD, was covered in Chapters 3, 4 and 7. In practice, for business processes the decisions about starting points are often complex. Conventional wisdom, as taught in some business schools, shows a business strategy being formulated before the definition of the required supporting information systems. In such a scenario, business process engineering 'should' precede everything else. Rarely does this happen in practice. It is rare to secure complete top-level support for a re-engineering exercise to the point that other re-engineering work will wait for the business planning results. Also, such a scenario tends to minimize the extent to which it is actually technological change that is the main driver for business process re-engineering – to respond to increased competitive pressure or to take advantage of new technological opportunities. The ISs are needed to capture and hold the business plans and provide the information for control and management. It is chicken and egg.

Scope and stages of development

We explain the fourth aspect, scope and stages of development, by giving structures that have been used by us, or others known to us, as further alternatives to Figures 12.9 to 12.11. Scope here includes the selection of software packages, subcontracting and timebox, as well as statistics such as queuing theory.

Incremental development

Incremental development builds up the complete set of business functions incrementally. It takes place typically when a core system and functions can be identified, and is then followed by iterations which add functionality or customizations to the original core.

The team members do a little work on perhaps several phases and activities on any day. There is no management view of sign-off of any phase. Figure 12.12 shows an outline structure.

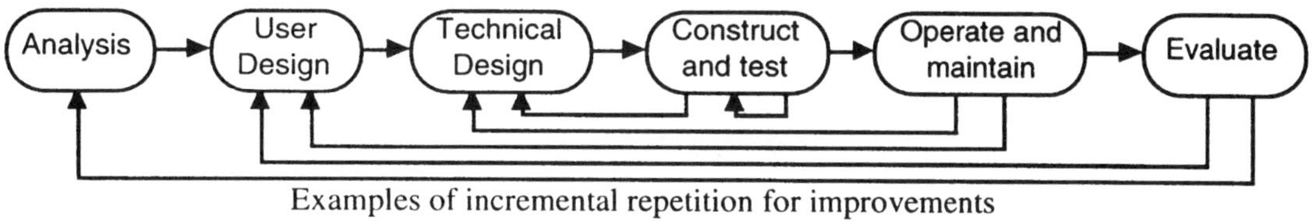

FIGURE 12.12 Pseudo phases but with incremental development.

Parallel development

Parallel development means making progress on many different areas as far as possible at the same time. Candidate areas for parallel working might be: bill of materials, routing, costing, inventory, material requirements planning, material and kit control, workshop loading, suppliers, customer orders and deliveries, invoicing, accounting, payroll, annual inventory checks, logistics. Similarly, progress might proceed in parallel on different areas of hardware, software, communications, standards, quality, and on determining how to merge existing systems.

Parallel development is appropriate where a system has clearly identified subsystems that can be satisfactorily developed in parallel. For example, if an accounts package is required, work on the accounts payable, accounts receivable, general ledger and user interface could all proceed in parallel. This is illustrated in the middle right columns of Figure 12.13 which shows a framework with four **styles of development**. Each is a column showing a time sequence of the starts of overlapped stages.

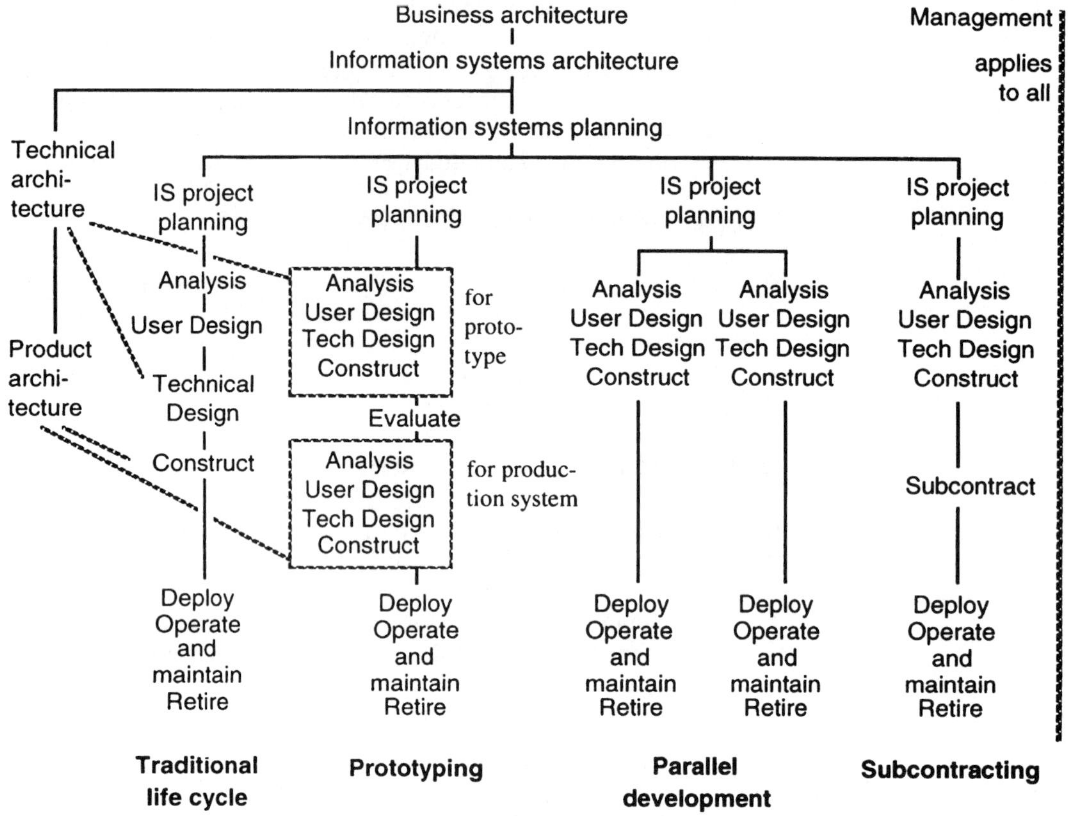

FIGURE 12.13
Framework showing four styles of development.

Package acquisition

A software package may be acquired to meet known requirements, to change the way business is done, to save time and avoid tying up other resources or because it is cheaper than developing an equivalent.

Such packages, which are often supplied with tailoring capabilities that allow users to modify the basic package and so deal with their own local variations, represent a fast way of providing a solution to a business problem with potentially little internal development resource involvement. The much reduced time normally associated with the implementation of a package is usually the primary factor influencing the consideration of this approach. However, many considerations should be taken into account over and above those of functionality and delivery date.

Subcontracting

After a little inhouse planning and feasibility study, the main work is subcontracted, perhaps to a software house or consultancy. Subcontracting demands strong project management of the overall project with particular experience of directing major subcontracts.

Much analysis and design activity must be done before the contracts are drawn up, and the work allocated. This is illustrated in the right column of the framework Figure 12.13.

Timebox

Having a **timebox** means a project is divided into discrete periods, typically 6 to 9 months, with simple rules. The overall project must be broken down into prioritized systems each of which appears feasible, capable of adding real value to the business and constructable within the timebox. The timebox period does not commence until all the necessary resources are available and committed to the project. At the end of the timebox there is an evaluation meeting, the date of which cannot be moved. A go or no-go decision is taken at each evaluation meeting. Postponement is not allowed.

Queuing theory

Queuing theory sometimes arises in the analysis and design requirements stage. Many people do not have sufficient understanding of statistical methods to apply them to estimating throughput, performance and the response time of a proposed technical design, e.g. as part of assessing its feasibility. Similarly, they fail to estimate how long each transaction or request for a service is likely to wait for the right person to deal with it. Queues can get unexpectedly long if this work is omitted.

Use of metamodels

Understanding metamodelling is valuable

Earlier in the book, we demonstrated several simple applications of metamodels but in practice applications are often much more complex.

The use of metamodels helps a range of activities.

(a) A thorough understanding of a metamodel that classifies and structures what is being talked about helps to create a population of instances of the metamodel. For example, a metamodel of strategic planning methods can be used to create a database of the results of a particular strategy exercise in a particular company.
(b) Metamodels can be developed to provide a formal benchmark against which to check a piece of analysis work.
(c) Tools for process engineering and information system design should have their metamodels defined and stated explicitly so that the analyst can know what the tool is suitable for.
(d) Metamodels can be constructed for the components of target systems, either business or information systems.
(e) Standards should have explicit metamodels declared.

In practice, we have found the comparison of metamodels a very powerful technique that can be used by practitioners for a variety of purposes. Table 12.2 gives some uses of metamodel comparisons.

First metamodel	Second metamodel	Usefulness of comparison
Populated database metamodel	Modelling tool metamodel	Know how much of the facilities of a tool has been used, and how much has not
Populated database metamodel	Functional specification metamodel	Know if the results of analysis so far are sufficient to meet the needs of a particular standard
Modelling tool metamodel	Functional specification metamodel	Know if a particular tool is suitable for compliance with an identified standard
Functional specification standard metamodel	Target platform metamodel	Know if a standard is suitable for anticipated target systems
Target platform metamodel	Analysis tool metamodel	Know if a proposed analysis tool is appropriate for the problem situation being handled

TABLE 12.2
Metamodel comparisons

Aspects of rationalizing something

Rationalizing a business process involves factor efficiency, factor substitutability, the overall system behaviour and the organizational learning curve. **Factor inputs** were explained in Chapter 5.

Factor efficiency concerns the resources used, e.g. cash, people, organization, property/real estate, equipment, energy, and information and knowledge. It also depends on the techniques used, e.g. low process added value, multiple processes with the same outputs, detecting isomorphisms - - i.e. processes that are essentially similar, inputs used by many processes, and data envelopment analysis.

Factor substitutability identifies the different factor combinations that are possible, builds scenarios, performs simulation and considers the automation of suitable operations.

The **overall system behaviour** should meet customer needs and do so efficiently and effectively, with appropriate quality and performance.

The **organizational learning curve** is how the process design gradually becomes embedded in the way the business does things.

How things are seen to be done

The above in combination lead to what people see as the way things are done. The added value is calculated. Flows of objects, products, services, knowledge, information, people, resources, equipment, and so on may be improved, speeded up and cost less. Impact analysis shows the effects of the changes on various other things. Migration planning is deciding how to change from the old arrangements to the new. Such a changeover may be gradual, with both in parallel for a period as a check, or a clean cutover. Actions in progress at the instant of cutover may need special arrangements. Data may need to be changed from one representation or structure to another. The new objectives may include better or optimum use of resources, if so, processes such as linear programming or scheduling or other optimizing arrangements may be needed. These may need appropriate modelling of the new system.

Specialists may be needed for cost accounting, operations

management, organizational design, job and work design, managerial cybernetics, ethnography and social anthropology.

Ways of measuring performance before and after the change should be comparable. The information systems should provide the facilities for these. Various measures of gaps in performance were explained in Chapter 3.

People see the points of control. Who can take what decisions? Do they have both authority and responsibility? How do the points of control fit into the organizational structures, the management reporting structure, the boards and committees, working parties and other meetings? The decision making criteria need to be determined and made known to the appropriate staff. To evaluate alternatives, as we explained under feasibility in Chapter 4, they need the appropriate information, therefore what information is needed by whom needs to be agreed. Channels of communication and processing power need to be of adequate capacity. Feedback is needed at each appropriate structural level and for each timescale.

Process improvement – quality and process

Enormous effort is expended by many organizations to define and improve their system development processes. An altruistic reason for this is that the result will be systems of higher quality. A pragmatic reason is that increasingly suppliers encounter terms and conditions of supply that include a requirement that the supplier is in some way certified to some process standard. There are the international ISO 9000 series of standards with national equivalents such as BS 5750. The software development world has the Software Engineering Institute's Capability Maturity Model (SEI CMM) process certification scheme.

There is little evidence that certification according to such schemes produces significantly higher quality of finished goods and services.

One of the main motives for initiatives in this area is so that managers can develop their beliefs that their *procedures and processes* are under control, documented and well understood. We have anecdotal evidence that where organizations are assessed and tested for the implementation of defined procedures and processes: (a) the managers are more likely to report that processes are followed, whereas; (b) consultants and practitioners are more likely to report that they convey the illusion to managers that the processes are followed, and; (c) in the meantime the practitioners must work around aspects of the defined procedures and processes that actually make doing the work more difficult.

The main defect in the procedure certification schemes is the lack of demonstrable evidence that the quality of finished goods and services is actually improved. We acknowledge that there is anecdotal evidence of both success and failure. A technical defect in the standards is that it is only necessary to demonstrate the existence and definition of a procedure or process and compliance with it, and it is not necessary to produce conclusive evidence that the defined processes actually yield satisfactory or higher quality.

So in the areas of methods for business process engineering and information system development, practitioners, managers and consultants are in serious difficulty about what to do.

Many organizations will be unable to avoid the need for some kind of certification, simply because it has become a business issue imposed by some contractual terms and conditions. It is important that organizations do not allow certification efforts to divert too much attention away from the real matters of quality and productivity. It is even more important that in the haste for certification, an organization does not institutionalize and enforce what is actually bad practice.

Quality involves a compromise between technical and economic factors. The most satisfactory approach is usually obtained when there is mutual agreement about the price to be paid for meeting agreed commitments. There may also be a need for absolute standards in some cases of health, safety and aesthetics. Process engineers need to understand how to take part in economic, psychological and political debates to establish what is likely to be appreciated (or not).

> Practitioners and managers should consider both quality and standards, and how they are related.

System development method selection

Many software development methods have been developed over the past 30 years or so, but strangely, there have been far fewer *system* development methods. This is a serious bias in the popular and professional management and computer literature which is likely to be corrected to some degree in the coming years.

To take a somewhat extreme view, the term **computer system** could be seen as an oxymoron; since computers do not have purpose they cannot be considered as systems. The same criticism applies to the term **information system** when used in a narrow sense of implying only the computers, software, networks and similar such artefacts. A computer needs a broader context before it is satisfactory to use the term system. Therefore, system design is concerned with not only the artefacts, but also the human and organizational context for their use.

From a practical point of view, this poses some serious problems. Firstly, there are very few system development methods. The practitioner will need to bring together a range of material from software development to organizational behaviour, and perhaps add a touch of additional subjects such as managerial cybernetics, human resources, finance and managing people.

Where organizations have adopted a formal software development method, we are tempted to offer the generalization that the usual thing to do is to consider a range of standard methods, and then select one for implementation. That usually involves training most people in various aspects of the method, issuing various manuals and standards and monitoring compliance during projects.

When a team of people is involved in a software development project, there are many degrees of freedom over how the work may be done and coordinated. There is a need for consistency in many aspects of system development such that there should be many standard ways of doing, representing and communicating the work; it would be no use having a team of people working together where everyone spoke and understood a different language.

Generally, defined methods are based upon prior experience as it is exceedingly difficult to define methods in anticipation of problems which have yet to be encountered.

Those who are currently engaged in business process engineering and information system development are frequently trying to do something innovative or of greater complexity than has been done before. Therefore in such cases it is to be expected that defined methods will lag behind in appropriateness for the latest problems being addressed.

For those who select and implement methods, an established method *may* be suitable where it can be demonstrated to be applicable to the range of problems likely to be encountered. For those who face increasing levels of novelty and complexity in the systems being built, the continual evolution of development methods is to be expected (and perhaps the occasional revolution).

We have observed in many organizations that the selection of a development method is frequently accompanied by a decision to withdraw support for initiatives on other methods. Generally this is not a good idea. It is important to retain a strategic capability to consider a broad spectrum of possible approaches that can contribute to the solution of problems in hand and those likely to be encountered.

We advocate a flexible methods framework, rather than the selection of a single development method. There are recent signs of the adoption of a **contingency** approach towards methods, changing from the use of one development method per organization to a broad methods capability used to provide appropriate methods, tools and techniques for the problems being addressed – sometimes resulting in a life cycle per problem.

More systems are evolving by transferring support for activities to a broadening infrastructure. There are greater levels of distribution and integration being achieved and this means that the idea of development methods directed at projects is less appropriate. Methods that are applied continually in support of evolving systems are becoming far more appropriate.

We see a need for a role we term **methods engineering**. A methods engineer is a person who is able to match methods, techniques and tools to problem situations, construct the life cycles of the products created in the solutions, and specify the various techniques to be used for different parts of the work. Here life cycle includes inherent characteristics, properties which can be explained, depicted and analysed, and the whole story from creation to removal of each product.

Professional analysts and practitioners

A well-defined profession for system development has not yet emerged

Sadly, the average general level of expertise and professionalism in analysis and ISD is not as high as people outside might desire. A generally acceptable standard has not emerged for several understandable reasons.

One reason is the way in which the adoption and deployment of ISD methods has behaved more like a fashion industry than an evolving profession founded on an established body of knowledge. Various 'structured' methods in popular use lack systematic justification of their wholesale adoption. Many projects have proved to be much more difficult to do because of the intrusiveness and disruption caused by methods that have been imposed on the development groups. Often these do not solve the problems. The scalability and applicability of proprietary ISD methods is not understood. Many managers and organizations have merely assumed that the prescriptive techniques contained in their adopted methods are sufficient for the purposes. Sadly, in many cases this assumption is wrong.

IT evolves rapidly. Computing platforms and software are not yet stable and international standards lag. This may continue for many more years because of the rapid evolution of technology. Unfortunately, organizations take premature decisions about over-simplified technology platforms and this leads to serious difficulty in providing computer support for emerging problems. For example, many organizations have built a database strategy around relational database management systems (RDBMSs) even though RDBMSs are unsuited to many kinds of information storage and retrieval systems. Operating systems are now so complex that organizations have little choice and cannot easily change, even where they understand their requirements before choosing. Technology exerts a greater influence on what is available than requirements exert an influence on technology. So practitioners spend time learning the facilities of new products and versions, and advising and helping users with their problems.

In many organizations, ISD is essentially one team of people doing all the work – including analysis, design, construction and testing. The range of skills needed for such extensive practice is usually too great for the individuals involved. Few practise the skills continually for a sufficient period of years to build up the necessary competence. Relatively few practitioners acquire a broad spectrum of skills from appropriate experience and even several years of experience in structured techniques is not sufficient.

Evolution of facilities

Technical progress determined feasibility

We now summarize technical progress in Table 12.3, showing how the feasibility of various methods and computer applications followed it. To some extent hardware developments were pressured by software ideas, e.g. to improve operating system facilities with interrupts, and to create computer sales by new applications and features. These affected which processes became feasible at different times.

1950–57 • One-off computers in research laboratories • Slow input and output, and no operating system • Hardware unreliable, e.g. mercury delay lines, racks of circuits of thermionic valves, several engineers per computer	• No ISD methods, no software • Computers very expensive for any application • User = both programmer and operator • Research maths applications mainly • Crude Assembly language or machine instruction code • Manual business processes, typewriters
1958–67 • Slow input and output, paper tape, punched cards; one job run at a time; magnetic drums, magnetic tape, no disks, no online terminals, no multiprogramming, crude lineprinters e.g. uppercase only • No longterm online storage of user's data, only sequential files on magnetic tape stored offline • Hardware improving, e.g. small ferro-magnetic core store, 2 hours scheduled maintenance daily, one or two maintenance engineers per computer	• Autocode, Fortran, Cobol, Algol • User = programmer; some separate operators employed • One computer per large company or university • Some commercial applications, e.g. accounting in big firms, where size over 250 staff, £1m turnover p.a. • Computing was a postgraduate activity • Maths, science, and engineering applications • No terminals, no users online
1968–75 • Mainframes and minicomputers, interrupts at end of transfer passed control to privileged operating system, central i/o improved by spooling (simultaneous peripheral online loading) • Online terminals (slow, keyboard and printer), modems for using telephone lines to such • Operating system facilities, impression of several concurrent users • Mainframes and dedicated networks, data transmission	• Files and disks, start of holding user's data online • Transistor hardware could run without engineer on site • Separate operators, users no longer operate • Some users online at keyboard slow-printer terminals • Computing became an undergraduate subject • Structured programming Structured design • Life cycle, growth of systems analysis, process analysis • Many applications, e.g. stock control, invoicing
1976–80 • Operating systems allowed many concurrent jobs with swapping, mainframe disk drives improved • Online VDU terminals, e.g. 24 lines of characters • Screen-based editors	• Data analysis • DBMS, many concurrent users at VDU terminals sharing suitably structured database • Structured analysis • Word processing on mainframe from terminals
1981–86 • Growth of micros, standalone PCs, networks, floppy disks; widespread terminals to mainframes • Colour terminals, TV screen as output	• Computer games, computers bought for home entertainment, some computers in schools, school subject • Hardware could run for years without regular maintenance
1986–95 • IT = convergence of communications and computer technology; small disks, better displays, CDs • Large application packages feasible on desktop standalone computers connectable to networks • Better word processing, fonts, styles, graphics, spreadsheets, E-mail, windows	• More integrated set of tools, workbench tools, CASE • Framework of methods • Modern structured analysis (mid 1980s) • Object-Oriented (OO) analysis (late 1980s) • Organization-wide IS planning, instead of for each business functional area

TABLE 12.3
History of development of features of hardware, software and ideas

Total computing power has increased by about a factor of 2 every two years, or around 10 times every six to seven years. This arose from a mixture of chip technology, CPU speed, size of stores, peripherals, communications and other features. This pattern has continued from the late 1950s to the 1990s.

Prior to the mid-1970s, systems analysis was by narrative

specifications – hard to read, understand and maintain. Machine processable methods were hardly feasible. Structured analysis in the mid-1970s to mid-1980s had early versions of graphical models and emphasis on modelling the current system before modelling the new – as hidden training. The late 1980s included object oriented and real-time techniques.

The trend is increasingly sophisticated software, and relatively less concern with differences between hardware.

Self check

Please spend some time reviewing what you have read and doing the questions below.

Objectives

After reading this chapter you should be able to do the following.

- explain the organization's dilemma in choosing a method to standardize on, and the problematical consequences of standardizing badly;
- explain and apply aspects of contingency and styles of development, including: the selection of phases and activities; sequencing, interleaving life cycles, starting points; and choosing whether to use packages, subcontracting, and/or timebox;
- justify the use of metamodels in a range of appropriate situations;
- contribute to discussions about rationalizing; process improvement; and selecting between different techniques for the analysis for different perspectives such as data, processes and dynamics;
- explain a few points about organizational design and stability;
- explain how the evolution of computers and IT facilities has continually affected what is feasible and worthwhile and how current ISD methods have tended to match what was currently feasible.

Questions

12.1 (i) Suggest some areas for possible standards.

(ii) To what extent do the tools and proprietary methods ensure that the design, development, production, installation and testing conform to quality standards – such as BS 5750 or ISO 900x?

(iii) Do the tools and methods ensure that the software produced, e.g. source code, conforms to standards for the appropriate programming languages?

13 Conclusions and advice to practitioners

We hope you have found the contents of this book interesting, challenging and somewhat different from other books that cover the many topics we have touched on.

We have not said many things that we would like to have said, and indeed much material that is available has been omitted due to constraints of space, and to make this book available earlier rather than later.

We are aware that there will be inevitable shortcomings and topics that readers would like to have seen covered. We welcome comments and suggestions that can be considered for subsequent editions.

In the meantime, we offer this final chapter to achieve two objectives:

- present a summary of key conclusions;
- offer advice to practitioners which we feel will help the wide range of readers and students of this book – this section also aims to present some of our observations based on practical experience.

Conclusions

The following summarizes many of the points in the book, but *not* in the order in which they occurred in the chapters. Many of the points below bring together related points from different chapters in new ways, and thus may give you further insight into why and how some requirements explained in an early chapter are met by details explained in a later chapter.

Framework

We have gradually explained a framework into which many aspects should fit together. Hence you should understand the reasons for many kinds of actions.

We recommend a **contingency** approach, in which people should retain the flexibility to do what appears best in their current situation – faced with perhaps incomplete knowledge, limited facilities and time pressures. People should be able to pick from the many approaches, methods, techniques, tools, models, diagrams and ways of handling problems.

Staff

For success assemble a team of people who have the right qualities. The ability to lead, good decision making, integrity, reliability, conscientiousness, willingness to study and learn properly, being good at human relations and working with others, and having the ability to analyse, to synthesize and to get detail right, are all essential.

Staff need facilities and jobs that as far as possible give them some sense of satisfaction and achievement, even if it be in small things. Most staff prefer business processes and ISs to have frequent small improvements, not large discontinuities. They also need and appreciate good training.

Many staff can suggest ideas for potential improvements or areas that should be looked at and managers should listen to suggestions. Relatively few staff have the ability to create cost-effectively the tools, methods and processes needed for actual improvements. Staff should contribute to the continuation of a satisfactory management style and organizational culture.

Organizational goals and approach

Enterprises usually need continual improvement and evolution. Successful small steady enterprises should not try to make sudden big risky leaps. Medium and large ones need to have relatively more people watching their environment and their measures of performance (including external-value metrics), recommending and deciding strategy and tactics by ongoing planning.

People should plan for and have the IS facilities for information exploitation, not just an MIS-centric IS and/or ISs for operational efficiency. Improvements to business processes need management commitment, a champion, new ways of doing something, time, resources and work, and the aim should be for significant improvements. People should research things that are likely to give a worthwhile improvement and return on investment.

Performance measurements should be measurable in terms of quantifiable variables, measured each time period and related to achievable objectives. External-value metrics measure the perceived impressions of customers and others in external organizations.

Business functions are classes of processes and other actions proper to the enterprise's purposes.

Large organizations, more than small, need ways of controlling what is happening. In their developments of business systems and ISs this shows as more formal project control with written scheduling of activities and reviews, rather than allowing the developers to do as they think best from day to day.

Optimizing the organization and improvements

Organizations have a collective organizational problem of how to optimize who should do what, and how to do so on a continual basis. Except in small organizations this leads to resource optimization problems that cannot be properly solved. In large organizations the ISs cannot even bring together all the information about the organization's current state on a continual basis. Compromises are needed and yet managers rarely face this organizational problem and try to think it through. The usual solution is a management reporting structure, perhaps combined with working parties, teams, projects and matrix structures.

Information flows 'vertically', not only as directives, plans and objectives from management decisions flowing downwards, but also as bids and suggestions flowing upwards. These flows form parts of control loops, they generate options to be evaluated against criteria when choosing between alternative courses of actions, and flows are also part of human interactions, including monitoring, assessment, reviews, management style and social networking.

Information flows 'horizontally' in coordinating the activities of people and systems in different areas of an enterprise, and for social networking. It would not be feasible for such information to flow up a chain to some higher manager and down another chain to where it is needed.

The development of IT-based ISs has significantly affected the patterns of information flows. Many flows that used to occur at meetings, in memos and by telephone have been replaced by flows resulting from input to and reports from central computer systems. This yields far less human contact and to some extent trust and commitment are lost or reduced. People rarely or never see those they are in fact dealing with. The same applies in dealings with other organizations such as suppliers and customers where purchasers meet sales staff less often, orders being placed and accounts settled by automatic transfers between computers. Middle managers have less control over information flows since flows through the computers can bypass them. The middle manager just receives a copy.

Opportunities for middle managers to create added value by appropriate expertise, amplification and attenuation have been reduced. With increased IT-based ISs, managers can be made responsible for relatively more staff yet have fewer meetings with each of them, relying on the IT for reports of progress and of exceptions that need action. Fewer middle managers are needed for a particular size of operational staff and so the management structure becomes flattened. Managers lose their jobs.

IT allows new kinds of operational processes and automation to be created. Fewer operational staff are needed with clerical jobs becoming IT-based and so fewer clerks are employed.

A business system may be improved slightly in the short term through good staff and improved operations. But such improvements within the existing resources are usually very limited, and have little effect on the performance of the enterprise. More significant improvements need changes to the resources, tools, equipment and processes, with medium-term planning and timescales. Really big improvements need major thought and work, planning, analysis, and changed tools, facilities, ISs and processes. Such improvements cannot be achieved overnight. The work involved in planning, analysis, development and provision of the new facilities and processes is often far more than each subsequent operation that uses them.

Planning and management

Business strategic planning involves shaping the future destiny of the business and knowing whether a particular course of action will be worthwhile in a particular organization. Usually it is necessary for such planning to be a continuous activity in large organizations. It needs commitment by top managers, with clear terms of reference, scope and prerequisites, and it needs resources. There are many steps covering mission, objectives, SWOTs, critical factors, measures of performance, gaps, deriving strategies, decisions, responsibilities and plans. From these come the ISs strategic plans and the business systems strategic plans, and the corresponding tactical plans and projects for each system.

An object–property–relationship metamodel of strategy, strategic business units, SWOT factors, metrics and objectives, together with their relationships, shows how consistency and completeness checks may help to indicate what aspects have not been thought through.

Management means directing, organizing, initiating the right work, reviewing and controlling; and ensuring that the right facilities are provided, including the provision and the use of business systems and the ISs.

Management styles impact the business systems and ISs, often making the difference between success and failure.

Cost analysis

Managers need to be able to analyse costs; to set cost objectives; and to understand shared costs, opportunity costs, deferral of costs, allocation of overheads, process costing, variable and fixed costs, product costs and infrastructure costs. They also need an ability to measure costs in order to provide knowledge of production costs, value of stock, cost of design and development, and operating costs for estimating, budgeting and control purposes. Managers should ensure that when jobs are planned the need for cost analysis is appreciated and the main activities structured accordingly, with appropriate metrics defined for each activity and the relevant classifications of costs stated.

Information

People need knowledge and information for many purposes. Managers and providers of systems need to understand this, and not dismiss what might appear as informal but are in fact essential requirements. Information has to be meaningful and useful as effective communication to the person or system receiving it, and related to some purpose. Data is not the same as information.

Information systems should provide appropriate facilities for handling and storing information. Different users may want different views and structures and information should be appropriately selected to match their purposes and needs.

ISs have non-IT-based parts, including manual and automated non-IT parts. People's salaries generally cost more than the hardware and software, allowing for all running costs and depreciation. The benefits of improved hardware and software in terms of increased quality of products and services, reliability, flexibility and productivity often so outweigh the costs of provision and training that change is continually worthwhile.

Systems

Preoccupation with computers and IT tends to cause people to neglect the idea of systems and associated ideas.

Systems are connected assemblies of parts that work together, can adapt, have a purpose and are of interest. A system is viewed as having a boundary, interfaces and flows of objects. These objects include materials, power, energy, information, knowledge and control signals. They flow across a boundary at an interface. Subsystems have the features of systems. Different people may view a system and its boundaries, interfaces and flows differently. These views may all contribute usefully to analysis and provoke suggestions.

A system has a particular state at each instant. State transitions may be analysed and represented in state-transition diagrams. System variables can be measured and quantified, giving attribute-value pairs at each such measurement. A system may have one equilibrium state or several where each such state may or may not be stable. The system may evolve and converge towards a stable state, reaching it reasonably quickly, or it may oscillate about it without reaching it.

Business systems need points of control for their management. Managing resources in an environment needs continual decisions by the manager, using knowledge and information from higher-level objectives and plans, from the environment and from the current and past performance of the resources. These decisions, which may involve wisdom and complex optimization processes, should produce appropriate information that flows from the control to the resources. The resource system and the controlling system interact like real-time systems. Analysis and modelling of such interactions needs appropriate techniques such as those Ward–Mellor and Hartley–Pirbhai have devised, together with state-transition and other diagramming techniques. The diagrams have a standard notation for modelling and understanding such real-time control systems, and for developing models of proposals for future improved systems.

Systems have important intensive properties that make the overall value greater than the sum of the values of the parts. Some of the value of business systems lies in the skills, experience and knowledge of those involved. Other intensive values arise from features built in during analysis, design and implementation. The ISs should have many features that help in adapting by providing flexibility. Management care and an appropriate management style is needed to retain the skills, knowledge and flexibility that are essential to ensure long-term continuing good return from the whole.

Actions and actors

Actions, whether by George or Anna or their managers, have various features. They are triggered by events. Receipt of information, observation of situations, feedback from progress on current actions, new thoughts and timepoints, such as noon each Friday, are such events.

An action may need planning before undertaking it, and review and control during and after it. It is performed by an actor – a system, a person or a processor. It has a purpose, such as to produce some product or service or information to a client. The client may be the same as the actor. During and after performing the action both actor and client may need feedback to provide monitoring and control, and to ensure that product quality is maintained.

The ways that the client and actor interact when an actor is helping a client to solve a problem, their roles, thoughts, actions and responsibilities, need to be understood. Some aspects of these are often assumed without being explicitly stated or agreed, and disputes may arise from misunderstandings.

The management control cycle of an action may be repeated in various ways to gradually improve the product, avoid waste and correct errors. Decisions are needed as to what to do next and whether to stop or continue. Indeed discussing and deciding upon criteria for these may be worthwhile in some cases.

For larger actions the trade-off between relatively more work and control, or less work and greater risk of waste and delay, may be difficult to get right. In practice there may be so many variables that the optimum way of working may be far from obvious, and impossible to get right. This applies to making optimum choices between alternative ways of developing and improving business systems and information systems.

The feasibility of an action may be investigated as part of planning. For small actions this is often trivially easy. For some larger actions, such as an ISD, this feasibility study can become a major phase. As technology improves over a decade the feasibility, costs and benefits of something will almost certainly change completely.

Actions may be classified by size, importance, complexity and whether or not they are routine. They are classified into projects, developments, phases/stages, activities, tasks and operations. They may also be classified by what education, training, skills and managerial ability are needed. Each action may need techniques and tools.

Information systems development

ISs may be implemented in many ways, e.g. filing cabinets, simple computer programs and data, spreadsheets and database systems.

They might require relatively more or fewer people, and correspondingly fewer or more computers and communications equipment. Increased development complexity, costs and timescale might be offset by lower running costs. Software packages can be purchased, but such software might not have all the facilities needed.

Information system development (ISD) means the complete process of deciding about, planning and providing a new IS or an improvement to an existing IS. Business systems development is similarly defined. The planning, analysis, development and provision of improvements is so large that it needs its own planning, tools, specialists and management.

An ISD method should have a recommendable collection of thought out assumptions, scope, rules, actions, deliverables, techniques, and management. A business system development method should have the same. Since most business improvements involve improvements and/or changes to information patterns these two have become merged. Methods of analysis of business processes apply to information processes, and vice versa. The term methodology is widely used to mean a proprietary ISD method, though its original meaning is the science of method.

An approach is a way of starting to tackle some issue, giving outline suggestions without precision or details, and leaving considerable freedom to the actor.

ISD approaches include: the waterfall and later variants; interleaving and gradual development; systems; planning; data-analysis; prototyping; socio-technical; participative; product set; automated tools; and a structured approach using structured analysis, design and programming. In some situations, several of these can be combined.

ISD is usually described in terms of phases and different ISD methods have different named phases. We recommend that the distinction between phases need not be clear cut, and that phases and activities may overlap to give feedback and to avoid problems. Each phase has many activities involving many tasks and operations.

If an organization tries to standardize on a particular proprietary method that method will probably turn out not to be suitable for all its problems. However, to understand all of the problems first and then standardize on a proprietary method is impossible.

Managers should consider whether the business systems, the ISs and the processes should be designed and built with added flexibility in order to cope with changes to the less-stable aspects. These include unpredictable changes in enterprise objectives, strategies and tactics; and major changes such as restructuring, reorganization, mergers and takeovers. We regard these as relatively unstable in the long term. Adding that flexibility, however, increases implementation and running costs slightly and the extent to which such flexibility should be incorporated is a controversial issue. Middle managers and specialists will not suggest or create the flexibility features where they think their jobs and careers would be threatened if they were to do so. Hence the ISs in some large organizations do not have this flexibility, even though technically feasible, because of management attitudes.

Models and modelling

Models are developed as simplifications that show the essential features of something for some purpose. Dynamic models allow rules and structures in the model to change.

Diagrams and text are used to describe and explain aspects of current and proposed situations and systems.

The real world changes. From a model of it at some instant, a new model can be created that corresponds to the changed real world state. The new model may passively reflect the new situation or, if the rules are understood and modelled, from the first model a second can be derived that correctly predicts a future real world situation. In practice these two are combined. A model of a relevant part of the real world, the rules governing changes and a model of a changed state may be held in an IS.

Multiple models may be created and represented to correspond to alternative plans and proposals. The model's predictions can then be compared as a step towards deciding which alternative to choose. In complicated cases, each alternative might be investigated using queries such as what-if questions, retrievals using an appropriate query language, calculations using spreadsheets or other packages, and comparisons between the predictions and the current and past reality.

Future improved ISs are envisaged as the result of dynamic changes to existing systems. Here the existing IS is like the current real world and the new IS corresponds to a change from it, a change which can be modelled. People need to realize that they are discussing many alternative possible changes to ISs and business systems, and then trying to compare the alternatives and for this they need ways of describing the features. This is not just discussing the processes that the future IS could perform, but the way the whole will look to a user such as George and to a developer such as David.

This is achieved by using logical models. Various kinds of text and diagrams are created to show various aspects of the processes, data, behaviour, responsibilities, operating arrangements, security, control and management. These models involve many kinds of abstractions. David's logical models during design and implementation may be different from George's logical models at the time of use, but David's models, being more general, will be such that George's models will be derivable from them as special cases.

The features of a future IS should match the requirements and so people need models to record and explain the requirements. This is achieved with conceptual models, which also include text and diagrams.

The stating and understanding of the requirements is partly a soft issue. The requirements have soft aspects that derive from the management style, priorities, culture, organizational objectives, strategy and tactics for the various parts of the business. These are combined with relatively hard aspects of requirements such as rules, abstractions and generalizations, processes and data. Ultimately these soft and hard aspects have to be transformed into increasingly hard detailed specifications of facilities and processes for George. The specifications are transformed into implemented systems, facilities, documentation, training for George and knowledge such as that which Isobel has to have in order to help George.

Conceptual models, and the ways in which people create and discuss them, need to cater for these soft aspects during the early stages of a development. So to ease the analysis stages, people try to develop rule-free models and text descriptions. On the other hand the analysis products should capture all of the knowledge that needs to be carried forward to the later development stages. This soft–hard aspect causes difficulties for many people.

Prototypes are models. Prototyping can provide a way of getting people involved and speeding development and can bypass some of the modelling problems usually encountered by user representatives such as Idris and George. People can comment on demonstration prototypes instead of helping to create the underlying models and diagrams. However, behind the scenes they still need to understand the underlying models sufficiently well to judge whether they are correct and contain the right features. What matters is the correctness of the structures of the systems, processes, information, behaviour, and so on, not just the human–computer interface features such as commands and screen layouts which the prototypes tend to emphasize. Some prototypes are developed just to show certain features and are then discarded. Others are gradually developed into the final systems.

The transformations from a mental image and conceptual model through to logical model, physical model and implemented system should preserve the consequences of the requirements, and become increasingly closer to providing a useful system. In practice the models are rarely completed and the distinction between the models is not clear cut. To do so would not be worthwhile as Anna and David have conventions that avoid the need for full models and they prefer to interleave and gradually develop the systems and changes in ways that do not require full models at the start of a later stage.

Business systems integrate across departmental structures and areas of an organization and so do ISs. Analysts therefore need ways of gradually extending a model that was initially created to correspond to just one area so that it covers all relevant areas. Alternatively, models developed for different areas may need to be merged. Conceptual and logical models have the right features to allow both extending and merging and can also be developed into systems that have the right hooks for future improvements and for appropriate independence.

Business systems and information systems should preferably not be developed for each separate business function or department independently. To do so leads to stovepiped separate systems that have many facilities which are virtually duplicated. This is inefficient from the view of the whole organization and multiplies the costs of development and procurement. Moreover, the differences in each implementation will make future horizontal coordination and integration, if needed, far more difficult.

To be worthwhile and useful, models should be simpler, faster, easier to work with, relevant, and cheaper than reality. Working with models thus saves expense and waste on building useless full-scale systems.

Models used in analysis and design

Techniques for analysing business processes have considerable overlap with techniques for analysing information system requirements.

A business process has inputs about factors of production, including information, cash, people, materials and other resources, and an infrastructure.

Many aspects of a process may be modelled including when does something happen, why, who or what does it, who is responsible for it, under what conditions does it start and finish, how are processes chained, what are the inputs and outputs, and how does it decompose into subprocesses. Further details of processes may be explained in structured English, pseudocode, and various kinds of diagrams.

Analysts form metamodels concerning objects such as events, processes, conditions, data, interfaces, inputs, outputs, responsibilities and attributes. In the metamodels these are connected through relationships. An object–property–relationship metamodel carries further abstractions that may apply to many or all organizations. A particular organization or business system will have many rules that need to be discovered and modelled and, for each rule, a decision is needed on whether or not to build it into the business and information systems, and if so how. Building it in may produce huge improvements in effectiveness and save many errors by the Georges, but may reduce flexibility at unstable times of upheaval. Not building it in would save on development costs, but possibly cost far more eventually as a result of waste and undetected errors.

Analysts need to think about what knowledge needs to be captured and agreed during analysis and passed on to others doing the later stages.

Information flow diagrams show the people, systems, areas, and processes; and the logic of the information flows between them. Data flow diagrams are similar but show physical data flows and data stores.

Entity–attribute–relationship models show the types of knowledge and information handled. Some of these may be more stable in the long term than the processes currently used by George to handle them.

Simple models use only 2-entity relationships but many organizational rules really should be modelled in ways that associate more than two entity types. Practical business situations require more complex ways of analysing and structuring – with attributes into aggregates, normalized entities, relations, tables, and particularly relationships between more than two entities. Ways of transforming between alternative data models are useful. Object oriented aspects should be observed during analysis so that the implementations have the right unified facilities.

Analysts need consistency and completeness checks. Some arise from viewing the objects, properties and relationships being described, and others arise from viewing the development methods and techniques.

IT-based facilities

The IT-based parts of ISs are limited by what is theoretically computable, and within that by what can be achieved with current technology, and within that yet again by what is available to an actor in a particular organizational situation. These limitations form a complicated intersection with what is acceptable within an organization, and also with what is worthwhile. This all limits the tools available to an actor and may also limit the information and knowledge available or that can be obtained. The actions, processes and methods that the actor may use are similarly limited, and an actor can only do an action where the tools are available and the process or method is acceptable.

Where an actor does many similar actions he/she may gain familiarity and think of shortcuts or improvements. The facilities and tools ought, therefore, to evolve gradually to match. Database administrators can improve the physical layout of large collections of data to match changing patterns of access and use and people tend to use different combinations of commands as their understanding of a computer system improves. Analysts use shortcuts and metalevel rules and abstractions, and even create new ones and new forms to match.

Advice and discussion for practitioners

Advice for managers and consultants

- Be aware of the external environment, e.g. the competitive position of the business, the support of sponsors, customers/clients and the overall finances. Watch for signs that may change these.
- Think out the objectives, aims, strategy, mission statement and the scenario for a horizon several years ahead.
- Be aware of the needs of staff and other people, and how these are to fit in with the business needs.
- Think out tactics and plans for the next few months and then move flexibly towards the longer term objectives and horizon.
- Think out the criteria for decisions.
- Communicate with staff who need to know and understand things.
- Allocate your own and other people's time and resources sensibly.
- Try to add value to what is done, and to information.
- Try to create a culture that allows others to contribute to their full ability.
- Remember that ISs need gradual and continual evolution in order to take advantage of hardware and software developments, and to evolve as the business does.
- Remember that users of ISs may be frustrated by relatively trivial features. They need good training and a service where they can get help when stuck.
- Plan appropriate capacity, e.g. IT need not be utilized fully.

Advice for system developers

- Communicate effectively. Write lucid and correct specifications, designs, reports and memos.
- Ensure user representatives' continual agreement is obtained as the work proceeds.
- Listen to managers and users; observe; read thoroughly; make sure you understand correctly.
- Be aware of body language, hidden agendas, motivation and culture.
- Produce systems that work fully, not just proposals and half developed systems; don't leave or move during a project.
- Plan to continue your responsibility for a system after it goes live, so that users get help from the right system experts during early use, and so that you get feedback from users' early experience.
- Try to make realistic guesses at how long a project will take, e.g. estimate minimum, expected and maximum times; do enough work to be sure of the estimate before submitting it; state assumptions about, e.g. leave, sickness, resources, technology, or any uncertain factors.
- Don't promise anything that cannot be delivered.
- Try to say no where appropriate, e.g. do not take on more than can reasonably be achieved with certainty; avoid overstress and the need for continually working long hours for more than a short-term crisis.
- Wherever possible make design choices that build in flexibility to cope with future changes, e.g. modularity, standard interfaces and independent blocks.
- In selecting and procuring tools to help your development work, try to get ones that can be used for several likely future projects, not just for the current need.
- Understand the objectives and strategy of your organization.
- Try to be aware of and keep abreast of technical developments.
- Realize that you will probably need continuing education and training throughout your career, and that the kind of work you do will continually evolve.
- Try to assess your own personal strengths and weaknesses. What are you best at? How do you create large programs, e.g. by writing a lot or a little code initially, by adding features to a working core, by testing in small sections and by using what tools, languages, and why? How fast can you create new program code? How much is correct first time? Do you prefer to be given a detailed specification or can you help develop the specification of what is needed? Can you analyse to other people's satisfaction? How easy do you find learning something new, e.g. a new package? How well can you work alone; how much do you need to be supervised? How good are you at leadership, management and decision making? How reliable are you? How conscientious are you? How good are you in a team? Do you become frustrated by a poor leader/manager above you? How good is your memory, e.g. for

details such as the exact words used? How good are you at re-expressing something in different words to aid communication? Are you a good teacher and explainer with a helpful and encouraging style? Are you approachable and willing to help others? Think how others perceive your abilities and be concerned with the impact of what you do.

Other discussion and advice to practitioners

At the risk of seeming to be prescriptive, we discuss and offer some practical advice here to practitioners.

The answers to many questions about practical business process engineering and information systems design should be prefaced by a comment such as 'Well, it depends on ...'. However, we are frequently asked to summarize a set of recommendations, despite all the cautions and caveats that should accompany summary advice.

The following subsections offer some key thoughts for senior managers, practitioners and consultants, based on our experiences in a range of practical situations, and taking into account literature we have found particularly helpful. We apologize in advance if many of the comments seem overly prescriptive or opinionated – after all, expressing personal opinions is one opportunity available to authors who succeed in publishing their work! We shall be very interested to share the experiences and opinions of others who have struggled with the topics below.

Many topics could have been selected. We mainly comment about those that seem to recur over relatively long periods of time and in many different organizations.

> Our advice is to ensure the formation of a small broad-based team. Desirably they should between them have the extensive analytical skills to handle all sorts of objects – such as: objectives, requirements, strategy and planning; processes, data, behaviour and responsibilities; finance, costing and operations; essential business processes, flexible and unstable organizational structures; points of control and management. Their education and skills should cover all the types of analysis, structured and object oriented techniques, statistical methods, optimization and project control.

Many of the traditional organization and methods (O&M) techniques from previous generations of analysts are coming back into vogue again with the increased pressure for business process re-engineering. Much contemporary BPR is old O&M rediscovered and directed at a different audience, with increased impetus from more readily available computing.

It is unlikely that the range of analytical techniques needed can be found in one person, therefore teams are necessary to provide the required broad base. In addition, there need to be people with good literacy in a very wide range of analytical techniques and who are able to know which techniques to use when.

Process description forms

The process description forms we outlined in Chapters 5 and 6 revive an approach that has been in use in many ways over the past few decades. We make no apology for their simplicity and the initial use of paper. They have proved to be very helpful indeed in many organizations. Analysts and users have found that the forms have encouraged simplicity and a degree of completeness that only enhances their understanding of the processes they are describing.

There are many ways in which the information collected on such forms can be rendered into a machine readable form, and many programmers and users will probably enjoy creating their own scheme to do so. Let us offer the advice that it is more difficult creating a general reporting capability on instances of the metamodels, than it is creating a way to store the information itself.

Create and use simple forms that have the right structure.

Business strategy, business processes, information and information technology

Business process engineering work is frequently linked to: (a) the formulation of business strategy and; (b) opportunities for process redesign offered by the use of computers and related technology. In our experience, many of the techniques used for information systems are indeed useful, they are necessary but not sufficient.

We recommend a trend towards applying the analytical techniques used in information system development to business objectives and strategy work and to business process engineering. The practitioner should develop literacy in a broader range of techniques, including more traditional statistical and financial approaches.

It is relatively naïve to propound that a business should define its strategy and then summon the technology needed to support that strategy. Many organizations today are undergoing rapid change more as a consequence and response to technology evolution, than as a result of a conscious decision to deploy more technology.

The practitioner in process engineering will be well advised to keep up to date with major trends in technology in order to anticipate both opportunities and pressures for changes to the way things are done at present.

There is a serious bias in the popular and professional literature towards seeing problems related to the management and use of information in business processes as mainly concerned with IT. Many organizations spend 50% or more of total cost on what can generally be termed 'knowledge work'. IT spending may be as low as 1–2% of total cost in commodity intensive industries such as oil, or as high as 7–8% of total cost in information intensive industries such as banks. Therefore the spending on the management of information and knowledge is usually at least *ten times greater* than spending on IT.

> For this reason even if no other, the information systems specialists and consultants should have a far broader base than IT. IS consultants who talk mainly about computers and the applications of computers are only doing a minor part of the whole job.
>
> Process engineers need to understand this point as well. Although business process engineering has IT as one of the enabling technologies, much of the process engineering work is concerned with people, organization and non-computer aspects of process.

There is no clear evidence of which we are aware showing that those companies with business strategies are actually more successful than those that do not have strategies. By this we mean articulated strategies that are described as such. We believe that the information systems should present measures of the parameters which reflect the external market situation of the organization. The more these are measured, the less the need for articulated strategy. The metrics will indicate whether the performance, processes, products and services need to change and how.

> In designing information systems to support business strategies and processes, the practitioner should develop information systems with:
>
> (a) performance measurements;
> (b) external-value metrics;
> (c) achievement of objectives;
> (d) progress towards implementing strategies; and also
> (e) the continuing applicability of the strategies.
>
> Few people do (d) and (e).

Oversimplification

The analyst and modeller face a difficult dilemma, as represented by the fundamental problem described in Chapter 2. The work of analysis and modelling is essentially that of abstraction and simplification. This is important to obtain a broad view of what is happening.

> People need models to get an overview of something that would otherwise be far too complex to comprehend.

On the other hand, human behaviour is infinitely varied. People are very ingenious at devising ways to work around rules and techniques that are overly restrictive, and that hinder doing work (similarly, some people are very adept at working around well designed processes!).

The practitioner needs to be very wary of techniques that deliver oversimplification. By that term we really mean abstract descriptions and analysis of processes which are just 'wrong'. For example, many approaches to describing process flows make assumptions about the sequencing of smaller processes. When practitioners such as ethnographers and anthropologists look at how work is actually done, terms such as 'interruption' start being used. Sometimes this is strange because the interruptions may indeed be the essence of the work. Therefore what is it that is being interrupted? The wrong simple model is that of abstract concepts of how people think that the processes 'ought' to work. A major problem with process flow diagrams is that the way processes are linked together may not be known until 'runtime' when the response to a particular event is created. George controls the behaviour. George interrupts himself and others. George makes the process work despite the wrong oversimplifications in the tools and processes provided to him.

Another area of oversimplification is in the realm of ISD method selection. Frequently the problem of method selection arises not because of any inherent difficulties in the way problems are currently being tackled, but because someone has been appointed to manage the system development activity. Where an organization is attempting to handle a wide range of problems, and where the problems are of increasing novelty and complexity over time, then a wide variety of methods and techniques will be needed.

> Managers may be under considerable pressure towards oversimplification in several different ways. The consultant needs to understand such pressures and develop an ability to keep technical and business issues as separately identifiable as possible. The practitioner needs to be sure that different levels of detail and abstraction can be mapped to each other, and that there is a clear knowledge and understanding of what is missing, or possibly even misleading, at the various levels.

Non-MIS-centric information systems planning

Some information systems planning (ISP) literature considers the problem of ISP as essentially how to define the information systems

(ISs) needed to implement and support the strategy of the company. The practitioner needs to be wary of this as a prime concern of ISP. Clearly such a concern is fundamental and must be incorporated but there are other concerns that can have a profound impact on the nature of ISP.

Many organizations are moving towards greater recognition of information as an intangible asset. This means that the information has market value or its use can generate income – information exploitation.

An alternative approach to ISP is to take the point of view of the system users or 'victims'. The main rationale of ISP is to put in place the information systems needed to meet the needs of users, who include the managers controlling resources. This is MIS-centric.

These alternative objectives of ISP can lead to substantially different results. Information systems that maximize cash flow to the company by the utilization of information assets are very different from the MIS-like systems needed to support the existing management structure of the company. Similarly, an approach to ISP of putting the needs of external customers first is very different because needs arising from a business strategy are then subordinate to those of the market. It is easy for companies to fail while their managers are blindly implementing an ill-conceived strategy!

> A difficult task facing the practitioner is to rectify the traditional MIS-centric approaches to ISP.

Scope of information technology

Increasingly these days, people may feel a bit guilty if computers are *not* used to support certain tasks.

The practitioner must maintain great care to treat all artefacts used to deal with information as part of the whole set of things that are the concern of information technology. The literature has a bad bias towards defining IT in terms of computers, communications and related artefacts only.

> The practitioner needs to understand that the term **technology** refers to the study of how artefacts are used to achieve objectives and purposes such as products and services; it does not refer to just the artefacts themselves.

Therefore in this sense, it is not correct to refer to computers as one kind of information technology. It is the study of the use of those computers to achieve effects that is a more accurate depiction of the term **technology**. The word technologies is used in a colloquial sense to mean just the collection of different kinds of artefacts.

Epilogue

This book points out to the practitioner and the manager a long and difficult journey. We have touched on a wide range of approaches, models, actions, methods and techniques that we believe to be of use to those concerned with business process engineering and information systems development. We have tried in places to explain what to do, how and why. Severely limited by book length and price we do not cover everything we would have liked.

We hope you have found this book helpful, and have gained some pleasure from the achievement of increased understanding. We also hope that its ideas may be applied in ethically desirable ways that increase happiness.

Appendix A
Notes on chapters

Chapter 1

Chapter 1 introduced various ideas and assertions for which additional discussions and sources are available in published literature.

The idea of information being some kind of useful communication is based on information theory and its applications, as in Cover and Thomas (1991), Darnton (1992). For Computer supported collaborative working (CSCW), see Bowers and Benford (1991). Grindley (1991) usefully discusses keyboard-level IT issues.

For the emergent properties of systems, general literature about systems is helpful, including Klir and Valach (1987), Jackson (1983), Flood and Carson (1988) and Beer (1979, 1981, 1985). Useful work on organizations and information includes Savage (1990) and Morgan (1986, 1993).

A common error is to consider ISs mainly or wholly as IT systems or as computer systems, with the serious but not misleading oversimplification 'companies spend 20 times as much on managing information as on managing IT' – for discussion of this see Darnton (1992) and Vincent (1990). Our book discusses information systems generally, and is not focused specifically on, or restricted to, IT-based systems.

The originator of the classical waterfall model of information system development is sometimes cited as Royce (1970), but an earlier exposition was given by Canning (1956). Maddison (1959) had a completely independent version with six iterative stages covering the broad outline, analysis of needs, forming a mental model, design, programming and testing, and running the old and new in parallel; and overlapped these as in the story at the start of Chapter 2.

The section on *Business process and analysis issues* gave many questions about aspects of Anna and other people's actions, which led to the justification of ISD methods in the following section. Maddison *et al.* (1983) discussed over 100 such questions about ISD methods. Maddison *et al.* (1983, 1989, 1993) are the sources of some of our definitions.

Chapter 2

The term 'universe of discourse' was used by Venn (1881) and by Carroll (1896). It was also used in meetings leading to Griethuysen (1982), which had overlapping membership with the Meyer and Morse (1982) working party.

At the start of *Modelling issues – many representations* we said data analysis methods and techniques were improved in the late 1970s. This included the ideas of entity–attribute–relationship diagrams and data structures, the distinction between conceptual models, logical models and physical models, normalization as in Chapter 11, and the ways to provide the software for data dictionaries and databases.

Before the definition of framework we said we stand back from the details of proprietary ISD methods. A few authors – Maddison *et al.* (1983, 89, 93), Olle *et al.* (1988) – have stood back from the detail and sought an overall framework and rationale.

Chapter 3

The material is an extension of and consistent with Maddison *et al.* (1984, 1989, 1993). The gaps and measurements of productivity were described by Beer (1979, 1981) and Kovacs (1974, 1982). The first definition of BSP on p. 95 is from Maddison *et al.* (1993), the alternative definition is based on Darnton (1992), p. 110.

BSP may need any of the following techniques, tools and methods: Five forces model, Generic strategies, Value chain analysis (Porter, 1980, 1985); Locating the core business, Logical incrementalism (Mintzberg & Quinn, 1991; Mintzberg, 1994); Information architecture (Darnton, 1992); Systems audit (Earl, 1989); Soft systems (Checkland, 1981).

Other references include: Anderla and Dunning (1987), Anthony (1965), Beer (1984), Cash *et al.* (1983, 1988, 1991), Espejo and Harndon (1989), Galliers (1992), Harrington (1991), Hartley and Pirbhai (1988), Johansson *et al.* (1993), Kertzner (1992), Kotler *et al.* (1988), Lovelock (1983), Maddison *et al.* (1984, 1989, 1993), Martin (1989), Ovum (1993), Remenyi (1991), Scott Morton (1991), Savage (1990), Synott and Gruber (1981), Vetter (1987), Vincent (1990), Ward *et al.* (1986) and Wilson (1992).

Chapter 4

Books on management include Arnold and Hope (1990), Boehm (1989), Cash *et al.* (1983, 1988, 1991), Cooper (1987), Drury (1992), Earl (1989), Handy (1985), Hill (1991), Horngren and Sundem (1987), Innes and Mitchell (1990), Kertzner (1992), Kotler *et al.* (1988), Maddison *et al.* (1989, 1993), Mayer (1986), Melan (1993), Morgan (1993), Savage (1990), Schroeder (1982), Synott and Gruber (1981), Voss *et al.* (1985) and Wilson (1992).

Chapter 5

The early ideas about processes in Section 5.1 are based on Davenport (1992), Hammer and Champy (1993), Harrington (1991), Johansson *et al.* (1993). Other references about process and re-engineering include Donovan (1993) and Melan (1993). Other references about human resources, organizational behaviour or processes and their management include Clegg *et al.* (1985), Handy (1985), Levitt (1972).

In our syntax of Idris's computer-processable text descriptions of a process the following words are optional and carry no meaning, they are called noise words:

```
a an and are as at be being by for from in is it
  of on the this to which with
```

A colon is noise where it introduces a list. Reserved terms such as 'process' and other names may have synonyms and abbreviations such as 'proc' and 'prc' which mean exactly the same thing. No process descriptive information is carried by the use of upper versus lower case, or layout or font.

The rules of Anna's generalizations are nearly the same.

The original version of PSL/PSA™ and System Encyclopaedia Manager™ were produced at the University of Michigan. They are software products to handle descriptions such as our Inventory-control-system assertions that conform to prestated rules (Teichroew and Hershey, 1977; Teichroew *et al.*, 1980).

Most data dictionary systems have a built-in hierarchy of metalevels. If an occurrence, e.g. Order number 26734, is metalevel 1, then the term `Order_entry` is metalevel 2. The term **process** is metalevel 3. The generalized terms Object, Property and Relationship are metalevel 4. All the descriptive assertions about the organization are at the same metalevel 2, using terms such as 'Order-entry'. These must conform to a set of rules at the higher metalevel 3 using terms such as 'process', as with Anna's generalizations. In some software packages these metalevel 3 rules are preset or built in, having been precoded in terms of an even higher metalevel 4 using terms such as object, property and relationship. This arrangement has the advantage of initial simplicity as in our metalevel 2 descriptions of the inventory control system. The disadvantages show later, e.g. the user cannot enter anything that does not conform to the preset rules. The user usually cannot easily alter the rules or create, except as unprocessable text, assertions that involve things at different metalevels such as: 'J Smith (metalevel 1) usually performs Order entry (metalevel 2)'. Similarly there are difficulties with rules involving several metalevels such as: Every metalevel 1 occurrence of a process, data, memo, input or output (a metalevel 2 list) should have a person responsible for it, and at different times it may be a different person.

A fuller collection of objects and rules was implemented as a package for students. Its features and rules were given in Maddison and Gawronski (1985). Unlike most data dictionary systems, this package, called DADICS, overcame the problem of having a hierarchy of metalevels by not having any built in. DADICS allows the user to store arbitrary assertions such as sentences. Its rules are sentences similar to Anna's and meaning that certain kinds of other sentences (at a next lower metalevel) may or should occur. The user may do commands: (a) to select all sentences involving a particular object; (b) to check for consistency, e.g. find every sentence for which there is no rule allowing that sentence, and; (c) to check for completeness, e.g. find rules and objects for which appropriate occurrence sentences are missing. DADICS used triples.

Systems using **triples** – such as subject, verb and multiple objects in each assertion – have advantages (of flexibility and avoiding metalevels) over EAR models, relational databases and network-based databases with fixed schemas.

Chapter 6

More detail about process description and analysis forms are presented in a pack obtainable from: Knowledge Management Consultants Limited, 34–36 The Square, Titchfield, Fareham, Hants, PO14 4AF. This pack contains a copy of several additional forms, and instructions for their use to build up detailed business process and information system descriptions. There is also a form that can be used to register a licence for the purchaser to make copies of the forms for use internally within the purchaser's organization.

Further information about the techniques of metamodelling described in this chapter can be found in: Teichroew (1977, 1980) and Maddison and Gawronski (1985). Other references about methods, information flow diagrams, systems analysis and data analysis include: Aktas (1987), Avison (1988), Chen (1976), Couger and Knapp (1974), DeMarco (1978), Daniels and Yeates (1982), Date (1986), Davis (1993), Gane and Sarson (1979), Parnas (1972), Veryard (1984), Vetter and Maddison (1981) and Yourdon (1989).

Chapter 7

Maddison *et al.* (1983) and Boehm (1989) gave spiral models. CommonKADS, from the ESPRIT project P5248 KADS-II, is a risk-driven model-based methodology for knowledge-based system development, and has a spiral of risk, plan, do, monitor and review. KADS stood for Knowledge analysis and design system (Gustafsson *et al.*, 1994).

Empirical research by Boehm (1976, 1981, 1989), indicated that the human and organizational issues are usually more important than technical ones in determining an information system's success or failure, its relevance or waste of resources, and its acceptability or inappropriateness to users and managers.

The traditional structured analysis development of the four current and new logical and physical models is explained in Yourdon (1989, Chapter 17). Information architecture references include Darnton and Giacoletto (1992), Toffler (1990), Zachman (1987) and Zuboff (1988). Software engineering and CASE references include Boehm (1981, 1989), Brooks (1986), Charette (1986), Conte, Dunsmore and Shen (1986), Fairley (1984), GEC (1986), Gehani and McGettrick (1986), Gibson (1989), Halstead (1977), Jones (1986), King and Pardoe (1985), Manley (1984), McDermid (1991), Pressman (1988), Rock-Evans (1989), Rock-Evans and Engelian (1989), Royce (1970), Shooman (1983),

Sommerville (1989), Teichroew (1989), Umar and Teichroew (1987) and Yourdon (1979). Other references include Ashworth and Goodland (1990), Avison and Fitzgerald (1988), Baber (1987), Bannon (1990, 1991), Beer (1984), Bentley *et al.*(1992), Bergland (1981), Budde and Zullighoven (1983), Candullo (1985), Case (1986), Checkland (1981, 1990), Cutaia (1990), DeMarco and Lister (1987), Eason (1988), Hice, Turner and Cashwell (1978), Mumford and Weir (1979), Royce (1970), Sackman (1983), Schmidt and Bannon (1992) and Schulmeyer and McManus (1987).

Chapter 8

No notes.

Chapter 9

Maddison *et al.* (1984, 1989, 1993) gave fuller descriptions of possible activities and products for the various phases. Typically each project only needs some subset of the various possible activities and products. Maddison *et al.* (1983, 1993) gave details of the ISD methods whose scopes are illustrated in Figure 9.6.

Some developers of real-time systems found methods for commercial systems inadequate for their needs, hence real-time extensions to structured ISD methods were created, as in Ward and Mellor (1985) and Mellor and Ward *et al.* (1986). Other methods or techniques are described in Avison (1988), Conte, Dunsmore and Shen (1986), Grudin (1990), Page-Jones (1988), Sloman and Kramer (1987), Stevens *et al.* (1974), Wasserman (1980), Yourdon (1989, 1990) and Yourdon and Constantine (1979).

Chapter 10

For further detail of costing see: Arnold & Hope (1990), Drury (1992), Horngren and Sundem (1987), Innes and Mitchell (1990) and Slemaker (1985). For customer orientation of products, and marketing see Dibb *et al.* (1991) and Lovelock (1983).

Chapter 11

The data analysis, aggregates and normalization techniques are partly based on Vetter and Maddison (1981). Other references include Coad and Yourdon (1990), Cohen, Harwood and Jackson (1986), Meyer (1988) and Rentsch (1982).

Chapter 12

The two main groups of authors of analyses of ISD methods are Olle *et al.* (1982, 1983) Olle, Sol and Verrijn-Stuart (1986), Olle, Verrijn-Stuart and Bhabuta (1988), Maddison (1985) and Maddison *et al.* (1983, 1984, 1989, 1993). Creators of frameworks include: Maddison *et al.* (1983, 1984, 1989,1993), Avison (1988) and Olle *et al.* (1988).

Figure 12.8 was first presented by Richard Maddison at the CRIS conference in November 1983.

For Ashby's law see Ashby (1956). References on ethnography or cybernetics include Business (1993), Hughes *et al.* (1991) and Rheingold (1993). For contingency, life cycle, and standards see IEEE Standard 1074.

Chapter 13

A more detailed discussion of the scope of information technology can be found in Darnton and Giacoletto (1992).

Appendix B
Solutions

Chapter 1

1.1 (a) False. Business processes are not the basis for structuring staff into departments. If you did not get this correct please reread the section on business processes. Departments traditionally correspond to terms such as accounting, marketing, production, research and development, warehouse, public relations and publicity.

(b) Partially correct. A business process may start when all the appropriate information reaches the appropriate person, but a person may start a process when only some information has been received and, as part of the process, try to obtain the further information needed for the completion of the process.

(c) True. Analysing *information* (relevant understandable data received) about past sales may create *data* that is not useful for planning future marketing (so is not useful information).

(d) Muddled and incomplete. An information system is an assembly of parts, but not necessarily involving computer and communication system parts. It has interfaces for information to flow across its boundary and it provides facilities to its users. Also it has some purpose, the parts work together, and the whole is of interest when viewed as a system.

(e) Wrong. A person and/or other people in that person's organization is/are responsible for the provision of satisfactory information handling facilities for that person's work.

(f) Misses the point. Information is not just a representation of some knowledge about the real world; it is communicated to a person who needs it for some reason and purpose.

(g) Wrong. An organization has a hierarchical structure as a first approximation to managing and delegating responsibilities for different parts of its activities. This structure may or may not be the way of ensuring that each item of information can be passed to the right person to deal with it.

(h) Maybe, but misses the point. The problem of allocating people to tasks optimally *might* be solvable mathematically, but it is not feasible to do so. The difficulties include collecting data about all the required tasks, collecting data about all the available people, solving the allocation problem with all its constraints, doing the whole quickly enough to be useful, and the human issues of whether such an approach would be acceptable to staff.

(i) Wrong. It muddles vertical and horizontal. Information flows horizontally between staff in different groups to ensure coordination between the groups. Horizontally means where neither group reports to the other.

(j) True. Each organization has a problem of providing information systems and services for its staff to use for their work.

(k) Incomplete. Receipt of a communication sometimes causes action. Junk mail, for example, is received but is not useful and does not trigger action other than to discard it.

(l) False and misleading. If an organization's business processes were fully documented so that every aspect of what should be done in all possible situations is covered, the staff would have no authority or responsibility nor be allowed any initiative. No one could think out all the possibilities needed to create such full documentation, and few people would want to work in such an organizational environment.

(m) True. Analysing data about past sales can create information that helps the planning of future production.

(n) False or muddled. Enterprise revenue is extensive, being the arithmetic sum of the revenues at lower levels. Board-level goals are intensive, not being the crude sum of those at lower levels. Entrepreneurial ability is intensive, as the ability of the staff in teams is more than the sum would be if each person were working alone.

1.2 Staff need information for the reasons in the solutions to exercise 1.4 (p. 10). Please check your answer with those.

1.3 Information systems facilities need to change sometimes because: needs change, procedures change, people become more experienced and so could use or would like improvements, technology improves, the relative costs and benefits of alternative technology changes, e.g. prices fall, new staff may request different equipment, expectations change, and external pressures may encourage change – e.g.

to keep up with competitors or conform to new standards or improve safety.

1.4 We cannot know your situation. But some of the kinds of information that you and your colleagues send and receive will concern business operations or your studies, other information will be about the planning and management of this, and yet other information will be about human issues. The kinds of information should have purposes related to the needs of the people for doing their jobs, to initiate actions such as the appropriate business processes or the correct study, and to keep records for future use. You cannot know or ensure that each incoming piece of information to your organization gets to the right person and is also understood and dealt with satisfactorily. But for information such as instructions to your George that you initiate, you need both two-way communication during the sending of the information to be sure he understands what is wanted and what to do, and feedback afterwards to you about his performance, preferably giving a measure of it.

1.5 In some computer applications the essence is processing to ensure completeness and consistency of a document produced, and the correct representation of reality. People would be dubious of a nearly identical document produced by a clerk with a word processor but without the ability to process associated information accurately. For example, an organization's accounts, bank and building society statements (which must represent the various transactions correctly), invoices (which must correspond to what has been supplied), airline tickets (which must correspond to actual available flights and bookings), weather forecasts (which should predict the weather as a result of recent observations and calculations), and manufacturing production plans (which should be based on recent orders, stock, work in progress, and so on).

The common features are: that each document produced must be reliably derived from processing a collection of data, much of which may have initially been in other forms and representations – e.g. quantities, measurements, time, units, messages, and physical objects; and that the transformations required involve more understanding than just copying and rearranging words.

1.6 Situations where IT-based facilities would be harder to provide and use include: ordinary conversation, meetings of groups of people, telephones, handwritten short notes from one person to another, face-to-face teaching and discussions involving questions and answers, human control of simple equipment such as a trowel, lawn mower, bicycle or car, and the reading (as opposed to the production) of newspapers, magazines and books.

Most such situations have in common: that the existing arrangements and skills evolved before computers; that they are suited to people's hands, eyes, brains and body;

that to provide a computer-based alternative would be costly and complicated to develop, and perhaps awkward to use; and that an IT-based alternative might not be as acceptable or enjoyable.

1.7 To save space we have not given a mind map. Summaries are given after the preface, in the chapters, and in the conclusions in Chapter 13.

1.8 A **systems approach** means: regarding the whole as a collection of adaptable systems and subsystems, where each subsystem or part is arranged to contribute to the whole, rather than optimizing its own performance in isolation. Sometimes, choosing what to regard as a system is debatable and people disagree over where each boundary should be. Similarly, agreement over what to include in what to optimize may sometimes be impossible.

Chapter 2

2.1 (a) Essentially true, but the IS may also hold data representing plans and alternatives that are different from reality.
(b) Essentially true.
(c) No. The amount of planning is not proportional to the length of the action. It is more nearly proportional to the complexity.
(d) No. If the opposite variation were made perhaps the result would be better.
(e) No. Meetings are needed to discuss things, to maintain social contact, to ensure confidence and participation, and to communicate face-to-face in ways that cannot be achieved even by telephone.
(f) No. A framework is an overall structure that is an abstraction from experiences and methods.
(g) Not quite. Hard problems cannot necessarily be programmed, as the method of solution might not be algorithmic. But soft problems, having uncertainties, usually cannot be usefully programmed.
(h) Wrong way round. Characters may be data. Data may include coded characters. Other symbols may also be data.
(i) Muddled and misses the point. Conceptual models are an abstraction of the real world or UOD situation as requirements, not constrained by rules or features of current software and hardware. Logical models should correspond to how functions, structures, behaviour and processes will appear to users, and may take into account the constraints of software and hardware.

2.2 Nowadays Anna would find the whole far more technically feasible and cost-effective. The development work and time would be far less. If Richard had not been doing it as research he would have stopped long before he did, so if costs nowadays were the same as they were in 1959, Anna would similarly stop. Anna might be able to find a suitable software package. A desktop computer in the accounts office should suffice instead of using a computer bureau.

2.3 See Figure B2.1. The point is to include in the figure a box for each idea that occurs in the scenario. So each real world state should appear – the current and the two alternatives for a year ahead. Each strategy should appear as a box. Each model and all the various changes must be correctly linked to reflect the logic. Physical layout on the paper is relatively unimportant except to help understanding and effective communication.

FIGURE B2.1
Solution to Question 2.3.

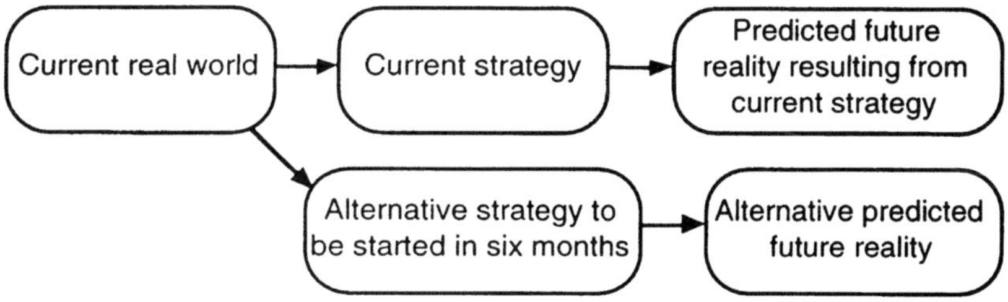

2.4 To a child playing, the real world is part of adults' wider real world, limited to the part that the child understands. The child makes mental hypotheses, e.g. invents rules of games and of how to interact with toys. These are combined into the UOD, which is what the child imagines. The child is aware of the objects around, and mentally augments these by whatever he/she imagines for the purposes of play. The rules can change from minute to minute, changing the UOD. The more general rules about such rules and changes can also change from minute to minute.

If two children pretend to phone each other with toy telephones, each hears what the other says, the sound being transmitted through the air as usual. But they hold the handsets and pretend to dial, and maybe have other agreed rules for the purposes of their actions. For example in their UOD they pretend not to hear each other unless both are holding their handsets to their heads after one has dialled the other. Their words will mirror adult phone calls, including, e.g. 'Hello', 'Goodbye', and smalltalk.

2.5 The aim of the organization's ISs is to help the organization to achieve its objectives and each IS may be regarded as a tool to be used for this purpose. With a systems approach the ISs are seen as parts of the whole organization, so their performance is not optimized in isolation. Each IS may also be viewed as a resource that, like people and other tools, can do various things; and it involves and incurs costs. Its purposes are to produce benefits such as improvements in products and services, including their timing and quality, beyond what might otherwise be achieved. The resource is justifiable if its benefits exceed its costs. Hence with appropriate ISs the organization should be more likely to achieve its objectives and targets more effectively.

2.6 People may have differing views of information systems. Different users will use its various facilities in differing combinations. They will have different mental images of the data it holds and of the way it works, and also of its facilities, costs and benefits. Some may view it as a way of storing data – e.g. as a database with associated facilities. Others may view it as a method of sending and receiving information as messages, which may only be checked against the database as an incidental effect. Others may see it as a way of planning, predicting and evaluating performance against plans. Others may use it as a way to acquire knowledge and information relevant to their work.

2.7 The data `020920` might be the date 2 September 1920, or 2 September 2020, or 20 September 1902 or 2002, or even data representing the letters of the word 'bit', or the time, 2 hours 9 minutes and 20 seconds. `15:53:47` certainly seems more likely to be a time on a 24 hour clock. `London` looks like the name of that UK city but it could be some other London such as the one in Ontario, Canada.

The underlying principle is that a particular string of data may represent different things in different contexts. But in a particular context it is desirable to avoid confusions that could arise from having more that one meaning for a string of data.

2.8 'The Eiffel Tower' has three different meanings: the tower itself – i.e. the metal and other parts; the logical name of the tower to identify it or refer to it in a message that is information, or in recorded knowledge such as a book; and a string of characters as data that may represent the tower or the logical name.

2.9 International and national telephone numbers have a structure and coding so that local numbers can be dialled with fewer digits than more distant places. The designers have made the assumption that most calls are local and most of the rest are within the caller's country.

International Standard Book Numbers (ISBNs) have digits that indicate the country of publication, the publisher, and a check digit.

2.10 An example of an infinite UOD, starting from a set of 10 objects, is constructed by allowing as further elements the association between any two, then also allowing associations between any two from those so far defined, and so on. The set is infinite in the same way as is the set of all numbers that can be formed by adding two numbers.

The computer system may be arranged to be unlikely to run out of storage space by only storing representations of the actual objects that George explicitly creates. Presumably Anna has estimated the maximum that George is likely to create in a finite time.

2.11 The purpose of this question is to check that you think about all the kinds of analysis. In a manufacturing business ... with fairly satisfactory business processes and information systems, all the kinds of analysis are likely to have been done satisfactorily in the past. Where competitive businesses are beginning to grow, the kinds of analysis likely to be needed to maintain sales income are those that concentrate managers and analysts minds on changing objectives and appropriate methods. This suggests business process analysis, perhaps re-engineering, analysis of responsibilities and rethinking business strategy as in Chapter 3.

2.12 We regard these as hard or soft as follows.

(a) A structured analysis and structured design method is hard. It requires the analyst to concentrate on the structure of some process to be analysed, and the designer to create a correspondingly structured single solution.

(b) A waterfall, having stages separated by milestones, is hard. The stages are prescribed; no alternatives are allowed.

(c) Using semi-automated computer aided tools is hard. The tool must be used. Its rules and procedures must be followed to produce the solution or product.

(d) Prototyping, creating a simple version and extending it based on the result obtained from the current version, is hard. The procedure is to deal with the current result. Each such result needs a single solution to the current situation, and the implementation of that solution; with appropriate repetition.

(e) Conceptual modelling is soft and rule-free thus permitting various solutions. It allows for several ways of drawing or specifying the conceptual model.

(f) A method of starting that aims to get people to understand a problem situation, with an intention later to initiate some action towards improvement, but with no attempt to decide the solution yet, is hard. There is one objective, to get people to realize that the problem exists. Whether there is one or a choice of many methods to solve it, and whether there is one or many solutions is not yet relevant.

2.13 Question 2.12 is hard. It demands a single solution to each part.

2.14 (a) To be **acceptable**, an IS should be imagined by each user and manager to be preferable to the main alternatives (such as past methods of working, or non-IT based methods of handling the relevant information). 'Preferable' here means any combination of: higher quality, easier, quicker, cheaper, providing better goods and services, better cash flow, reduced costs, increased revenue, various benefits, products and services available sooner, competitive advantage.

Acceptable also implies acceptable within the organization, to its staff and to people generally, and acceptable externally to other organizations. Something acceptable in one country is not necessarily acceptable in others, cultures and legislation differ.

(b) As (a) but for 'an IS' read 'a process'. Sometimes satisficing processes and behaviour is preferable to some maximum. **Satisficing** means acting so as to satisfy the minimum requirements, such as satisfacory processes, profit and growth rather than maximum productivity or profit.

2.15 See Figure B2.2. Further extensions of ER diagrams and notations are given later (pp. 161–8, 188–195 and Chapter 11).

FIGURE B2.2
Solution to Question 2.15.

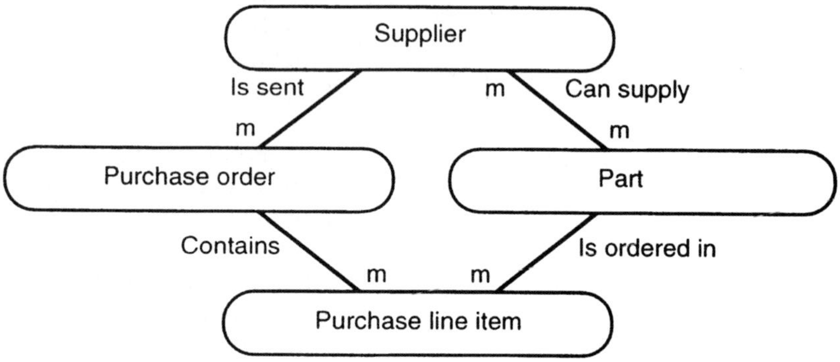

Chapter 3

Each * means half a mark. Generally there is one mark for the appropriate phrase correctly used in the appropriate context making a point within a sentence, then another mark for reason or example. The solutions may give several ways of obtaining full marks, or even more than full marks.

3.1 Internal means within the organization*, and also that staff and managers have significant influence* over internal factors, forces and decisions**. External means outside the organization*, and also where they have little* or no* such influence*.

3.2 The ISs have impact on:

- people and their work*, e.g. changing their skills* and methods of working*;
- jobs, how many staff employed*;
- management style*, centralizing or devolving decision making* and information availability*;
- flattening* the management structure, fewer levels*, more people reporting to a given person*;
- changing patterns of vertical* and horizontal* information flows, with more flowing through the IT equipment*;
- more management time than years ago is spent on how to provide the ISs*, and on discussing needs*;

- the services and products that are the organization's main business change far more often* and evolve more*, both as a result of IT affecting the products and services themselves*, and from IT affecting how the organization works and is arranged to provide the products and services*;
- the organization's strengths and weaknesses*.

3.3 The main forces driving continual IT developments are the following.

- IT suppliers want to stay in business* and make profits* and therefore they continually make new products to try to maintain their share of the market*, or increase their market size*, as the total IT market continues to grow*.
- People's changing general perception produces forces for further change*, partly to improve organizational productivity*, products and services*, and partly for the deeper intellectual satisfaction and status of staff*.

3.4 If you are a student you may find it interesting to visit some organizations. They may be reluctant to tell you their detailed business strategy and tactics, regarding these as highly valuable. But you may get some flavour of how they tick and how they evolve. Visitors are sometimes given a rosier picture than the reality.

If you are an employee, you may be aware or unaware of appropriate information to think about the issues in this question. That may itself illustrate the management style, e.g. whether and about what the staff are kept informed, are consulted or participate.

3.5 (a) A reductionist approach is hard*. It prescribes what to do*. It tackles the following in order: business strategy and objectives, business processes, functions, systems, subsystems, ...**

(b) Information exploitation is soft* and unbounded*. It is not clear what the problem is, how to solve it, what resources and timescale, or who will be involved.**

3.6 BSP focuses on core competencies for success, so that the organization can respond well to customers, clients, suppliers and other partners. BSP involves strategic planning for all parts of the organization – leading to information needs, ISSP, the information systems themselves and their use for the operations and management of the business, feedback and to more BSP.

BSP may be regarded as a central strategic service that performs the activities and produces the products described. These activities are continuous and iterative. The BSP products evolve. BSP and other strategic planning interact with ISSP because ISSP concerns those ISs needed to support the whole organization. Part of BSP should determine the roles and place of ISs in the organization, including their allocation of resources within the corporate budget.

BSP should be the first in a set of stages. It forms the

overall strategy as a prerequisite for other stages and levels of management, e.g. strategic, tactical and operational planning for each business unit; and ensures that management structures fit the strategy. As much behaviour as possible is directed to implementation of the strategy. For ISs, BSP is the first stage of a set of stages from forming business objectives and strategy to implementation and use of the ISs. This is a **reductionist** ideal BSP, but we recommend that the stages overlap and iterate, with feedback.

3.7 The minimum prerequisites to start BSP are: top management commitment*, middle management agreement to participate enthusiastically*, someone to be responsible – a champion*, the right team*, and available resources* (as in the text). Most enterprises do not have a formal business strategic plan and those that attempt one generally encounter great difficulty in assembling the right group of people. Hence the above list is ideal.

3.8 No solution.

Chapter 4

4.1 Something in E could move to any of C, J, I, D, A or G if the organization's culture and managerial style does not change*;* or could move to L for example if the culture changed to make it worthwhile but not within the skills and expectations of the staff*;* or to B, H, K or B if not culturally acceptable and not worthwhile**. Something in F is theoretically impossible so will remain impossible; it is culturally acceptable and may or may not remain so**.

4.2 The food manufacturer wanted to merge and integrate certain facilities of its division's ISs as there would be far more outlets, and all these outlets needed to have the same procedures for all foods. The existing IT systems were too incompatible, causing major problems. (3)

4.3. The oil holding company insisted that each company must provide its accounts for each country in a centrally specified structure and format by specified dates, to make the work of the holding company accounts and computer staff not just feasible but easy and technically straightforward. (3)

4.4 In the Venn diagrams, Figures 4.2 and 4.3, the solid sets are nested. Those named in plain font are well defined, independent of the state of any particular organization. Whether or not an idea falls within each of the italic-named sets depends on the state of the organization. The dashed sets are soft since what is inside each depends on human judgement, whereas the solid ones are mathematically related. (3)

4.5 D had separate ISs for physical distribution and sales analysis in each of its operating divisions*,* because that reflected their management style* and because the kinds of people employed there after many years expected that style and created the ISs they thought appropriate*. Each division made its own IS investment decisions* and was allowed to purchase separately*. (2)

HC had a single* centrally imposed* IS for physical distribution, and a single sales analysis IS* covering all its operations*. Top managers insisted on this standardization*. Other aspects of management style may have been relevant, but this was not asked in the question*. (2)

4.6 This is subjective and people may have different opinions. We think you should have put 3 to 5 in the cells marked Impact in Table B2.1. The partial impact cells indicate you should have put about 2 or 3. The others should be 2 or less or are irrelevant. Count how many correct entries, including the no-impact ones, and divide by four to give marks out of 7. The table has 31 cells, 3 or 4 minor errors still gets full marks!

	... its organizational objectives	... its management style	... its product / service	... the market for its products	... its selection of IT applications	... successful use of its ISs
The organizational objectives affect ...			Impact		Impact	
Its management style affects ...		-			Partial impact	Impact
Its external environment affects ...	Partial impact	Partial impact	Impact	Impact	Impact	Partial impact
The market for its products affects ...	Partial impact		Impact	-	Impact	
Its selection of IT application areas affects ...		Partial impact	Impact		-	Impact
Successful use of its IT-based ISs affects ...	Partial impact	Partial impact	Impact			-

TABLE B2.1
See Solution 4.6

4.7 At first sight the answer to this would be that an organization that delegated responsibility* would allow such spreadsheets for local planning*. But the spreadsheets will all be different* and so they cannot easily be combined* to give appropriate vertical flows upwards* of bids, e.g. with totalling and fast decision making relating to the budget and cashflow of the whole*. Similarly, vertical flows downwards* cannot easily be arranged to generate the variety of local spreadsheets when products, services, strategy, tactics and objectives change**. So local response to centrally needed changes will be slow*,* probably disadvantaging the organization. (4)

4.8 The effect of good IT-based ISs on lower to middle

managers may depend on their personality and experience*, and perhaps how near retirement they are*. But generally, with better information than they had previously*, they do not need to get performance feedback directly from their staff so often* and therefore meet them less often*. In addition, the flattening* effect means that they also have more staff reporting to them* and so have to reduce the time spent speaking to each*.

Top managers, being more remote from operations, and having to work with better informed middle managers*, may become more participative*. But if they reliably receive improved IT-based information on performance*, and anything else that they may need to act on*, they need to see the middle managers less often* and may bypass them*. They may then use the IT systems to get information from computer produced reports*, without the information going through the middle managers*. They may, however, enjoy human contact and need to find new ways of justifying it*, in which case meetings will continue*.

With better informed managers the organization may become more transparent, i.e. easier for more people to understand and to contribute to decisions, at least where the people have access to the relevant information and have appropriate influence.** The more an IS depends on a person the more power that person has* and, conversely, the more a person depends on an IS, the less influence that person will have*. So certain middle managers, whose activities are central to the business functions and success of the organization, will gain increased power from the IT-based ISs*. Those whose activities are peripheral will lose power*. (10)

4.9 The attenuation and amplification activities of middle managers have been substantially semi-automated by IT in the last ten years*. They can take a document received in an IT-based form and edit it* before passing it on*, or use it as the basis for what they pass on*. This has also enabled such managers to manage more staff on average*, flattening the management structures*, and so fewer middle manager jobs exist for a particular size of workforce*.

Chapter 5

5.1 Figure B2.3 shows our opinion of the stability of various business actions.

5.2 Figure B2.4 shows our opinion about the stability of various engineering aspects of information systems.

5.3 (i) See Figure B2.5 (p. 390).

(ii) Doing this exercise should have suggested to you that the text is far from complete. The text does not give *all* the details of the process, despite its initial apparent detail. This shows what a lot can be specified about each process, if it is worthwhile doing so.

Organization structure	Business functions	Business planning	Business processes	Business routine operations
Restructuring	Marketing	Production scheduling	Accounting	Answer enquiry: 'Was bill paid?'
Takeover	Production		Invoicing	Payroll
Bankrupcy	New products, new services		Stock control	

Less stable ——————————————— *More stable*

FIGURE B2.3
Varying stability of business actions.

Information technology	Computer platform			Elementary computing operations
Hardware	User interfaces	Software	Program structures	Data structures
	Features of packages		Functions of packages	

Less stable ——————————————— *More stable*

FIGURE B2.4
Varying stability of engineering aspects of information systems.

5.4 Anna uses the metamodel term **object** for any of the following classes:

action activity association attribute communication computer condition contribution data element entity event group information input interface knowledge memo message object operation output plan person process processor product project property relation relationship resource responsible_object role service set specialist structure system system_parameter task time unit undefined

This list is not definitive. Other things may be added, such as the concepts in Figure 1.4 and mathematical, scientific and social terms, e.g. integer, speed and management. Some of the terms in it are explained later, but for convenience we have collected all the terms together here.

Chapter 6

6.1 (i) See Table B2.2 (p. 390).
(ii) Far from an IFD/ DFD being worth 1000 words, it needs 1000 words of descriptions of the processes and data flows to support it. IFDs/DFDs may help in the initial analysis and understanding, but they hardly help the later stages of development unless a lot more detail is given.

6.2 (i) Table 6.3 names all the processes at each of three sublevels below the name Inventory_control_system.

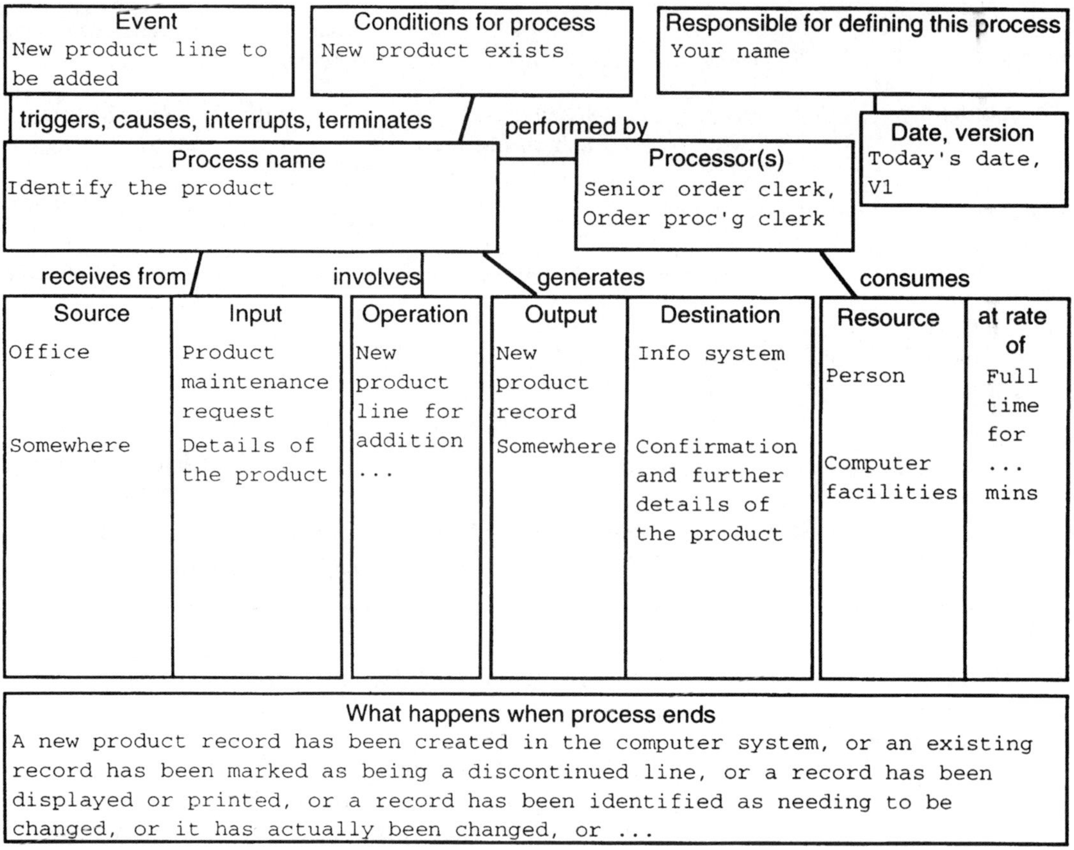

FIGURE B2.5
Process identification form for identifying the product.

Information from IFD/DFD	*Program component*
Some information, further information may be available by cross-checking with the data dictionary entries	Declaration
DFD just shows a named box, need information from process specification as description or structured English	Transformation
Overall control information is missing; some hints may be in the process descriptions; need to look at behaviour and system dynamics, and get frequency information from volume and volatility analysis results	Control structure
Names of other systems shown in IFD/DFD, but that is not enough; need details of formats of incoming and outgoing data to satisfactorily interface to existing systems, and desirable screen layouts for staff to use	Environmental message

TABLE B2.2
Solution to 6.1 (i)

(ii) An alternative would be a collection of diagrams like tree structures, which might be difficult to draw and use.

6.3 A data flow diagram has four metalevel objects: external entity, process, data store and data flow. These can be put as a matrix as Table B2.3 shows, with the intersections showing the relationships. Only one half of the matrix is needed as it is symmetrical except for active and passive names.

	External entity	Process	Data store	Data flow
External entity	Not regarded as relevant	Sends information to; receives information from	Not permitted	Sends/generates; receives
Process	Sends information to; receives information from	Sends data to; receives data from; consists of; part of	Updates; reads; maintains; uses	Sends; receives
Data store	Not permitted	Maintained by; used by; updated by; read by	Not permitted	Maintained by; used by
Data flow	Sent/generated by; received by	Sent/generated by; received by	Maintains; uses	Not permitted; (in some situations could be consists of)

TABLE B2.3
Solution to 6.3

Chapter 7

7.1 The approaches that include creating conceptual models of processes and/or data, and the prototyping and participative approaches aim to have representations that staff can understand and comment on.

7.2 **Hard problems** are easily definable. The rules are fully known. An appropriate solution is also relatively easy to recognize as correct. Examples include problems in school arithmetic, differentiating an algebraic expression, providing a payroll system and developing a stock control system.

Soft problems are difficult to define and an appropriate solution is not clear, for example what systems to build for the order-fulfilment activities in a large company, or how to change the existing systems, if at all.

Hard approaches and methods have structured steps, concentrating on how to develop a system, particularly the technical aspects. For example, the reductionist steps and normalization of data models.

Soft approaches emphasize human relations, organizational issues and deciding what is needed, but not on how to do the later work dealing with providing a system. Examples include the soft proprietary methodologies and the participative approach.

Bounded approaches and methods will have known resources and timescale, and will ignore human issues. Examples include: Timebox – where a review is scheduled for a fixed date that will not be postponed under any circumstances; each waterfall stage, especially where done by a different contractor; having a fixed number of staff in a section and no subcontracting allowed; and buying a product set.

Unbounded approaches aim to get people to work together, without specifying the amounts of their time needed or any other resources to solve the whole. The participative approach is usually unbounded. Some work in voluntary organizations and their fundraising is unbounded.

7.3 The following are examples of soft issues that the manager may have thought of.

- **Interpersonal** relations – how people get on together. Some people are concerned with the impact (CWI) of what they do and say.
- The **turbulent environment** – e.g. unexpected fast external change.
- Organizational politics, power struggles and **hidden agendas**.
- **Unknown** aspects of organizational **policy** – e.g. analysts, specialists, managers and users not being fully aware of internal policy or priorities.
- Unknown aspects of **criteria** – such as how to make optimum and acceptable choices between alternatives at every step.
- The **culture** of the organization – unstated but accepted ways of behaving.
- How various people in the organization are likely to respond to various kinds of proposals, and how to play on the politics to gain acceptance of a proposed solution.
- How the provision of, or improvement to, ISs may affect people's jobs – fears of unemployment and concern about career development, training and retraining.
- How the provision and growth of ISs may affect organizational structure – e.g. flattening it by making it possible for more staff to report to someone, and making it easier for a manager to obtain information on performance earlier and in more easily usable forms.
- How the provision and growth of ISs may affect people's activities in doing their jobs – e.g. they may obtain the same information as their boss but slightly earlier, thus having time to initiate actions to put unsatisfactory things right, and to know what to say to the boss. The availability of time-triggered selective information can thus improve organizational performance even without managerial action.

7.4 The soft versions would emphasize human aspects, be somewhat vague and use terms that are themselves soft or difficult to define precisely, such as 'meaning', 'useful', 'good', or 'stupid'. A hard version would be more technically oriented, quantified, definite, testable and have a definite structure. For example, the definition of information in *Information and information systems reviewed* in Chapter 2 (pp. 78–9) at first sight seems hard, but in fact involves many fuzzy and somewhat undefinable terms such as: useful, relevant, understandable, form, language that can be understood. These terms are soft.

In practice most people would give something between these extremes. But those more concerned with impact and aware of soft issues would match their style to their audience.

7.5 Prototyping is a mixture of hard and soft. It is hard in that some product and/or result is produced at each step. But the participation of George and Graham is softer. This combination makes prototyping very useful for establishing requirements fairly accurately, and it helps early identification of possible technical difficulties. But these softer aspects make it difficult to apply in contractual situations as estimating is difficult, and the end product and timescale are also difficult to predict. Thus with prototyping, project control techniques such as PERT are harder to apply than with a traditional waterfall approach with clear activities and milestones for project reviews at the completion of each stage.

Both approaches are therefore towards the hard end of the spectrum, with prototyping being less hard than the waterfall.

7.6 The examples of diagrams and text in earlier chapters assume one person, Idris, specified what was needed. In practice each person could create a different assertion. So every metalevel rule that Anna made in Chapter 5, such as A process may be triggered by an event or any of several events becomes generalized to a person may assert that a particular process is triggered by a particular event or any of several events. We decided for simplicity not to apply that generalization to every assertion of Anna's in Chapter 5. We made the assumption that Idris and all his colleagues agreed on what was required. In practice most software packages for holding models of requirements do not allow for multiple, and perhaps contradictory, assertions from different managers or user representatives, since resolving such contradictions is a human issue. Curiously PSL/PSA™ allowed such contradictory assertions about the properties and characteristics of attributes, but not about any other object, object type or rule.

7.7 The term **logical** has several connotations, as shown in Table B2.4 (p. 394).

7.8 The four models were and are not satisfactory. They assumed that computing students had not learnt business concepts, but that the growth of IT had created jobs for them. So analysing the current situation is performed as hidden training for them. The four models also assumed that the user representatives were initially incapable of working on a new logical model until they had received hidden training, and that they were suspicious of analysts

- The intention is to describe **the way that the implemented system is viewed by people** – analyst, designer, programmer, end user representative, end user. This is implementation dependent, not a rule-free conceptual model.
- The logical model is structured so as to **fit the constraints of current computers**, software packages, discs, printers, files, records, input and output devices, peripherals, operating systems; and the **constraints of non-computer technology**, communications, mail, transport. Processes were represented by boxes in diagrams and described by text that roughly matched what could be programmed. Fitting all these constraints was sometimes hidden, not openly stated.
- Logical model diagrams show how interrelated parts of the system work together. Many details may be omitted, such as common-sense checks, security, error correction processes. Logical models of data matched in a hidden way the available-software structures and access methods of files of records and/or logical database structures. Physical proximity or position is *not* shown.

TABLE B2.4 Connotations of logical models

apparently unfamiliar with the business. The models also assumed that transforming a current logical model into the required new one would not require much work, just the addition of a few user features. Management and users therefore expected little delay in producing the new IS but, in fact, it took many months and sometimes years.

7.9 The assumptions are that the data types are the most stable aspect of the business and that, as the years roll by, the business structures, processes and systems will change. So the data structures used in ISs must be such that the various kinds of independence allow many kinds of change without reprogramming. This means that Anna and Idris should look for rules about data and inherent structures that are likely to continue for many years. Normalization and pure normal forms may help but need not be used in early conceptual models where people's participation is paramount. Anna should be able to apply the principles later when it is appropriate to do so. That may help clarify data structures and rules. The data types should be checked for completeness and consistency with the entity life history rules and processes, e.g. as obtained from the methods of Chapter 5 or from structured analysis.

Chapter 8

Here we cannot know about your organization, so we indicate principles that you should have applied and give illustrative examples.

8.1 (i) Business functions are named classes of activities pertinent to the organization's purpose, e.g. sales, sales order processing, accounting; and/or a meaningful unit of business work as seen by clients of a system. Business functions may be analysed and decomposed. You should have described and justified perhaps four to ten of them.

(ii) Systems are used where feasible and cost-effective. Management needs information for business planning, directing, initiating work, control, assessing performance and to reward and give feedback to staff.

(iii) The system should have purposes that relate to the organization's objectives, strategy, tactics and functions. A system may serve several functions and integrate them, e.g. by providing coordinated horizontal information flows.

(iv) We hope you chose an appropriate approach and also thought out how much work and planning would be appropriate, particularly in a small organization.

(v) See Table B2.5.

Situation	*Client's role*	*Roles involving both*	*Specialist's role*
1 A new requirement exists	2 Recognize the requirement and describe it	3 Agree that a system will be produced or changed so that the client can use it for the new requirement	4 Do the work to produce a system that can be used as required
	6 Receive training	5 Install and handover the system, and show the client how to apply it	
7 Each case arises	8 Use the system for each case		

TABLE B2.5
Actions of client and IS provider, simplified

8.2 (i) Many of the activities in a large organization are concerned with providing products and services to other parts of itself, only ultimately contributing to supplying external products and services. In most organizations the products and services gradually improve long term.

(ii) The way a product or something is identified might have to change to allow for coding the country of origin or country of use, or to conform to new standards.

8.3 (i) Administration subsystem, divides into subsubsystems for personnel, hiring and contracting, ...; finance and accounts similarly into budgeting, purchasing, accounts receivable, ...; accounts receivable then interfaces with sales order processing, ...

(ii) The structure should be a table with three columns for named main type of data, origin (from) and destination (to). If such a table were completed every area should have something flowing in and something flowing out, otherwise it is not usefully integrated with the rest.

(iii) Figure 2.4 shows the style, except that you should have many boxes and named flows, like Figure 6.9 (p. 177).

(iv) and (v) The effect of introducing IT-based ISs is generally to cause far more information flow into and out of the computers, replacing many of the flows that in the past occurred between people, sections, departments, and so on. So some of the flows in your input–output diagram perhaps go through the computer.

(vi) Capture the data as near as possible to its real origin. Have validation checks wherever possible, e.g. in data entry processes, in order to ensure that values are within the allowed ranges and formats. Conduct stock checks occasionally, comparing actual quantities, values and so on with the computed and computer-held equivalents. Have processes and checks that ensure that all data reaches its destination, e.g. that all incoming relevant information is input into the computer and no items are lost or omitted, and that this occurs without delay. Ensure that all information flow is consistent and based on the most recently received data. Have recovery mechanisms and processes.

8.4 (i) Staff-no, National Insurance-no, Passport-no, Patient-no, Part-no, Order-no, Date-of-..., Telephone-no, have well-defined precise formats and ranges of allowed values. **Identifiers** are chosen to be unique, easy to use and known when an entity is created. Dates can be used to select. Part numbers may have embedded coded characters that indicate features and can be used to select all parts with some particular feature.

(ii) Addresses, names, postcodes and similar data items have varying formats such as varying length, number of lines of address, and so on. Some addressees have a house name, some have a flat number, some have a village and a nearby town or city. A student may have several addresses, e.g. at college, at lodgings during term, normal home address, temporary address during a job or holiday, and so on. Different students may have differing numbers of such addresses. People's names vary with more or fewer firstnames and/or initials, and the name they are known by may or may not be the first, or may even be a nickname that is not part of their proper name. In some countries the equivalent of surname is not the last. Different countries and cultures have different ways for people to change names on marriage, and so on. Postcode structures vary with country.

(iii) Text, graphics, pictures, lists, matrix structures, tables, reports and messages do not have a standard length and format.

(iv) Information and data flowing vertically typically includes: objectives, policy, planning, directives, control, feedback, performance, quality, exception reports, emergencies, non-routine, restructuring, proposals, bids, budgets, approvals and summaries.

Chapter 9

9.1 Here is a soft, people-oriented explanation of what an information system is. ISs are facilities* for people to communicate* both informally*, with social information, as well as formally* for planning*, organizing*, directing, controlling* and other business needs*. An IS may be a group of clerks* with files or may involve computers. Its behaviour is affected by its environment*.

9.2 Here is a hard, technically oriented explanation of what an information system is. An IS is a system composed of parts* that together can receive* information, hold representations as data* from the moment received until needed*, and carry out processes* on the data to generate new information*. Nowadays most ISs are IT-based – using computers, communication facilities* and complex software*. The behaviour would be affected if any part were to be changed*.

9.3 (i) Where an IS includes people the user will phone for help. With a completely computer-based system the user would usually use a help command.

(ii) In both cases, the IS help should ideally include both an explanation of the current situation that the user has reached, and an explanation of the various options available to the user to continue. Unfortunately many computer systems only give an explanation of the various commands, and do not relate these to the current state and what to do next, which is what a tutor alongside the user would do during user training.

(iii) Table B2.6 (p. 398) gives the roles and actions.

9.4 (a) The structured approach is hard – prescriptive structures created.

(b) The participative approach is soft – human participation is emphasized.

(c) The waterfall approach is hard – defined stages.

(d) Conceptual modelling is soft – rule-free.

(e) The planning approach is both – having human and technical aspects.

(f) The prototyping approach is fairly hard – building a definite product and improving it from comments.

(g) The systems approach is soft – different people see different purposes and subsystems.

(h) The socio-technical approach is both – having human and technical aspects.

(i) The automated tools approach, such as CASE, is hard – with well defined preprogrammed rules of modelling and building.

9.5 People differ in their ability to attend to detail. Some can invent ideas, but cannot carry them through all of the detail to acceptable and successful implementation. Others can concentrate and check details carefully. Some can handle a broad idea but not apply techniques to model and describe it. Others can study and apply the techniques. People vary in their ability to create correct abstractions. Those who attend to detail will put in the correct qualifiers. People also vary in their abilities at human relations, concern with impact, thinking of motivations, analytical reasoning, finding out new information, management styles,

Situation	*User's role*	*User's thinking*	*Roles involving both U and IS*	*Isobel's thinking*	*Isobel's or the software's role*
1 U gets stuck	2 U recognizes that he is stuck and needs help	3 U thinks of phoning or trying the help command	4 Isobel or software receives request/ command. Isobel will discuss and U will clarify on the phone to be sure that Isobel understands	5 Isobel envisages U's situation. Isobel may ask U for clarification of the current state of affairs, to be sure she understands correctly	6 Isobel may look up details in her copy of a manual, or do commands on her computer to be sure of the details; or may recall from her memory. Or the software looks up and/or generates the response text
7 Response knowledge to be communicated to U is known to Isobel, or is displayed	10 U listens to the explanation, and indicates understanding to Isobel as feedback, affecting what Isobel says. Or U reads the displayed reply	11 U envisages doing the actions Isobel recommends. Or U thinks whether the displayed description of the facility matches what he wants	9 Isobel explains the solution to U. Or the software transmits the text and U reads it	8 Isobel realizes that she has to communicate effectively to U what has happened and how to proceed, and preferably generalize to help U avoid similar situations in the future	
12 U tries the action suggested	13 If U is still stuck, he continues the phone call with Isobel	14 If U is stuck and only has the software help, U knows he will get the same display again if he does the same help command again!	15 Isobel may stay on the phone while U tries the action	16 Isobel hopes that U is happy. Isobel is concerned with impact	

TABLE B2.6
Actions and roles where help is needed

leadership, integrity, conscientiousness, reliability, assertiveness, perseverance, willingness to work long hours and behaviour in meetings.

9.6 (a) At first sight these may seem incompatible, but they are in fact compatible. The fact that the staff are in various buildings does not imply there must be a particular kind of distributed system. The physical distribution of facilities may be mostly hidden from the staff, to whom the logical facilities are what matters.

(b) The method assumption aims to provide systems that have certain interfaces standardized so that systems can be integrated. But the organizational delegation is incompatible with that.

(c) The management style is uncaring. Contrary to the organization's officially stated standard personnel policies, the developers believe that they do not have good career development prospects and that they cannot take holidays without losing the opportunity to attend the course. They might feel resentment, they might not be promoted and could take their backlog of due leave perhaps to look for another job.

Chapter 11

11.1 The normalized entity types are as follows. Underlining indicates the identifiers, on which all other attributes in that particular entity type are fully functionally dependent.

```
Trip(TripNo, VehType, TripDate)
VehicleType(VehType, VehVolume, VehWeight)
Shipment(ShipNo, TripNo, CuNo)
ShipmentPkg(ShipNo, PackNo)
Package(PackNo, CuNo, PkgVol, PkgWt,
  ProdNo, ProdQty, PackDate)
Customer(CuNo, CuName, CuAddr)
CuTel(CuNo, CuTelNo)
Product(ProdNo, ProdDesc, ProductGroup)
ProdMethod(ProdNo, MethodNo, LeadTime)
ProdMethodComponent(ProdNo RoleLarger,
  MethodNo, ItemNo, ProdNo, RoleSmaller,
  Quantity)
```

The logical data model for a relational database software package could be essentially the same, except that there would then be problems with void values where entity occurrences did not have all attributes known. For that aspect, Aggie's points in solution 11.3 below are an improvement.

Working with a collection of tables structured as above and in a spreadsheet would be very difficult for staff. But in theory all facts could be represented in a consistent way.

11.2 Figure B2.6 (p. 400) gives an EAR model. All relationships are one-to-many or none-or-one-to-many downwards, this being omitted for clarity. The attributes marked ? are optional. If they are included they help understanding. If they are omitted then the model shows each attribute in only one place, which may form the basis of a logical data model which has no redundancy as each value will then only occur at one place. That would serve as a first draft of a schema for a corresponding database.

The various entity life histories and the various views corresponding to (a) to (g) can all be catered for by choosing the appropriate subsets of the entity, attribute and relationship types in the diagram. These would correspond to subschemas of the database schema structure. Each subschema could be used by appropriate application programs.

11.3 Aggie would have extra relations corresponding to identifiers, allowing the creation of a representation of an

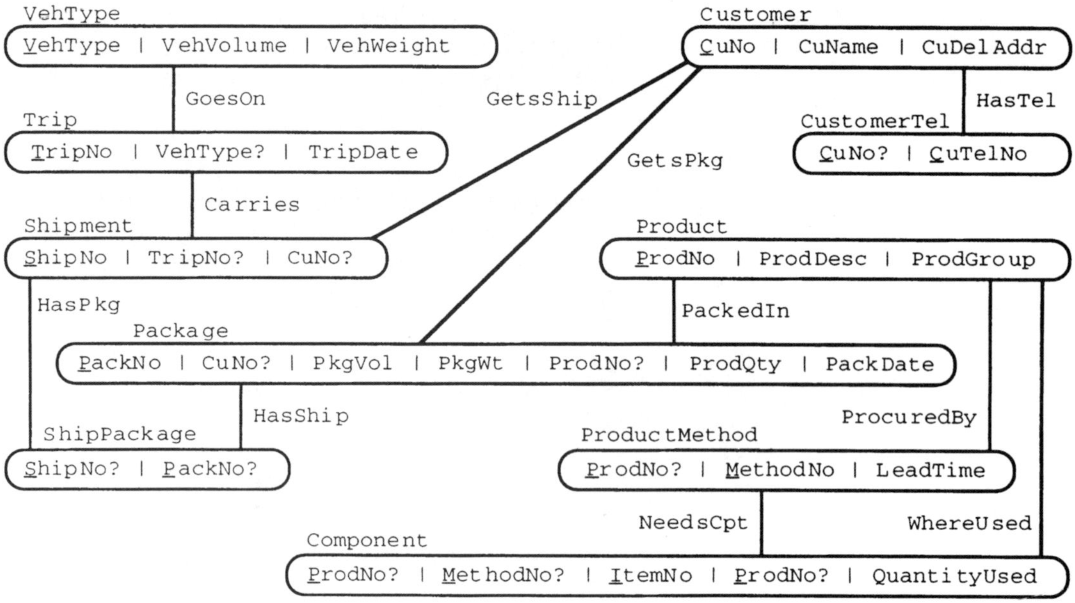

FIGURE B2.6
EAR model for shipping and manufacturing company.

entity occurrence when only its identifier is known, and no other facts are yet known, e.g.:

```
TripId(TripNo)
VehicleTypeId(VehType)
ShipmentId(ShipNo)
PackageId(PackNo)
CustomerId(CuNo)
ProductId(ProdNo)
ProdMethodId(ProdNo, MethodNo)
ProdMethodComponentId(ProdNo RoleLarger,
  MethodNo, ItemNo, ProdNo RoleSmaller)
```

These would allow for the creation, discussion and use of entity occurrences before all their details were settled. For example, a shipment can be discussed and its ShipNo referred to before its TripNo and/or CuNo are decided. Similarly the next free CuNo can be allocated, e.g. during a phone call before the name and delivery address are recorded. A next method can be created for a product before its leadtime is known. All these avoid imagining some artificial representation of an unknown. Aggie does not create anything extra for ShipmentPkg or CuTel, as these are all key. David should provide the equivalents in the logical model.

11.4 Obadiah will notice the two dates, PackDate and TripDate. These have the same features, representations and processes that can be used on them. Staff should be able to search for entities associated with any range of dates in the same way whether it is a PackDate or a TripDate.

There are various identifiers. For each, a new value can be created at any time to correspond to another entity occurrence. The staff processes and the computer processes to create all such entities should be the same. Staff should never have to deal with temporary blank values. The ways that entities cease to exist should be uniform. Programmers should not have to include code that tests for representations of void in their programs for each process on each entity type. Constructor and destructor routines should cater for all that in a uniform way.

Obadiah will also notice the similarity between HasShip and HasPkg. These relationships will have similar conditions and processes.

Obadiah will notice Delivery address, and perhaps ask about other addresses, e.g. invoice address, staff home address, and so on that may be modelled later or elsewhere. The ways that these are represented and handled should be unified. For example if envelopes of all sizes can be produced for selected addresses of one type then that facility should be the same for all types of address. More subtly, the way that CuDelAddr is related to CuNo in the model should be the same as the way StaffHomeAddr is related to StaffNo, and the way InvoiceAddr is related to InvoiceNo. Modelling each by relationships, and with associated dates during which the addresses are valid, may be preferable to having the addresses as attributes as in Eric's and Nora's models above.

Similarly with all telephone numbers, Obadiah may ask if each CuTelNo is associated with a different person in the customer's organization, and perhaps that should be modelled like ABC's staff names and telephone numbers.

11.5 The scenario and models are perhaps not as general as would be desired for a typical organization. We give some examples.

(a) In most organizations more than one product might be packed in a package, whereas ABC does not pack more than one product in a package.

(b) The way that packages and shipments relate to orders needs further analysis. Maybe different orders or different items within an order need to be delivered to different addresses where a customer has several buildings. Orders or items within an order may have promised delivery dates and even times. How are delivery instructions handled?

(c) The way that product occurrences are identified needs further analysis. Perhaps each item made has a serial number and that indicates which item occurrence is packed in which package for which customer. Products may have further attributes: perhaps a status such as obsolete or still current design; a stock unit or unit of measure such as kilograms, metres, each, inner; and associated cost information. Each serial item made will have version number, date and so on.

(d) The relationship between customer and shipment looks unsatisfactory and may need further analysis. It seems that in ABC a Ship-package can be associated with a customer in two ways, through Package and GetsPkg, or through Shipment and GetsShip. This cannot ensure consistency. Perhaps the reason in ABC for GetsShip is to allow the sales and manufacturing people to tell the transport people that a shipment is coming for an urgent delivery to an important customer on a particular date, so they must schedule a trip to that customer on that date. But the product is not yet made and the package details are not yet known, so the Package and GetsPkg occurrence cannot be created.

(e) The CuName may give difficulties. For large organizations it will be the name of the organization. But ABC's staff may want to hold the name of the particular person within the customer's organization who is responsible for the order. That person's name will have an associated telephone number. So CustomerTel needs further analysis.

11.6 Obadiah would notice that wagons and locomotives are not treated the same by their various staff. Locos have a value for miles since last maintenance, but wagons have one for miles till next maintenance. Locos can have a major or minor maintenance service, but wagons cannot. What about carriages and passenger trains? What about the round-trip trains, are its loco and wagons all serviced together? Or can such a train occasionally be separated and a few different wagons put in? What about other railway vehicles, e.g. cranes, track maintenance and inspection vehicles? Wagons are scrapped in a workshop, but what about other vehicles? How do new vehicles come into existence? How are new loco and wagon numbers allocated? Is the creation process the same for all the kinds of vehicles?

Obadiah generalizes wagons, carriages and locos into vehicles, and says that all such should be treated the same both in the modelling and in the processes that the staff perform.

11.7 In our Table B2.7 we have made particular assumptions about how the object oriented issues were resolved, e.g. each vehicle has a miles till next maintenance, and the workshops know whether, at a particular mileage, a vehicle will want a major or minor service without that being modelled here. For consistency with the scenario, we have allowed LocoNo and WagonId, whereas a more consistent object oriented view might have treated all as say Id, but that might not have fitted with common use. An important point is to put only fully functionally dependent attributes in the column for such.

The table is not correctly normalized. For some column entries there may be several entries in some column to its right. The table is a convenient way to show derived dependencies.

View	*Entity*	*Identifier*	*Functionally dependent attributes*	*Multivalued entity or attribute*
a	Loco	LocoNo	LocoClassNo	
			MilesTillMtce	
	LocoClass	LocoClassNo	MilesBetMtce	Loco
			Power	
b	Wagon	WagonId	WStatus	
			LcnId	
			OriginLcn	
			DestLcn	
c	Wagon	WagonId	WagonClId	
			MilesTillMtce	
	WagonClass	WagonClId	MilesBetMtce	Wagon
	LocoClass	LocoClassNo	MilesBetMtce	Loco
d	Location	LcnId	LcnName	Wagon
			LcnAbbrName	
			LcnRespFor	
	WagonLcn	WagonId	LcnId	
			OriginLcn	
			DestLcn	
e	RouteMiles	FromLcn, ToLcn	RouteMiles	
	Wagon	WagonId	MilesTillMtce	
f	Train	TrainId	DepTime	
			ArrTime	
	TrainRun	TrainId, Date	MinsLate	Loco, Wagon
		LocoNo, Date, Time	TrainId	
		WagonId, Date, Time		

TABLE B2.7
Table for Solution 11.7

11.8 Figure B2.7 (p. 404) shows an EAR model for the trains.

11.9 The proposed structure is unsatisfactory in several ways. It has an implied direction from the one location to the other, which perhaps should not appear in the structure. It does not group the loco classes. Also the fact that a driver has been passed for a particular loco class cannot be stored until he is passed for some route for which it is appropriate. It needs structures corresponding to each separate rule, e.g. {DriverLocoGroup(StaffNo, LocoGroupId), LocoGroup(LocoClassNo, LocoGroupId), DriverRoute(StaffNo, RouteId)}; and RouteId has to be held in another structure.

11.10 The **purposes of normalization** are to: eliminate redundancy; avoid potential inconsistency, such as anomalies in representations of facts about reality; make it easier to change models later, provide flexibility; and simplify data structures.

A more complete set of **reasons** includes the following. It eliminates certain anomalies, including: deletion side effects, insertion side effects, update side effects, read side effects and archive side effects. It allows developers to

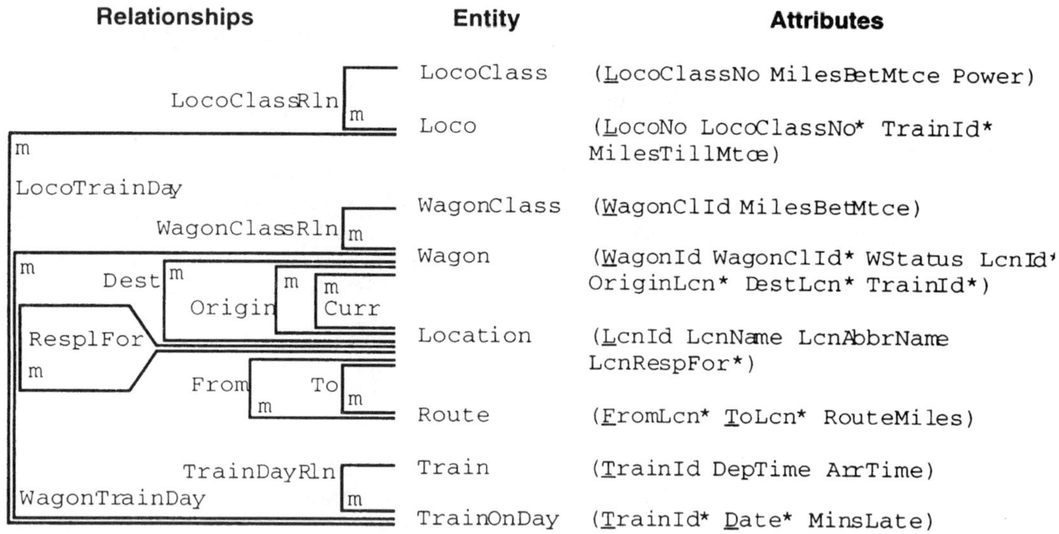

FIGURE B2.7
EAR diagram for trains, solution to Question 11.8.
To-many is marked m.

standardize the data models independently of the applications and the business under investigation, and to make different things comparable. It helps to make the data models understandable for non-technical users, because users are in general familiar with table representation and manipulation. It gets a good mathematically sound logical data model and even if the implemented logical model is slightly different for some reasons, it gets a good starting point for physical data modelling independent of the selected database system. Implementation of a fully normalized model often causes performance problems. The fully normalized model may be denormalized later, with the reasons clearly stated.

The **principles** are functional dependencies, forms of normalization and non-loss decomposition. Normalization should minimize future changes to the complete conceptual model and the complete logical model. A fully normalized model can be an intermediate stage in the progression towards a physical implementation of the data model and this should be a target responsibility of the analyst.

Chapter 12

12.1 (i) Some areas for possible standards are shown in Figure B2.8.

(ii) Generally the tools and proprietary ISD methods do not ensure that the design, development, production, installation and testing conform to quality systems BS 5750 or ISO 9000 (1987) and related standards. These standards are mainly concerned with procedures, and do not ensure the adequacy of the final product such as an IS.

Strategy Planning Analysis Design Documentation Completeness Consistency

Testing Coding Training Installation Release Data Operations Support

Organizational performance | System performance | Project management | Retirement and migration | Risk management

FIGURE B2.8
Areas for possible standards.

(iii) Generally, whether the software produced, e.g. source code, conforms to the standards for the appropriate programming languages is only determined by testing the systems, although the compilers and software packages contribute by having many software checks. Ultimately it relies on the conscientiousness and attitudes of those involved. Some people are better than others at programming complicated subjects.

Appendix C
Bibliography

These are our sources, not necessarily suggested further reading.

Aktas, A.Z. (1987) *Structured Analysis and Design of Information Systems*, Prentice-Hall, Englewood Cliffs, NJ.

Anderla, G. & Dunning, A. (1987) *Computer Strategies 1990–9*, John Wiley, Chichester, UK.

Anthony, R.N. (1965) *Planning and Control Systems: A Framework for Analysis*, Harvard University Press, Cambridge, MA.

Arnold, J. & Hope, T. (1990) *Accounting for Management Decisions*, Prentice-Hall, Englewood Cliffs, NJ.

Ashby, W. Ross (1956) *An Introduction to Cybernetics*, Chapman & Hall, London. Reissued Methuen (1964).

Ashworth, C. & Goodland, M. (1990) *SSADM: A Practical Approach*, McGraw-Hill, New York.

Avison, D.E. & Fitzgerald, G. (1988) *Information Systems Development: Methodologies, Techniques and Tools*, Blackwell Scientific, Oxford.

Baber, R.L. (1987) *The Spine of Software: Designing Provably Correct Software Theory and Practice*, John Wiley, Chichester, UK.

Bannon, L. (1991) From human factors to human actors: the role of psychology and human–computer interaction studies in system design. In *Design at Work: Cooperative Design of Computer Systems*, ed. J. Greenbaum *et al.*, Lawrence Erlbaum, Hillsdale, NJ.

Beer, S. (1979) *The Heart of Enterprise*, John Wiley, Chichester, UK.

Beer, S. (1981) *The Brain of the Firm*, John Wiley, Chichester, UK.

Beer, Stafford (1984) The Viable Systems Model: its provenance, development, methodology and pathology. *Journal of Operations Research*, **35** (Included in Espejo & Harnden, 1989).

Beer, S. (1985) *Diagnosing the System for Organizations*, John Wiley, Chichester, UK.

Bentley, R. *et al.* (1992) *Ethnographically-informed Systems Design for Air Traffic Control*, Proceedings of CSCW 1992, Toronto.

Bergland, G. (1981) A tour of program design methodologies. *IEEE Computer*, **14** (10) (October).

Boehm, B.W. (1976) *Software Engineering*. IEEE Transactions on Software Engineering. Vol. C-25 No. 12 (December) pp. 1226–41.

Boehm, B.W. (1981) *Software Engineering Economics*, Prentice-Hall, Englewood Cliffs, NJ.
Boehm, B.W. (1989) *Software Risk Management*, IEEE Computer Society Press, Los Alamitos, CA.
Bowers, J.M. & Benford, S.D. (1991) *Studies in Computer Supported Cooperative Work*, North Holland, Amsterdam.
Brooks, F.P. (1986) *No Silver Bullet: Essence and Accidents of Software Engineering*. In H.J. Kugler (ed.), *Information Processing 1986*, North Holland, Amsterdam.
Budde, R. & Zullighoven, H. (1983) *Socio-Technical Problems of System Design Methods*. In U. Briefs, C. Ciborra & L. Schneider (eds), *Systems Design For, With, and By the Users*. Proceedings of the IFIP WG 9.1 Working Conference 1982. North Holland, Amsterdam.
Business Intelligence (1993) *The Groupware Report 1993*. Business Intelligence, London.
Candullo, C. (1985) *System Development Standards*, McGraw-Hill, New York.
Canning, R.G. (1956) *Electronic Data Processing for Business and Industry*, John Wiley, Chichester, UK.
Carroll, L. (C.L. Dodgson) (1896) *Symbolic Logic*, **I**, II. iii, 14.
Case, A.F. (1986) *Information Systems Development*, Prentice-Hall, Englewood Cliffs, NJ.
Cash, J.I. et al. (1983, 1988, 1991) *Corporate Information Systems Management: Text and Cases*, Richard D. Irwin, published by Dow Jones–Irwin, Homewood, IL.
Charette, R.N. (1986) *Software Engineering Environment: Concepts and Technology*, McGraw-Hill, New York.
Checkland, P. (1981) *Systems Thinking, Systems Practice*, John Wiley, Chichester, UK.
Checkland, P (1990) *Soft Systems Methodology in Action*, John Wiley, Chichester, UK.
Chen, P. Pin-Shan (1976) The Entity-Relationship Model – towards a unified view of data. *ACM Transactions on Database Systems*, **1** (1), 9–36.
Clegg, C. *et al.* (1985) *Case Studies in Organizational Behaviour*, Paul Chapman, London.
Coad, P. & Yourdon, E.N. (1990) *Object-Oriented Analysis*. Yourdon Press, Englewood Cliffs, NJ.
Cohen, B. Harwood, W.T. & Jackson, M.I. (1986) *The Specification of Complex Systems*, Addison-Wesley, Reading, MA.
Connor, D. (1985) *Information System Specification and Design Road Map*, Prentice-Hall, Englewood Cliffs, NJ.
Conte, S.D., Dunsmore, E. & Shen, V.Y. (1986) *Software Engineering Metrics and Models*. Benjamin Cummings, Mealo Park, CA.
Cooper, R. (1987) The two-stage procedure in cost accounting. *Journal of Cost Management for the Manufacturing Industry*.
Couger, J.D. & Knapp, R.W. (1974) *System Analysis Techniques*, John Wiley, Chichester, UK.
Cover, T.M. & Thomas, J.A. (1991) *Elements of Information Theory*, John Wiley, Chichester, UK.

Cutaia, A. (1990) *Technology Projection Modelling of Future Computer Systems*, Prentice-Hall, Englewood Cliffs, NJ.
Daniels, A. & Yeates, D. (1986) *Basic Systems Analysis*, Pitman, London.
Darnton, Geoffrey & Giacoletto, Sergio (1992) *Information in the Enterprise: It's More Than Technology*. Digital Press, Burlington, MA (1992); Butterworth-Heinemann, Cambridge, MA (1994).
Date, C.J. (1986) *An Introduction to Database Systems*, Addison-Wesley, Reading, MA.
Davenport, Thomas H. (1992) *Process Innovation: Reengineering Work Through Information Technology*. Harvard Business School, Cambridge, MA.
Davis, A.M. (1993) *Software Requirements: Objects, Functions, and States*, Prentice-Hall, Englewood Cliffs, NJ.
DeMarco, T (1979) *Structured Analysis and System Specification*, Yourdon Press, Englewood Cliffs, NJ.
DeMarco, T & Lister, T. (1987) *Peopleware: Productive Projects and Teams*. Dorset House, New York.
Dibb, S. *et al.* (1991) *Marketing*, Houghton Mifflin, Boston, MA.
Donovan, J.J. (1993) *Business Re-engineering with Technology: An Implementation Guide*. Cambridge Technology Group, Cambridge, MA.
Drury, C. (1992) *Management and Cost Accounting*, Chapman & Hall, London.
Earl, Michael J. (1989) *Marketing Strategies for Information Technology*, Prentice-Hall, Englewood Cliffs, NJ.
Eason, K. (1988) *Information Technology and Organizational Change*, Taylor & Francis, London.
Espejo, R & Harnden, R. (eds) (1989) *The Viable Systems Model: Interpretation and Application of Stafford Beer's VSM*, John Wiley, Chichester, UK.
Fairley, R. (1984) *Software Engineering Concepts*, McGraw-Hill, New York.
Flood, R.L. & Carson, E.R. (1988) *Dealing with Complexity*, Plenum Press, New York.
Galliers, R.D. (1992) *Information Systems Research: Issues, Methods and Practical Guidelines*, Blackwell Scientific, Oxford.
Gane, C. & Sarson, T. (1979) *Structured Systems Analysis: Tools and Techniques*, Prentice-Hall, Englewood Cliffs, NJ.
Gehani, N. & McGettrick, A.D. (eds) (1986) *Software Specification Techniques*, Addison-Wesley, Reading, MA.
General Electric Company (1986) *Software Engineering Handbook*, McGraw-Hill, New York.
Gibson, M.L. (1989) The CASE philosophy. *BYTE*, **14** (4), p. 209.
van Griethuysen, J.J. (ed.) (1982) *Concepts and Terminology for the Conceptual Schema and the Information Base*. ISO TC97/SC5/WG3, American National Standards Institute, New York.
Grindley, K. (1991) *Managing IT at Board Level*, Pitman, London.
Grudin, J. (1990) The computer reaches out: the historical continuity of interface design. *Conference on Human Factors in Computing Systems: Evolution and Practice in User Interface Engineering.* ACM, New York.

Gustafsson, Maria *et al.* (1994) *An Overview of CommonKADS*. ESPRIT KADS-II P5248. (March), 18pp.

Halstead, M.H. (1977) *Elements of Software Science*, Elsevier North Holland, New York.

Hammer, Michael & Champy, James (1993) *Reengineering The Corporation: Manifesto For Business Revolution*, Nicholas Brealey Publishing, London.

Handy, C.B. (1985) *Understanding Organizations*, Penguin Books, Harmondsworth.

Harrington, H.J. (1991) *Business Process Improvement: The Breakthrough Strategy For Quality, Productivity And Competitiveness*, McGraw-Hill, New York.

Hartley, D.J. & Pirbhai, I.A. (1988) *Strategies for Real-time System Specification*, Dorset House, New York.

Hice, G.F. Turner, W.S. & Cashwell, L.F. (1978) *System Development Methodology*, North Holland, Amsterdam.

Hill, T. (1991) *Production/Operations Management: Text and Cases*, Prentice-Hall, Englewood Cliffs, NJ.

Horngren, C.T. & Sundem, G.L. (1987) *Introduction to Management Accounting*, Prentice-Hall, Englewood Cliffs, NJ.

Hughes, J.A. *et al.* (1991) CSCW: discipline or paradigm? A sociological perspective. *Proceedings of ECSCW'91*. Kluwer, Dordrecht.

IEEE Standard 1074-1001 (1991) *Standard for Software Life Cycle Processes*. IEEE, New York.

Innes, J. & Mitchell, F. (1990) *Activity-Based Costing*. The Chartered Institute of Management Accountants, London.

Jackson, M. (1983) *System Development*, Prentice-Hall, Englewood Cliffs, NJ.

Johansson, Henry J. *et al.* (1993) *Business Process Reengineering: Breakpoint Strategies For Market Dominance*, John Wiley, Chichester, UK.

Jones, C.B. (1986) *Systematic Software Development Using VDM*, Prentice-Hall, Englewood Cliffs, NJ.

Kertzner, H. (1992) *Project Management: A Systems Approach to Planning, Scheduling, and Controlling*, Van Nostrand Reinhold, New York.

King, M.J. & Pardoe, J.P. (1985) *Program Design Using JSP – A Practical Introduction*, Macmillan, London.

Klir, J. & Valach, M. (1967) *Cybernetic Modelling*, Iliffe Books, London.

Kotler, P. et al. (1988) Marketing Management: Analysis, Planning, Implementation, and Control, Prentice-Hall, Englewood Cliffs, NJ.

Kovacs, A.I. (1974) Information systems for project management. Paper presented at INTERNET Congress, Paris.

Kovacs, A.I. (1982) Information systems for management structure design – A challenge for OR. Paper presented at OR Society Conference, Bristol.

Levitt, T. (1972) Production-line approach to service. *Harvard Business Review* (September–October).

Lovelock, C.H. (1983) Classifying services to gain strategic marketing insights. *Journal of Marketing*, **47**.

Lovelock, C.H. *et al.* (1981) Some Organizational Problems Facing Marketing in the Service Sector. In Lovelock, C.H. (ed.) (1981) *Managing Services*, Prentice-Hall, Englewood Cliffs, NJ.

Maddison, R.N. (1959) Commercial Applications of Computers. Thesis, Oxford.

Maddison, R.N. *et al.* (1983) *Information System Methodologies*. Wiley Heyden, Chichester, UK.

Maddison, R.N. *et al.* (1984) *Information Systems Development: A Flexible Framework*. The Open University, Milton Keynes. [Now superseded by 1993 edn].

Maddison, R.N. (1985a) Information system methodologies. *The Corporate Database State of the Art Report 13 3*. Pergamon Infotech, Oxford, pp. 51–74.

Maddison, R.N. & Gawronski, A.J. (1985b) A data dictionary for learning data analysis. *Computer Journal*, **28** (3), 270–281.

Maddison, R.N. *et al.* (1989/93) *Information Systems Development for Managers*, 1st edn 1989, 2nd edn 1993. The Open University, Milton Keynes. [Maddison *et al.* (1993) is not generally available through booksellers. To obtain a copy phone UK 01234 21 22 93, or from outside UK +44 1234 21 22 93, and send a cheque for £12 to Dr Richard N. Maddison, 4 Balmoral Avenue, Bedford MK40 2PT.]

Manley, J.H. (1984) Computer-Aided Software Engineering (CASE): foundation for software factories. *IEEE Compcon Fall Conference of the Small Computer Evolution Proceedings, September 1984*. IEEE Computer Society Press, Los Alamitos, CA.

Martin, J. (1989) *Strategic Information Planning*, Prentice-Hall, Englewood Cliffs, NJ.

Mayer, R (1986) *Production and Operations Management*, McGraw-Hill, New York.

McDermid, J.A. (1991) *Software Engineering Reference Book*, Butterworth-Heinmann, Oxford.

Melan, Eugene H. (1993) *Process Management: Methods for Improving Products and Services*. McGraw-Hill and ASQC Quality Press, New York.

Mellor, S.J. & Ward, P.T. (1986) *Structured Development for Real-Time Systems*, vols 1–3. Yourdon Press, Englewood Cliffs, NJ.

Meyer, K.H. & Morse, C.C. (eds) (1982) *Data Dictionary Software Working Party Journal of Development*. British Computer Society, London.

Meyer, B (1988) *Object-Oriented Software Construction*, Prentice-Hall, Englewood Cliffs, NJ.

Mintzberg, H. & Quinn, J.B. (1991) *The Strategy Process: Concepts, Contents, Cases*, Prentice-Hall, Englewood Cliffs, NJ.

Mintzberg, H. (1994) *The Rise and Fall of Strategic Planning*, The Free Press, New York.

Morgan, G. (1986) *Images of Organization*, Sage, Beverly Hills, CA.

Morgan, G. (1993) *Imaginization: The Art of Creative Management*, Sage, Beverly Hills, CA.

Mumford, E & Weir, M. (1979) *Computer System in Work Design: The Ethics Method*, Associated Business Press, Manchester, UK.

Olle, T.W., Sol, H.G. & Verrijn-Stuart, A.A. (eds) (1982) *Information*

Systems Design Methodologies: A Comparative Review, North Holland, Amsterdam.
Olle, T.W., Sol, H.G. & Tully, C.J. (eds) (1983) *Information Systems Design Methodologies: A Feature Analysis*, North Holland, Amsterdam.
Olle, T.W., Sol, H.G. & Verrijn-Stuart, A.A. (eds) (1986) *Information Systems Design Methodologies: Improving the Practice*, North Holland, Amsterdam.
Olle, T.W., Hagelstein, J., MacDonald, I.G., *et al.* (1988) *Information System Methodologies: A Framework for Understanding*. Report prepared by CRIS Task Group of IFIP Working Group 8.1: Design and evaluation of information systems, Addison-Wesley, Reading, MA.
Olle, T.W., Bhabuta, L. & Verrijn-Stuart, A.A. (eds) (1988) *Computerised Assistance During the Information Systems Life Cycle*, North Holland, Amsterdam.
Ovum Ltd. (1993). *Groupware: Market Strategies*, Ovum, London.
Page-Jones, M. (1988) *The Practical Guide to Structured Systems Design*, Prentice-Hall, Englewood Cliffs, NJ.
Parnas, D.L. (1972) On the Criteria to be Used in Decomposing Systems into Modules. *CACM*, **15** (2) (December) 1053–1058.
Parnas, D.L. (1977) *The Use of Precise Specifications in the Development of Software*. Proceedings of the IFIP Congress 1977. North Holland, Amsterdam.
Porter, M.E. (1980) *Competitive Strategy: Techniques for Analysing Industries and Competitors*, Free Press, New York.
Porter, M.E. (1985) *Competitive Advantage*, Free Press, New York.
Pressman, R. (1988) *Software Engineering. A Practitioner's Approach*, McGraw-Hill, New York.
Remenyi, D.R.S. (1991) *Introducing Strategic Information Systems Planning*, NCC, Manchester, UK and Blackwell, Oxford, UK.
Rentsch, T. (1982) *Object Oriented Programming*. ACM Sigplan Notices, **17** (9) (September) p. 51.
Rheingold, H. (1993) *The Virtual Community*, Addison-Wesley, Reading, MA.
Rock-Evans, R. (1989) *CASE Analyst Workbenches*, Ovum, London.
Rock-Evans, R. & Engelien, B. (1989) *Analysis Techniques for CASE: a Detailed Evaluation*, vols. 1 & 2. Ovum, London.
Royce, W.W (1970) Managing the development of large software systems. *Proceedings of IEEE WESCON West Coast Conference*. (1970). Reprinted in R.H. Thayer (ed.) *IEEE Tutorial on Software Engineeering Project Management*. IEEE Press, Los Alamitos, CA.
Sackman, H. (1983) Problems and promise of participative information systems design. In U. Briefs, C. Ciborra & L. Schneider (eds), *Systems Design For, With, and By the Users*. Proceedings of the IFIP WG 9.1 Working Conference 1982, North Holland, Amsterdam.
Savage, C.M. (1990) *Fifth Generation Management*. Digital Press, Burlington, MA.
Schroeder, R.G. (1982) *Operations Management, Decision Making in the Operations Function*, McGraw-Hill, New York.
Schulmeyer, G.G. & McManus, J.I. (eds) (1987) *Handbook of*

Software Quality Assurance, Van Nostrand Reinhold, New York.
Scott Morton, M.S. (1991) *The Corporation of the 1990s: Information Technology and Organizational Transformation*, Oxford University Press, New York.
Shooman, M.L. (1983) *Software Engineering*, McGraw-Hill, New York.
Slemaker, C.M. (1985) *The Principles and Practice of Cost/Schedule Control Systems*, Petrocelli Books, Princeton, NJ.
Sommerville, I. (1989) *Software Engineering*, Addison-Wesley, Reading, MA.
Stevens, W. *et al.* (1974) Structured design. *IBM Systems Journal*, **13** (2).
Synott, W.R. & Gruber, W.H. (1981) *Information Resource Management*, John Wiley, Chichester, UK.
Teichroew, D. & Hershey, E.A. (1977) PSL/PSA: A computer-aided technique for structured documentation and analysis of information processing systems. *IEEE Transactions Software Engineering* (January) 41–48.
Teichroew, D., Macasovic, P., Hershey, E.A. & Yamamoto, Y. (eds) (1980) Application of the entity-relationship approach to information processing systems modelling. In P.P.S. Chen (ed.), *Entity-Relationship Approach to System Analysis and Design*, North Holland, Amsterdam.
Teichroew, D. (1989) Systems Engineering and CASE in the 1990s. In *Taking CASE into the 1990s. Geneva Conference Proceedings*, Digital Equipment Corporation, Geneva.
Toffler, A. (1990) *Powershift: Knowledge, Wealth and Violence at the Edge of the 21st Century*, Bantam Books, London.
Umar, A. & Teichroew, D. (1987) A support environment for distributed application systems. *CASE Studies 1987 Conference Proceedings*, Ann Arbor, MI.
Venn, J. (1881) *Symbolic Logic*, vi, p. 128.
Veryard, R. (1984) *Pragmatic Data Analysis*, Blackwell Scientific, Oxford.
Vetter, M. & Maddison, R. N. (1981) *Database Design Methodology*, Prentice-Hall, Englewood Cliffs, NJ.
Vetter, M. (1987) *Strategy for Data Modelling*, John Wiley, Chichester, UK.
Vincent, David R. (1990) *The Information Based Corporation*, Dow Jones–Irwin, Homewood, IL.
Voss, C. *et al.* (1985) *Operations Management in Service Industries and the Public Sector*, John Wiley, Chichester, UK.
Ward, P.T. & Mellor, S.J. (1985) *Structured Development for Real-Time Systems*, Prentice-Hall, Englewood Cliffs, NJ.
Ward, J. *et al.* (1986) *Strategic Planning for Information Systems*, John Wiley, Chichester, UK.
Wasserman, A.I. (1980) *Principles of Systematic Data Design and Implementation – Software Design Techniques*, pp. 287–293, IEEE Computer Society Press, Los Alamitos, CA.
Wilson, D.C. (1992) *A Strategy of Change: Concepts and Controversies in the Management of Change*, Routledge, London.
Yourdon, E.N. (ed.) (1979) *Classics in Software Engineering*. Yourdon Press, Englewood Cliffs, NJ.

Yourdon, E.N. & Constantine, L. (1979) *Structured Design: Fundamentals of a Discipline of Computer Program and Systems Design*, Prentice-Hall, Englewood Cliffs, NJ.
Yourdon, E.N. (ed.) (1982) *Writings of the Revolution: Selected Readings on Software Engineering*, Yourdon Press, Englewood Cliffs, NJ.
Yourdon, E. (1989) *Modern Structured Analysis*, Prentice-Hall, Englewood Cliffs, NJ.
Yourdon, E. (1990) *The Yourdon Structured Method (YSM) – An Introduction*, Yourdon Press, Englewood Cliffs, NJ.
Zachman, J.A. (1987) A framework for information systems architecture. *IBM Systems Journal*, **26** (3).
Zuboff, S. (1988) *In The Age of The Smart Machine*, Heinemann Professional Publishing, Oxford, UK.

Appendix D
Glossary

To IS specialists or others a term here may have a special meaning – with connotations slightly different from the natural English language meaning. Thus for some terms we distinguish:

(ENL)	English natural language meaning – e.g. as in an English dictionary
(IS)	Information systems specialists' meaning
(GST)	meaning within general systems theory
(CS)	meaning as in computer science
(Math)	Mathematical meaning
(T)	Technical or technology meaning.

Different meanings are either numbered to distinguish the end of one meaning from the start of another, or start with one of (ENL), (IS), (GST),... or are separated by |. The notation |... means other meanings (usually in ENL) are omitted.

Many terms can have 'type' or 'class' added: e.g. 'entity', 'entity type', 'entity class'. The terms 'entity type' and 'entity class' mean a collection or set of entity occurrences that are similar. In written text and speech the word 'type' or 'class' is often dropped, e.g. where no confusion should arise and the context should imply whether an entity occurrence or an entity type is being discussed. Generally an 'entity type' means a *named* class of 'entity' occurrences.

An asterisk indicates that it is unnecessary to restrict to IS usage.

Access control*: (IS) mechanism ensuring who and what is allowed what access to what – e.g. by doors with keys or software checks.

Access path: (IS1) method of finding information or data, e.g. from its association with some quotable key. (IS2) method of finding further data, e.g. from its association with data already found.

Access right*: conceptual model of privacy, e.g. who has the right to access what data in what access mode.

Action: (ENL) term used to cover anything that can be done; any of development, phase, activity, task, operation.

Activity*: (T, IS1) action, taking time and resources, as in PERT or CPA (Programme Evaluation and Review Technique, Critical Path

Analysis), e.g. 'build east wall', 'test system'. (IS2) group of actions or tasks, usually associated with a particular business function in an organization, e.g. 'process sales order 1234'.

Actor: one who acts, does actions.

Aggregate: (ENL) to collect into a whole | to assemble | formed of parts that combine into a whole. (IS) named collection of e.g. attributes, data items; e.g. 'Date' is an aggregate of Year, Month, Day.

Aggregate entity type: (IS) named entity type in 3NF, 4NF or 5NF with full identifier shown. All the non-identifying attributes are fully functionally dependent on the identifier; the aggregate may be created by collecting together such attributes according to what each attribute is fully functionally dependent on.

Aggregate model: (IS) model that is like an EAR model but with each entity type shown as an aggregate entity type; the attributes being grouped together according to what they are functionally dependent on.

Algorithm: a set of steps to do something and where it is known that the whole must finish in a finite time.

Analysis phase*: the phase or stage of development during which analysis is done.

Analyst: a person who contributes to business analysis and/or information analysis; | role of doing analysis; | person skilled in doing such; | job title of person doing planning, analysis, design in system development generally.

Application program: (IS, CS) program for servicing a particular type of transaction, e.g. to update stored addresses at each change of address.

Application type*: class of similar transactions and operations, e.g. apparently serviced by one program, using different data for each occurrence.

Attribute*: property, quality or quantity assigned to or associated with an object or entity. An attribute may be optional, e.g. some people have a telephone number, some do not.

Attribute type: (IS) named recognized class of similar attribute occurrences, e.g. 'Year-of-birth'. Equivalently a type of quality or quantity for which each occurrence of a particular entity type has or may have a value, e.g. each Person has a Year-of-birth.

Attribute-value pair: a named attribute type and an occurrence of its value e.g. 'Date of order' is '7 Jan. 1987'.

Behavioural objective: the reason for the behaviour and intended outcome.

Bounded: see Table 2.4.

Breakpoint: a significant achievement in performance.

Business event: typically something that happens outside or inside an organization and that may or should influence what the organization does. A business event may be a regular occurrence, e.g. receipt of a customer's order, or an irregular occurrence, e.g. a change in VAT rates. A business event will trigger one or more activities and/or business functions.

Business function: class of activities proper to the organization's purpose | ... a meaningful unit of business work, as perceived by an end-user of a system. Business functions may be analysed into lower-level units, also termed business functions, to any useful number of levels.

Business function data model: represents a subset of the data described by the System Data Model. It describes information required to support a particular business function.

Business procedure: the (predefined) actions and/or decisions to be taken under various circumstances that might occur in a business, reflecting detailed work design, typically in circumstances where staff have limited discretion to take decisions.

Business process: A collection of interdependent actions that together produce outcomes that contribute to the business success of an organization. Used in a wider sense than 'business procedure'.

Business process improvement: the process of deciding about, planning, building, and providing an improvement to a business process, usually in incremental steps.

Business process innovation: business process improvement, but by radical or fundamental change rather than incremental.

Business process re-engineering: business process improvement by changes of methods, techniques and tools, rather as in engineering.

Business system: a system for a proper part of the business of an organization.

Candidate identifier/key: (IS1) possible identifying attribute type (or composite group of attributes) such that for each entity occurrence the attribute(s) have unique (distinct) values, e.g. National Insurance numbers or National Health Service numbers could identify employees, chassis numbers or Registration numbers could identify vehicles. (IS2) as IS1 but not selection as the preferred identifying attributes.

Cardinality: (ENL, IS1) how many occur. (IS2) cardinality of a relation means how many tuples.

Class: (ENL) a rank or order of things or persons, e.g. 'high class' | a scientific classification | to form methodically into a class or classes | ... (Math1) collection of things (= the elements or members) with at least one common property. (Math2) Equivalence class: a group of elements/members such as 'all Mondays' which satisfy a mathematical equivalence relation; all Tuesdays is another equivalence class occurrence; the class of all dates subdivides into seven such classes.

Closed system: system that has a boundary.

CODASYL: (IS) Conference On Data And System Languages, various years.

Compound, **composite**: collection of two or more of something, e.g. two named attribute types, usually without having a name for the collection; e.g. 'Order-no, Part-no'.

Composite function: two functions performed one after the other.

Conceptual: (ENL) appertaining to a 'mental image', an idea formed in the mind. (IS) same but especially appertaining to an analyst's, developer's or user's image of the 'real world' and concentrating on the meaning. Please distinguish: (1) a 'real world' object or process, e.g. I threw a 6 with a particular dice at 7.20 p.m. on a particular date; (2) the mental image that you have of that (you did not see the dice); (3) a representation as symbols, e.g. '19:20: RNM threw 6'.

Conceptual model, **CM***: a model describing the allowable (= UOD) objects, information, processes, flows and the interrelationships of these; e.g. what is used where, when, how and why. (The information and processes need not be computerized.)

Conceptual process model, **CPM***: the structure of the types of processes and flows, whether computerized or not.

Conceptual schema, **CS**: (IS1) an agreed central full description of all relevant information types, i.e. the necessary propositions covering the whole of the relevant part of an organization, the allowable universe of discourse, and resolving users' views before design of an implemented IS. Equivalently, a formal description of all rules and structure that apply to a UOD; a set of semantic rules – i.e. stating the meaning. (IS2) the conceptual schema of a database means its fundamental structure, determining what data is allowed to be stored and what operations are allowed.

Concurrent working means more than one operation or constituent parts of different actions are performed during the same time interval. This term is only applicable to the working of a connected system such as an IS or computer system or connected system of computers.

Contingency: (ENL) depending on something else | continually choosing appropriately between many methods and techniques, depending on the context and situation.

Corporate data model: (IS) is initially formulated during strategic planning or at the start of a major design project involving multiple system phases that have not been preceded by a strategic planning phase. It must be simple and clear, in business terms, as it acts as the route map for determining the scope and inter-relationship of the more detailed data models based upon it.

Cybernetics: the theory of control mechanisms, particularly the special case of systems that show self-regulation; study of communication and control mechanisms in machines, in living creatures, and in organizations.

Data administration: (IS) organization-wide coordination of information systems and standards.

Data analysis: (IS) analysis and documentation of the structure of information types, e.g. as local and global CDMs leading to logical data models. The act of ensuring that a data resource is accurately, completely and consistently documented. It may be documented in a data dictionary.

Data assurance: (IS) responsibility for ensuring that stored data is accurate, up to date, secure, protected, consistent.

Database: (IS1) a collection of data items structured to be used for many applications, with controlled redundancy. (IS2) as IS1 controlled through a DBMS. (IS3) a collection of many such databases forming an information system. (IS4) such a collection representing information for a specific universe of discourse. Users need to distinguish what represents the actual real world from other allowable possibilities.

Database administrator, **DBA**: (IS) administrator of database, DBMS and service to users, maybe including data assurance.

Database management system, **DBMS**: (IS) software package for controlling databases, providing application program interfaces, performance monitoring, security, recovery, evolutionary use.

Data description: (IS1) processable representation of the names, structure and use of data types. (IS2) full descriptions, e.g. with text and diagrams for easy understanding.

Data description language, **DDL**: (IS) processable language for data descriptions.

Data dictionary, **DD**: (IS) repository for all meta information, e.g. about CMs, CSs, logical models, SSs, processes, programs; with sources, authors, dates, reasons.

Data dictionary system, **DDS**: (IS) a computerized DD service, with facilities for queries, updates.

Data flow diagram, **DFD**: (IS) diagram showing data flows between activities, equipment, and functional areas; may show storage, i.e. show information bases. A diagram showing sources and destinations of data, logical processes, data stores, and flows between these.

Data independence: (IS) facilities in a DBMS to change independently, where consistent: any subschema, schema, storage schema, without attention to anything whose purpose is unaltered.

Data manipulation language, **DML**: (IS) language for programming updates, retrievals and other database operations.

Data model: (IS) a formalized description of the structure of the types of elements within a data resource.

Degree of relation: (IS) how many named attribute types; i.e. how many domains and roles; i.e. how many columns.

Degree of relationship: (IS) rule of allowable cardinalities of association between occurrences of the two entity types; e.g. one to many.

Design phase*: the work of fully specifying what is to be implemented, e.g. as the target system. Compare Analysis phase.

Domain: (ENL) what territory one has dominion over | the scope or range of a subject or sphere of knowledge | ... (Math, IS) the collection of values to which a mathematical mapping can be applied. A mathematical function is a mapping from one set of values (= the domain) to another set (= the codomain). An object (in the domain) maps to one or more image(s) (in the codomain). The collection of all actual images is called the **range**. E.g.: Sue dances Mon & Thurs, Jo dances Fri, domain = {Sue, Jo}, codomain = {Mon, Tues,... Sun}, Range = {Mon, Thurs, Fri}, Image of Jo = Fri. (Database) the named set of values that can occur in a column in relation (= table), e.g. Days-of-the-week | the named set of values that a data item can take.

Dynamic model: model that allows the structure and rules of the model to change.

End-user, **EU**: (IS) anyone in the role of user of a computer or an IS; issues messages, including commands, to the information system and receives messages from it; but not developer or provider.

Entity: (ENL) a thing that really exists (as opposed to its qualities and associations) | ... (IS1) any concrete or abstract thing of interest, including an association among things. This means any thing in the universe of discourse, i.e. including things that might have existed or happened but did not. (IS2) the denotation of a meaningful item of data, e.g. the house at the address given in the data item, or the person identified by a string of characters.

Entity attribute relationship model, EAR: (IS) model representation for CDMs with named entity, relationship and attribute types.

Entity identifier: (IS) the attribute or composite collection of attributes selected and preferred to identify and distinguish the occurrences of an entity type.

Entity life cycle, ELC: (IS) creation, changes to, and end of existence of each entity occurrence; checking that all these are possible for all entity types.

Entity model: (IS) brief synonym for ER or EAR model.

Entity occurrence: (IS) same as entity IS1 and 2, occurrence of an entity type.

Entity relationship attribute model, ERA: (IS) same as EAR.

Entity relationship model, ER: (IS) model like EAR but initially concentrating on entity types and relationship types, assuming attribute types may be added later.

Entity type: (IS1) named class of similar entities, especially in EAR, ER models, so each occurrence has the same attributes and does or may have the same relationships; usually derived or produced by analysis. (IS2) as IS1, but maybe artificial or normalized, so as to have some particular useful properties.

Event analysis*: the identification of business and system events and the types of activities and functions which are triggered by an occurrence of each type of event.

Existence condition*: rule about entity occurrences.

External-value metric: a measure of some external factor relevant to the organization, such as the value of a product or service as perceived by a customer, client, supplier or other external organization.

Factor substitutability: how the same outputs can be produced using different combinations of factor inputs.

Flattening: fewer lower managers and fewer levels of management are needed.

Full functional dependency: (IS) an attribute is fully functionally dependent on others if all the others are needed.

Functional analysis*: analysis oriented to business functions.

Functional area*: that part of the organization responsible for a single business function.

Functional decomposition*: functional analysis done in steps of increasing detail.

Functional dependency: (Math, IS) an attribute B is functionally dependent on others if quoting values for them implies which value of B corresponds.

Functional dependency analysis*: analysis concentrating on the interdependence of business functions – nothing to do with functional dependency.

Functional primitive: process that is well understood so needs no further decomposition.

Functionality*: what processes the system is capable of doing.

Fundamental organizational problem: to produce good working business processes and information systems that support people in their work.

Global CDM: (IS) a global CDM may be derived by merging or extending local CDMs for areas.

Hard: see Table 2.1.

Horizontal information flow: information flows between people/areas not reporting to each other, e.g. to coordinate work.

Identifier: (ENL) a way by which something can be recognized and referred to. (IS1) entity identifier. (IS2) composite attributes that another attribute is functionally dependent upon.

Independence*: facilities so something can be changed without affecting something else, e.g. data independence.

Information base: (IS) a collection of assertions/sentences that are consistent with each other and with the conceptual schema, and that express the propositions other than the necessary propositions that hold for a universe of discourse.

Information exploitation: information is seen as assets, and business processes are constructed to make a business around exploiting the use of those assets.

Information flow: (IS) message or information from one area or process to another. It may flow indirectly through many systems on the way.

Information flow diagram, IFD: (IS) diagram showing (named) information flows between areas, systems, people, activities; shows the logic not the physical flows.

Information–process relationship: (IS, CS) association between information type and process type, e.g. what used where.

Information system, IS: (IS) a system (a collection of people and/or equipment) that handles knowledge and information appropriately, catering for flows, storage and processing of all relevant information; may or may not use computers.

Information system development, ISD: the development and provision of an IS; widened to include analysis of strategy and requirements, maintenance, and removal.

Information system development method: a method for ISD with recommended steps, deliverables, techniques, tools, management, and preferably also an underlying rationale; sometimes called 'ISD methodology'.

Information systems planning, ISP: all of ISSP, ISTPs, and ISPPs. Ongoing.

Information systems strategic planning, ISSP: Strategic planning for all ISs. Ongoing.

Information system tactical planning, ISTP: Tactical planning for one IS.

Information system project planning, ISPP: Planning for one project within one ISTP.

Information technology, IT: means the study and use of the artefacts of the technologies associated with handling information; using computing, communications, electronics and related technologies.

Integrity*: wholeness, uprightness, honesty | consistency during and before and after processing, so all information flows between each user and the system are consistent.

Isomorphic systems: (GST) Two or more types of systems that can be described by the same models of behaviour.

Life cycle: a set of phases and activities to be performed in a specified sequence, e.g. to develop a new business process.

Life cycle model: a candidate life cycle abstraction that might be recommended for many system development projects, giving a structure of phases, and activities.

Logical: (IS) fitting the rules of available analysis techniques; not conceptual; not physical; showing the logic.

Logical database description: (IS) schema, or diagrammatic and descriptive equivalent.

Management oriented documentation: (ENL) working paper(s) relating to project reports, present status, policy and organization, costs and benefits, contractual agreements and interviews.

Management reporting structure: organizational structure showing who reports to whom.

Meta: (CS) appertaining to the description or structure of something; e.g. rule about the structure of the something. Used in terms such as metalanguage, metalevel, metamodel.

Methodology: the science of method in scientific procedure; a body of methods used in a particular subject.

Metric: a quantitative measure of something, e.g. the value of a product or service.

MIS-centric: view of information systems planning seeing the problem mainly as one of identifying what information systems are needed.

Mission statement: a business oriented assertion statement of long-term intentions.

Model: (ENL) an object representing something else, usually a simpler equivalent preserving the main features. (IS) mapping of the real world, usually simpler but preserving important relevant features.

Network: (Math) nodes and arcs | structure of such (IS) similar structure e.g. entity and relationship types; communication paths; generally more complex than a hierarchy.

Network model: (IS) model as network; e.g. EAR, schema for a DBMS based on a CODASYL standard – having records that are associated through relationships that have a network structure; not a hierarchy or tree structure.

Normalization: (IS) technique for deriving entity types in 3NF, 4NF, 5NF; three main methods: 1 from unnormalized through 1NF, 2NF, 3NF …; 2 programmed procedure; 3 via aggregates.

Object class: (IS) class of such; named type, but not necessarily entity type in CDM.

Object oriented, **OO**: concentrating on objects, so features of properties and associated processes common to a class of similar objects are preferably only coded once; so the user sees the same features and processes for each similar object occurrence.

Object–Property–Relationship (OPR): model similar to EAR model, but the meaning being an abstraction as a metamodel of EAR models.

Open system: (GST) system that either has no well-defined boundary, or interacts with its environment in ways that cannot be ignored.

Organizational information systems problem: how best to provide and use information systems and services to support the people and activities within the organization.

Organizational unit: (ENL) a part of an organization; e.g. company, division, department, section, group.

Parallel working means the performance of a set of operations at the same time or during the same time interval.

Parameter: a data item value made available to a process.

Performance indicator: (ENL) a variable whose value shows whether or to what extent a goal or objective has been achieved, e.g. percentage of products available on promised dates.

Performance measurement: a variable that is quantified and measurable for a time period, or which gives a measure of comparison. Its value shows to what extent a performance objective has been achieved, or gives a useful comparison.

Physical model: buildable, as it actually is or will be.

Population: (ENL, Math) how many members of a class or set.

Primitive: (ENL) first cut version; crude first attempt at; skeleton version | atomic concept; e.g. entity, entity property, property value, relationship from which other concepts are built.

Process analysis*: analysis oriented to input, output, processing rules, models of such.

Process type*: named class of similar processes.

Property: (IS) named characteristic of an entity or object.

Property-value pair: A named property and its value.

Pure data model: fully normalized model.

Query language, QL: (IS) easy method of coding queries, enquiries, retrievals.

Relationship occurrence*: an association between entities or objects.

Relationship type*: a class of such; named in one or both directions; having degree and existence conditions.

Retention: (IS) rule about allowable changes to currently occurring relationship occurrences.

Retention class: (IS) class or rule for all occurrences of a particular relationship type.

Reverse engineering: translating one level of abstraction (of a model) to a higher level of abstraction.

Rule-free: no particular rules are imposed, such as rules of software packages or unnecessary diagramming techniques, to help nonspecialists to explain.

Schema: (IS) logical data model, processable by DBMS.

Set: (Math) a collection of elements or members.

Soft: see Table 2.1.

STEEP: Social, technical, economic, environmental, political.

Storage schema, SS: (IS) physical storage structure description, processable by DBMS.

Stovepiped: each of these applications and processes will be biased to its business function and so they will not be well integrated. (Lots of stovepipes, not one chimney.)

Subentity type: (IS) subclass of an entity type, e.g. 'clerical staff' within 'staff'.

Subschema: (IS) view of part of a schema relevant for an application; occurrences derivable by DBMS.

System data model*: a subset of the types of data described by the system group data model; it describes information which is of interest to a system development project team. It is first formulated in summary draft, as a subset of the corporate system group model. Later, during systems design, it becomes more detailed and refined in order that it is able to support the business function data models.

System event*: (IS) typically something that will cause a processing function to act. For example, the production of a 'report request record' by an online program can be used to trigger production of a report.

Systems analysis: set of techniques for the analysis of systems; actions of so doing.

Third normal form: (IS) entity type or relation structured so every attribute (or collection of such) that any other is functionally dependent on is a candidate identifier.

Transaction*: piece of business performed; logical unit of equivalent input, processing and results.

Tripartite assumption: everything relevant could be specified and modelled as one of processes, data, and behaviour. It is not true.

Tuple: (IS) row of relation; n-tuple; in each tuple of a relation the order of the columns is the same.

Unbounded: see Table 2.4.

Universe of discourse, UOD*: all those objects that have been, are or ever might be, and within some hypothesis, plan, proposal, or reality.

Variable: a name or an identifier associated with a data item.

Venn diagram: diagram showing the logic of membership of various sets by having overlapping boundaries.

Vertical information flow: information flows that are up and/or down a management reporting structure.

Index